The Homeowner's Ultimate Tool Guide

Choosing the Right Tool for Every Home Improvement Job

SANDOR NAGYSZALANCZY

The Taunton Press
Inspiration for hands-on living®

The Taunton Press
Inspiration for hands-on living®

The Taunton Press, Inc., 63 South Main Street, PO Box 5506, Newtown, CT 06470-5506
e-mail: tp@taunton.com

Distributed by Publishers Group West

EDITOR: STEFANIE RAMP
COVER DESIGN: HOWARD GROSSMAN
INTERIOR DESIGN: ROBIN WEISS
LAYOUT: CATHY CASSIDY
PHOTOGRAPHERS: SANDOR NAGYSZALANCZY,
            SCOTT PHILLIPS (p. i)

LIBRARY OF CONGRESS CATALOGING-IN-PUBLICATION DATA

Nagyszalanczy, Sandor.
    The homeowner's ultimate tool guide : choosing the right tool for
    every home improvement job / Sandor Nagyszalanczy.
        p. cm.
    Includes index.
    ISBN 1-56158-582-3
  1. Dwellings--Remodeling--Equipment and supplies. 2.
Dwellings--Maintenance and repair--Equipment and supplies. 3. Tools.
I. Title.
TH4816 .N34 2003
643'.7--dc21

                                                    2003005648

Printed in the United States of America
10 9 8 7 6 5 4 3

The following manufacturers/names appearing in *The Homeowner's Ultimate Tool Guide* are trademarks: Academy Awards®, Anti-Vibe®, Betadine®, B-I-N®, Bondo®, Bosch™, Bucket Boss®, Carborundum®, Chinex®, Cordura®, Corian®, Craftsman®, Delta™, Dremel®, DeWalt®, Festool®, Formica®, Jorgensen™, Kevlar®, Lamello®, Leatherman®, Lego®, Lexan®, Makita™, Mapp®, Masonite®, Melamine®, Milwaukee®, Mycitracin®, Oscar®, Panasonic®, Peltor®, Plexiglas®, Porter Cable®, Power Painter®, Prazi®, Putty Chaser™, RascalRule®, Ridgid™, Robertson®, RoboGrip®, Robo Hammer®, Rockwell®, Rolodex®, Romex®, Ryobi®, Sawzall®, Scotch-Brite®, Sealcoat®, Sears®, Sheetrock®, Skil®, Skilsaw®, Stanley®, Styrofoam®, Surform®, Swiss Army Knife, Targa, Teflon®, 3M®, Torx®, Uvextreme®, Velcro®, Victorinox®, Vise-Grip®, Wagner®, Wilton®, Wood Grenade®, Worktunes®, and X-Acto®.

Working with wood is inherently dangerous. Using hand or power tools improperly or ignoring safety practices can lead to permanent injury or even death. Don't try to perform operations you learn about here (or elsewhere) unless you're certain they are safe for you. If something about an operation doesn't feel right, don't do it. Look for another way. We want you to enjoy the craft, so please keep safety foremost in your mind whenever you're in the shop.

To Helen Albert, my Editor at The Taunton Press *(and an excellent craftsperson), who gave me the inspiration and guidance that brought this book into existence. Through thick and thin, she has remained both my most dependable ally and my good friend.*

Acknowledgments

How does one acquire all the tools, machines, and knowledge it takes to create a tool book of this size and scope? Beyond my 25 years of experience in the trades and 16 years in publishing, testing, and reviewing tools and machinery, my most important aids were (1) a Rolodex® containing the names of professional tool designers, makers, and users and (2) a garage the size of a dirigible hanger to house all the tools and equipment included in this book during the course of the project.

As a small token of my appreciation, I'd like to thank all the folks that assisted directly and indirectly with the creation of this book (as some nervous Oscar® winner says at the Academy Awards® every year: "I apologize in advance to anyone I've accidentally forgotten to mention").

First, the tool manufacturers and public relations folks who helped me acquire tools and technical information: Dave Hazelwood, Emerson Electric; Peter Hayward, Ridge Tools (Ridgid™); Ken Kueter, Leigh Anthony Communications (Sears® Craftsman®); Jacek Romanski, Wilton Tool Company; Frank Burgmeier, Frank Burgmeier Company (Vaughan-Bushnell); Barton Schindler, Toolfactoryoutlet.com; Mark Schroeder, Franklin International; Todd Langston, GMR Marketing Inc. (Porter-Cable®, Delta™); Matt Jones, Makita™ USA; Chris Carlson, S-B Powertools (Bosch™); Joanne Bertsch, S-B Powertools (Skil®); Karen Powers, Freud; Christian Oltzscher, Toolguide (Festool®); Bob Hillard, Fein Tools; Peggy Brunet LeMay, Dremel®; Dave Powell, DMT; Todd Walter, SWB&R (DeWalt®); Dan Holman, Adjustable Saw Company (Pony, Jorgensen™); Debra Cifreo, Hitachi; Kathleen Oberleiter, Colonial Saw (Lamello®); Richard S. Peterson, Blue Horse Inc. (Milwaukee®); Jim C. Ray, McFeely's Catalog; Wally Wilson, Lee Valley Tools (Veritas); John Otto, Jet Machinery; Rickard Brånby and Yvonne Caruso, Gränsfors Bruks; Mike Sherriff, Ryobi® America; Mark Duginske, FasTTrack; Brad Witt, Woodhaven; Ken and Steve Grisley, Leigh Jigs; Jim Swann, Advanced Machinery Imports Ltd. (Hegner); Richard Wedler, MicroFence; Dan Sherman, CMT USA; and David Williams, Panasonic®.

An extraspecial thanks goes out to Leonard Lee, owner of Lee Valley Tools Ltd., and Mike Managan, of MKM Communications (Sears/Craftsman), for their steadfast support and prodigious assistance.

Finally, kudos to my friends and colleagues who generously shared their personal and professional tool-using experiences with me, as well as offering heaping helpings of encouragement: Jerry Bowden, Curtis Bowden, Michael Dresdner, Michael Schweit, Jeff Traugott, Kevin Ireton and Charles Miller at *Fine Homebuilding* magazine, Rick McKee, Sven Kalmar, Robert Weiner, and last but not least, my parents, Maria and Lorant Nagyszalanczy, and my wife, Ann Gibb.

Contents

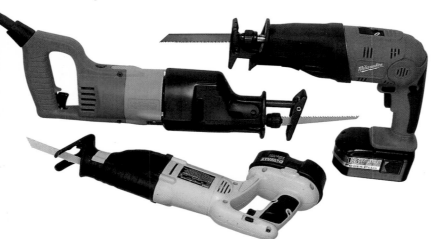

Introduction

The home-improvement game is no different than the rest of life. The person who can pick the right tools for a job—and use them most effectively—stands a good chance of being a winner. If you consider yourself a "winner" who already knows all there is to know about tools, then you might be in for a shock. Unless you've recently spent time checking into the latest crop of tools on the market, you probably know less than you think. The reason is that most kinds of tools—woodworking, metalworking, masonry, and finishing hand and power tools and machines—have changed more in the past few years than they have in the previous few hundred years. In fact, the shelves of your local hardware store or home center are currently stocked with so many new and innovative tools that, to borrow a phrase from a recent auto ad, "it's no longer your father's hardware store."

Need examples? Walk in and ask a home-center clerk for a tape measure and he or she is likely to ask, "Mechanical, electronic, or laser?" Scan a hardware store's racks for a simple framing hammer, and you're likely to find *dozens* of choices, including antivibration, ergonomically designed, all-titanium, and convertible striking-cap models. And things don't get any less confusing when it comes to choosing among cordless drills ("Do I really need a high-voltage model with a computerized charger for around-the-house repairs?"), paint sprayers ("Is a piston-pump airless sprayer a better choice for painting my house than a power roller or HVLP system?"), or even glass cutters ("Does an oil-lubricated diamond-wheel glass cutter really cut more cleanly than an inexpensive carbide cutter?").

THE CHANGING WORLD OF TOOLS

What has happened in recent times that has changed today's tools so significantly? There are a few significant areas of development that have had a profound impact on the design and construction of modern hand and power tools.

Improved Manufacturing

Rapid prototyping and CAD design have led to many speedy innovations in the tool field. Before, when you were designing a new tool or machine, you had to make models and physical prototypes, which were costly and only revealed so much about the final manufactured version of the tool. Now, designers create remarkable,

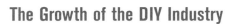

virtual versions of their tools on the computer, using advanced software and futuristic peripheral devices, such as hard-copy machines, which can actually produce a 3-D plastic model of a tool directly from a computer file. Designers make changes and improvements to a tool in the computer, and then use it to bring the design directly into manufacturing. This process makes tool development much quicker and makes it easier for designers to incorporate the latest technological advances into their tools.

Advanced Materials

The latest engineered-alloy metals and fiber-reinforced plastics have made modern tools not only stronger and lighter but also safer and cheaper to manufacture than their more traditional counterparts. Space-age materials such as titanium, superhard carbide, Kevlar, vibration-absorbing gel, and carbon fiber–reinforced epoxy and polycarbonate plastics are now found in a wide range of consumer tools, from hammer handles to knee pads, chainsaw chaps to dry-cut metal saws, and screw guns to oscillating spindle sanders.

High-Tech Electronics and Optics

The computer revolution has had an impact on literally every aspect of modern life, and the contents of our toolboxes aren't exempt. Electronic innovations have improved cordless tools, through high-capacity battery packs and computerized chargers, as well as corded tools, through soft-start controllers and electronic motor feedback circuitry. Many new tools operate by advanced electronics and/or electrical-optical means, including stud finders, circuit testers, sonic distance measures, rotary lasers, and laser-actuated measuring tools.

The Growth of the DIY Industry

What once comprised a small number of people taking on an occasional home-improvement project has burgeoned into a *multibillion-dollar* DIY (do-it-yourself) industry. The result is that thousands of consumer-grade tools and machines, once only available as expensive industrial items, have come to market. Examples include oscillating spindle sanders, auto-feed screw guns, specialized carbide blades and bits, and air tools. The thriving DIY market has also fostered the development of ingeniously designed tools, including patent inventions like folding layout squares, improved pry bars, and multipurpose tools such as the Leatherman.

Ergonomics

Advanced studies in how we hold and use tools have led to remarkable advancements that have made newer tools safer and more pleasurable to use than ever before. New ergonomic handles on hammers, pliers, and wrenches increase user comfort while reducing vibration, stress, and fatigue, which can lead to repetitive stress injuries such as carpal tunnel syndrome.

Safety

Modern hand and power tools are safer than ever—the upside of living in a litigious society where companies are financially responsible for even the most inexperienced tool users. Examples include tools with built-in "on" indicator lights, which help stop you from picking up a hot soldering iron or glue gun and burning yourself; stationary and benchtop tools with locking on/off switches, which prevent unauthorized use; and electrical GFI (ground-fault interrupt) circuitry, which prevents accidental shocks.

The downside of this wealth of improvement in our tools is that choosing the right tools for any particular job is more confusing than ever. This situation is bad enough for professionals and advanced amateurs who pore over the latest tool reviews and ads in magazines and catalogs. But if you're new to the tool game and have recently joined the ranks of the weekend warrior, the confusion is even worse: Do you feel intimidated by walking into the tool corral at your local home center? Have you ever failed to ask a question because you didn't want the clerk to laugh at you? Then you know exactly what I'm talking about.

To stem the tide of confusion about the tools we use to build our projects and maintain, repair, and improve our homes, I've written this book that gives you all the information you need to "walk the walk" and "talk the talk." The first goal of this book is to help you build your knowledge and recognition of both traditional tools and the latest and most advanced modern tools and to help you develop the vocabulary you'll need when asking for these tools and their accessories. Second, the book will help you build a thorough understanding of just what specific tools do and which tools you need to tackle most projects around the house or workshop.

ORGANIZATION

To achieve these goals, this book is organized into chapters arranged by the kinds of jobs that different tools do: pound and pry, shape and shave, drill and drive, etc.

Each chapter contains sections that cover specific tools, describing in detail what the basic tool does, the tool's features and range of styles, and useful accessories for the tool. The text, photos, and a variety of features will not only help you identify tools but also learn to choose the right tools for the job. It will also help you differentiate similar-looking tools that perform different functions—for example, a drywall hammer and a roofing hatchet. You'll also find plenty of advice on how to purchase tools wisely, including recommendations on what kinds of things to buy, what not to buy, and what to rent instead of own.

The opening chapter contains various tool kits, a rundown of all the tools you'll need for doing specific jobs: basic carpentry, electrical work, plumbing, drywall installation, painting, tile repair, etc.

Obviously, a book of this size can't possibly describe every tool on the planet, but I've attempted to be comprehensive in my coverage of the tools that even the most ambitious home-improvement enthusiast will want for working with wood, metal, plastics, tile, glass, concrete, brick, and other masonry materials.

Limited space also prohibits an extensive discussion of how every tool is used. There are, however, plenty of action photos, tips, and sidebars to give you a good idea of how a tool is used effectively and safely. Additionally, a safety chapter at the end of the book includes all the protective gear you'll need (and should *always* use) to work with even the most hazardous tools in safety and comfort.

When most folks think about having a complete set of tools in their home workshop, they think about having a single tool chest or cabinet, jammed full of all the hand and power tools needed for all kinds of repairs and projects around the home—fixing a leaky faucet or a broken door, laying a new parquet floor, changing the sparkplugs on the Corvette, or building a tree fort (if your tinkering goals are more

modest, perhaps you're imagining a big, tool-stuffed drawer in the utility room).

But while your big tool chest or drawer might have some of the tools you need to get you through some basic repairs or home maintenance tasks, wouldn't it be nice to have *exactly the right tools* you need for the job, organized and ready to go? That's the idea behind creating Tool Kits for specific kinds of jobs around the house—carpentry, roofing, electrical, painting, etc. By organizing a collection of task-specific tools into a dedicated box, chest, tote, or bag, you'll have everything you need in a container that you can easily take with you to wherever you're working—that means fewer trips back to the garage or workshop for tools you forgot or just discovered that you need.

The following chapter contains a dozen tool kits designed to handle most common home repair, maintenance, and improvement tasks (there's even a kit that'll help with roadside auto repairs). Each tool kit section contains a list of all the basic—and some not-so-basic—tools needed for the job. The list includes a brief description of what each tool does and a reference to the chapter and page in the book where the tool is discussed in greater detail.

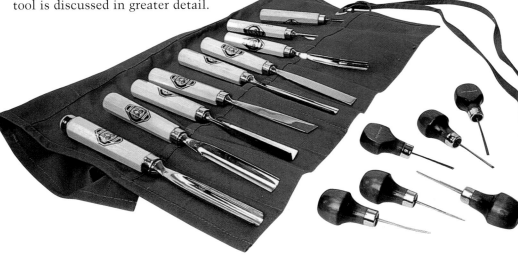

HOME MAINTENANCE & REPAIR

Even if your building superintendent or a hired professional handles all your major and significant household repairs, a home tool kit is something every renter or homeowner should keep on hand. Easily stored in a small toolbox, kitchen drawer, or (my favorite) a plastic tote tray, this kit contains all the basic tools you need to handle daily home repairs and maintenance duties.

Want to hang a picture frame? Put up drapery rods? Replace a water filter or broken electrical outlet plate? Assemble a knockdown television stand? The tools shown in the photo on the facing page and outlined in the chart below are likely to do the trick. To save space (and expense), the kit contains some multipurpose tools, (e.g., screwdrivers and wrenches) instead of sets of separate tools. For more advanced repairs, you can always add tools to your kit from one of the other tool kits described in this book.

TOOL	PURPOSE	PAGE
Small Claw Hammer (12 oz. to 16 oz.)	Drive nails, brads, and tacks; pound small parts	155
Hand drill or cordless drill/driver (with set of twist drills, ¹⁄₁₆ in. to ¼ in.)	Drill holes for mounting hardware	138, 143
Cordless screwdriver with driver bits	Drive screws quickly	145
Multidriver or screwdriver set	Tighten/loosen screws	147
Precision screwdriver combination tool	Tighten/loosen small screws	151
Utility knife	Slice packaging; cut up materials	121
Scissors or utility shears	Cut thin materials	109
Awl	Poke holes in materials, starter holes in walls, etc.	200
Wood chisel (¾ in.)	Install hinges and hardware	67
Tape measure (12 ft. to 16 ft.)	Measure for carpeting, drapes, etc.	194
Torpedo level	Level pictures, curtain rods, etc.	210
Cutting needle-nose pliers	Grasp nuts, bolts, and hardware; cut and strip wire	35
Locking pliers	Grasp hard-to-turn nuts and bolts	36
Slip-joint pliers	Fasten/loosen pipe fittings, large fasteners	33
Adjustable wrench (8 in. to 10 in.) and/or emergency gas shutoff valve wrench	Tighten/loosen nuts and bolts; turn off gas in an emergency	40
Allen wrench set	Tighten/loosen Allen fasteners and set screws	45
Half-round file	Round over sharp edges and remove burrs	73
Flashlight	Illuminate work area	261
Safety glasses and work gloves	Protect eyes and hands	261, 269

Utility shears

Locking pliers

Safety glasses and work gloves

Work gloves

Rechargeable flashlight

tting
edle-nose
ers

Half-round
file

Wood
chisel

stable
ch

Awl

oint

Multidriver

Small claw
hammer

less
wdriver

FISKARS

Hand
drill

Allen
wrench set

Twist drills

STABILA

Torpedo
level

cision
ewdriver
mbination
t

Tape
measure

Utility knife

HOME MAINTENANCE AND REPAIR TOOL KIT Unless you've got a handyman who takes care of your place, everyone needs to have a well-equipped home maintenance and repair tool kit.

CARPENTRY

A carpentry tool kit has all the tools you need to make small improvements to the basic structural elements of a house: stud walls, decks, stairways, doors and windows, indoor and outdoor trim, and the like. The kit shown here includes the measuring tools and hand tools you'll likely need, as well as a couple of portable power tools I consider to be modern essentials, including a circular saw and cordless drill (hand-tool equivalents are included, in case you're on a tight budget). For larger, more involved jobs, such as room additions or major remodeling projects, additional power tools maybe desirable, including a table saw, reciprocating saw, etc.

TOOL	PURPOSE	PAGE
Portable circular saw (or panel saw)	Rip and crosscut lumber, plywood, and other sheet materials	79, 92
Powered miter or compound miter saw (or backsaw and miter box)	Accurately crosscut and miter studs, trim, and moldings	80, 101, 102
Handsaw (toolbox or Japanese style)	Cut in locations where power saws won't fit; finish cuts in corners	80, 83
Keyhole saw (or folding utility saw with wood and drywall blades)	Make cutouts and notches in wood or drywall	85
Jigsaw (or coping saw)	Cut curved edges and parts	85, 88
Cordless drill/driver, 12 volts to 24 volts (or brace or hand drill)	Drill holes; quickly drive screws and fasteners	138
Driver bits and drill bits (twist, spade)	Drill holes; quickly drive screws and fasteners	136
Screwdriver set (or single with interchangeable bits)	Tighten/loosen fasteners	148
Tape measure (16 ft. to 25 ft.)	Measure parts; lay out cuts	194
Folding rule (or yardstick)	Measure parts; lay out cuts	193
Carpenter's pencils	Mark cuts; label parts	N/A
Speed square (or combination square)	Mark square and 45-degree cuts	204, 206
Framing square	Lay out and check for square; calculate rafter angles	205
Bevel square	Measure and mark angled cuts	208
Levels (18 in. to 36 in., and torpedo)	Make sure parts are level or plumb	208
Utility knife	Cut and trim materials	121
Hammer: 16 oz. to 20 oz. (and/or air-powered nail gun)	Drive and remove nails; do light demolition work	155, 219
Nail puller/ripping bar	Remove fasteners	170

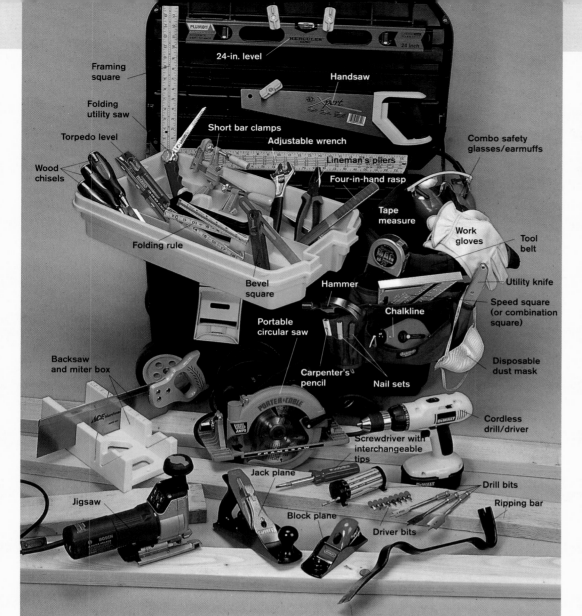

Framing
square

24-in. level

Handsaw

Folding
utility saw

Short bar clamps

Torpedo level

Adjustable wrench

Combo safety
glasses/earmuffs

Wood
chisels

Lineman's pliers

Four-in-hand rasp

Tape
measure

Work
gloves

Tool
belt

Folding rule

Utility knife

Bevel
square

Hammer

Speed square
(or combination
square)

Portable
circular saw

Chalkline

Carpenter's
pencil

Nail sets

Disposable
dust mask

Backsaw
and miter box

Cordless
drill/driver

Screwdriver with
interchangeable
tips

Jack plane

Jigsaw

Block plane

Drill bits

Ripping bar

Driver bits

CARPENTRY TOOL KIT A modern
marriage of hand and power
tools in this carpenter's tool kit
has everything you need to take
on most home-improvement and
remodeling projects.

TOOL	PURPOSE	PAGE IN TEXT
Nail set	Countersink finish nails	168
Handplanes: block and jack sizes (or power plane)	Trim wood ends, edges, and surfaces	61
Four-in-one rasp	Shave and smooth edges	75
Wood chisel set	Mortise for hardware and fasteners	67
Lineman's pliers	Bend or hold hardware and fasteners	33
Adjustable wrench	Tighten/loosen nuts and bolts	40
C-clamps or short bar clamps	Clamp work to benchtop; glue parts together	48
Tool belt	Keep most-used tools with you on the job	N/A
Safety glasses, earplugs or earmuffs, dust mask, work gloves	Protect eyes, ears, lungs, and hands	261, 264 265, 269

MECHANICAL

Depending on the kind of repairs you wish to do, a mechanical tool kit could consist of just a few dozen tools in a tool roll or hundreds of tools. The kit shown here is a general set of tools, which will equip you for a wide range of mechanical tasks, such as assembling a bicycle, changing a spark plug in your lawnmower, or rebuilding your car's carburetor.

TOOL	PURPOSE	PAGE
Set of screwdrivers, slotted and Phillips	Tighten and loosen machine screws	148
Set of precision screwdrivers, slotted and Phillips	Tighten and loosen nuts and bolts	151
Right-angle screwdrivers, slotted and Phillips	Tighten and loosen nuts and bolts	152
Set of wrenches (open-end, box, and combo)*	Tighten and loosen nuts and bolts	39
Set of box wrenches*	Tighten and loosen nuts and bolts	39
Socket wrench driver and socket set**	Tighten and loosen nuts and bolts	44
Set of nut drivers*	Tighten and loosen nuts and bolts	153
Torque wrench	Tighten and loosen nuts and bolts to specified tightnesses	43
Adjustable wrenches (6 in., 8 in.)	Tighten and loosen nuts and bolts	40
Set of Allen wrenches*	Tighten and loosen Allen fasteners	45
Strap wrench	Remove large-diameter parts (e.g., oil filters)	44
Pliers: engineer's and needle-nose	Hold, remove, or tighten fasteners and parts	33, 35
Slip-joint pliers, straight and curved jaw	Hold, remove, or tighten large fasteners and parts	33
Locking pliers, assorted	Remove rusted or frozen fasteners	36
Snap-ring pliers set	Remove and replace locking rings	37
Diagonal cutters	Cut wires and thin parts	112
Wire strippers	Repair automotive wiring	118
Ball peen hammer	Drive chisels and punches, set pins, etc.	163
Mallet	Pound assemblies apart, drive tools	165
Pry bar	Pry assemblies apart, align parts	170
Cold chisels	(½ in., 1 in.) Cut off rusted fasteners	69
Pin punch set	Drive out pins that hold on shafts, pulleys, etc.	169
Hacksaw	Saw fasteners and parts to length	86
Files, assorted	Smooth rough edges, repairing fastener threads	73
Mechanic's gloves	Protect and cushion hands	270
Tool bags, boxes, and chests	Store and protect tools	N/A

Imperial or metric, depending on your needs.
**Includes socket extension, universal drive, and deep spark-plug socket, as needed.*

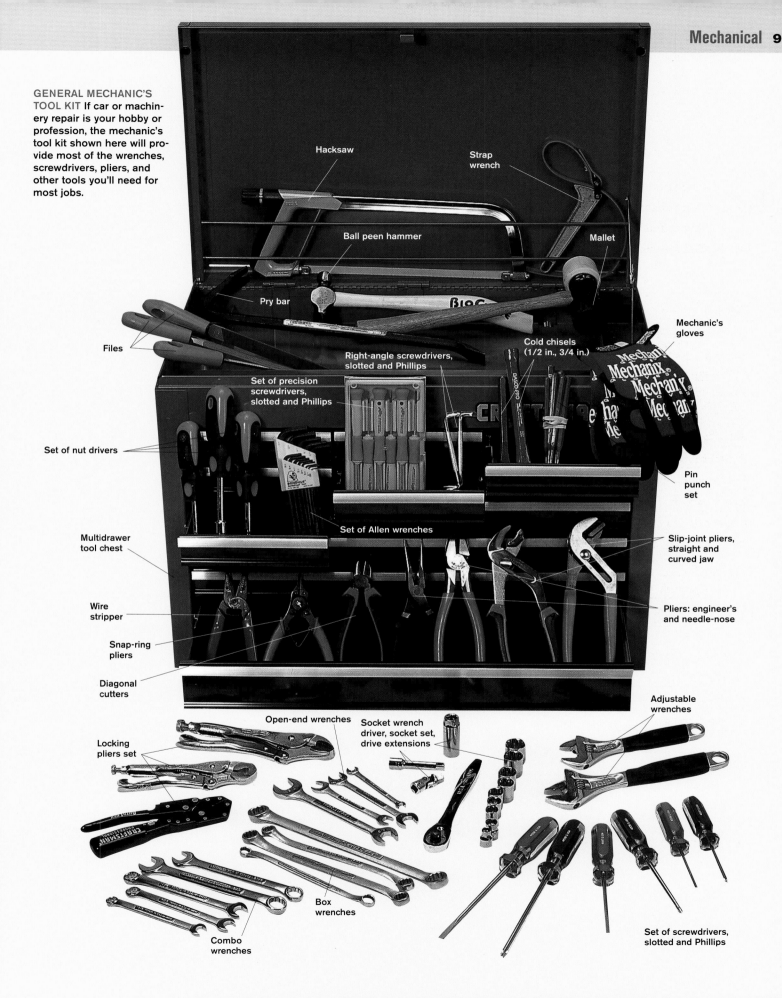

GENERAL MECHANIC'S TOOL KIT If car or machinery repair is your hobby or profession, the mechanic's tool kit shown here will provide most of the wrenches, screwdrivers, pliers, and other tools you'll need for most jobs.

Hacksaw

Strap wrench

Ball peen hammer

Mallet

Pry bar

Mechanic's gloves

Files

Cold chisels (1/2 in., 3/4 in.)

Right-angle screwdrivers, slotted and Phillips

Set of precision screwdrivers, slotted and Phillips

Set of nut drivers

Pin punch set

Set of Allen wrenches

Multidrawer tool chest

Slip-joint pliers, straight and curved jaw

Wire stripper

Pliers: engineer's and needle-nose

Snap-ring pliers

Diagonal cutters

Adjustable wrenches

Open-end wrenches

Socket wrench driver, socket set, drive extensions

Locking pliers set

Box wrenches

Combo wrenches

Set of screwdrivers, slotted and Phillips

AUTOMOBILE

The minikit shown here stores right in your car's trunk. It has all the tools you'll need to perform basic roadside repairs, like replacing a fan belt, tightening a loose alternator bracket bolt, or changing your oil. These tools will fit into a small soft-sided bag, plastic box, or even into a jumper cable bag, as shown in the photo.

TOOL	PURPOSE	PAGE
Combination screwdriver	Tighten and loosen screws	147
Multitool	Provide needle-nose pliers, strippers, etc.	153
Combination wrench set*	Tighten and loosen nuts and bolts	39
Adjustable wrench	Tighten and loosen nuts and bolts	40
Allen wrench set*	Tighten and loosen Allen fasteners	45
Compact socket set (Wilton®)*	Tighten and loosen nuts and bolts	41
Slip-joint pliers	Hold parts; tighten and loosen fasteners	33
Locking pliers	Remove rusty or frozen fasteners	36
Disposable gloves (preferably nitrile)	Keep hands clean	272
Flashlight (preferably head-worn)	Provide light (while keeping hands free)	261
Duct tape and plastic ties	Emergency repairs	N/A
Jumper cables	Jump power to weak battery to start car	N/A

Imperial or metric, depending on your needs.

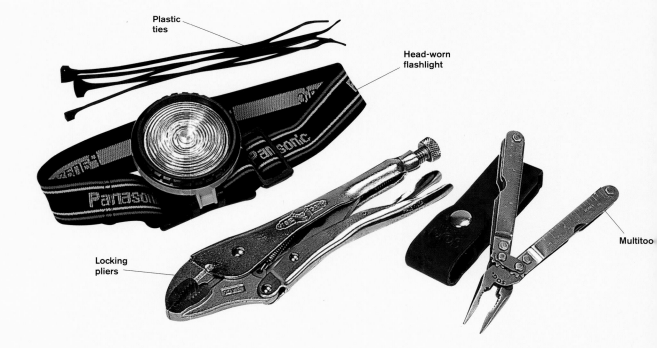

Plastic ties

Head-worn flashlight

Locking pliers

Multitoo

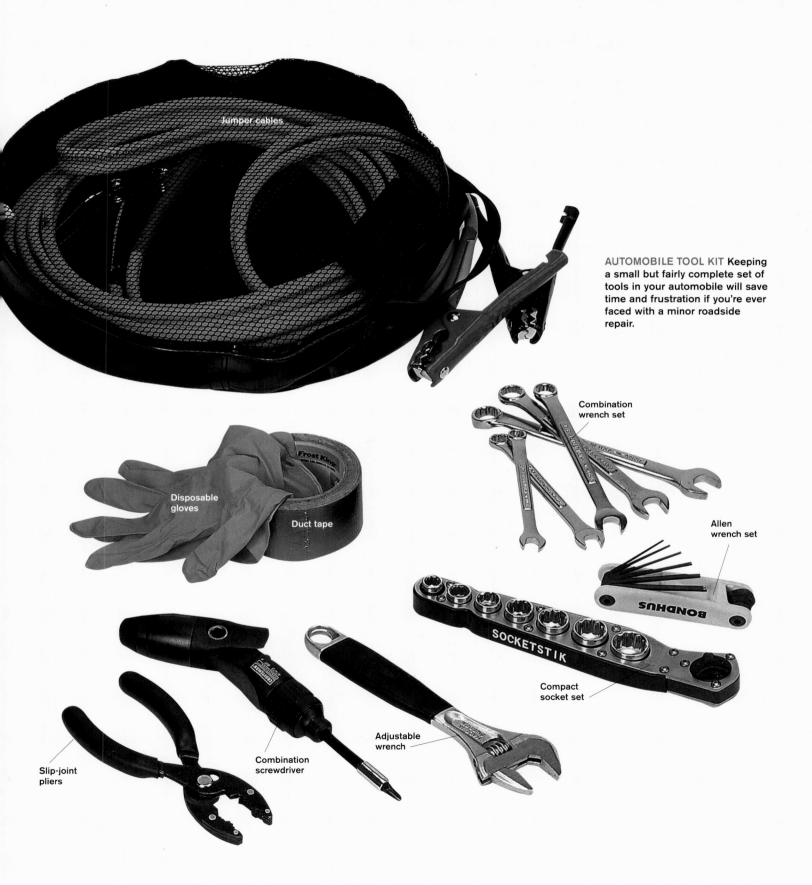

Jumper cables

AUTOMOBILE TOOL KIT Keeping a small but fairly complete set of tools in your automobile will save time and frustration if you're ever faced with a minor roadside repair.

Combination wrench set

Disposable gloves

Duct tape

Allen wrench set

SOCKETSTIK

BONDHUS

Compact socket set

Slip-joint pliers

Combination screwdriver

Adjustable wrench

ELECTRICAL

If you need to repair a broken electrical outlet or want to exchange a regular light switch for one of those neat dimmers, you'll find all the tools you need in the kit shown here and described in the chart below. If you're even more ambitious (and always take the proper precautions when working with household AC current), there are tools in this kit for running new circuits in your home or workshop, as well as for connecting wiring to new outlets, switches, light fixtures, and appliances.

For more electric-savvy users, the kit also contains electronics tools to find and check live circuits for correct wiring or for troubleshooting wiring problems and doing simple diagnostics on faulty electric or electronic appliances.

TOOL	PURPOSE	PAGE
Lineman's pliers	Grab and turn parts; remove slugs from electrical boxes	33
Needle-nose pliers	Form loops on wire ends; grab and turn small parts	35
Diagonal cutters	Cut wires, cables	112
Wire strippers (or automatic or combination stripper)	Remove insulation from wires	118
Cable strippers (and/or cable ripper)	Remove sheathing from electrical cable	120
Screwdrivers (small and large slotted and Phillips)	Tighten and loosen screws for fixtures, wall plates, etc.	148
Offset screwdrivers (slotted and Phillips)	Tighten screws inside electrical boxes	152
Cordless screwdriver	Fasten wall plates; secure fixtures	145
Utility knife	Cut wire sheathing	121
Electricity checker and/or circuit checker	Warn of live electricity or wiring problems	216, 217
Multimeter or ammeter	Make electrical measurements; check electronics circuitry and components	214
Fish tape	Pull wiring through finished walls	217

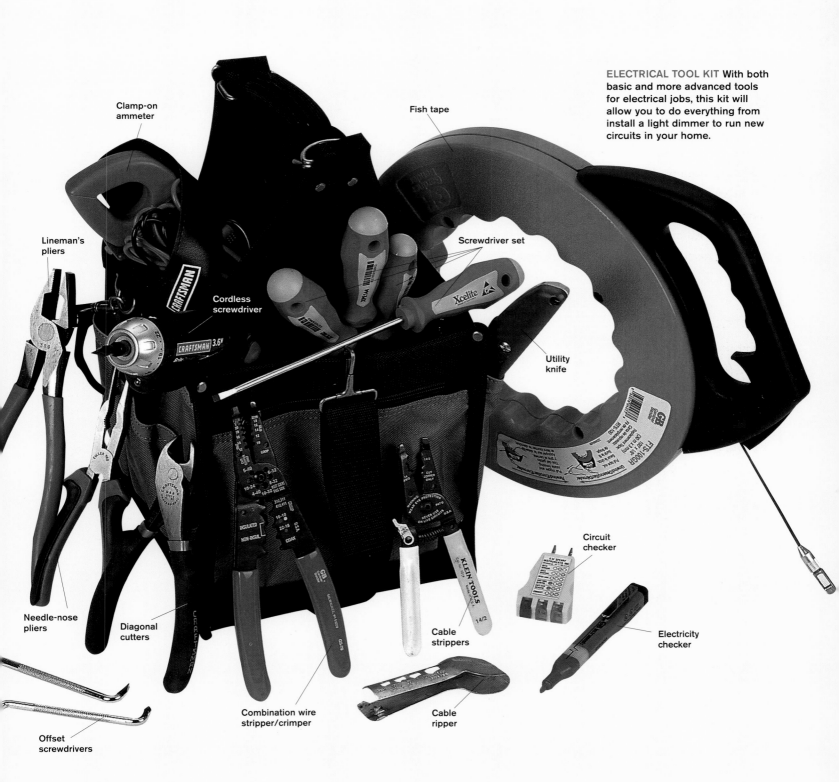

Clamp-on
ammeter

Fish tape

ELECTRICAL TOOL KIT With both
basic and more advanced tools
for electrical jobs, this kit will
allow you to do everything from
install a light dimmer to run new
circuits in your home.

Lineman's
pliers

Cordless
screwdriver

Screwdriver set

Utility
knife

Needle-nose
pliers

Diagonal
cutters

Circuit
checker

Cable
strippers

Electricity
checker

Combination wire
stripper/crimper

Cable
ripper

Offset
screwdrivers

PLUMBING

The assortment of tools and supplies in the basic kit, shown in the photo on the facing page and listed in the chart below, includes everything you need to deal with most common household plumbing repairs and emergencies. These include the repair or replacement of pipes in household water supply, pumping, and/or heating systems, as well as the repair or replacement of common household faucets, traps and drains, toilet valves, and ball cocks. The kit is intended to help you deal with three of the most common "DIY-friendly" types of household pipe: galvanized steel, copper, and PVC or ABS plastic. (Tools for working with older-style cast iron, vitrified clay, and asbestos cement sewer pipes have been omitted

because they're difficult to deal with. When these need attention, call a plumber.)

If you're up for taking on more advanced plumbing repairs and improvements, there are three advanced tool kits (all shown on pp. 16 and 17) you might need, each with tools and supplies specific to one type of pipe. The galvanized pipe-threading tool kit lets you thread the ends of raw pipe to make custom lengths for any new installation or repair. The copper pipe tool kit has a torch and tools to allow you to cut pipe to length and sweat (solder) connections. Finally, the plastic pipe tool kit includes saws and special snips for cutting straight pipe to length and special cements for assembling plastic pipe components.

TOOL	PURPOSE	PAGE
Pipe wrenches, pair (10 in. to 14 in., for general work and repairs)	Assemble pipe fittings	46
Adjustable wrenches (two sizes: 6 in. and 8 in.)	Tighten/loosen hex-head nuts and bolts	40
Closet spud wrench	Tighten/loosen flanged nut, slip nuts, etc., on drainpipes, sinks, and other plumbing fixtures	47
Strap wrench	Tighten/loosen/hold plated pipes without scratching them	44
Basin wrench	Tighten/loosen nuts that attach faucets to sinks	47
Tongue-and-groove pliers (8 in. or 10 in.)	Tighten/loosen large flange, slip, or lock nuts on drains, fixtures, and fittings	34
Locking pliers	Tighten/loosen stuck or rusted fasteners	36
Screwdrivers, slotted and Phillips	Install/disassemble plumbing fixtures	148
Half-round file	Remove burrs from pipes and fixtures	73
Valve seat removal and/or seat resurfacing tools	Repair leaking faucets	77
Toilet force pump (plunger)	Unclog toilets	N/A
Drain auger	Unclog sink drains	N/A

(continued on pp. 16–17)

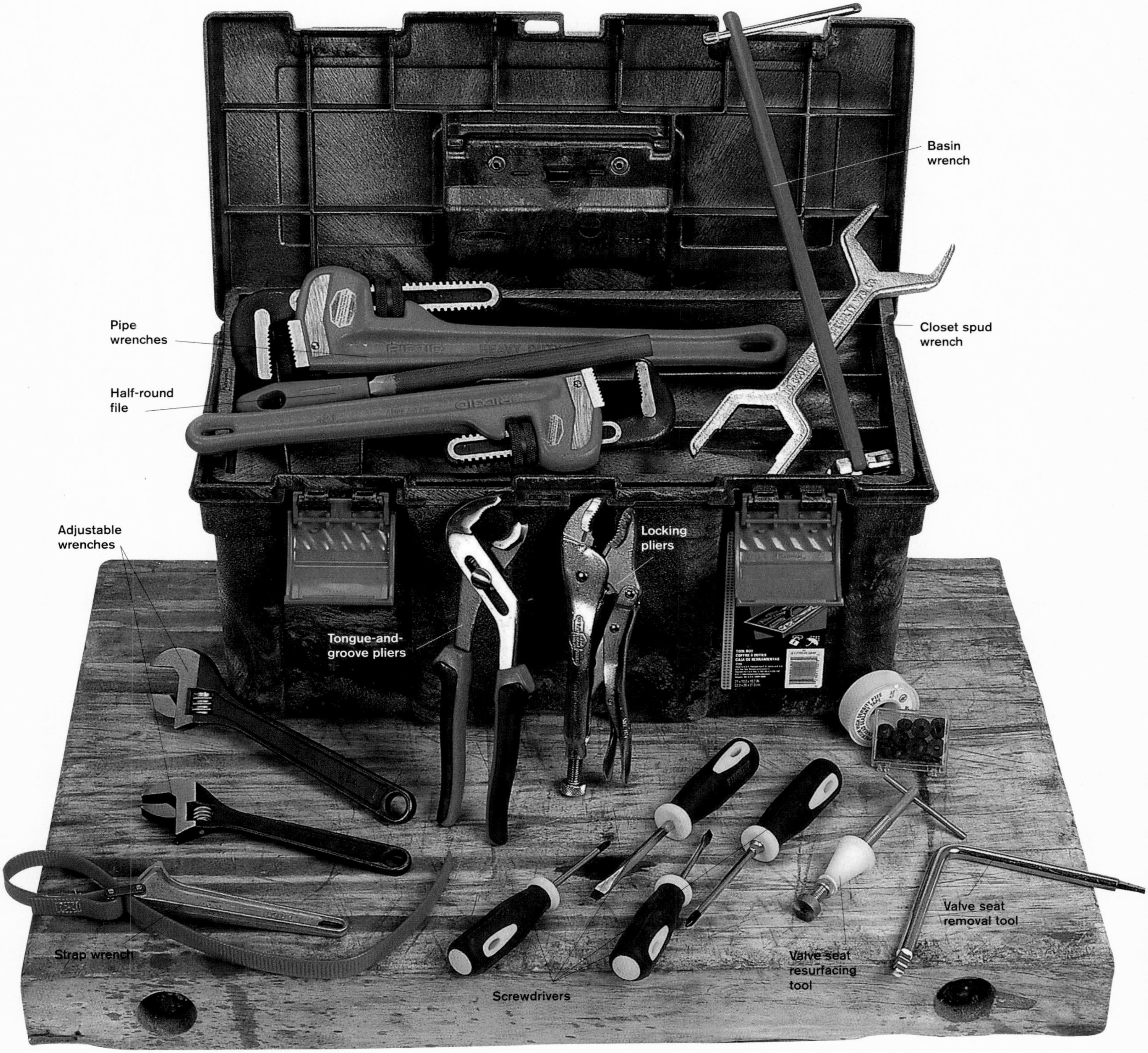

Basin wrench

Closet spud wrench

Pipe wrenches

Half-round file

Adjustable wrenches

Locking pliers

Tongue-and-groove pliers

Strap wrench

Screwdrivers

Valve seat resurfacing tool

Valve seat removal tool

BASIC PLUMBING TOOL KIT
The kit shown here has plumbing tools to fix every leaky pipe and faucet, as well as to repair drains, toilets, and other fixtures.

PLUMBING *continued*

GALVANIZED PIPE-THREADING TOOL KIT

TOOL	PURPOSE	PAGE
Small claw hammer	Hold pipe securely during threading	155
Pipe-threading dies and handle	Cut threads on straight-pipe ends	130
Pipe reamer	Remove burr from end of cut pipe	76
Pipe cutter	Cut steel pipe to length	115

COPPER PIPE TOOL KIT

TOOL	PURPOSE	PAGE
Tubing cutter	Cut copper pipe to length	116
Propane torch	Sweat copper pipe and fittings	229
Flaring tool	Flare ends of copper pipe for attaching to fittings	131
Flux brush	Apply flux when sweating copper pipe	N/A

PLASTIC PIPE TOOL KIT

TOOL	PURPOSE	PAGE
Miter saw (or miter box and backsaw, or compound miter saw)	Cut large-diameter plastic pipe to length	81, 102
Pipe-cutting snips	Cut small-diameter plastic pipe to length	116
Smooth-jaw tongue-and-groove pliers (12 in.)	Tighten/loosen slip nuts when connecting plastic fittings	34
Utility knife	Clean up cut-pipe ends	121

GALVANIZED PIPE-THREADING TOOL KIT These heavy tools are designed for threading the ends of steel pipes.

Pipe-threading dies and handle

Pipe vise

Pipe reamer

Pipe cutter

Propane torch

PLASTIC PIPE TOOL KIT It's quicker and easier to install plastic pipe and fittings if you have a few special tools on hand.

Miter saw

Flaring tool

Tubing cutter

Utility knife

Half-round file

Flux brush

COPPER-PIPE TOOL KIT It takes a torch and a few special tools to cut, flare, and sweat copper-pipe fittings together.

Smooth-jaw tongue-and-groove pliers

PAINTING

Covering a surface with paint is usually the last step in a process that's often tedious. For example, a drywalled interior wall requires taping, joint and fastener hole filling, sanding, and texturing—all before the first coat of primer goes on. The painter's tool kit shown here and described in the chart below has all the tools you'll need to paint the interior or exterior of a house, garage, or shed.

The tools include applicators (brushes, rollers) and protective equipment (masking applicators, drop cloths), as well as accessories (paint lids, pry bars) that help make any finishing job easier. Modern alternatives to traditional tools, such as paint pads and power painters, are also included for consideration.

TOOL	PURPOSE	PAGE
Wide paint brush (or wide paint pad)	Paint wider surfaces; do fine finish work	237, 240
Narrower, skewed brush (and/or narrow paint pad)	Paint trim, details, narrow surfaces	237, 240
Small touchup brush	Touch up missed areas	237, 239
Paint tray or bucket	Hold paint for application	241
Paint-can cover lid/ring	Make it easier to dispense paint from can	241
Roller frame and cover (and/or powered painting device)	Paint large surfaces quickly	241, 244
Roller tray and tray liners	Load roller with paint; ease cleanup	241
Roller extension handle	Reach high or low areas easily	241
Ladder or scaffolding	Paint ceilings or high walls	N/A
Masking applicator (and/or painting shield)	Protect surfaces not being painted	238
Plastic, paper, or canvas drop cloth	Protect floors and furniture	N/A
Small pry bar	Open paint cans	170
Safety glasses or goggles	Keep paint splatter out of eyes	261
Disposable gloves	Keep paint off hands	272

Ladder

PAINTING TOOL KIT Painting and wall papering tools can last for years if properly cleaned after use. Invest in good quality brushes and they will be a pleasure to use time after time.

Canvas drop cloth

Disposable gloves

Paint can cover lid/ring

Roller extension handle

Power painter

Masking applicator

Small pry bar

Roller tray and tray liner

Roller frame and cover

Narrow paint pad

Safety goggles

Painting shield

Narrower, skewed brush

Wide paint brush

(Not shown: Small touchup brush, paint tray)

DRYWALL

Are you adding a closet to your bedroom, or do you need to repair a hole in the living room wall? Then you need some or all of the drywall installation and repair tools shown in the photo and listed in the chart. The kit includes tools for measuring, marking, and snapping drywall (gypsum board, plasterboard, etc.) sheets to size; screwing or nailing it up; applying joint compound; and sanding joints. (Once repairs or installation is done, you'll need brushes, rollers, and trays to finish it; see p. 18.)

Note that this kit *doesn't* include tools for taping, texturing, and finishing vast expanses of drywall that would be found, for example, in a large room addition. Specialized tools—like a drywaller's banjo (used to quickly apply joint tape), drywall sander, and a texture spray gun (to coat drywall with texture material)—take skill and experience to use properly. Unless you're ready to spend the time necessary learning how to use these tools correctly, save yourself grief and hire a professional drywall crew to do big jobs.

TOOL	PURPOSE	PAGE IN TEXT
Tape measure	Measure room; lay out cuts	194
Utility knife	Cut paper to snap sheets; do small trimming jobs	121
Drywall square	Snap sheets in two; mark large cutouts	207
Chalkline	Mark panel position for correct alignment	201
Rotary saw	Trim around windows, doors, electrical fixtures, etc.	94
Drywall saw (or nest of saws)	Notch edges or make small cutouts	85
Surform® rasp (or four-in-one)	Clean up ragged panel edges	76
Screw gun (or hammer)	Drive screws (or nails) to attach drywall to studs and joists	146
Screwdriver	Drive/adjust individual screws when setting/adjusting a drywall sheet	148
Aviation snips	Cut metal corner-reinforcement strips	110
Wide-joint knife, corner knife, and mud pan	Apply joint compound to drywall seams	253
Narrow joint knife or putty knife	Fill in nail and/or screw holes	252, 253
Sanding block and/or pole sander	Sand joints after tape and joint compound is applied	N/A
Tool belt and bags, with drill holster and bags for fasteners	Keep tools, screw gun, and fasteners handy	N/A
Ladder and/or scaffolding	Install drywall overhead	N/A
Safety glasses	Protect eyes while using power tools or when working overhead	261

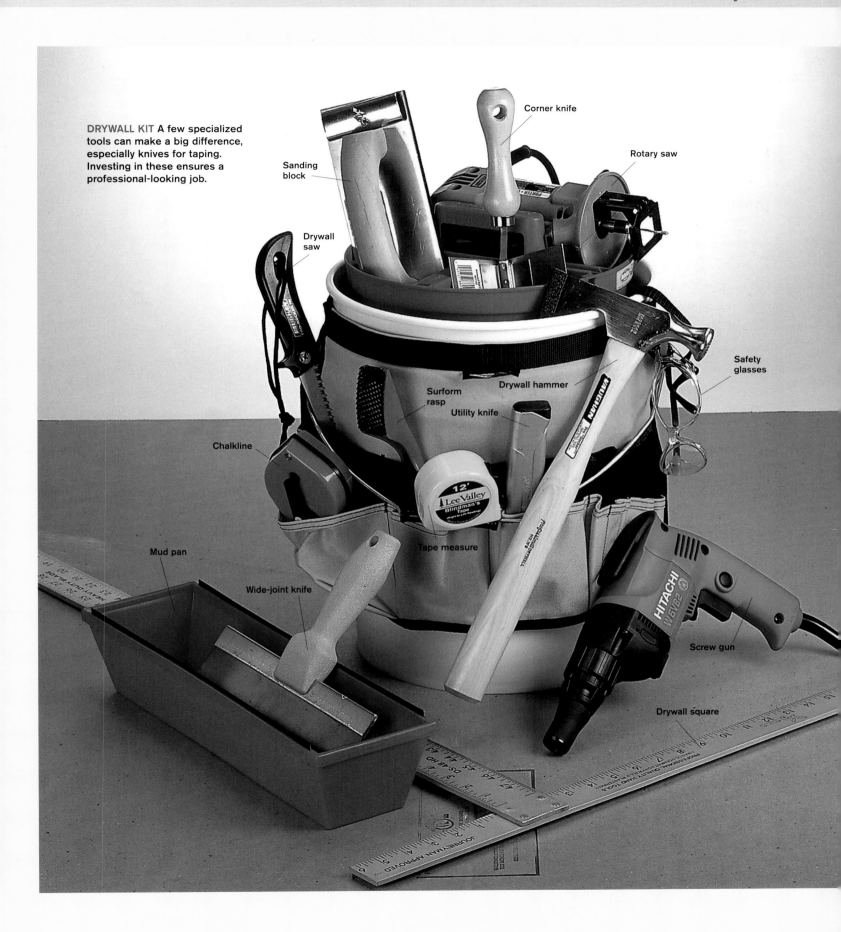

DRYWALL KIT A few specialized tools can make a big difference, especially knives for taping. Investing in these ensures a professional-looking job.

Corner knife

Rotary saw

Sanding block

Drywall saw

Safety glasses

Drywall hammer

Surform rasp

Utility knife

Chalkline

Tape measure

Mud pan

Screw gun

Wide-joint knife

Drywall square

DEMOLITION

Ready to rip out that lime green vanity and remodel your old bathroom? Using a kit of tools (shown in the photo and described in the chart) designed for rough-neck work will make this task, or any demolition job, easier and safer. A small assortment of hand tools, listed below, will allow you to slice or chop through many other building materials you'll encounter. And to protect your hands and eyes, gloves and goggles should be included when doing any kind of demolition work.

The reciprocating saw is the versatile king of demolition and remodeling tools. Fitted with the correct blade (see p. 91), this saw quickly cuts through nails, slices openings in walls, and chops through old pipes, electrical conduits, lumber, and rebar.

Break up a brick patio, concrete walkway, or mortar-bed tile shower with a sledgehammer, and rip out structural framing and trim work with a framing hammer and an assortment of wrecking bars, nail pullers, and ripping chisels. (If you're no John Henry with a sledge, consider renting or buying a rotary hammer; see p. 135). If you must remove an old roof or floor, a roofing mutt demolition tool (see p. 170) makes the job a lot easier.

TOOL	PURPOSE	PAGE
Reciprocating saw	Cut away walls, lumber, metal, etc.	90
Sledgehammers, large and small	Break up foundations, walkways, and masonry	164
Heavy framing hammer (with rip claw)	Rip into drywall; yank boards apart; remove nails	155
Wrecking bar	Tear down walls; pry up flooring, etc.	169
Pry bars, ripping chisels	Pry boards apart; tear through sheathing, drywall, etc.	170
Nail pullers: impact and cat's paw	Yank out nails and other fasteners	170
Roofing mutt	Lift and remove old roofing and flooring	170
Wood chisel, wide	Chop out wooden trim and framing	67
Bolt cutters	Cut rebar and fasteners that can't be removed	113
Cable cutters	Cut thick electrical cables and wires	113
Utility knife	Cut through roofing paper, insulation, etc.	121
Safety goggles and work gloves	Protect eyes and hands from flying debris	261, 269

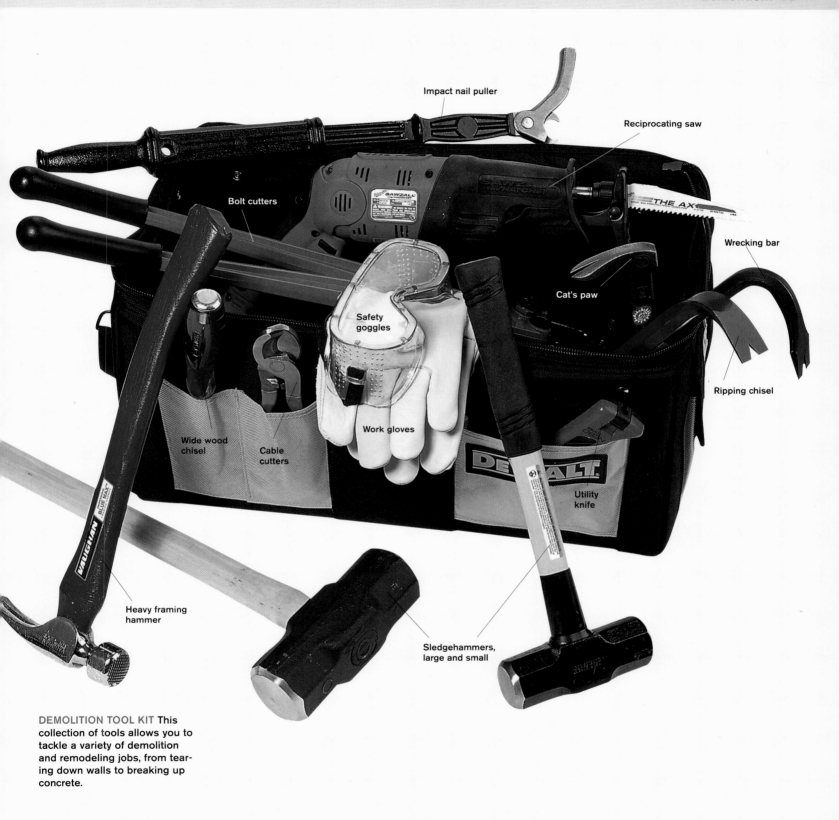

Impact nail puller

Reciprocating saw

Bolt cutters

Wrecking bar

Cat's paw

Safety goggles

Ripping chisel

Work gloves

Wide wood chisel

Cable cutters

Utility knife

Heavy framing hammer

Sledgehammers, large and small

DEMOLITION TOOL KIT This collection of tools allows you to tackle a variety of demolition and remodeling jobs, from tearing down walls to breaking up concrete.

SHARPENING

S harp tools are easier to use, making all of your cutting jobs go more smoothly. Keeping tools well sharpened is essential in any wood-shop or well-equipped home workshop. The sharpening kit shown in the photo and described in the chart below includes all the gear you'll need for regular sharpening and honing of most common tools—knives, chisels, blades, and the like—by hand. They may also need occasional regrinding on a bench grinder (see p. 183). Other special tools for sharpening drill bits, scrapers, and chainsaw blades are described at the end of the chart.

TOOL	PURPOSE	PAGE
Benchstones (oil or water) and/or diamond stones; one medium, one fine	Refine and hone sharp edges on cutting tools	186
Plastic container with sealable lid*	Keep waterstones immersed between uses	N/A
Abrasive plate with coarse abrasive	Restore nicked edges; flatten and deglaze benchstones	N/A
Angle-setting gauge and roller jig	Maintain bevel angle on blades and chisels when sharpening	180
Pocket stone (or honing rod or sharpening steel)	Keep knives and small edge tools honed	186, 188
Handheld sharpener	Hone knives and scissors	185
Files: flat mill, triangular, and round	Joint and sharpen handsaws, axes, and chainsaw blades	189
SPECIAL TOOLS		
Drill-bit sharpener	Restore sharp cutting tips on twist drill bits	190
Scraper jointing and burnishing tools	Sharpen cabinet scraper blades	191
Rotary tool with chainsaw sharpener accessory	Sharpen chainsaw teeth	190
Bench grinder	Remove nicks and restore angle on beveled cutting tools (planes, chisels, etc.)	183

*Only needed for waterstones

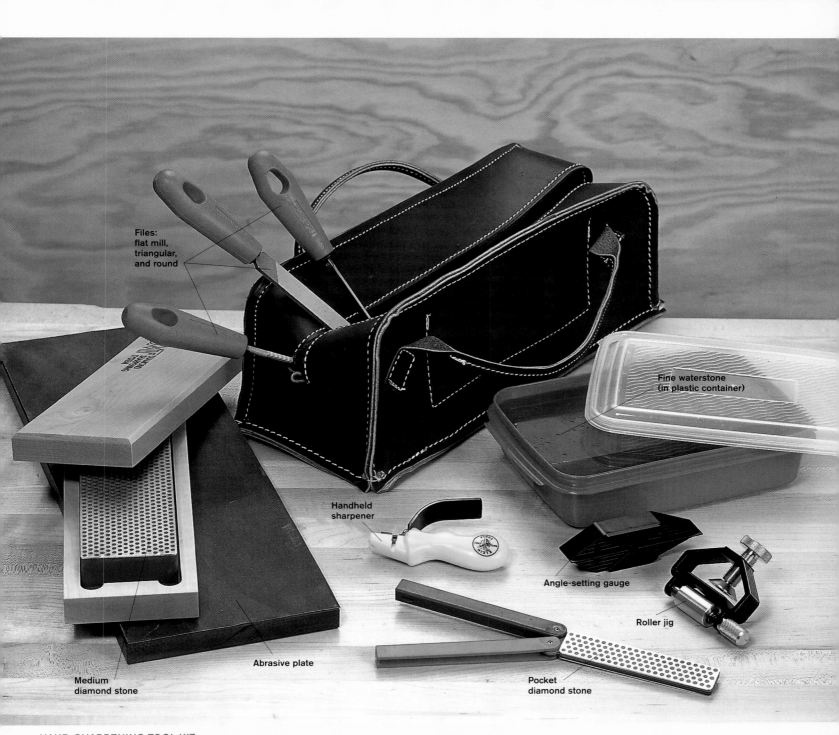

Files:
flat mill,
triangular,
and round

Fine waterstone
(in plastic container)

Handheld
sharpener

Angle-setting gauge

Roller jig

Abrasive plate

Medium
diamond stone

Pocket
diamond stone

HAND-SHARPENING TOOL KIT
Stowing a complement of hand-
sharpening tools in a drawer or
cabinet near your work area
makes it easy to hone your
edged tools often and keep
them cutting at their best.

TILE

A skillfully tiled kitchen countertop, bathroom vanity, or tub enclosure is a thing of beauty— at least until the grout starts to crack and discolor or the tiles chip and break. When it's time to spruce up the tile in your bathroom or install a new tile floor in the family room, the kit shown here has everything you'll need.

The tile kit includes the tools needed to cut and set tile, as well as the measuring and layout tools necessary for preparing walls, counters, and floors for tile installation. It also includes the trowels and other tools needed to create a mortar-bed foundation for tile or to cut and install a concrete backerboard foundation.

TOOL	PURPOSE	PAGE
Level (solid-bodied, not open I-beam style)*	Check counter, walls, and floor for level	208
Plumb bob*	Check vertical surfaces for plumb	213
Large folding square*	Check walls, floor, and counters for square; lay out work	207
Tape measure	Measure and lay out work	194
Chalkline	Mark layout lines	201
Scoring tile cutter (or electric wet tile saw)	Cut tiles in two; trim to size	107, 115
Tile nippers and/or tile saw	Notch or trim tiles to fit around moldings, obstructions	87, 117
Grout saw	Remove old grout	87
Scoring tool (or circular saw with abrasive blade)	Score and snap concrete backer board	92, 115
Hammer	Nail backer board to walls	155
Carbide hole saw	Drill hole for pipes, wires, etc.	85
Rubbing stone	Grind down sharp edges from cut tiles	N/A
Flat trowel (with notched edge) or flat and notched trowels	Spread mortar, thinset, and mastic	251
Margin trowel	Mix grout, thinset; butter backs of large tiles	251
Rubber mallet	Tap tiles into position	166
Grout float	Pack grout into joints between tiles	250
Bucket	Mix thinset, mortar, and grout; clean up	N/A
Large sponge	Clean off excess grout from tiles	N/A
Cheesecloth	Remove grout residue	N/A
Rubber gloves	Protect hands from mortar, thinset, grout, etc.	270
Dust mask	Prevent inhalation of dust when cutting backer board	265
Safety glasses; earplugs or earmuffs; work gloves	Protect eyes from flying chips; ears from power-tool noise; hands from sharp edges	261, 264, 269
Knee pads	Protect knees when setting floor tiles	272

*You can use a multibeam laser or rotary laser instead; see p. 211.

Cheesecloth

Large sponge

Bucket

Large folding square

Rubber gloves

Scoring-type tile cutter

Knee pads

Grout float

Flat trowel

Work gloves

Margin trowel

Carbide hole saw

Scoring tool

Solid-bodied level

Notched trowel

Safety glasses

Rubbing stone

Tape measure

Disposable dust mask

Plumb bob

Earplugs

Tile nippers

Rubber mallet

Chalkline

TILE TOOL KIT Ready to replace your plastic-laminate counters with high-class tile? This kit has all the lay-out, surface preparation, installation, and finishing tools you'll need.

ROOFING

To keep the rain out, any roof must be watertight and kept in good repair. Whether you're putting a new wood shake or composition shingle roof on your home, workshop, or utility shed or just replacing a few shingles, the kit shown in the photo has all the basic equipment you'll need for the job.

For fastening roofing, the kit outlined in the chart offers the option of choosing an air-powered roofing stapler or going manual with a shingling hammer. Other basic tools consist of layout, installation, and safety equipment, including safety glasses and antislip knee pads. If you must remove the old roof first, you'll also want to use the special demolition tool discussed and shown on p. 170.

TOOL	PURPOSE	PAGE
Air-powered roofing nailer or stapler (or shingling hammer)	Nail shingles; align rows	162
Nail pouch/tool belt	Hold loose roofing nails and/or clips for air nailer/stapler	N/A
Hammer tacker	Fasten roofing felt to sheathing	162
Tape measure	Lay out shingle rows	194
Chalkline	Strike layout lines for aligning rows of shingles	201
Utility knife	Cut roofing felt	121
Aviation snips	Cut roof flashing	110
Caulking gun	Seal around vent pipes and skylights	254
Knee pads (treaded cap)	Protect your knees; prevent you from slipping	272
Safety glasses/ear protection	Protect eyes and ears	261, 264
Ripout tool *	Remove old shingles and nails	170

*Only needed when removing old roof

Knee pads

Caulking gun

Aviation snips

Shingling hammer

DeWALT

Nail pouch

Air-powered roofing stapler

Tape measure

Hammer tacker

Chalkline

Utility knife

Ear plugs

Safety glasses

(Not shown: ripout tool)

ROOFING TOOL KIT Need to repair or replace a shingle roof? The collection of tools shown here includes almost everything you'll need, including a belt and pouch for nails or staples.

FLOORING

Other than a new coat of paint on the walls, nothing spruces up the look of a room better than a shiny new hardwood floor. Fortunately, thanks to new flooring products manufactured just for do-it-yourselfers, attractive wood (and woodlike laminate) floors have never been easier to install.

The kit shown in the photo contains the basic tools you'll need to lay out and install most common types of flooring. The kit, described in the chart, also includes many optional tools you may need, depending on the type of flooring you're installing: unfinished tongue-and-groove strips and

TOOL	PURPOSE	PAGE
Circular saw (or table saw)	Cut flooring strips or squares to size/width	92, 97
Miter box and saw (or powered crosscut saw)	Cut strip flooring to length	81, 100
Jigsaw (or coping saw)	Notch flooring to fit around doorjambs and obstructions	85, 88
Flush-trim saw	Trim bottom ends of doorjambs, casings; trim flush with new floor	83
Small pry bar (with wide end)	Remove baseboards; remove nails from wall or subflooring	170
Mallet	Knock flooring strips tightly together (use with a wood block)	165
Small finish hammer and nail set (or air-powered brad nailer)	Nail up baseboards and trim	160, 168
Knee pads (hard cap)	Protect your knees yet let you slide freely around the floor	272
Safety glasses/ear protection	Protect eyes and ears	261, 264
Contour gauge	Transfer profile when cutting flooring to fit around trim	203
SPECIAL TOOLS		
Air-powered or manual flooring nailer*	Fasten flooring to subfloor (can be rented)	219
Large layout square**	Ensure parquet tiles are installed square with walls	207
Notched trowel**	Apply adhesive for gluing down non-self-stick floor tiles	252
Floor roller (150 lb.)**	Press down flooring to assure proper adhesion	N/A
Belt sander, orbital sander, random-orbit sander#	Touch up areas left rough by drum and edge sanders	175, 176, 177
Drum and edge sanders#	Level and smooth wood flooring before finishing	N/A
Putty knife#	Add putty to knots and gaps	252
Ripout tool^	Remove old tile or linoleum flooring	169
Heat gun^	Soften old vinyl tile for removal	255

For installing tongue-and-groove flooring
**For installing prefinished parquet tile or ⅜-in.- or 5⁄16-in.-thick prefinished strip flooring*
For finishing unfinished flooring
^ *For removing old flooring*

floor tiles or prefinished parquet floor tiles and strip flooring. A flooring nailer, necessary for nailing down tongue-and-groove flooring strips, is discussed on p. 223. Tools for coating unfinished wood floors are discussed on p. 252. Also mentioned in the chart are tools used for the removal of old flooring, as well as specialized tools—such as floor sanders and drum rollers—which are needed for completion of some types of floors; these are typically rental items beyond the scope of this book.

Small pry bar

Mallet

Small finish hammer

Nail sets

Flush-trim saw

Circular saw

Jigsaw

Knee pads

Notched trowel

Safety glasses/ear protection

(Not shown: putty knife, heat gun, belt sander, orbital sander, random-orbit sander, contour gauge, drum and edge sanders, 150-lb. floor roller, large layout square, and ripout tool)

FLOORING TOOL KIT The kit here contains most of the tools you'll need for installing basic strip or parquet-tile wood floors. You'll need special tools and finishing supplies to complete some installations.

CHAPTER 1

Tools That Grab, Tighten & Hold

You can't get much work done if you can't hold on to the parts or materials you're working on. Sometimes, you need to keep a workpiece steady while you saw, plane, or pound on it—a job for a sturdy vise. Other times, clamps provide just the degree of hold necessary for pressing parts together during assembly. Bending, twisting, or cutting parts held freehand is a job for a good pair of pliers, with jaws sized and suited to the task. And there's an extensive variety of wrenches to choose from when it's time to put the grip on fasteners—nuts, bolts, plumbing fittings, etc.—that require tightening or loosening.

▲ASSORTMENT OF PLIERS Older pliers (rear) have attractive grips but are difficult to hold compared to the ergonomically shaped and padded grips found on modern pliers (front).

PLIERS

Take two metal rods, with shaped handles at one end and jaws at the other end of each, join them with a pivot pin, and you have a basic pair of pliers. Ranging in size from a mini 4-in. tool to the 20-in. super-heavy-duty giants, pliers are primarily made for gripping things—pipes, nuts and bolts, wires, rods, sheet-metal parts—to turn, bend, hold, or press them together. Although pliers' jaws often include a cutter, some types, such as diagonal pliers, or "dikes," are specifically designed to be cutting rather than gripping tools (see diagonal cutters on p. 112).

Pliers fall broadly into three categories: those with a single, fixed-pivot pin (lineman's, needle-nose, fence); those with a repositionable pivot (slip-joint, tongue-and-groove); and those that are adjustable with multiple pivots, such as locking pliers. Although older pliers had knurled or raised designs to provide better grip on their cast-metal handles, most modern pliers have ergonomically designed handles with padded grips (see the photo on the facing page).

Lineman's Pliers

Lineman's pliers got their name from electrical linemen, who liked the tool's streamlined head design because it easily slid in and out of their tool belts. Also called engineer's or side-cutting pliers, lineman's pliers are incredibly handy tools for all kinds of electrical installation and repair work. The tool's stout, serrated jaws have a flat section near the end to hold and twist bare wires together or to tear off knockouts from metal junction and fuse boxes. The jaws on most models have a curved section, for gripping and turning rods, as well as a built-in side cutter that's powerful enough to snip through thick copper wire and cable.

A 7-in.- to 9-in.-long pair is appropriate for general work (the bigger the pliers, the

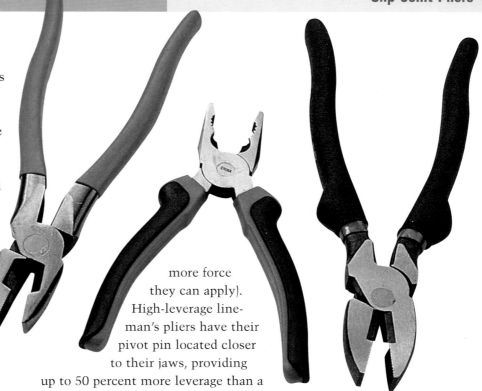

more force they can apply). High-leverage lineman's pliers have their pivot pin located closer to their jaws, providing up to 50 percent more leverage than a standard pair. If you plan to use lineman's pliers mainly for high-voltage electrical work, it's worth paying extra for a model with specially insulated handles (often referred to as electrician's pliers), which conform to standards for 1,000-volt shock protection (see the tip on p. 118).

Slip-Joint Pliers

If you're looking for a basic pair of pliers for a home or automotive tool kit, a pair of slip-joint pliers definitely fits the bill. Also called combination pliers, most slip-joint pliers have both flat and curved serrated jaws, so you can grab and hold either flat or round stock and even turn nuts or bolts in a pinch (of course, to avoid damaging the fastener, you *should* use the proper-size wrench). What gives slip-joint pliers their name is also what makes them unique and useful: When you need to hold larger, thicker work, the halves of the pliers expand at the pivot pin, thus allowing the jaws to open wider than usual (see the top photo at on p. 34).

A 6-in.- to 8-in.-long pair is good for light work around the house or shop. Better pairs are made from drop-forged steel,

▲**TRIO OF LINEMAN'S PLIERS**
Combining a strong wire cutter with a pair of stout pliers, lineman's pliers are a great tool for electrical installations and repairs.

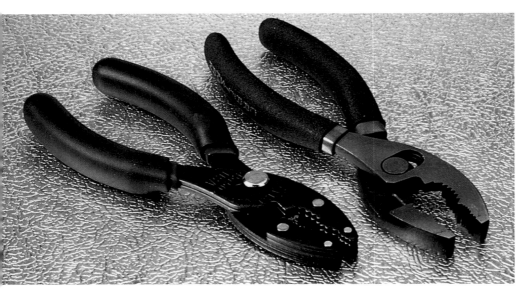

▲SLIP-JOINT PLIERS These two pairs of slip-joint pliers aren't alike: The pair on the right is made with durable drop-forged construction, while the lighter-duty pair on the left is made with economical laminated-plate construction.

Tongue-and-Groove Pliers

Tongue-and-groove (T&G) pliers have an adjustable joint that enables the tool to adjust to the size of the workpiece. But unlike slip-joint pliers, T&Gs have long handles, generating lots of leverage, that articulate on a series of semicircular joints, which adjust the jaws from five to eight positions, allowing a single tool to fit a wide range of fastener sizes (some models use a push-button locking mechanism that secures the slip joint at the desired setting; shown at far right in the photo below). A large 12-in. to 14-in. pair can grip objects ranging from a paper-thin width to 4½ in. thick. Their versatility makes tongue-and-groove pliers a must-have tool for a wide range of tool kits, including plumbing, mechanics, and home maintenance/repair. They're especially handy for grasping and turning large pipe connections, such as the drainpipes and P-traps used for household sinks, showers, and bathtubs.

while less expensive pliers are often built with laminated-steel-plate construction (shown at left in the photo above). Most slip-joint pliers have a shear-type wire cutter, which doesn't cut nearly as well as lineman's pliers or dikes but is handy in a pinch. Some models have handles with a flared slip guard to prevent your hands from slipping toward the jaws when applying forward pressure.

Sometimes called Channel locks (after a major brand that produces them) or adjustable gripping pliers, T&G pliers come in many different jaw styles. Straight-jaw pliers are for gripping sheet stock and flat objects; most have serrated jaws, with the exception of smooth-jaw pliers designed specifically to fasten chrome and plastic plumbing fixtures without marring them.

▼TONGUE-AND-GROOVE PLIERS With slightly different jaw shapes and sizes, each of the five pairs of tongue-and-groove pliers shown here is best suited for a different job.

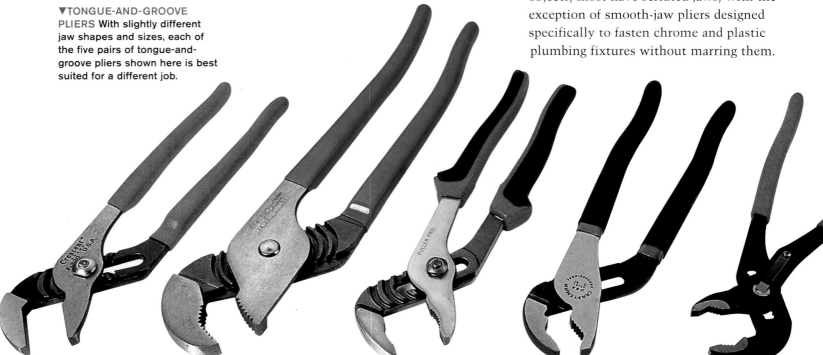

Curved-jaw pliers (a.k.a. water-pump pliers) are for gripping pipes, rods, and bolts; they have semiround serrated jaws that were originally designed for gripping pipe work. Other styles include alligator pliers, with V-shaped, self-gripping jaws designed to grip hexagonal nuts and bolts without slipping, and parrot-jaw pliers, with teeth specifically made to grip and bust loose, worn, or rusty fasteners.

Needle-Nose Pliers

Also called long-nose pliers, needle-nose pliers have a long, tapering snout, typically lined with fine serrations for a better grip. Needle-nose are much better than slip-joint or lineman's pliers for bending bare wire ends before attaching them to the screw terminals on electrical switches, outlets, and circuit breakers. They're also indispensable for installing tiny electronic components and jewelry findings, as well as for removing and replacing cotter pins and other small fasteners. Many needle-nose pairs also have a built-in side cutter for light wire-snipping duties.

Peruse a well-stocked tool-, electronics-, or jewelry-supply store, and you'll find more needle-nose shapes than at a plastic surgeon's office: long, short, bent, flat, recurved, etc. Long-nose pliers are obviously best for reaching into places with restricted clearance—say, when performing an automotive repair in a cramped engine compartment. But shorter-nose models make it easier to grip small objects. Curved styles are bent at an 80-degree angle, making them handy for reaching around objects. A variety of other special-shaped needle-nose pliers are used by jewelers,

Cool Tools	ROBOGRIP® PLIERS

ROBOGRIP® PLIERS may, at first glance, look like regular pliers, but they're the product of some serious brainpower. Designed by a team of ergonomic specialists and leading university engineers, RoboGrip pliers adjust like standard tongue-and-groove pliers, to fit a range of different-size workpieces. However, RoboGrips (also know as "smart pliers") are automatic, self-adjusting tools with a unique cam mechanism. All you do is slip the jaws over the work and press the handles; the jaws stay roughly parallel while adjusting to fit the thickness of the work.

The jaws on a 7-in. pair open up to ¾ in. wide, while a 9-in. pair opens up to 1½ in. wide. Available with straight, curved, or V jaws, RoboGrip pliers offer one-handed operation that makes them easy to use, even by people that aren't tool savvy. In fact, they're so user friendly that they've become the single most successful hand tool ever sold by Sears, Roebuck in its 75-year history.

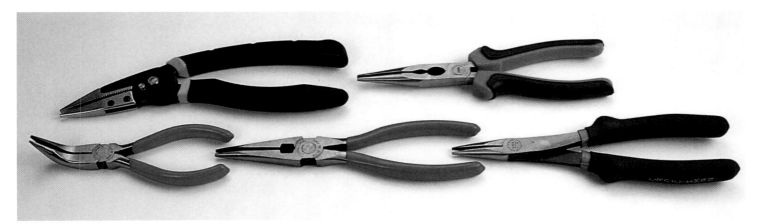

▲NEEDLE-NOSE PLIERS Whether they have short, long, bent, or locking jaws, needle-nose pliers are the tool of choice for bending wires, grabbing small parts in cramped locations, and much more.

To reduce hand fatigue, buy a pair of needle-nose pliers with a built-in leaf spring. The spring opens the pliers' jaws automatically when you release pressure, so you don't have to do hand gymnastics every time you need to grip a new object.

telephone workers, and even weavers, for specific operations. Parallel-jaw models (shown at top left in the bottom photo on p. 35) are more expensive, but they allow you to grip both thick and thin objects securely.

Locking Pliers

If there's only one pair of pliers you can take with you to a deserted island (or on television's *Survivor* challenge), make it a pair of locking pliers. Originally developed as the Vise-Grip® brand pliers by Vilhelm "Bill" Petersen in 1924, locking pliers are one of the handiest tools you can own. What makes them so handy? They combine the gripping jaws of a regular pair of pliers (most pairs also have a built-in wire cutter) with an adjustable locking mechanism. Once you lock on to an object—a bolt, pipe, pin, rod, etc.—you don't have to

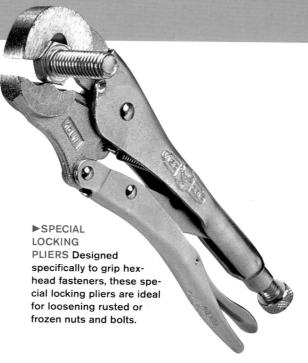

►SPECIAL LOCKING PLIERS Designed specifically to grip hex-head fasteners, these special locking pliers are ideal for loosening rusted or frozen nuts and bolts.

▼LOCKING PLIERS With an iron grip that clamps to the part you're holding, locking pliers have jaws designed to fit workpieces of different sizes and shapes.

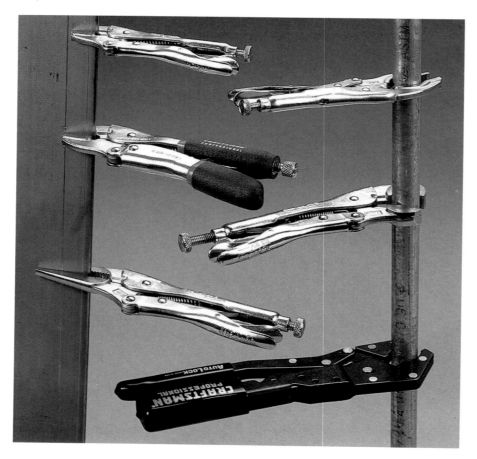

continue squeezing while you pull, twist, or turn it.

Available in several sizes and more than a dozen jaw configurations, locking pliers are a truly versatile tool that's useful not only as a pair of pliers but also as a pipe wrench, an adjustable wrench, a wire cutter, a ratchet, or a clamp. In addition to the conventional straight-jaw pliers, they also come in curved-jaw, long-nose, and bent-nose styles. You can also buy specialty locking welding clamps and chain clamps (for use on pipes and other round objects). There's even a locking wrench model, which firmly grabs hexagonal nuts or bolt heads without scarring them.

Here are just a few ideas how you could use a pair of locking pliers around the house, garage, or home workshop: to turn nuts, bolts, and studs; to hold metal parts for soldering or brazing; to clamp small wood objects for gluing; to close the links on chains; to crack Brazil nuts and pecans; to crimp wire connectors; to extract broken bolts and screws; to hold small items while drilling or cutting; to remove bottle caps; to loosen round oil-drain plugs; and to unscrew broken lightbulbs (and I'm just getting started).

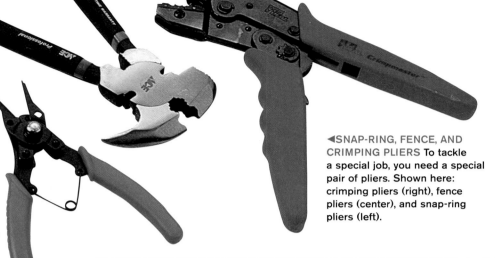

Specialized Pliers

While the majority of pliers are for general use, some pairs are designed for highly specialized purposes (making jewelry, assembling and repairing electronic components, etc.). There are three pliers discussed in this section, each with a form and feature specific to a particular task or range of tasks—setting and cutting fence wire, installing and removing snap rings, and attaching electric connectors.

FENCE PLIERS If you have to run fence wire around your yard or property, a pair of fence pliers is about all you need to do the job. Especially designed for installing and maintaining wire fence on metal or wood posts, this odd-looking tool (shown at center in the photo above) is really several tools in one; hence, it's alternately called a multipurpose fence tool. It has a heavy-duty wire cutter that cuts though even double-strand barbed wire, along with oval-face jaws for gripping and twisting wire or pulling it tight between posts. Although some fence pliers lack them, most models also have a built-in corrugated hammer-head on one jaw, for hammering staples and nails, and on the other jaw, a hook-shaped prong for pulling staples.

SNAP-RING PLIERS You can drive a nail with a rock or remove it with a pair of pliers in a pinch. On the other hand, a snap ring—a retaining or locking ring frequently used in automobiles and in machinery with all kinds of gear, bearing, and shaft assemblies—requires a specialized tool for removal and installation. Also known as lock-ring or retaining-ring pliers, snap-ring pliers come in three basic types: Internal pliers com-

◄SNAP-RING, FENCE, AND CRIMPING PLIERS To tackle a special job, you need a special pair of pliers. Shown here: crimping pliers (right), fence pliers (center), and snap-ring pliers (left).

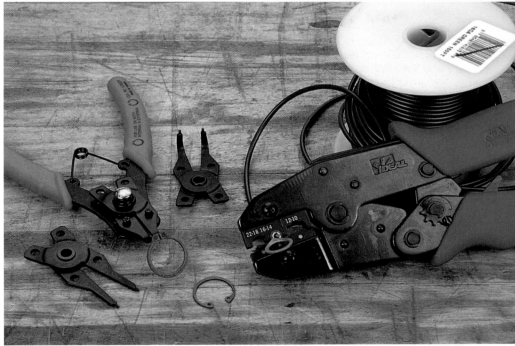

press rings that snap inside of hollow components (bearings, gears, etc.); external pliers expand rings that fit on the outside of shafts; and combination pliers have reversible jaws that convert, compressing internal rings in one position and expanding external rings in the other. A pair of combination pliers is the most practical tool for casual users because it allows you to deal with most snap rings that are

▲SNAP-RING AND CRIMPING PLIERS With its interchangeable heads, a snap-ring pliers set (left) is used to remove or install all styles of snap rings. The pair of crimping pliers (right) have jaws for setting three different sizes of crimp-style electrical connectors.

encountered when repairing home-work-shop machinery and household appliances. It is also the most versatile tool because it comes with several sets of interchangeable jaws (shown at left in the top photo on p. 37) to fit a wide range of situations.

CRIMPING PLIERS If your electrical or electronic projects involve lots of wiring, you've probably discovered the convenience of using solderless connectors. After slipping one of these components onto a bare-wire end, you use a special crimping die to fasten it permanently in place. Most multipurpose wire strippers (see p. 118) include a crimping feature that's good for light use. But you'll get better results by using a dedicated pair of crimping pliers. These are heavy-duty tools designed to handle both insulated and uninsulated terminals, lugs, and splices, making them useful for automotive, computer, home-electrical, appliance, audio, and electronic wiring jobs.

Because different-size insulated connectors fit a specific range of wire sizes, most

crimping pliers have color-coded dies; you use the blue die for blue connectors, red die for red connectors, etc. Ratcheting-style crimpers (shown at right in the top photo on p. 37) use a compound-lever action that puts more crimping power into each squeeze, assuring a reliable, uniform crimp every time. The pliers' jaws release automatically when the crimp is complete. For television and home-theater connections using coaxial wire, employ special crimpers that are designed for the hexagonal connectors used with coaxial wiring.

WRENCHES

Peek into a professional machinist's or auto mechanic's tool chest, and you'll see more types of wrenches than you ever imagined possible. Most are esoteric wrenches designed to serve specific tasks, including spanner wrenches, flare-nut wrenches, Saltus (open-end/socket-end) wrenches, bent obstruction wrenches, tappet wrenches, ignition wrenches, and more. Fortunately,

▼**WRENCH ASSORTMENT Not all wrenches are made to turn nuts and bolts. The assortment here includes (left to right): Allen, adjustable, socket, gas shutoff, pipe, and quick-action wrenches.**

▲OPEN-END, COMBINATION, AND BOX WRENCHES Depending on the accessibility and force with which you want to turn a nut or bolt, choose a box (bottom right), combination (middle right), or open-end (top right) wrench.

the majority of us only need a few basic types of wrenches—box, open-end, adjustable, pipe, etc.—to perform most of our daily tasks: to change the oil in a lawn-mower or spark plugs in an automobile, to tighten a V-belt on a table saw or clothes dryer, or to replace a leaky pipe on a pool pump and filter.

Box, Open-End, and Combination Wrenches

Box, open-end, and combination wrenches are the three most basic, nonadjustable wrenches out there for tightening and loosening hex-head nuts, bolts, and fasteners. A box wrench (shown at bottom right in the photo above) offers the surest grip because its 12-point-socketlike head (see "Socket Wrenches" on p. 41) surrounds the fastener's head on all sides. They're indispensable for dealing with stuck bolts or nuts that require high torque to loosen or tighten. The latest box wrenches have a special

design that drives the side of the hex nut or bolt, not the corner, helping you avoid rounding over rusted or damaged fasteners.

When a box wrench won't fit or the end of the nut or bolt isn't accessible, an open-end wrench (shown at top right in the photo above) is the next-best choice. This wrench's parallel jaws grip only two sides of a hex-head bolt (they also fit square nuts and bolts, which are often used in farm equipment), so care is required when applying lots of force, as slipping off can not only damage the fastener but also result in bloody knuckles. Offset box wrenches have sharply offset ends for improved hand clearance in tight work spaces.

A combination wrench (shown at center right in the photo above) simply has a box wrench at one end and an open-end wrench at the other—both the same size. (Box wrenches and open-end wrenches, on the other hand, have two different size wrenches

Cool Tools — SPEED WRENCHES

SPEED WRENCHES tighten or loosen nuts and bolts faster than regular wrenches allow. Pick from one of these three designs:

GEAR WRENCHES, shown at left in the photo below, come in sets of both metric and standard sizes and look much like regular combination wrenches. However, each wrench has a clever reversible ratchet mechanism that drives its box wrench with the ratcheting action of a socket wrench. The fine-tooth ratchet allows you to turn the wrench handle as little as 5 degrees for each tightening or loosening motion, which lets you work in very cramped places.

QUICK WRENCHES, shown at center in the photo, look much like regular open-end wrenches but feature an angular cutout in the wrench's jaw, which engages the bolt/nut head in only one direction, releasing it in the other. This design allows you to ratchet the tool around the head of a nut or bolt without having to completely remove the tool from the head for each and every turn. This saves time and frustration, especially when dealing with fasteners that you can't see or are hard to reach.

CLENCH WRENCHES, shown at right in the photo, are equal parts adjustable wrench, combination wrench, and pliers. The tool's spring-loaded, self-adjusting, pivoting jaws automatically adjust and lock onto different-size fasteners—the harder you pull, the tighter it gets. You can work one-handed and without repositioning the wrench after each turn, much the same as with the gear and quick wrenches.

Pro Tip

Inexpensive wrenches are fine for tool kits used occasionally, like for emergency roadside auto repair. But when equipping your home workshop or business, you can't go wrong buying the highest-quality tools you can afford. They won't rust, deform, or break during heavy use and will last for decades.

at either end, for example, 7/16 in. and 1/2 in. or 13mm and 15mm.)

All of these wrenches—box, open-end, and combination—have variations suited to special uses. Long-pattern wrenches have longer handles for better reach and greater leverage when loosening stuck nuts and bolts. Short-pattern wrenches give you greater access in confined spaces. These wrenches (as well as their quick-action and specialized variations—see "Speed Wrenches" above) also come in both standard fractional (also known as SAE) and metric sizes. Polished, chrome-plated wrenches are easier to clean and wrenches with rounded handle edges increase user comfort.

Adjustable Wrenches

Professional mechanics will tell you that turning a nut with a good box or open-end wrench is always preferable to using an adjustable wrench. But it's not always practical to carry a whole set of wrenches with you—in your car or bicycle bag, for instance. An adjustable wrench fits any size nut within its size range—both U.S. standard and metric—so a single wrench can serve the same duty as an entire set of fixed wrenches. Plus, an adjustable fits British Whitworth fasteners used on English bikes and equipment, as well as off-size nuts and bolts occasionally found on inexpensive machinery made in Asia.

Adjustable wrenches (sometimes called Crescent wrenches, after that common brand name) come in sizes ranging from a petite 4 in. long to a mammoth 24-in. length. The most practical size for average users is a 6-in. or 8-in. wrench, which will handle the largest fasteners you're likely to encounter. A large 12-in. to 15-in. wrench is a smart purchase for a workshop because it will turn large nuts used in shop machines and equipment, and it's cheaper to buy a single adjustable than an expensive set of large fixed wrenches.

While the majority of adjustables have bare, drop-forged steel handles, wrenches with plastic or rubberized coatings are more comfortable to grip, and insulated models can even protect you from electric shock (see "Lineman's Pliers" on p. 33).

Adjustables with thin heads are great for reaching into tight confines or for turning a pair of locking nuts, where two wrenches are used. Some newer models have measurement scales stamped into them (see right two tools in the top photo on the facing page), with inches on one side and millimeters on the other. These let you use the wrench as a handy caliper for sizing nuts, part thicknesses, and pipe or tube diameters.

▲ADJUSTABLE WRENCHES A single adjustable wrench can replace several fixed-size wrenches, making it a handy tool to have in your tool chest or kit.

Socket Wrenches

Like a box wrench, the body of a socket wrench surrounds the fastener, creating positive contact and sure driving. When used with a ratchet wrench, you also can use a socket wrench to drive a fastener more quickly than you can with a fixed wrench.

Each socket wrench fits only one size of fastener but is part of a modular system, with sockets and accessories mounting to a square, quick-release drive handle (see the bottom photo on p. 42). A typical set includes either metric or U.S. standard sockets and one or more driving handles. Sets are sized not only by the range of socket sizes they contain (e.g., 10mm to 19mm), but also by the size of the square-drive handle they fit. The three most common drive sizes are ¼ in., ⅜ in., and ½ in. A set with a ⅜-in. drive and ⅜-in. to ¾-in. sockets is the right size for most of the fasteners you'll encounter around the house.

Most sets come with accessories to increase driving versatility. These include: extensions, which increase the reach of a socket from the drive handle/ratchet wrench; universal joints, which allow the socket to be driven at an angle relative to the drive handle; and drive adapters, which allow, for example, a ⅜-in. drive handle to accept a ¼-in. drive socket.

Sockets, as well as special wrenches that fit standard ratcheting and other socket drive wrenches, come in many styles.

▲SOCKET SET AND DRIVE ACCESSORIES A full set of socket wrenches includes various-size sockets, drive handles, and accessories, including universal drives and extensions.

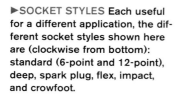

►SOCKET STYLES Each useful for a different application, the different socket styles shown here are (clockwise from bottom): standard (6-point and 12-point), deep, spark plug, flex, impact, and crowfoot.

Some are right for everyday jobs, like tightening or loosening nuts and bolts. Others are made for specific applications, such as installing spark plugs or for use with an impact wrench (see "Impact Drivers and Wrenches" on p. 147).

SOCKET TYPES Standard 12-point sockets are best for general nut-turning duties. Six-point sockets are stronger than 12-point sockets and offer firmer contact. Deep sockets come in 6-point and 12-point styles and drive bolts deep in recesses. Spark-plug sockets are long, like deep sockets with an inner foam-rubber sleeve. Flex sockets are shallow, 6-point sockets with a built-in universal joint and can be driven at an angle. Impact drive sockets are thick

walled and much stronger than regular sockets; they handle high-torque air-powered or electric-impact wrenches. Crowfoot wrenches aren't really sockets but rather cutoff, open-end wrenches that fit onto a socket drive extension; they can tighten or loosen nuts with zero clearance on one side.

SOCKET DRIVE HANDLES The beauty of a socket wrench set is that you can change the usefulness of any socket by attaching it to a different drive handle. The most useful and common are ratchet handles, which drive the socket in one direction yet allow the handle to return in the other. A small lever on the head lets you change drive direction for tightening or loosening. Better-quality fine-tooth ratchets have a short swing, so very little handle motion advances the fastener (important when you're working in a cramped space).

Variations on ratchet handles include short and thin profile (for tight spots), flex head (for off-angle driving), spider drive (for driving in tight spaces—cranking a handle at one end of the spider drive rotates a socket at the other end), and air-powered (see "Air-Powered Ratchet Wrench" on p. 44).

There are other, nonratcheting socket-wrench handles, including torque handles (described in the next section) that are use-

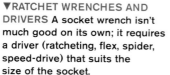

▼RATCHET WRENCHES AND DRIVERS A socket wrench isn't much good on its own; it requires a driver (ratcheting, flex, spider, speed-drive) that suits the size of the socket.

ful for both home and professional work-shops. Slide-bar or flex T-handles (some-times called breaker bars) are perfect for tightening or loosening high-torque nuts, such as the lug nuts on your car's wheels. A speed drive handle works like a brace-style drill (see "Braces and Hand Drills" on p. 143), allowing you to spin nuts or bolts with long threads very quickly. Screwdriver-type handles are perfect for driving small nuts, much like a nut driver (see "Nut Drivers" on p.153).

Torque Wrenches

The engine in a car, motorcycle, or lawn-mower is carefully engineered and bolted together. Whenever you take an engine—or other highly engineered mechanism—apart, you need to carefully tighten the bolts and nuts that hold it together, as specified by the manufacturer. Torque wrenches are designed to serve just this purpose. Torque wrenches are socket-wrench handles with a built-in meter that measures the amount of turning force—or torque—you exert as you tighten a nut or bolt. High-quality wrenches come in both micrometer and digital styles; both have an adjuster that lets you set the desired amount of torque.

On smaller wrenches, the setting is shown on a scale as ounce-inches or pound-inches, and on larger ones, it's shown as foot-pounds or pound-feet (some models have dual scales that also show metric newton meters). As the fastener is tight-ened, the wrench clicks and/or releases pressure when the desired torque setting has been reached. Less expensive

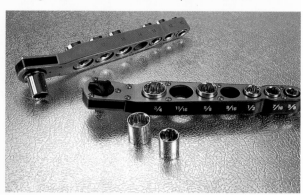

Cool Tools | **THE SOCKETSTIK WRENCH**

THE SOCKETSTIK SOCKET AND RATCHET SET combines a complete set of sockets and a ratcheting drive handle all in a single tool. The Socketstik's unique wrench has built-in storage compart-ments for the seven sock-ets included in the kit (both standard and metric sizes are available). Although considerably larger and less "hand friendly" than a standard ratchet wrench, this design keeps everything together in a compact, convenient kit.

▲TORQUE WRENCH Tightening bolts evenly and to the same degree on automobile engines and deli-cate machinery is a job for a torque wrench.

◄TORQUE-WRENCH SCALES The beam-style torque wrench (top) has a simple pointer and scale that shows how much torque is being applied. The micrometer wrench (bottom) is set to the desired torque by twisting the handle.

beam-type torque wrenches (shown at top in the bottom photo on p. 43) display foot-pounds or inch-pounds via a long pointer and scale. They're less accurate than micrometer or digital wrenches, but they are considerably less expensive and good enough for less sensitive tightening tasks, such as mounting lug nuts or installing spark plugs on the family car.

Strap Wrenches

This clever wrench doesn't look much like a wrench at all. Often used by mechanics for removing canister-style oil filters from gasoline or diesel engines and generators, a strap wrench is also a useful household tool for gripping, loosening, and tightening the lids on jars, bottles, pipe caps, and canisters. The tool's operation is simple: Just wrap the strap around an object, slip the strap's loose end into the wrench, and then pull the handle. The harder you pull, the tighter the strap grips the object, and the more leverage you have to turn it (people with weak hands really love this tool). The wrench lets you apply pressure judiciously, and the strap doesn't leave any tool marks the way a pair of pliers or a pipe wrench would. This makes a strap wrench the perfect choice for installing thin-walled, polished-chrome drainpipe.

Heavy-duty strap wrenches with cast-metal handles and straps made of rubberized webbing (shown at right in the photo below) can turn large-diameter pipes and large, difficult-to-grip objects. An even heavier-duty variation of this tool, used by plumbers for tightening pipes and fixtures, is called a chain wrench (it has a chain instead of a strap). In contrast, plastic wrenches with rubber straps are good for basic household, lid-turning chores

Allen Wrenches

You don't have to know who Allen was in order to make use of his fasteners and the wrenches that fit them. Also called Allen keys or hex keys (for their six-sided shape),

▶STRAP WRENCHES When you need to turn a pipe or open a jar without marring or damaging it, reach for a strap wrench.

▲ALLEN WRENCHES To suit every need, Allen wrenches come in three styles: T-handle, loose (set in a holder), and folding jackknife style.

Allen wrenches tighten and loosen machine screws, cap screws, and other fasteners with hexagonal-socket heads. Allen wrenches are also needed for installing/removing setscrews commonly used to lock pulleys, sheaves, and gears to their shafts.

Like other wrenches, Allens come in both standard and metric sizes. A set of simple Allen wrenches resembles different-size hexagonal bars, each bent into an L shape. You insert the long end of the L into a fastener for quicker turning, and you use the short leg when you need more leverage. To keep all the loose wrenches organized, most sets come with either a bag or a plastic holder, as shown at center in the top photo above.

Allen wrenches also come as T-handle wrenches (shown at left in the top photo above) with cushion-grip handles that provide more leverage and comfort than loose wrenches. Some loose-wrench and T-handle sets come with ball ends (see the bottom photo above), a useful innovation that allows the wrench to be off-axis from the screw as you turn it, enabling you to drive screws in confined spaces.

A folding Allen wrench set resembles a jackknife, in that individual-size wrenches hinge out of a metal or plastic handle (shown at right in the top photo above). While a folding set's short wrenches don't have the reach or leverage of loose or T-handled Allen wrenches, individual wrenches won't get lost, and you'll always have a full set of metric or standard wrenches on hand when you need them (they're handy for auto- or home-repair tool kits).

▲ALLEN WRENCH DRIVE TIPS
A standard Allen wrench (left) is great when you have clear access to a screw. A ball-drive Allen (right) has a special tip that lets you angle the tool as you drive hard-to-reach screws.

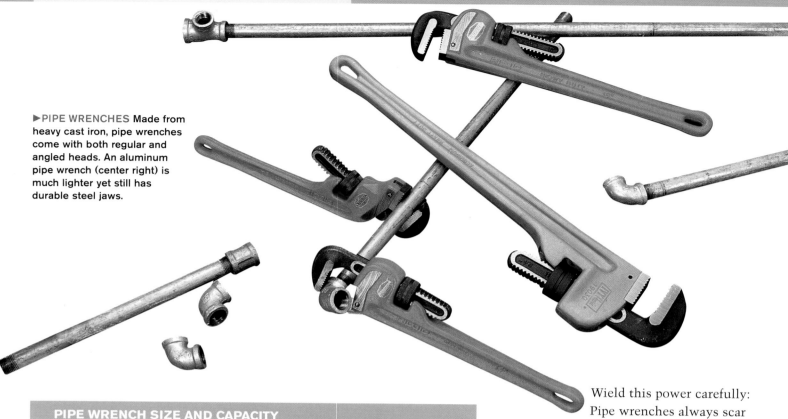

▶PIPE WRENCHES Made from heavy cast iron, pipe wrenches come with both regular and angled heads. An aluminum pipe wrench (center right) is much lighter yet still has durable steel jaws.

PIPE WRENCH SIZE AND CAPACITY

Length of Wrench	Diameter of Pipe/Fitting the Wrench Fits
6 in.	⅛ in. to ¾ in.
8 in.	⅛ in. to ¾ in.
10 in.	⅛ in. to 1 in.
14 in.	¼ in. to ½ in.
18 in.	¼ in. to 2 in.
24 in.	¼ in. to ½ in.
36 in.	½ in. to 3½ in.

Pipe Wrenches

When you have to remove, refit, or replace galvanized or black steel pipe and fittings, a pipe wrench is the tool for the job. A type of Stillson wrench, a pipe wrench is an adjustable wrench with one fixed jaw and one movable jaw. A large knurled nut moves the upper jaw until it's in light contact with the pipe. When the handle is pulled, sharp teeth that run across both jaws bite deeply into the metal, giving the wrench tremendous turning power—more power than any other wrench can develop.

Wield this power carefully: Pipe wrenches always scar the pipe with deep marks and so should never be used on plated pipes, soft copper or thin bronze pipe, or flat-sided fitting such as unions and valves. (When assembling threaded pipe and fittings—elbows, tees, couplings, reducers, etc.—say, to run water to a new bathroom or replace leaky pipes in a shower, you'll need to use two pipe wrenches. One wrench holds the pipe/fitting steady, while the other threads the new component in place.)

Standard pipe wrenches have jaws that are perpendicular to the handle and are good for most uses. Alternatively, offset pipe wrenches (shown at center left in the photo above) have angled jaws that are easier to slip on and off pipes located in tight areas, such as attics and crawl spaces.

Although they're adjustable, any particular size of pipe wrench can handle only a limited range of pipe and fitting sizes; the chart at left shows the maximum diameters that each size wrench can handle. A 10-in. pipe wrench is probably the smallest (and lightest) wrench that will work with ½-in. and ¾-in. galvanized pipes and fittings—the two sizes most commonly used in home and garden plumbing systems. If you need to buy a larger-size pipe wrench, consider paying more for a lightweight aluminum model (shown at center right in the photo on the facing page).

Special Plumbing Wrenches

With the possible exception of professional plumbers, most of us who do our own household plumbing need all the help we can get. When installing kitchen and bathroom fixtures, there are several kinds of specialty wrenches to make particular jobs a lot easier. The photo below shows several of these plumbing helpers, which are discussed in the following paragraphs.

BASIN WRENCHES Also known as a sink wrench or fixture wrench, a basin wrench (second from left in the photo below) is used to tighten coupling nuts and tailpiece mounting nuts when installing a kitchen or bathroom sink. Its funny bent shape is designed for reaching up and behind an installed sink, where it's nearly impossible to use any other wrench. A basin wrench's spring-loaded jaws automatically adjust to fit a wide range of nuts. The jaws grip the nut each time the wrench is turned or repositioned, without the need for any hand tightening.

CLOSET SPUD WRENCHES Also called a plumber's wrench, a closet spud wrench fits the large toilet spuds (flanged nuts), slip nuts, and lock nuts used to connect drainpipes to toilets, sinks, and other plumbing fixtures. The wrench, shown at left in the photo below fits 1¾-in., 2-in., and 2½-in. nuts.

ADJUSTABLE SLIP-NUT WRENCHES This versatile tool (shown at upper right in the photo below does the same thing as a closet spud wrench but adjusts to fit any flange, slip, or lock nut between 1¼ in. and 3 in. in size.

P.O. PLUG WRENCHES This odd-looking tool (shown at lower right in the photo below) unscrews and removes the strainers and drain fittings on kitchen sinks, bathtubs, and showers. It lets you tighten the strainer basket without ruining its chrome finish.

GARBAGE-DISPOSAL WRENCHES This wrench (not shown) fits down into a kitchen sink to engage the blades on a common garbage-disposal unit. Turning the wrench frees the disposal when it's stuck due to lodged debris.

> ### Pro Tip
>
> Standard cast-iron pipe wrenches are heavy—even in the smaller sizes. Aluminum wrenches have the same steel jaws and adjustment mechanisms as standard wrenches, but they weigh about 40 percent less. Less weight means you can work with them longer with less fatigue.

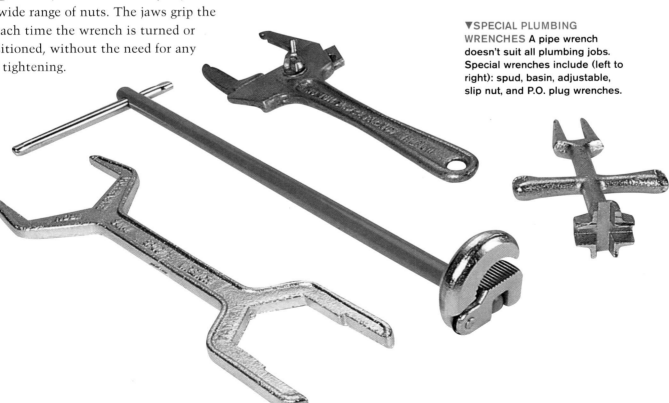

▼SPECIAL PLUMBING WRENCHES A pipe wrench doesn't suit all plumbing jobs. Special wrenches include (left to right): spud, basin, adjustable, slip nut, and P.O. plug wrenches.

▶**VISES AND CLAMPS** To hold work steady or secure workpieces to one another, nothing beats a sturdy vise or clamp.

▼**C-CLAMP ASSORTMENT** Large or small, deep-throated or regular, C-clamps are sturdy, versatile, and useful for all kinds of glue-up, holding, and assembly chores.

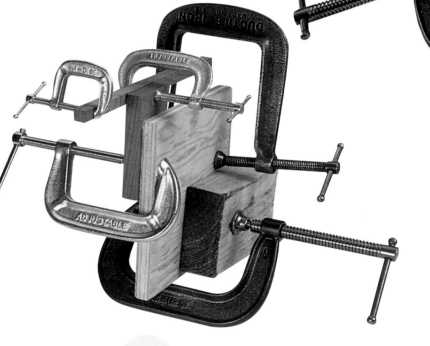

Pro Tip

When using C-clamps to press parts together during gluing, distribute the pressure by putting a scrap-wood block between the clamp and the work. The block also prevents the clamp from denting the work's surface.

CLAMPS AND VISES

You can't easily clench the separate parts of your project together or hold parts steady while working on them without achieving a good grip, and that's exactly what clamps and vises are designed to do. Clamps are useful for all manner of assembly, from gluing up wood cabinet doors or cabinets to firmly holding steel parts for welding. And to get the job done right, clamps come in a staggering assortment of shapes and sizes, from compact C-clamps and spring clamps to lengthy bar and pipe clamps.

Unlike clamps, which are most often used freehand, vises are rigidly attached to a bench or other sturdy workpiece. Their strong jaws grip parts securely and hold them rock solid during sawing, planing, pounding, and grinding. In addition to multi-purpose vises, which are handy for home hobbies and repairs, there are specialized vises designed for working with wood or metal.

C-Clamps

One of the simplest clamps is also the most versatile. With a metal frame shaped like the letter *C*, a C-clamp has a strong threaded screw that can concentrate tremendous pressure in a small area. It's widely used for clamping parts in place during gluing or for holding wood parts for sawing, routing, or planing. As they're made entirely of metal, C-clamps are also great for holding metal parts and assemblies in position during welding.

Sized by their capacity (the maximum thickness they can clamp) and throat depth (the farthest their jaws reach in from the edge of the work), C-clamps range from 1 in. with a 1-in. throat to 12 in. with a 4-in. throat. While even the smallest shop will want to have a good selection of different sizes on hand, you'll find that a couple of 3-in. or 4-in. C-clamps can handle a lot of the holding tasks you'll encounter around the house. Painted or nickel-plated clamps won't rust like bare-metal clamps, especially if they're kept in a damp garage or basement.

Two useful variations of the basic C-clamp are deep-throated clamps and edging clamps. Deep-throated clamps (shown at rear in the bottom photo on the facing page) have (big surprise) a deeper throat, so you can position the clamping jaws farther in from the edge of the work. Edging clamps look like C-clamps with an additional clamping screw set perpendicularly through the middle of the C-frame. The extra screw is for clamping banding, edging strips, or molding to the edge of a panel, counter, or tabletop—for example, a solid-wood strip that covers the raw edge of a plywood door or drawer front.

Handscrews

A very old style of clamp, which was once made entirely out of wood, modern handscrews have deep jaws that reach much farther than steel C-clamps. A handscrew's large wooden jaws also grip the work more securely and distribute pressure more evenly than clamps with small clamping faces. And since they're made of hardwood, you can use them to glue up wood parts without the need for clamp pads (see the tip on the facing page).

After quickly adjusting the clamp to the approximate size (see the tip at right), you tighten the clamp on the work by turning primarily the rear screw. Turning the clamp's two screws by different amounts angles the jaws to grip nonparallel surfaces and tapered, cylindrical, or odd-shaped workpieces—a neat trick that's useful to woodworkers, carpenters, and do-it-yourselfers alike.

Handscrews come in several sizes ranging from cute 4-in. clamps, useful to model makers and miniaturists, to massive 16-in. clamps that could be used for gluing construction lumber into a laminated beam. A couple of pairs of 6-in. and/or 12-in. handscrews would serve well in a small home shop. Although ready-made handscrews are expensive, more affordable kits are available that supply the metal screws and hardware; you craft the wooden parts yourself.

> **Pro Tip**
>
> The best method for quickly closing or opening the jaws of a handscrew is to grasp the clamp handles and rotate the entire clamp in front of you (see the photo below). Hold the handle that's closest to the jaws in your right hand and rotate the top of the clamp away from you to open the jaws.

◄HANDSCREW Tightening or loosening the jaws of a handscrew clamp is quick if you use both hands and rotate the clamp in front of you.

─── **Pro Tip** ───

Need to push an assembled cabinet or frame apart instead of clamping it together? You can reverse the movable clamping heads on most styles of pipe clamps—and on some bar and quick-adjusting clamps—to temporarily transform them into powerful spreader clamps.

Bar and Pipe Clamps

When you want to grip or clamp a large object that's too big for most clamps to handle (for example, C-clamps and handscrews), it's time to reach for bar or pipe clamps. Both styles of clamps consist of a pair of clamping heads: one stationary head with a threaded screw and handle that applies the clamping pressure and another head that slides up and down on the bar or pipe to adjust the clamping capacity. A self-locking clutch plate keeps this head from moving after it's positioned. By moving the sliding head, a long bar or pipe clamp can grip an object that's much narrower than the clamp's maximum capacity.

PIPE CLAMPS These clamps are best for gripping really long or wide work—a table and countertops, plywood and paneling, etc. That's because the length of a pipe clamp is only limited by the length of the pipe used—you buy the clamping heads

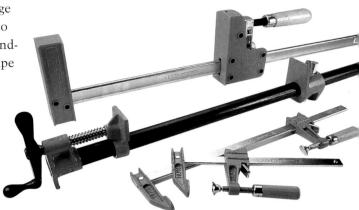

▲BAR AND PIPE CLAMPS
Gluing up wood projects requires strong clamps, including short or long bar clamps and/or pipe clamps, shown here.

Tool Helpers	**CLAMP PADS AND SOFT VISE JAWS**

The jaw faces of metal clamps and bench vises are strong, but they can also mash the objects they're gripping. Slide-on plastic clamp pads and soft vise jaws are an inexpensive way to protect wood, plastic, and even metal surfaces from scratches, dents, and dings. Interestingly, they can also prevent iron stains, which can occur when gluing tannin-rich woods, like oak and ash, with water-based glues. The pads are made to fit many different types and brands of clamps; most quick-action clamps already come with them. While they don't help distribute clamping pressure like clamping blocks do, they're much handier to use since they stay snapped in place until you remove them. Soft vise faces are also made of flexible plastic and are often held in place by magnetic inserts, so you can pull them off instantly when they're not needed.

and mount them to any length pipe (galvanized or black steel, with threaded ends) you choose. Models that fit ¾-in. pipe are for heavier clamping duties; ½-in. models are good enough for general work. Pipe clamps have a relatively shallow throat, but they're still terrific for gluing up door and picture frames, and all kinds of cabinets (you can fit them with special jaw extenders that increase throat depth up to 10 in., but they are expensive).

BAR CLAMPS These come in three basic styles: deep-throat, quick-adjusting, and heavy-duty. Deep-throat clamps have heads that ride on a flat steel bar that's 6 in. to 36 in. long. Their deep reach, adjustability, and relatively light weight make them a versatile and popular choice for general gluing and gripping tasks. Deep-throat clamps come in light-, medium-, and heavy-duty models, as well as a special parallel-jaw version, designed specifically for accurately clamping up cabinet assemblies and fine furniture projects (shown at rear in the photo on the facing page).

Bar-style quick-adjusting clamps resemble deep-throat bar clamps but have an innovative design that's easy to use, even single handed (see "Quick-Adjusting Clamps" at right).

Heavy-duty bar clamps look like pipe clamps but with a massive steel I-beam or square channel instead of a pipe. Available in 1-ft. to 6-ft. sizes, these weighty bruisers can generate enough pressure to clamp really beefy parts together—say, to glue up an enormous wooden entry door for your home.

Spring Clamps

One of the handiest things you can have around your house or home workshop is a spring clamp. It's like a big clothespin only with larger, padded jaws and handles. Spring clamps are so quick and easy to use that it would be impossible to list all the things they're handy for, but here are a few ideas: to clamp small parts together for gluing up a school project; to attach a blanket or sheet to a window frame to darken a room for a slide show; to route computer cables along the back edge of a desk; to quickly secure parts in position until heavier clamps are applied; to temporarily fix a template on top of a part on which you're tracing a pattern; to hold a small part during a sanding or grinding operation; and so on.

While early spring clamps were made of metal, modern ones are made from light-

Cool Tools — QUICK-ADJUSTING CLAMPS

QUICK-ADJUSTING CLAMPS let you get most clamping jobs done with a minimum of stress and fuss. Bar-style models (shown at front and rear in the photo at right) look like light-duty bar clamps, with one important difference: They have a built-in mechanism that lets you tighten the clamp by squeezing a plastic pistol-grip handle. All it takes is one hand to position the clamp and tighten—very fast and efficient.

Although they're not quite as powerful as traditional clamps with threaded screws, quick-adjusting bar clamps let you set the clamping pressure precisely, and they can't be overtightened. That, and the fact that clamping jaws of all models come with plastic pads, virtually eliminates the risk of marring the work's surface. Once the glue has set and you want to remove a quick-adjusting clamp—or to open its jaws larger—all it takes is a press on the clamp's quick-release trigger.

Another useful style of quick-adjusting clamp is called a ratchet clamp (shown at center in the photo). It looks something like a spring clamp but has a special ratcheting jaw that tightens and locks as you press the handles together. Like quick-adjusting bar clamps, you can position and tighten a ratchet clamp single-handed. Lightweight versions made of plastic are good for the same kind of light clamping jobs you'd use a strong spring clamp for. Stronger, metal models can handle the same jobs that C-clamps can.

weight reinforced polymer plastics and have swivel jaws that grip flat or odd-shaped surfaces more securely than metal ones. Spring clamps come in sizes from 2 in. to 12 in., and most users agree that it's worth having all of them; buying a combination or starter set that contains a couple of each size is an economical way to go.

▼SPRING CLAMPS There's a spring clamp that's sized just right for every light-clamping or temporary-holding job.

PRO CON

SERIOUS WOODWORKERS will tell you that you should concentrate on building a good collection of standard clamps (C-clamps, bar clamps, handscrews, etc.) before spending your money on gadgety quick-adjusting clamps. But modern quick-adjusting clamps are so easy to use that they might be a better choice for several repairs and temporary-holding duties around the house or workshop.

STANDARD CLAMPS
Pros:
• provide more clamping pressure for difficult assemblies (warped boards, e.g.)
• retain part alignment better than most quick models

Cons:
• are heavy
• are prone to rust
• will mar stock unless pads or blocks are used

QUICK-ADJUSTING CLAMPS
Pros:
• are lightweight
• can be quickly applied and positioned
• allow one-handed tightening or loosening

Cons:
• don't supply as much pressure as standard clamps
• may break apart due to plastic parts

Band Clamps

Also referred to as a web clamp, a band clamp consists of a long, woven fabric band (like a seat belt) and a mechanical tightener. You thread the strap around the parts you want to hold or glue together—a picture frame, a jewelry chest, or an odd-shaped assembly, for instance—then pull the strap taut using the tightener. Metal corners that come with most models distribute pressure to prevent denting the corners of square or rectangular assemblies.

Inexpensive band clamps have nylon webbing and a ratcheting tightener that's operated with a small wrench. This model is fine for small projects like regluing the rungs or stretchers on an old chair. Band clamps made for more serious shop duties, such as gluing up large octagonal planter boxes, have longer canvas bands and use threaded-screw tightening devices that generate tons of pressure.

Woodworking Vises

Mounted to a heavy workbench top, a woodworking vise is something that even casual woodworkers make use of on a daily basis. Their jaws are ample in size and strong enough to hold long boards or heavy parts securely during sawing, planing, carving, grinding, or machining operations. Larger woodworking vises with 9-in. or 10-in. jaws open wide enough to hold fairly large, assembled projects—such as dresser drawers, wood boxes, and chair seats—for finish-sanding or repair. Medium-size vises with 7-in. jaws typically open 8 in. to 10 in., wide enough for general work-holding duties, including nonwoodworking jobs like sharpening chainsaw teeth or truing up bicycle wheels.

Most vise jaws have holes for mounting wooden jaw faces to protect soft or delicate wood from dings and dents. One feature to look for in a woodworking vise is a rapid-action screw mechanism. This feature unlocks the vise's movable jaw, allowing you to pull or push it quickly to the desired position before tightening it down on the work.

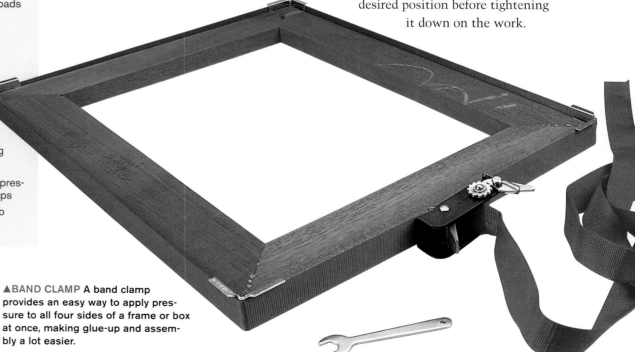

▲BAND CLAMP A band clamp provides an easy way to apply pressure to all four sides of a frame or box at once, making glue-up and assembly a lot easier.

Another useful feature built into most woodworking vises is a raisable bench dog, a metal pin that pops up from the movable jaw. By fitting a similar wood or metal dog into one of a series of holes drilled in the benchtop to which the vise is mounted, you can clamp a large or long board or part flat on the benchtop while you work on it. Good-quality woodworking vises aren't cheap, but they're a worthwhile investment if woodworking is your passion. You can save some money by buying a kit that contains the threaded screw and metal parts; you make the wooden parts of the vise yourself.

Bench Vises

If there's one tool that belongs in every single workshop, large or small, it's a bench vise. Securely bolted to the front edge or corner of a bench, counter, or worktable, a bench vise is a multipurpose clamping tool that grips, supports, and holds workpieces of all shapes, sizes, and materials—as well as small tools. Not only do bench vises work with all kinds of workpieces, they also work for all kinds of jobs, from filing, chiseling, pounding, and painting to fastening, soldering, and brazing.

The strong jaws on this versatile vise are flat, sometimes with small horizontal and vertical grooves to help hold thin or narrow parts. Just below their primary jaws, many bench vises sport a secondary pair of serrated pipe jaws for holding rods, pipes, and other round stock. Most vises are mounted on a rotating base so you can realign the jaws relative to the benchtop to suit the work. The vises also have a small, flat anvil located just behind the fixed jaw that's good for light pounding jobs, such as setting leather-working rivets, flattening clasps, or bending over cotter pins.

The size of a bench vise usually corresponds to the width of its jaws, with 3-in., 4-in., 5-in., and 6-in. models commonly available. But a vise's jaw size and its heft and capacity are often very different things. For example, consider that the two vises shown in the photo on p. 54 are both 4-in.

▲**WOOD VISE** Woodworking operations—like planing, sawing, routing, or sanding boards—are a lot easier to do if you have a wide-jaw wood vise bolted to your workbench.

Pro Tip

A vise is basically a clamp that's securely fastened to a benchtop, so there's no reason not to use a vise as a clamp whenever it's convenient. Even small vises have plenty of pressing power and enough capacity to clamp, for example, a small box or jewelry drawer for glue-up or a broken kitchen-utensil handle for repair.

▲BENCH VISES The jaw capacity of a vise doesn't tell the whole story: The two bench vises here are both 4-in. models, yet the vise at rear is much larger and heavier than the one in front.

models. Bigger, heavier vises are desirable for handling big, heavy workpieces. But unless you're a weekend mechanic or love to tinker with machinery, an average-size 4-in. vise will probably fulfill most of your needs. Quality is also an important consideration when buying a bench vise. Inexpensive "bargain" vises are often crudely made from soft steel and/or cast iron, with jaws and anvils that dent and gall easily.

Utility Vises

If your idea of having a workbench is clearing off one corner of the kitchen table or countertop, a utility vise might be just right for you. These small, inexpensive vises are designed to quickly and temporarily mount on a surface to provide a secure means of holding small workpieces. In the

well-equipped household, this kind of vise provides assistance for tackling all kinds of little repair and hobby jobs: mending eyeglasses, replacing batteries in a cellular phone or MP3 player, applying touch-up paint on a die-cast model car, or tying fishing flies.

Many utility vises clamp to the edge of a table or countertop with a threaded screw, as shown at right in the bottom photo on the facing page. Others models use a vacuum base to suction onto a smooth surface, while still others attach firmly via a detachable quick-mount (shown at left in the bottom photo on the facing page). A useful feature shared by many utility vises is a swivel head that allows you to angle the workpiece as needed to suit the available lighting and make the operation more comfortable to perform.

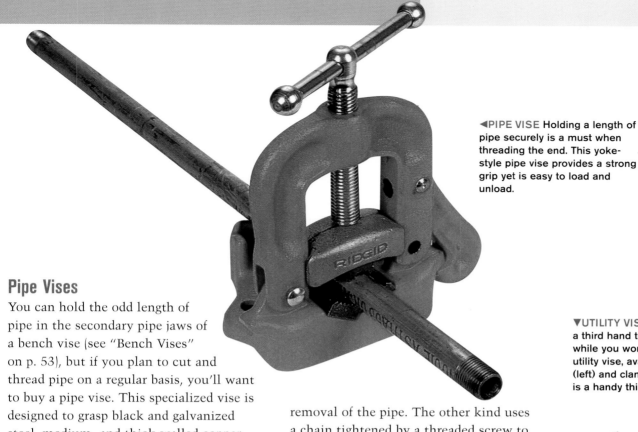

◀PIPE VISE Holding a length of pipe securely is a must when threading the end. This yoke-style pipe vise provides a strong grip yet is easy to load and unload.

Pipe Vises

You can hold the odd length of pipe in the secondary pipe jaws of a bench vise (see "Bench Vises" on p. 53), but if you plan to cut and thread pipe on a regular basis, you'll want to buy a pipe vise. This specialized vise is designed to grasp black and galvanized steel, medium- and thick-walled copper and bronze pipe, or rigid electrical conduit, preventing it from rotating as it is cut and threaded, or as fittings are screwed on. A V-shaped support located behind the jaws keeps long pipes steady.

There are many different styles of pipe vises, but two of them are the most common and suitable for home-workshop users. A bench-yoke vise has serrated jaws mounted to a quick-release frame, which opens for easy insertion or removal of the pipe. The other kind uses a chain tightened by a threaded screw to grasp the pipe. Both types sometimes have bending rollers or channels built into them, for bending thin-walled pipe. Most models can handle pipe from ⅛ in. to 2½ in. in diameter—more than enough to handle the piping found in the average home.

▼UTILITY VISES When you need a third hand to hold parts steady while you work on them, a small utility vise, available in plastic (left) and clamp-on (right) styles, is a handy thing to have.

CHAPTER 2

Tools That Shape & Shave

Most building and home-improvement projects require parts or raw materials that need to be shaped and shaved. For example, a rough board is planed smooth, flat, and straight, and then edge-routed to create a piece of trim or molding; or bricks or concrete pavers are cut and trimmed to fit snugly together for a garden path.

The do-it-yourselfer's arsenal of basic shaping and shaving tools includes both powered tools and machines—lathes, routers, jointers, and thickness planers—and hand tools—chisels, carving gouges and knives, planes, spokeshaves, scrapers, files and rasps, deburring tools, and reamers.

▲FIXED- AND PLUNGE-BASE ROUTER KIT Most routers are either fixed-base or plunge models. But if you don't want to buy one of each, choose a convertible router kit, which includes one motor unit that fits into either a fixed or plunge base.

ROUTERS

If you consider all the powered tools that shape wood, the router is the king of versatility. Want to shape the edge of a tabletop or create your own custom molding? Router bits come with dozens of different profiles (see "Router Bits" on p. 58), letting you create the shape you want. Other bits allow you to use a router to joint, trim, drill, and carve wood, as well as cut all kinds of wood-to-wood joints, from simple box joints to fanciful dovetails. A router provides a quick and easy way to cut slots and mortises for mounting hinges and other hardware or recesses for decorative inlays. Depending on the kind of work you wish to do, you can buy a router in three basic forms: fixed-base routers, plunge routers, and laminate trimmers.

Fixed-Base Routers

If you're looking for a basic, low-cost router for shaping parts and basic router-table work (see "Router Tables" above right), a fixed-base router is for you. The base of this tool mounts its motor and collet (the part that holds the bit) in a simple, stable base with a pair of knob handles that offer a firm grip. The base allows the motor/collet to be adjusted up or down, so you can set the cutting depth of the bit.

Fixed-based routers aren't as versatile as plunge models (see p. 58) but are generally less expensive and more compact, making them easier to handle. As is true of plunge routers, better fixed-base models feature variable speed, allowing you to set the motor speed to match the bit diameter (see the tip on p. 58), as well as a collet lock for convenient, single-wrench bit changes. When choosing a model, be sure to check its bit capacity: Most smaller, less powerful models accept only ¼-in. shank bits. For greater versatility, choose a bigger model that accepts either ¼-in. or ½-in. shank bits.

Tool Helpers **ROUTER TABLES**

More than any other accessory, a router table can greatly multiply the number of wood shaping, trimming, and joinery jobs that a router can perform. Whether it's shopmade or store bought, a good router table should have a smooth, sturdy top mounted to a floor or benchtop stand, a removable plate that supports a router mounted upside down, and an adjustable fence to guide stock past the spinning bit. The fences on better router tables feature a safety guard, dust shroud or port (for connection to a vacuum hose), and adjustable hold-downs, to keep the workpiece in contact with the table and fence during routing.

To make the height of the bit easier to adjust, many plunge-router manufacturers offer accessory knobs, which you crank to raise or lower a bit. Alternatively, you can buy a special accessory router plate that raises and lowers the entire router via a removable handle.

▲FIXED-BASE ROUTER **A standard fixed-base router is one of the most versatile woodworking tools you can buy. Accepting a wide range of bits, this tool can shape edges, plow grooves, cut joints, add decoration, and do much more.**

These routers have more power and can drive larger bits and can take heavy or deep cuts without slowing down.

A variation on the standard fixed-base model, a D-handled router replaces one of its knobs with a loop handle that contains the tool's on/off trigger, just like on a portable circular saw (see the bottom photo on p. 93). This offers superior control of the router and allows experienced users to run the router single handed.

Plunge Routers

A plunge router is much like a fixed-base router—with an important difference: You can change the cutting depth of a plunge unit while it's running. This allows you to feed a spinning bit down into the wood in a safe and controlled way, as is necessary for grooves, mortises, inlays, and decorative

▲PLUNGE ROUTER A plunge router adds a user-controlled, up-and-down plunging action to a standard router, letting you safely start and stop cuts in the middle of a panel.

Cool Tools | ROUTER JIGS

ROUTER JIGS are seemingly as numerous in a shop as various cocktail glasses are in a well-stocked bar. In fact, there are probably more jigs, guides, accessories, and joinery devices made for routers than for any other portable power tool. One of the most basic, everyday router accessories is an edge guide (see the bottom photo on the facing page), which mounts to a router's base and guides a bit at a fixed distance from an edge—say, to rout parallel grooves on a decorative column. Some edge guides double as circle jigs that allow you to rout circular disks or, with special accessories, rout oval grooves and plaques.

There are router jigs for cutting all kinds of wooden joints, including mortise and tenons, box joints, and dovetails. An adjustable dovetail jig (shown at right in the photo below) lets you set the size and spacing of pins and tails (the two interlocking parts of the joint) to make attractive joints for kitchen or dresser drawers, jewelry boxes, and blanket chests. As the drawer or box sides are clamped in the jig, metal fingers steer a guide bushing (attached to the base of the router) as the pins and tails are cut. By using additional templates, this kind of jig can also cut box joints and other decorative-wood-to-wood joints.

cuts in the middle of a board or panel. A stop mechanism on a plunge router's base lets you accurately plunge the bit to the same depth time after time. This is helpful when routing, for example, a series of letters or numbers on a wooden street sign for your home or office. A separate thumb-operated handle locks the router's up-and-down travel when the cutting depth is reached. Some models let you fine-tune cutting depth after the lock is set, which makes these routers handy to use in a router table (see "Router Tables" on p. 57). A depth-stop turret is another feature included on most models. This allows you to change cutting depth in fixed increments, handy when you have a cut that's too deep to make in one pass.

Router Bits

The main reason that routers are capable of cutting so many different shapes is the star-

▲ROUTER BITS The variety of router bits includes (left to right): straight bits, flush-trim bits, pilot bearing–guided bits, and special-purpose bits.

tling array of bits made for them. Bits, as these cutters are called, come in a wide range of sizes from huge shape-forming bits with ½-in. shanks to teeny detailing bits with ¼-in. shanks. While some inexpensive bits are made of high-speed steel, the majority of them have hard carbide cutting tips, so they cut smoothly for a long time before dulling. To get the most from any router, you'll want to have several kinds of bits on hand (shown from left to right in the photo above):

Straight bits come in many cutting diameters (⅛ in., ¼ in., ½ in., etc.) and are useful for cutting straight or curved grooves, dadoes (grooves across the grain), slots, and rabbets, as well as recesses and mortises for hardware or inlays. When running a straight bit, you usually guide the router with an edge guide, or with a fence when using a router table.

Flush-trim bits are just straight bits with the addition of a ball bearing on the bottom end of the bit (or, sometimes, fitted on the shank above the cutter). The bearing rides against the edge of the workpiece to guide the cut. Since the bearing's outside diameter is the same as the cutting diameter of the bit, a flush-trim bit trims off excess material above (or below) the bearing when creating laminate countertops or routing parts to final size using a pattern.

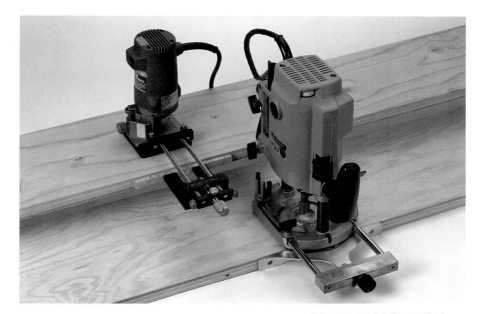

▲ROUTER EDGE GUIDES It's the job of an edge guide to keep a router parallel to an edge during a cut. Most router models have edge guides offered as stock or optional accessories (front), but you can also buy aftermarket models, such as the Micro Fence (rear).

Pilot bearing–guided bits come in an endless assortment of profiles, including roundovers, coves, ogees, chamfers, step cuts (rabbets), and slots. Guided by ball bearings that allow you to rout freehand, such bits are great for putting shapely profiles on the edges of tabletops, boxes, stool seats, and more, and they give any project a more finished look. You can also use these bits individually or in combination to shape your own decorative moldings.

Pro Tip

It's important to set a variable-speed router's rpm to suit the size of the bit. To find the correct rpm, multiply the bit diameter (in inches) by 0.262, and divide the result into 11,440. For example, for a 2¼-in.-dia. bit, multiply 2.25 by 0.262 (0.5895) and divide this result into 11,440 (11,440 ÷ 0.5895), which equals 19,406, rounding off to a safe 19,000 rpm.

Special-purpose bits are made for cutting various kinds of joints (dovetails, tongue and grooves, cope and sticks, etc.) or for shaping special profiles, such as bull-noses, drawer pulls, crown moldings, or raised panels. Often large in diameter, raised-panel bits (used for shaping the edges of door and drawer panels) should only be run in a router table using a variable-speed router set to the proper speed (see the tip at left).

Laminate Trimmers

Laminate trimmers were originally designed for trimming thin plastic counter-top materials like Formica®, hence their name. However, this tool is also a handy minirouter that's great for taking light cuts: routing narrow grooves, shaping small roundovers, or making shallow hinge mortises. A laminate trimmer's small size and light weight let you work deftly and without the strain of hefting a full-size router. Although you're limited to using ¼-in. shank bits, these trimmers have a neat trick up their sleeves; the motor/collet easily detaches from the standard base and mounts on any of three special bases: a tilt base, for routing at an angle relative to the work surface; a flush seam base, for trimming overlapping seams of plastic laminate sheets; and a corner-routing base, for routing or trimming deep into an inside corner.

▲LAMINATE TRIMMER AND BITS Laminate trimmers not only trim plastic countertop materials with aplomb but also accept a full range of small bits—as well as serving as handy minirouters.

▼LAMINATE TRIMMER KIT A complete laminate trimmer kit includes several interchangeable bases, which adapt the tool for both flat and angled routing, seam trimming, and work on inside corners.

PLANING AND SCRAPING TOOLS

Unless you like the look of rustic furniture and handcrafts built from twigs, branches, and logs just as Mother Nature grew them, the wood you use for your projects is processed into boards and planks that are smooth and flat. The group of woodworking tools used to dimension lumber to final thickness and give it faces and edges that are flat and square include

Pro Tip

With the exception of a few premium-priced handplanes that come ready for precise work right out of the box, most handplanes need tuning for maximum performance. Tuning includes sharpening the blade, along with a whole slew of mechanical tweaks and adjustments that are beyond the scope of this book. See *The Handplane Book*, by Garrett Hack.

▲HANDPLANES, SCRAPERS, POWER PLANES, AND SPOKESHAVES Need to shape or shave a surface? There's no shortage of planes (both hand- and electric-powered), scrapers (box, cabinet, and razor), and spokeshaves designed to tackle the job.

handplanes; power planes; jointers, which are used for truing the edges (and sometimes faces) of lumber and parts to be joined; and thickness planers, which are used to plane planks and parts smooth and to final thickness. Cabinet scrapers can create an even smoother surface, while box scrapers and razor-blade scrapers are handy for removing paint and old finishes.

Handplanes

If you prefer muscle power to electricity, then handplanes certainly belong in your tool chest. The sweet-smelling shavings produced by a sharp, well-tuned handplane are the stuff of romance that brings many wanna-be users to woodworking in the first place. Handplanes come in dozens of different forms, including highly specialized planes for rabbeting, jointing, dadoing, chamfering, molding, beading, and dovetailing wood (these aren't discussed

▲MODERN AND TRADITIONAL HANDPLANES Handplanes have evolved considerably from early transitional models (rear) into modern tools that are easy to adjust and use. Planes come in many sizes, but the two most useful are jack planes (front left) and block planes (front right).

here because they're highly specialized woodworking tools). Two of the most generally useful planes for trimming edges, fitting joints, and smoothing surfaces are jack and block planes. Even if you own a power planer and/or jointer, this dynamic handplane duo belongs in your tool kit for occasional touch-up work.

JACK PLANES These medium-size handplanes range from 12 in. to 15 in. in length and sport a 1¾-in.- to 2-in.-wide blade. They're great for cleaning up blade or knife marks from an edge or surface after sawing, jointing, or thickness planing, as well as knocking sharp edges off a panel or trimming a part

▼WOOD AND METAL HAND-PLANES While most modern handplanes are made from cast iron and steel, traditional wooden planes, preferred by some craftsmen for their feel, are still available.

to size or thickness. A jack plane set to take a deep cut can remove a large amount of wood surprisingly quickly. Yet the same plane, reset to take a fine cut, can leave a surface smooth, true, and ready for gluing.

While modern wood-bodied planes are still available, planes with cast-iron bodies are more common. Even moderately priced models have features that make them easy to adjust and use, such as a screw-type blade depth–setting wheel. More expensive planes with high-quality construction, thicker blades, and advanced features enable an advanced user to get stellar performance and to plane beautiful woods until they glisten, needing little or no sanding before finishing.

BLOCK PLANES As part of a traditional cabinetmaker's tool kit, block planes are primarily intended for planing wood's end grain. However, because of their compact size (typically only 6 in. long and 2 in. wide), woodworkers and hobbyists find them handy for many wood trimming, smoothing, and touch-up tasks (for example, cleaning up a splintery section on the edge of a birdhouse roof). Block planes are especially good for planing small parts (model makers love them) or for working in confined areas—say, inside a cabinet or drawer, where a full-size handplane won't fit. And because of their small size and low profile, inexperienced users often find block planes easier to handle than full-size planes.

While a standard block plane is good for general work, a

▶BLOCK PLANES Block planes come in two common styles: standard models (left), good for general trimming work, and low angle–bladed models (far right), which shear end grain and figured wood more cleanly and easily.

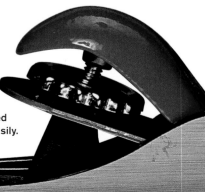

low-angle block plane
has an adjustable throat and a blade
mounted at a shallow angle—only 12
degrees to the sole—enabling it to cut
tough wood grain and dense hardwoods
more easily than a standard plane and to
shear end grain cleanly.

Power Planes

Nature gave wood a mind of its own and,
unfortunately, it has a mind to warp after
it's been cut into lumber. Since the majority of us don't have time to straighten and
true up boards with a handplane, a portable
power planer is a miraculous time-saver.
Add a motorized cutterhead to a handplane
and you have the basic idea of how a
portable power plane works. Its long sole is
like a handplane except that the front half
of the sole, instead of the blade, adjusts up
and down for deeper or shallower cuts.

Although power planes are primarily
part of a professional carpenter's kit,
they're a practical purchase for any home-
improvement do-it-yourselfer who does a
lot of wood trimming and fitting work. Say
you're replacing all the doors in your home
with nice, solid-wood doors or fitting new
cabinets or windows as part of a major
home remodel; a power plane lets you

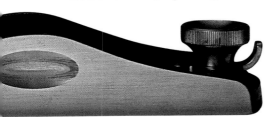

trim those doors, win-
dows, panels, and cabinet edges to fit
much faster and more easily than you
could with a handplane.

While smaller cordless models are available, most power planes are corded tools
with cutterheads in the neighborhood of
3¼ in. wide. That's wide enough to plane
2x lumber or the thickest doors. To ensure
that edges are trimmed square and true,
there's a fence below the sole that guides
the plane and stabilizes it against the side
of the work. Some models have a shallow
groove that runs the length of the sole,
which is there to guide the tool during
chamfer cuts, when it's held at 45 degrees
relative to the edge (see the photo above).

Benchtop Jointers

Take a power planer, turn it upside down,
give it a bigger cutterhead, and make it
longer and more powerful and you've just
created a jointer. While big, floor-standing
jointers are essential machines in serious
woodworking shops, benchtop jointers are
affordable enough for hobbyists and home-
improvement mavens yet are compact
enough to fit into part-time work spaces,
such as the family garage.

The most important job a jointer does is
put a straight, true edge on a board so it's
ready to run safely along a table saw's rip
fence. With its long table and fence that
support and guide the work, even a pint-

▲POWER PLANE
**Basically a small, portable jointer,
a power plane uses electric-
motor power to drive a small
cutterhead that quickly smoothes
and flattens rough wood edges
and surfaces.**

▲BENCHTOP JOINTER A benchtop jointer does a good job of straightening and flattening all but the longest boards yet fits easily into the smallest workshops.

you can plane in a single pass. Made from lightweight alloys, 6-in. benchtop jointers are portable and easily storable, making them popular with small-shop users. While not as powerful as floor models, benchtop jointers have tilting fences for beveling or chamfering edges and have variable-speed universal motors that let you change cutterhead speeds to suit the material you're jointing: slow for plastics, medium for softwoods, and fast for hardwoods.

Portable Thickness Planers

You *could* flatten and smooth a rough board with a handplane. But unless you've got the skill and patience of Norm Abram, you'll do it more quickly and accurately with a thickness planer—the tool of choice for cleaning up rough wood surfaces and planing lumber to final thickness. Once only available as expensive stationary machines, newer portable benchtop models are affordable enough for occasional users yet have enough power and capacity to do most lumber surfacing for small- and medium-size projects. As a bonus to small-shop users, their lightweight and compact size make them easy to stow away—under a bench or in a closet—when they're not needed.

▲PORTABLE THICKNESS PLANER A portable thickness planer makes it easy to plane rough lumber—from thin, narrow strips to wide, thick planks—flat and smooth.

size benchtop jointer can straighten planks 10 ft. or longer—a difficult job using a handplane or power plane. Besides dealing with crooked edges, a jointer also flattens cupped, bowed, or twisted boards on one surface, a necessary preparation before running them through a thickness planer (see the following section).

All jointers are sized by the length of their knife, which limits the widest board

Modern portable planers have noisy but powerful universal motors with powered feed rollers, which drive the board past a cutterhead that can slice $\frac{3}{32}$ in. of wood in a single pass. Most models handle lumber (or glued-together panels, cutting boards, etc.) up to 12 in. or 13 in. wide and from $\frac{1}{8}$ in. to 6 in. thick.

These technologically advanced machines pack in a slew of features that

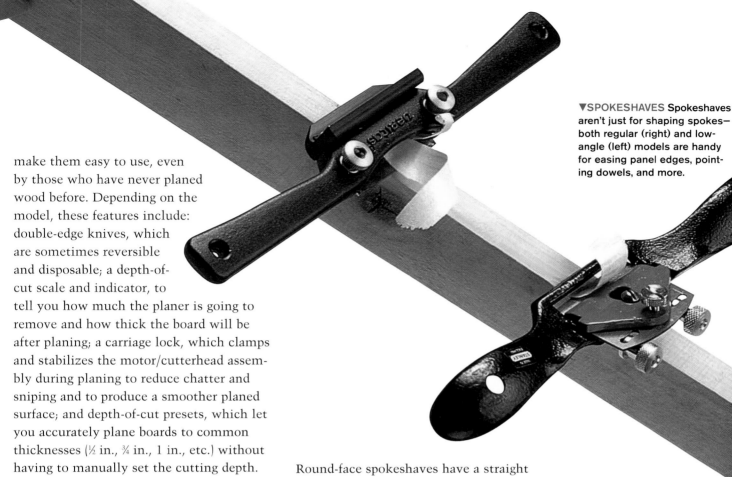

▼SPOKESHAVES Spokeshaves aren't just for shaping spokes— both regular (right) and low-angle (left) models are handy for easing panel edges, pointing dowels, and more.

make them easy to use, even by those who have never planed wood before. Depending on the model, these features include: double-edge knives, which are sometimes reversible and disposable; a depth-of-cut scale and indicator, to tell you how much the planer is going to remove and how thick the board will be after planing; a carriage lock, which clamps and stabilizes the motor/cutterhead assembly during planing to reduce chatter and sniping and to produce a smoother planed surface; and depth-of-cut presets, which let you accurately plane boards to common thicknesses (½ in., ¾ in., 1 in., etc.) without having to manually set the cutting depth.

Spokeshaves

Named for their now-outdated use of shaving wooden spokes for carriages and carts, spokeshaves are still excellent tools for hand-shaping all kinds of things, from walking sticks to stirring spoons to chair legs. Resembling a short metal plane flanked by two handles, the tool is pulled over the work as a shaving is taken. Spokeshaves come in flat-face, low-angle, round-face, half-round, and radius styles, each for shaping a different profile.

You can use the straight edge of a flat-face spokeshave like a small handplane to plane flat surfaces, or you can create a convex profile by taking a series of narrow cuts and then rounding and smoothing the surface by scraping or sanding. Low-angle spokeshaves also have flat soles, but they work like low-angle block planes to shear wood fibers and end grain more easily.

Round-face spokeshaves have a straight blade and a lengthwise, rounded sole that's good for scooping wood with the grain— say, to shape a concave chair back. Half-round spokeshaves are best for shaving round handles and large dowels or for rounding over edges on counters or table-tops. Radius spokeshaves have a relatively small-radius (2 in.), curved blade that's good for hollowing a chair seat or scooping out a curved channel or gutter.

Cabinet Scrapers

Although the wood surfaces of fine cabinets, furniture, and household wares are most often smoothed with sandpaper, scraping provides an interesting alternative. While a handplane or power plane can hog wood from a rough surface, a cabinet scraper is designed for an already flat, relatively smooth surface. A simple scraper is just a flat, rectangular piece of high-carbon steel roughly the size of a 3x5 index card.

Pro Tip

If you plan to build lots of solid-wood cabinets or furniture, you can save money by buying unsurfaced, rough lumber and dressing it yourself. After straightening edges and flattening one surface on a jointer, run each board through a thickness planer, flipping it over between passes, until it's smooth and ready to use.

▲CABINET-SCRAPER BLADES AND HOLDER A thin piece of steel with a hook-shaped edge, a simple cabinet-scraper blade (right) can smooth a flat or curved wood surface while creating little dust. A cabinet-scraper holder (left) makes a flat blade easier to hold during extended use.

Cool Tools   RAZOR-BLADE SCRAPERS

RAZOR-BLADE SCRAPERS are some of the most useful yet least expensive tools you can buy. Basically a plastic handle that holds a standard single-edge razor blade, this small scraper is handy for lots of around-the-house jobs: removing price stickers, bumper stickers, old tape, and the residue they leave behind. If you're painting your house, a razor-blade scraper is the ideal tool for removing paint drips and spatter from window glass (it's also good for cutting off paint and varnish drips at the bottom edges of doors and panels). For larger glass-scraping jobs—say, removing overspray from unmasked areas—buy a large-size glass scraper. Its wider blade lets you do these big jobs in short order.

In skilled hands, a scraper can leave the sides of a new dresser or the top of a table silky smooth and ready for finishing. You can also use one to remove old varnish or sensitively remove stains or ink marks. To scrape curved or irregularly shaped surfaces—bowls, chair seats, etc.—you can buy a curved gooseneck scraper, shaped like a squat French curve.

Before it will shave properly, the edge of a scraper must be flattened, smoothed, and burnished. A burnisher is a hard steel rod that's pressed along the edge of the scraper to draw the edge over into a hook-shaped cutting edge. You can use a screwdriver for this, but it's easier to get consistent results with a burnisher (see "Scraper Jointing and Burnishing Tools" on p. 191). As the scraper is pushed or pulled across the surface of the wood, this tiny hook on the edge removes fine shavings. For best results, the blade should be bowed slightly during use. You can do this manually by holding the blade by the edges and applying pressure to the middle with your thumbs while you scrape, but it's made much easier if you mount the blade in a scraper holder (see the top photo at left), which uses a screw to set and adjust the bow of the blade.

Box Scrapers

You could call a box scraper a cabinet scraper's coarser, less refined brother. Basically a flat-edge blade mounted to a handle, a box scraper is the right tool for many quick-and-dirty surface-scraping jobs: scouring old, peeling paint from a boat hull or house siding; removing old shipping labels from a wood crate; scuffing off layers of old varnish from a parquet floor. A box scraper's sharp (though not hook-shaped) edge leaves a surface that's clean and relatively smooth, though it may require a bit of sanding depending on the desired finish. Old-fashioned box scrapers (shown at rear in the photo on the facing page) have square, four-sided blades that are easy to

▲PAIR OF BOX SCRAPERS Box scrapers are good for removing everything from labels and decals to old floor finishes. Traditional models (rear) have mul-tisided steel blades, while modern styles (front) have long-lasting, replaceable carbide blades.

▲CHISELS AND CARVING TOOLS Chisels and carving tools come in various styles and shapes, made for shaping, trimming, or slicing through materials, including wood, masonry, and metals.

resharpen with a stone, file, or belt sander. Modern scrapers (shown at front in the photo above) have replaceable, disposable, twin-edge blades or long-lasting carbide blades.

CHISELS AND CARVING TOOLS

Handplanes enclose a cutting blade in a body that controls the edge's depth of cut. In contrast, chisels and carving tools, such as gouges and knives, are simply narrow blades with handles designed for freehand shaping and trimming. Although most chisels, gouges, and knives are designed to work with a specific or narrow range of materials—carving gouges for wood, brick chisels for masonry, etc.—the freehand nature of these tools makes them extremely versatile. For example, using a set of carving gouges or knives, you could sculpt or whittle anything from a small wood whistle to a life-size statue of the Venus de Milo.

Chisels

There are chisels made for cutting and shaping specific materials, including wood, metal, and masonry, and most of these are general-duty tools. For example, wood chisels are important tools for tackling most common (and some not-so-common) woodworking and carpentry chores, brick chisels are used for trimming bricks and masonry, and cold chisels are used for cutting and shaping metal stock or parts.

WOOD CHISELS For such a simple tool, a wood chisel can do a lot of complex jobs: cut mortises for hinges that will hang a new cabinet door; chop a notch in a 2x4 to make way for a new water pipe; square up the round corners of a routed slot or drilled hole; or carve out and trim wood joints for fine furniture. While there are literally dozens of chisels made for specialized woodworking duties (mortising, paring, framing, etc.), general-duty wood chisels (sometimes called bench chisels), which are available at any hardware store, are good for all these tasks and more (less conventional uses include scraping off old finish and opening paint cans).

Pro Tip

The edge sharpness of any chisel is important for both performance and safety. When regrinding the edge bevel, avoid using a high-speed grinder, which may overheat the edge. Also, if the struck end of an all-steel cold chisel or brick chisel becomes spread and mushroom shaped, reshape it with a file.

Pro Tip

If you work with standard inches and fractions, make sure to buy wood chisels that are fractionally sized; it's easiest to chop a ½-in. hinge recess with a ½-in. chisel. This may seem obvious, but many European- and Japanese-made chisels are metric sized (10mm, 15mm, etc.) and don't match up precisely to fractional measurements.

▶ERGONOMIC WOOD CHISELS Wood chisels with modern, ergonomic, rubber-padded handles are comfortable to use, especially when heavy pounding is required—say, for chopping hinge mortises in a door frame.

▶WOOD CHISEL SET A set of basic wood chisels contains both narrow and wide tools for all kinds of carpentry and woodworking chores, from chopping grooves to trimming miters.

Better chisels are made from durable alloyed steels, such as chrome vanadium, which hold a sharp edge yet resist rust and corrosion better than the high-carbon steels of yesteryear. Fitted with high-impact plastic handles or wood handles reinforced by metal ferrules, wood chisels are made to be pushed by hand or struck with a hammer or, preferably, a mallet (see "Mallets" on p. 165). Models with fat, ergonomic handles and cushioned rubber inserts are more comfortable and less fatiguing to grasp, especially when applying lots of hand pressure.

Wood chisels are sized by their width and are sold individually or in sets. A full set (a good purchase for a home woodshop) will include seven or eight chisels, ranging in size from around ¼ in. to 1 in. or more, and a box, case, or roll for storage. If you can only afford two or three chisels, ½-in., ¾-in., and 1½-in. sizes are handiest for the widest range of carpentry and home-improvement chores (see the tip at left).

Regardless of what kind or how many chisels you get, don't forget to buy a good sharpening stone or two (see "Choosing a Sharpening Stone" on p. 186) to keep the chisels' edges razor sharp and able to cut cleanly.

▲BRICK CHISEL AND DRILLING HAMMER To trim and shape bricks, concrete pavers, and other masonry, all you need is a brick chisel and a drilling hammer. A safety chisel, shown here, has a guard to protect your hand from misplaced blows.

Pro Tip

If you're faced with a big job that includes a large number of bricks in need of cutting—when laying an entire brick patio, for example—consider renting or buying an electric power saw with a masonry blade, which is specifically designed to cut bricks, pavers, and other masonry materials. You'll not only get cleaner cuts but also make them more quickly.

BRICK-DRESSING CHISELS A brick set or brick chisel is used for scoring and cutting bricks, concrete, and cinder blocks as well as for clearing away old mortar when repairing brick or concrete-block walls. Similar to a mason's chisel, a brick chisel has a 1½-in.- to 4½-in.-wide blade that's beveled on one side. To use it, first mark the brick on all four sides, and place it on a sandbag or soft ground. Use the chisel to score all the way along the line, with the edge bevel facing toward the waste side. Once scored, a strong whack on the line cuts the brick through. Always use a small sledgehammer or drilling hammer to strike a brick chisel—never use a nail or bricklayer's hammer. For safety and striking comfort, it's best to buy a brick chisel that has a built-in, plastic hand guard, as shown in the photo above.

COLD CHISELS When you can't cut through a metal bar or section of sheet with a hacksaw or power saw, it's time to pull out a cold chisel. This rugged tool, which is little more than a hexagonal bar

▲COLD CHISEL AND BALL PEEN HAMMER Pounded by a ball peen hammer, a cold chisel's stout, hard cutting edge will slice through most metals, including mild steel.

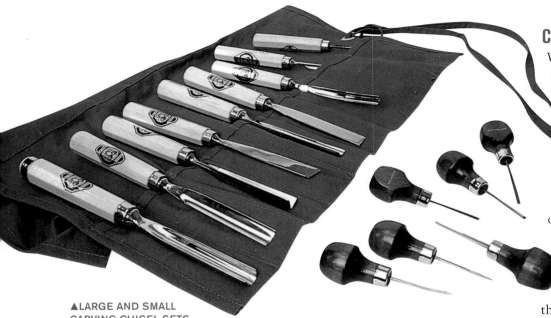

▲LARGE AND SMALL CARVING CHISEL SETS
Carving chisels and gouges come in different sizes: Sets of large tools (shown left, in a canvas tool roll) are best for shaping heavy sculptures, while smaller tools (right) are made for fine detail carving.

Pro Tip

To save you from trauma and a trip to the emergency room, always wear a pair of protective Kevlar® gloves when using a knife, short chisel, or gouge to carve wood (see "Hand Protection" on p. 269). Should the tool slip, these gloves can prevent deep cuts and stab wounds.

with a flared edge at one end, was designed to shear through unheated metal, hence the word "cold" in its name (saws were not readily available until the 1900s, so all metal cutting was done with a chisel). Struck by a ball peen hammer, cold chisels are useful for cutting, shaping, and removing metal stock or hardware made of mild steel, cast iron, aluminum, bronze, or copper. Although the chisel's edge is hardened and tempered, it won't cut through hardened tool steel and shouldn't be used on masonry, such as stone or concrete.

One of the most common uses for cold chisels is slicing through studs and bolts that have rusted or frozen in place (for example, the hasp bolted to a garden gate). For this job, choose a chisel with an edge that's about twice as wide as the diameter of the bolt. For general uses, it's good to have at least two cold chisels in your tool kit. Start with ⅜-in.- and ¾-in.-wide sizes, then add ½-in.- and 1-in.-wide sizes if the need dictates. Unless you can find cold chisels with hand guards (similar to those found on brick chisels—see the top photo on p. 69), always protect your hands with heavy gloves when using them.

Carving Tools

While most woodworking endeavors involve owning a shop's worth of tools, woodcarving requires few tools indeed: a set of carving gouges and chisels, a good wooden mallet, and a few accessories (the skill required to use them effectively and artistically not included). In order to allow the user to create a full range of sculpted shapes and profiles, basic carving-tool sets include a complement of both straight- and skewed-edge chisels and curved-edge gouges.

Carving knives can be added to expand the usefulness of a basic carving set or can be used on their own.

CARVING GOUGES AND CHISELS Although primarily made for working wood, carving gouges and chisels are different from regular, straight wood chisels (see "Wood Chisels" on p.67). Carving gouges and chisels are implements designed for hewing sculptures, shaping furniture and cabinet details, and creating knickknacks and whittled objects in wood, soapstone, and other soft materials.

Gouges are like chisels with bent or curved cutting edges. Gouges are sized by both their blade width and their edge curvature, or "sweep," which ranges from an almost-flat #1 sweep to a semicircular #9 sweep. Carving chisels are like gouges with no sweep, and they have a flat blade like a standard wood chisel.

Beyond the basic gouges and chisels, there are endless kinds of specialized carving tools, such as fishtail, spoon, and bent gouges, along with veiners, V-parting tools (sometimes included in basic sets), dog-leg chisels, and macaroni tools (I didn't make that one up—really!). These specialized tools are best used by more advanced carvers who have specific needs for them.

To carve a full range of shapes and curvatures, you need to have at least a basic set of gouges, chisels, and (for advanced work) specialized carving tools. Different carving sets contain tools sized to suit a particular scale of work: A large-size set containing wide-blade tools with 10-in.- to 12-in.-long handles is good for removing large amounts of material, as when sculpting large figures "in the round." These are typically struck with a mallet when big cuts are taken and hand-pushed for detail work. A small-size carving set has shorter tools with 4-in.- to 6-in.-long handles and narrower blades, which are better for shaping small figures and fine details in relief-carved decorative plaques and linoleum-block carvings. Small carving tools often have squat "mushroom" handles (shown at right in the top photo on the facing page) made for gripping with the palm of your hand, which puts the tool in a good position for doing fine detail work.

WOOD LATHES

One of the most clever wood-shaping machines ever devised, a wood lathe's parts are few: A headstock secures and drives a wood-turning blank; a tailstock provides support for long turnings; a bed joins the two ends together and provides a mount for the tool rest; and the rest supports hand-held turning tools that are used to shape the spinning work.

Lathes range in size from tiny desktop models useful for turning pens, spinning tops, and drawer pulls to superheavy-duty lathes, which professionals use to turn giant bowls and stairway posts. At the mid-point of the spectrum, benchtop and midi-size lathes are small enough to occupy a small corner of a garage shop (or store under a bench), yet they have enough capacity to create useful-size vessels, such as salad bowls, or long objects, such as flutes or chair legs.

▼WOOD LATHE AND TURNING TOOLS While wood lathes come in all sizes, a midi-size lathe, shown here, is useful for shaping medium-size bowls or spindles. No lathe is complete without a good complement of turning tools, shown in the foreground.

Pro Tip

Since most files and rasps have a sharp tang (a pointed end for a handle) that can inflict serious injuries, always mount them in tight-fitting handles before use. If you don't want to fit all your files with separate handles, buy an adjustable handle with metal clamping jaws that will securely grip any size of file tang.

A lathe's "between-center" capacity signifies the longest piece that you can mount and turn between the headstock and tailstock—say, to turn a spindle. A lathe's "swing-over" size indicates the largest diameter work you can turn over the bed— say, to turn a bowl. Some modern lathes employ a pivoting headstock design that rotates the head around so it's perpendicular to the bed. This lets you turn platters or bowls larger than the lathe's swing-over dimension normally allows. While all basic lathes have a belt and pulley arrangement for speed changes (similar to a drill press), some modern lathes are driven by a variable-speed motor that lets you "dial in" just the right speed to suit the size of the work or the nature of the cut—very convenient!

Turning Tools

Stretch a set of carving tools to make them longer, and you've created chisels and gouges just right for shaping wood that's spinning on a lathe. Turning tools cut much like carving tools, only you press them against a spinning wood blank and let the motorized lathe provide the cutting power. Their longer length gives the user more leverage, necessary when applying cutting force to a bowl, spindle, or vessel that's spinning with lots of inertial force.

Like carving tools, turning tools (see the photo on p. 71) come in many shapes and sizes, each right for a particular type of cut or size of workpiece. While specialized and custom tools abound, there are only four basic types of turning tools. Gouges, sometimes called bowl gouges, are good for removing stock rapidly, hollowing vessels, and creating concave forms. Turning scrapers are often used to clean up the wood's surface after it's been roughed out with a gouge. A parting tool cuts small, flat areas, reduces a section of a turning to final diameter (such as a bead on a spindle) before it's refined, and cuts (parts) a finished turning from the lathe. A skew chisel is essential for cutting beads and rounded forms on a turned spindle. Tools are best bought separately, since a purchased set may not provide the particular tools you need for the type of turning you wish to do—large bowls require different tools from spindles.

FILES AND RASPS

What has metal teeth and eats practically anything? A rasp or file, of course. These versatile shaping tools come in many styles, with teeth that are either coarse, to gobble up material in a hurry, or fine, to smooth and refine surfaces and take out scratches left by cruder tools. Files of various types and sizes are useful for jewelry making and metalworking, as well as for sharpening edged tools (see "Files" on p.189), while rasps are mostly used for tackling projects made of wood.

Tool Helpers FILE CARD

Just like a handsaw or circular-saw blade, a file or rasp needs sharp teeth that are clean and clear of debris to cut properly. Cleaning files is occasionally necessary, especially after filing aluminum, plastics, or other soft materials that tend to gum up the teeth (fine-cut files, such as mill bastards, gum up more easily than coarse files). A file card, also called a file cleaner, is a small, wood-handled paddle covered with short, stiff wires that will keep all your files and rasps clean and cutting well. By scrubbing the file or rasp, the wires scour out debris—known as pinnings—that get lodged in the teeth (use an awl to pick out tiny clumps that the card doesn't get).

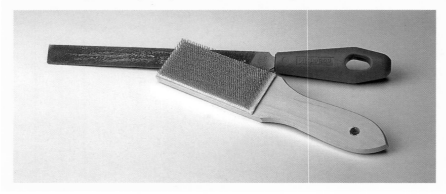

FILE ASSORTMENT To suit a wide range of shaping jobs, files come in many sizes and shapes, including (left to right): round, half-round, flat, and triangular.

Files

Files are used for shaving, smoothing, and fitting metal parts and for basic sharpening of things like axes and lawnmower blades. While most are made from hardened metal with teeth cut into them, diamond files (see "Diamond Stones and Hones" on p. 187) use abrasive diamond particles instead of teeth to do the cutting.

There are several factors that distinguish files from one another: their size, their shape, the cut of their teeth, and their tooth coarseness. Sizes range from huge files that are 12 in. long (and longer), for heavy metalwork, to petite 4-in.- to 6-in.-long needle files, designed for jewelry and detail work. Common file shapes include flat, half-round, round, knife-edge, square, and triangular. Additionally, a file may be tapered, decreasing in width from one end to the other, or blunt, the same width for its entire length.

There are four basic file styles (referred to as cuts): single, double, rasp (described on p. 74), and curved-tooth. Single-cut files, often referred to as mill files, have a single series of parallel rows of teeth running across them that look like a diagonal pat-

▲NEEDLE FILE SET A set of needle files includes many file shapes (round, flat, triangular, etc.) that you need for doing jewelry work, model making, or other fine work.

tern of lines. Double-cut files (also called machine files) have a second set of teeth, running 45 degrees to the first set, which resemble a checkered pattern. Curved-tooth files feature teeth that are milled in an arc.

Mill files leave a smoother finish than machine files but cut more slowly. Single-cut mill files are used on sawteeth and metals where a good finish is required. Double-cut files are used primarily on metals where rapid stock removal is necessary

Which One? CHOOSING A FILE

All the different factors that distinguish one file from another—shape, tooth cut, and coarseness—can make it difficult to know which file is best for a required task. Here are some of the most frequently used file types, identified by their common names, with the jobs they're best suited for.

FLAT BASTARD FILES with double-cut teeth are aggressive tools and great for:
• shaping or refining metal parts
• removing heavy burrs or flashing from parts

HALF-ROUND BASTARD FILES have one flat side and one curved side, making them best for:
• shaping or refining concave edges
• removing burrs on the inside edges of large-diameter pipe and tubing

FLAT MILL FILES with a single cut are versatile tools and good for many smoothing jobs including:
• removing light burrs from sheet metal, bars, and flat stock
• removing scratches on parts left by coarse grinding
• sharpening axes, knives, and shears

KNIFE BASTARD FILES are slightly tapered with a single sharp edge, making them good for:
• creating or enlarging narrow slots
• filing fine notches or division markings

TAPERED ROUND FILES come in various diameters and are well suited for:
• removing burrs from the inside edges of pipe and tubing
• enlarging holes in sheet metal, plastics, and hardwoods

TRIANGULAR FILES, also known as cantsaw files, are useful for:
• sharpening teeth on western panel saws and crosscut saws
• creating or enlarging V-grooves in metal, plastics, and hardwoods

NEEDLE FILES are small in size and come in many shapes; they're good for:
• cleaning up edges and profiles on jewelry and small parts
• shaping or refining model components and precision parts

CHAINSAW FILES are round, untapered files that are designed for:
• sharpening round- or square-hooded chainsaw teeth

and a rough finish is adequate. Curved-tooth files are good for rapid removal of soft materials and are a staple in auto-body shops for smoothing repaired fenders and body panels.

Files are available in four levels of coarseness: coarse, bastard, second, and smooth cut. Coarse and bastard cuts are used on heavy work, while second and smooth cuts are used for finishing or more exacting work.

Wood Rasps

A wood rasp is a powerful shaping tool for curved or rounded parts. Really a kind of file with individually formed, pointy, aggressive-cutting teeth, a rasp can make quick work of rounding over sharp edges—on a stool seat or butcher-block table, for instance—or shaping an ordinary block of wood into a custom umbrella handle or drawer pull. Despite its name, a wood rasp does a lot more than just work wood. It will also shred rigid foam (such as Styrofoam®), plaster, soapstone, leather, and even soft metals, including copper and aluminum.

▶WOOD RASPS AND RIFFLERS
Wood rasps come in both standard (center) and Japanese styles (rear) and are great for quickly rough-shaping edges or wood parts. Rifflers (front) come in different shapes and are terrific for refining carvings and detail work.

Wood rasps come in several useful shapes, including flat, half-round (with one flat and one rounded side), and round, ranging in length from 6 in. to 14 in. Hardware stores usually stock only the coarsest, bastard-cut version of each shape. A bastard-cut rasp is great for quickly rough-shaping parts or edges, but its big teeth leave lots of scratches, which require extensive sanding to eliminate. Designed for two-handed use, a Japanese-style rasp is another type of course rasp (shown at rear in the photo below). It has a crisscross matrix of toothed blades that removes stock quickly.

Woodworking-supply catalogs often sell finer-toothed second-cut rasps as well as smooth rasps with even finer teeth. Sometimes called cabinetmaker's rasps, both of these tools are good for refining parts shaped with a bastard-cut rasp or other tool that leaves a less-than-smooth surface. Supply catalogs also sell petite needle rasps and riffler rasps (shown at front in the photo on the facing page), both of which are perfect for refining carved details or for shaping small parts used for miniature models or doll furniture.

Four-in-One Carpenter's Rasps

This wood shaper's multitool combines two rasps and two files into a tool that conveniently fits into your pocket or apron pouch. A 4-in-1 carpenter's rasp (shown at right in the photo below), also called a hand file or a shoe rasp, is an 8-in.- or 10-in.-long metal bar that's flat on one side and half-round on the other. Each side has a rasp at one end and a file on the other. The rougher rasp ends are for removing wood quickly—to rough-trim a joint or knock a sharp corner off the end of a rafter or railing, for instance. The file ends are used to refine and smooth the rough surface left by the rasps. Although the files look relatively coarse, they produce a surprisingly fine finish that sands smooth easily.

Another handy carpenter's multitool combines a wood chisel with a flat wood rasp on one side and a half-round wood rasp on the other (shown at left in the photo below). You can use the chisel to chop out slots and mortises, while the rasps are perfect for removing material quickly, shaping parts, and enlarging holes.

▼FOUR-IN-ONE RASP AND RASP/CHISEL TOOL A four-in-one rasp (center right) or rasp/chisel combo tool (left) are handy to carry in a carpentry tool belt and good for easing sharp wood corners or smoothing edges.

Surform® Rasps

A Surform rasp uses many rows of small, slicing teeth to shape wood, plastics, leather, and soft metals. An opening behind each tooth allows waste to pass though, which helps prevent the clogging that regular rasps are prone to. This makes a Surform a terrific tool for rasping down gummy materials like excess auto-body filler or epoxy putty from a repair before it has completely hardened.

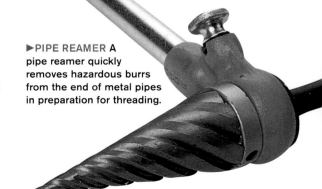

▲SURFORM RASPS A Surform rasp is like a cheese grater for wood, with lots of sharp teeth that quickly shape wood, foam, and other soft materials.

REAMING AND RESURFACING TOOLS

There are lots of handy little tools that serve to ream, deburr, or resurface parts and workpieces—shave holes, clean up metal edges, and resurface valve seats. Tapered reamers are useful for cleaning up or enlarging drilled holes, while deburring tools are handy for cleaning burrs from tubing or sheet-metal edges. Pipe reamers are specialized deburring tools specifically made for pipe-threading work. Valve-seat regrinding tools are specialized devices for resurfacing and repairing the seats of water faucets.

Tapered Reamers

Is the hole you drilled just a little too small for the bolt you need to fit into it? A tapered reamer is just the tool to make holes larger to accept bolts, dowels, rivets, and pins. Most effective with thin sheet goods (sheet metal, Peg-Board, thin plywood, and the like), a reamer's long, tapered shape fits into holes between ⅛ in. and ½ in. in diameter. By rotating the tool, its cutting edges shave the hole. Shave a little and you'll remove burrs and clean the edges of the hole; shave a lot and you'll enlarge the hole's diameter. Reamers should be kept in a sleeve or pouch to prevent the edges from dulling.

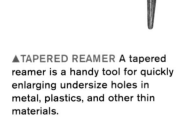

▲TAPERED REAMER A tapered reamer is a handy tool for quickly enlarging undersize holes in metal, plastics, and other thin materials.

PIPE REAMERS A pipe reamer has one purpose in life: to remove the burr left on the end of metal pipe after it has been cut with a pipe cutter (see "Pipe Cutters" on p. 115). This type of burr is sharp enough to render a nasty cut and should always be removed before threading the pipe's end. While a pipe reamer is an expensive, specialized tool, it's worth buying if you're doing a job that involves cutting lots of pipe—say, replacing the water pipes in your home or adding irrigation pipes to your yard.

A pipe reamer has tapered cutting edges just like a tapered reamer (see the previous section), but it's much larger and is able to handle steel pipe between ⅛ in. and 2½ in. in diameter. The reamer is pressed into the end of the pipe and rotated by its long ratcheting handle; its spiral-cutting edges feed into the end and slice off the burr, leaving a smooth, lightly chamfered end that's ready for use.

►PIPE REAMER A pipe reamer quickly removes hazardous burrs from the end of metal pipes in preparation for threading.

VALVE-SEAT WRENCH

A valve-seat removal wrench is designed to loosen the valve seat so you can replace it. There are two styles of valve-seat wrenches—tapered and stepped—both of which fit numerous sizes of the square-shaped sockets found in valve seats.

Don't know if your faucet has a replaceable valve seat? To find out, remove its handle and cap nut (if it has one) and remove the valve stem (the part that the handle attaches to). Now look down into the faucet: If you see a square hole, the seat is removable; if not, it needs regrinding and a new washer to remedy the leaking.

◀**VALVE-SEAT REGRINDING TOOL** Fitted with the right-size cutting wheel, a valve-seat regrinding tool is the tool for fixing most leaky faucets.

Valve-Seat Regrinding Tools

You can stop the steady drip, drip, drip of a leaking faucet without the hassle and cost of replacement by removing the faucet's valve and regrinding the valve seat. A valve-seat regrinding tool (shown at upper left in the photo above) comes in a kit that contains all the parts and accessories you need to regrind the brass seats on several different sizes of faucets. Most kits also contain an assortment of replacement washers. If your faucet lacks a cap nut, as most small bathroom-faucet fixtures do,

you'll need a valve-seat regrinding kit that includes a plastic guide cone to align the seat grinder. This kit is often sold as a double-cone reamer. To repair leaky faucets that have a removable seat, you'll need a valve-seat wrench in lieu of a regrinding kit (see "Valve-Seat Wrench" above).

CHAPTER 3

Tools That Saw

With the right tools, there's more than one way to saw through a board—or a tile, or a piece of flat iron, or drywall. Muscle power and sweat have traditionally provided the force for sawing through most materials, using handsaws and coping saws for wood and hacksaws for metal. But while there are still occasions when a handsaw will do, portable power and stationary saws are quickly turning many old saws into mere wall-hanging decorations. Modern powered wood-cutting saws, metal-cutting portable and cutoff saws, tile saws, and their brethren let us saw practically any material with more speed and greater accuracy than ever before.

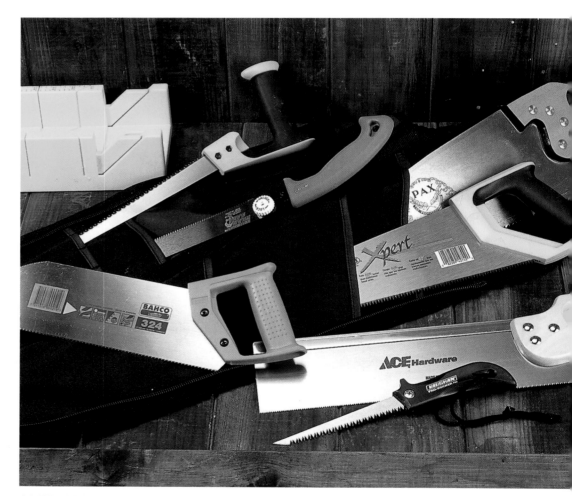

▲A FEW GOOD HANDSAWS When a power saw just won't cut it, reach for a handsaw–panel, rip, keyhole, flooring, Japanese-style, drywall, or backsaw–to get the job done.

HANDSAWS

Despite the profusion of power saws—table saw, radial-arm saw, portable circular saw, sabersaw—there's still a place for the traditional handsaw in every workshop. Even if it's only brought out on occasion (to finish a pocket cut, trim a tenon, or flush-cut molding, for instance), a sharp, well-tuned saw is a pleasure to use.

Like so many other tools, handsaws have evolved over the years in shape, size, and style, and the multitude that now exist guarantees you'll find one that perfectly suits your needs. In addition to traditional western-style panel saws, you'll now find a bevy of cleverly designed Japanese hand-saws, as well as short, aggressive-cutting, toolbox-size saws at your local hardware store or home-supply center.

Panel Saws

Carpenters, boatbuilders, cabinetmakers, and woodworkers of all sorts once used panel-type handsaws (at rear in the photo below) for many of their wood-cutting tasks: sawing planks and panels to size, trimming parts, and cutting out pockets and large joinery. Most panel saws are 20 in. to 26 in. long, with teeth specialized to cut wood either across the grain (cross-cutting) or along the grain (ripping).

Nowadays, crosscut saws are the most commonly available. Their teeth typically number 7 tpi to 12 tpi (teeth per inch). Fewer teeth produce a faster, rougher cut edge, while more teeth cut more slowly but leave a smoother surface. A crosscut saw is not only good for cutting solid lumber pieces to length but also for sawing ply-wood parts, which you can cut in any direction. A fine-tooth (12 tpi) saw is best for delicate hardwood plywoods. Some

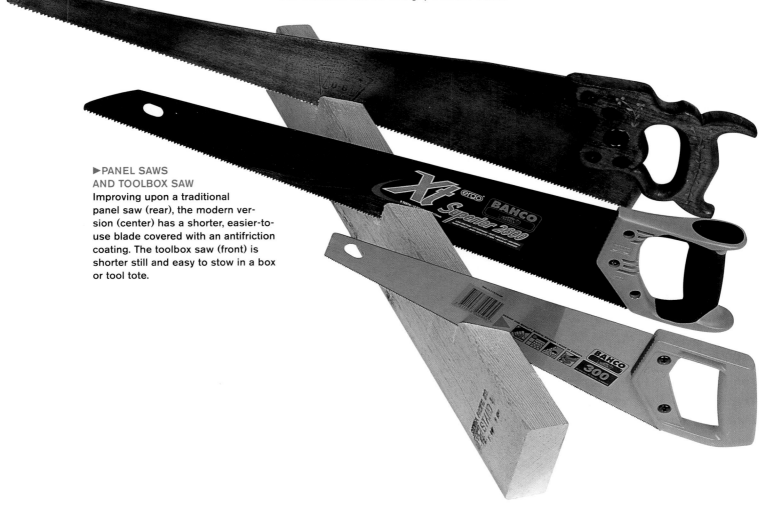

▶PANEL SAWS
AND TOOLBOX SAW
Improving upon a traditional panel saw (rear), the modern version (center) has a shorter, easier-to-use blade covered with an antifriction coating. The toolbox saw (front) is shorter still and easy to stow in a box or tool tote.

modern saws even have a low-friction coating (shown at center in the photo on p. 79) that makes the saw glide more easily through the cut.

Panel saws designed for ripping typically have large (4-tpi to 7-tpi) teeth, shaped to plow through wood fibers like little handplanes. This is the tool for sawing solid-wood planks and panels along their length.

Toolbox Saws

Panel saws can be difficult to use for the uninitiated and inexperienced, primarily because of their long length: Jamming the

teeth or binding the blade can buckle (and ruin) an expensive saw in a flash. Thus, many of the newer handsaws on the market have shorter—10-in. to 14-in.— blades (shown at front in the photo on p. 79). Not only does the shorter length create a shorter work stroke, making these saws easier to use and less subject to bending and buckling, but they also fit into medium-size toolboxes (hence the nickname toolbox saws).

Most of these nontraditional saws sport nontraditional, three-sided teeth that cut *very* aggressively. They're just like the teeth found on Japanese-style pull saws (see p. 83), but they're reversed, so they cut on the push stroke, which most Western carpenters and woodworkers are used to.

Backsaws

Another type of handsaw that is still useful in a modern workshop is the backsaw. The name of this saw comes from the steel or brass stiffening strip that's formed around the rectangular blade's back (top) edge. This back strip reinforces the blade, keeping it

---

HOW TO SAW LIKE A PRO

To get a good, clean cut with a handsaw, start by setting the board, plank, or panel on a sturdy surface, like a benchtop or sawhorses. Clamp or hold the work so the part you wish to cut overhangs the support. Start by aligning the blade teeth with your marked line of cut and take a few strokes, pulling or pushing the saw opposite the cutting direction of the teeth. Placing your thumb aside the blade (above the teeth) will help stabilize it. Once you've created a small kerf (cut), begin sawing with long, full strokes, using as much of the length of the blade as is comfortable. Switch to shorter, lighter strokes as you get near the end of the cut, and support the cutoff portion so it doesn't drop off and tear or splinter.

▲BACKSAW With its stiff back, short length, and fine teeth, a backsaw is great for accurate cutting.

straight and preventing buckling. Most backsaws have fine teeth (11 tpi to 14 tpi) along a rectangular-shape blade that's 10 in. to 14 in. long. The saw's stiff blade and fine teeth allow for straight and accurate cuts—perfect for cutting wood joinery, for instance—but the blade back prevents deep through cuts like those you would make with a panel saw. Backsaw teeth are primarily shaped for crosscutting, but you can also make cuts with the grain. The most popular general use for backsaws is making accurate crosscuts using a wood or plastic miter box, as discussed in "Miter Boxes" at right.

Razor Saws

Resembling miniature backsaws, razor saws have blades that are short (4½ in. to 6½ in.) and incredibly thin (0.008 in. to 0.015 in.), backed by a steel spine for greater stability. They're great for cutting delicate materials, such as decorative wood banding or balsa wood (for model making), without splintering. Model makers love razor saws for their versatility; their miniscule, tempered teeth (as small as 54 tpi) easily cut through plastic and are hard enough to slice through thin-wall brass tubing and other nonferrous metals. Combine a razor saw with a mini-miter box, and you'll get accurate square and 45-degree angle cuts on all your narrow stock.

Miter Saws

If you prefer to make your crosscuts sans power but a simple miter box won't cut it (pun intended), consider purchasing a miter saw. Available in both large and small sizes, these precision tools use special tensioned blades (much like a hacksaw) supported and aligned by a set of guideposts. Sliding guides ride on the posts, allowing the blade to move up and down and back and forth during a cut while keeping the

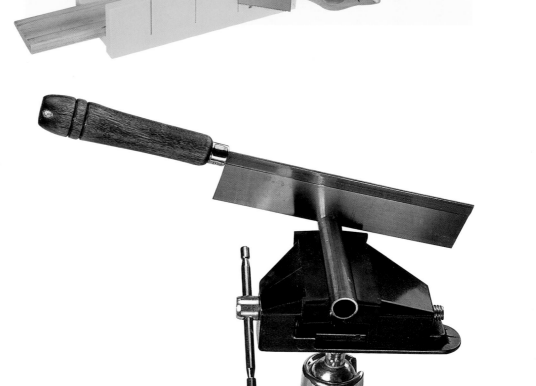

Tool Helpers | **MITER BOXES**

A good miter box and sharp backsaw go together like hot pizza and cold beer—they're just made for each other. A U-shaped strip about a foot long made from either wood or rigid plastic, a miter box has three or more narrow, vertical slots, each made to accurately align and guide the saw through a standard cut: 90 degrees (square) or 45 degrees in either direction.

Although you could build your own large or small miter box to suit your special needs, commercially made miter boxes are sized for cutting stock no bigger than 3¾ in. wide by 2¼ in. thick. They provide an economical means of cutting reasonably accurate miters when cutting out picture frames or trimming moldings for cabinets and interior woodwork.

▲**RAZOR SAW** For clean, accurate cuts in metal tubing or flat stock, a razor saw's thin, fine-tooth blade does the trick.

▼MITER SAW A step up from a backsaw and miter box, a miter saw has a thin, tensioned blade and a turntable that you can accurately set for cuts between 45 degrees and 90 degrees.

angle precise. The posts are attached to an assembly that pivots the saw relative to a cast-alloy base and fence, which support the workpiece.

Just like a powered miter saw (see p. 101), you can set a miter saw to cut any angle between 90 degrees (square) and 45 degrees in either direction, allowing you to miter either end of a narrow board or long molding strip. The pivoting base locks accurately at common angles—such as 90 degrees, 22½ degrees, and 45 degrees—making for accurate picture-frame corners and other joints for interior trim and molding. You can also lock in the saw for cutting odd angles, useful when fitting moldings on walls or around windows and doors that are out of square. Even if you already own a powered crosscut saw, a miter saw is handy to have around for cutting small, thin, or delicate workpieces too difficult or dangerous to cut on a power saw.

Dovetail Saws

Resembling pint-size backsaws, dovetail saws have rectangular blades ranging from 6 in. to 10 in. long and *very* fine teeth—15 tpi to an ultrafine 26 tpi. Fitted with back-stiffening strips (often made from attractive brass), dovetail saws are just the right tool for taking fine, straight cuts in solid hardwoods with a minimum of splin-

▲DOVETAIL SAWS Whether short or long, dovetail saws have thin blades and fine teeth capable of making the delicate cuts necessary for hand-cut wood joinery.

tering. While traditionally used for accurately sawing joinery—such as dovetails, lap and finger joints, miters, and other wood-to-wood joints—dovetail saws are also handy for all kinds of odd cuts and trimming jobs, whenever cleanness and accuracy is of the utmost importance.

Japanese Saws

A different culture inspired the carpentry tools developed in the Far East, producing many that are quite distinctive from those born of the European traditions with which we are familiar. Some, like the Japanese handsaw, are useful in any workshop. Unlike most Western saws, all Japanese saws have teeth that cut when the saw is pulled toward the user. Why cut on the pull stroke? Pulling the ends of a narrow strip of paper demonstrates that a blade, put into tension, can be extremely thin and still have enough rigidity not to bend and buckle while sawing wood. The thin, highly flexible blades and aggressive teeth char-

acteristic of Japanese saws have some distinct advantages over Western-style saws (see the Pro/Con box at right).

Traditionally, Japanese saws have oval-shaped wood handles covered with rattan or even sharkskin, to give the user a good grip with both hands. Newer saws have cushioned plastic grips for one-handed use (more familiar to Westerners). These are angled and shaped for better ergonomics and comfort. Better still, many of these newer saws have heat-treated teeth that are hard and durable enough to saw dense hardwoods (many traditional saws are meant only for sawing softwoods). Plus, the saws have replaceable blades, thus eliminating the problem of keeping their difficult-to-sharpen teeth sharp. Both traditional and newer-type Japanese saws come in many styles, each specifically designed for ripping, crosscutting, or both operations. There is even a special saw made just for sawing plastic stock or pipe used in plumbing work.

▲JAPANESE HANDSAWS All equipped with thin blades that cut on the pull stroke, the four types of Japanese saws shown here are (clockwise from top): *ryoba, azebiki, dozuki,* and a *kugihiki*-style flush-cut saw.

▲FLUSH-CUT SAW With nonset teeth that won't scratch the surface, a *kugihiki*-style flush-cut saw is ideal for trimming pegs or dowels.

▲JAPANESE-STYLE SAWS Based on traditional *ryoba* and *dozuki* designs, these modern Japanese-style saws have cushioned handles. The saw at right is for crosscuts, while the saw at left has crosscut teeth on one edge and rip teeth on the other.

JAPANESE CROSSCUT SAWS Compared to Western sawteeth, the teeth on Japanese-style crosscutting blades are most unusual, with three bevels per tooth and each tooth sharpened on all three edges. While this makes them more practical to replace than to resharpen (modern saws have replaceable blades), it allows them to slice through wood fibers with great vigor. One common style of Japanese crosscut saw, traditionally known as a *dozuki* saw, has a reinforcing back strip (just like a backsaw) and small, razor-sharp teeth designed for fine miter cuts and for cutting joinery, such as dovetails.

More popular now, backless-style crosscut saws aren't as stiff, but they allow the saw to cut all the way through its width, good for crosscutting wide or thick lumber and trim. Longer saws with larger teeth (9 tpi, for example) are handy for quickly zipping through thicker planks and even small tree branches. Shorter saws with finer teeth (14 tpi to 17 tpi) are terrific for cutting fine hardwood or plywood parts cleanly and accurately.

There are two specialized Japanese crosscut saws that are also useful. The *abeziki*

(see the left photo on p. 83) has a short (3-in.) curved blade with teeth on both edges designed to start a cut in the middle of a panel, perfect for pocket cuts or joinery. The small *kugihiki*-style flush-cut saw has a thin, flexible blade with tiny teeth specifically designed for flush-trimming jobs. By keeping this saw's blade flat on the work and tilting the handle up, you can cut off protruding pegs or dowels flush with a surface or trim the bottom of door casings and trim flush with the floor.

DUAL-PURPOSE JAPANESE SAWS A unique Japanese dual-purpose saw, known traditionally as a *ryoba* saw, has two rows of teeth on either edge of the blade: One side has large chisel-style teeth for ripping, and the other has three-sided teeth for crosscutting. While the crosscut teeth are just like those found on regular Japanese crosscut saws, the ripping teeth on dual-purpose saws are graduated in size. The smaller teeth closer to the handle make starting a cut easier, while the larger teeth near the end of the blade provide a more aggressive cutting action. Like traditional *ryoba* saws, modern dual-purpose saws have an oval-shape handle (but one covered with soft-grip plastic, rather than rattan). This provides a grip for both hands so that both arms power the cut, allowing you to work with less fatigue.

Keyhole, Compass, and Drywall Saws

While panel saws and backsaws are large saws designed for straight cuts across boards, panels, and trim, keyhole, compass, and drywall saws are the tools you need for sawing cutouts and curves across—or in the middle of—boards and panels. All three have long, thin blades that come to a sharp point.

The smallest of the three is the drywall saw (also called a jab saw), which typically has a short (5-in. to 7-in.) blade with coarse teeth specifically designed to quickly carve through—you guessed it—Sheetrock® and drywall. It's the best choice for making cutouts for pipes, trim, electrical boxes, and fixtures when drywalling a room.

Keyhole saws (sometimes called compass saws) have slightly longer (10-in. to 12-in.) blades, with 7 tpi to 10 tpi. They're perfect for cutting tight curves in solid wood or plywood in lieu of a jigsaw. Like drywall saws, keyhole saws have sharp, self-starting points, which let you start cuts in soft and thin materials (soundboard, drywall, wood paneling, etc.) without drilling a starting hole: Carefully jab the point in, and take a few short strokes to start a cut in the middle of a panel. Although the keyhole saw's blade is relatively thick and sturdy, the teeth cut on the push stroke, so you must saw carefully to avoid bending the blade.

If you need a more versatile saw, buy a "nest of saws"—that is, a handle that comes with a set of interchangeable blades, including a keyhole-type saw and several tapered steel blades of different lengths and teeth sizes (for cutting metal, wood, and other materials).

Coping Saws

How are you going to cut out that curved solid or plywood part when there's no electricity for your jigsaw? Try using a coping saw. This inexpensive saw is nothing more than a U-shaped frame with a handle that tensions a narrow blade, much like a hacksaw (see the following section). To cut tight curves, you turn either (or both) the saw or the workpiece, which is supported by a V-block, as shown in the photo at below.

▼**COPING SAW** With the work supported on a V-shaped block that's clamped to the work table, a coping saw's thin blade and a deep throat allow it to take curved cuts in thick or thin materials.

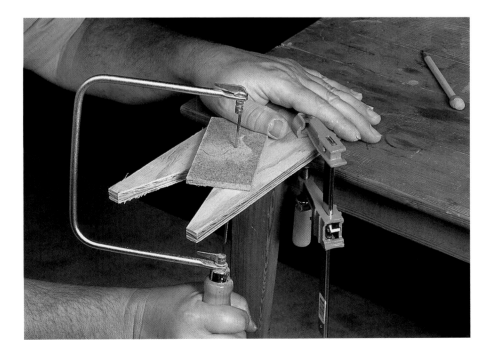

▲**KEYHOLE, DRYWALL, AND UTILITY SAWS** For cutting small slots and holes, use a keyhole saw (lower right) in wood materials or a drywall saw (upper right) in gypsum wallboard. A nest of saws (left) has a handle and several blades for multiple tasks.

Cool Tools | FOLDING UTILITY SAW

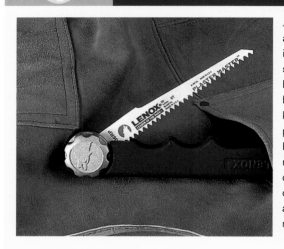

A FOLDING UTILITY SAW allows you to stick a handsaw in your pocket—as odd as that sounds. It sports a compact blade that folds up, like the blade of a jackknife, so you can keep it handy in your tool bag, pants' pocket, or apron pouch. Because the saw uses standard reciprocating-saw blades, you can choose blades designed for cutting drywall, wood, metal, and other materials as your needs dictate.

▲**THREE HACKSAWS** A high-tension hacksaw (left) has a sturdier frame than a standard hacksaw (right) and holds its blade more stiffly, for a cleaner cut and longer blade life. The close-quarters hacksaw (bottom) is for cuts in tight spots where a regular saw won't fit.

Pro Tip

If you've bought a high-tensioned hacksaw, always use a bimetal blade with it. Bimetal blades (hard steel teeth on a more ductile metal backing) are designed to withstand the stretching forces imposed by high-tensioned frames. Never use standard hacksaw blades, which can suddenly shatter during demanding cutting operations.

A coping saw's fine-tooth blade has small cross pins on the ends, which are held by the ends of the frame. To make inside cuts (cuts that don't reach the edges of the workpiece), remove the blade from the saw, and thread one end through a hole drilled in the work. To cut farther from the edge of the stock, a coping saw's blade holders can be rotated so that the blade cuts perpendicular or at an angle relative to the frame.

Hacksaws

A basic hacksaw consists of a frame with a simple threaded screw and wing nut that tensions the blade. Most saw frames are sized for 12-in. blades (the most common size), but some frames adjust to accept 10-in. and 8-in. blades as well.

A good hacksaw is characterized by a strong frame that keeps a narrow blade in tension during cutting. Although it's the traditional tool for hand-sawing both non-ferrous metals and mild steel, a hacksaw fitted with a fine-tooth blade will also cut most plastics, fiberglass, and other dense materials quite handily. Also, special wire blades with imbedded carbide chips let you cut tile, ceramics, and even glass.

The latest hacksaws have high-tension frames. These employ a strong cast or formed frame-and-cam mechanism that gives the blade about twice as much tension as a simple hacksaw frame. The higher tension keeps the blade taut and prevents twisting during heavy cuts, helping you make straighter and more accurate cuts in thick stock or other difficult materials.

Regardless of frame style, most hacksaws provide a means to angle the blade relative to the frame. This provides clearance between blade and frame in cases where a deep cut is needed on a long workpiece or when a cut must be made sideways. Some hacksaw models store extra blades in the hollow top tube of the frame.

A close-quarters hacksaw (shown at bottom in the photo above) has a blade holder that accepts either a full or half blade, mounted in a handle with a short arm that reinforces the back of the blade at midspan. This tool is handy when you need to cut away broken pipes or fasteners in areas where a full-size hacksaw just won't fit.

Tile and Grout Saws

To make long, angled cuts or to split ceramic tiles in two, you'll get the best results with either a scoring-type cutter (see "Scoring-Type Tile Cutters" on p. 115) or an electric tile saw (see p. 107). But when you need to cut a notch in tile or make a curved cut, you need to use a tile saw. This tool's simple U-shaped frame holds a special blade: thick, wire-embedded carbide chips that abrade their way through ceramic tiles and terra-cotta pavers (or even china dishes and flowerpots) without excessively chipping at the edges of the cut.

To prevent breakage, keep the tile saw's blade vertical during the cut and support the tile on a V-board (a short, rectangular board with a V-shaped cutout at one end,

which supports the tile while providing cutting clearance for the sawblade). To accurately mark cuts where tiles must fit around obstructions (where a tile must fit around a faucet fixture, light switch, or drainpipe, for instance), use a profile gauge to transfer the pattern (see "Contour Gauges" on p. 203).

The grout lines between tiles look lovely when they're fresh and new, but they can really look awful when they're old, cracked, crumbling, or discolored. When it's time to regrout, a grout saw (shown at left in the photo below) provides the easiest means of removing old, hardened grout. The tool's sharp, carbide-coated blade abrades the grout in much the same way that a rasp cuts through wood. The saw's narrow profile lets you get all the way to the bottom of each grout line without nicking or chipping the tile on either side. For big jobs that require a power solution, you can get a grout sawblade that fits into a reciprocating saw.

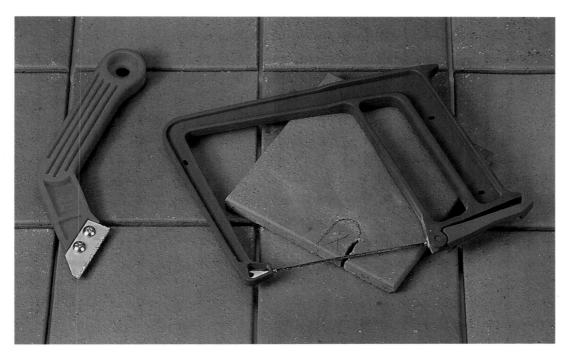

▲**TILE SAW AND GROUT SAW** Removing grout and hand-trimming tiles are jobs made less tedious with the right tools, such as the grout saw (left) and the carbide-bladed tile saw (right).

PORTABLE POWER SAWS

In the evolution of tools, few innovations have had greater impact than the harnessing of an electric motor to drive a sawblade. While stationary saws—table saws, bandsaws, and the like—have an important job in a woodshop, it's the portable tools that have revolutionized the speed and accuracy with which even relatively inexperienced users can tackle all manner of projects and household improvements and repairs. There's a portable electric saw for just about every type of cutting imaginable: circular saws for straight cuts and jigsaws for curved cuts in lumber and plywood; chainsaws for slicing up firewood and rough lumber; reciprocating saws for hacking through nail-embedded wood and metal; and rotary cutters for zipping through drywall, wallboard, and more.

Jigsaws

Modern jigsaws have the power and features to make them curve-cutting machines, which run like sewing machines and cut like chainsaws. Using a narrow blade that pumps up and down rapidly, a jigsaw cuts all manner of curves, circles, and scroll cuts (think of Victorian gingerbread decorations) in solid wood or plywood. Known alternatively as a sabersaw or a bayonet saw, a jigsaw also can do

▲PORTABLE POWER SAWS Whether corded, cordless, or gas-powered, portable circular saws, jigsaws, reciprocating saws, and chainsaws are ready to take on any construction or repair project in and around the house and yard.

straight cuts. But unless you're taking advantage of its compact size to cut in tight quarters, a jigsaw isn't the ideal tool for straight cuts, which are better left to a circular saw or table saw. One of the jigsaw's most impressive talents is plunge cutting: Tilt the saw forward on its base and slowly allow the blade to slice into the middle of a panel—say, to make a cutout in a plywood countertop when installing a kitchen sink.

While wood constitutes a jigsaw's usual diet, most saws have features that enable them to make an occasional meal of plastic, cardboard, fiberglass, and even metal. Fitted with the right blade (see "Jigsaw and Reciprocating-Saw Blades" on p.91), a jigsaw can cut wood up to 2¾ in. thick, aluminum ¾ in. thick, and even ¼-in.-thick mild steel. Variable speed allows you to reduce the blade speed, necessary when cutting dense or delicate materials. An orbital blade mechanism moves the blade in a slightly circular motion as it reciprocates. Setting the orbital action adjusts how aggressively the saw cuts: lots of orbit for faster, rougher, or straighter cuts;

straight up and down for slower, finer, or curvier cuts.

CHOOSING A JIGSAW Jigsaws come in both corded and cordless models. Corded saws come in either a top-mounted D-handle or in the European barrel-grip style, where one hand holds the saw around the motor housing. (Both work well; it's a matter of personal preference.) Battery-powered saws are safer and handier to use when you're away from power or working in damp or wet conditions where electric shock is possible.

Regardless of which style you choose, there are some common features to look for when buying a new jigsaw: a toolless blade holder for rapid blade changes without scrounging for a wrench or screwdriver; a tilting base for making beveled cuts (the blade angled relative to the work); a built-in dust blower to clear sawdust so you can see the cutting line better; a port for connecting a vacuum hose, to collect sawdust as you cut; and a scrolling feature, which lets you rotate the blade while keeping the jigsaw itself moving in one direction, making delicate, curvy cuts easier.

▲ **JIGSAW** For cutting gradual or tight curves in solid wood, plywood, and other sheet goods, a jigsaw's aggressive cutting action gets the job done.

Reciprocating Saws

Although its blade moves in and out much like a jigsaw's, a reciprocating saw is an entirely different animal. A jigsaw has a large base and narrow blade best suited to cutting flat stock that's firmly clamped to the benchtop. A reciprocating saw (or "recip" saw) has a small base (called a shoe) and accepts blades ranging from narrow to wide (see the top photo on p. 92) making it suitable for cutting flat or curved work that's horizontal, vertical, or even at an odd angle overhead.

Its basic design and wide range of blades make the recip saw a remodeler's dream tool, capable of sawing jobs both ordinary and odd: cutting out a wall for a new window or a roof for a skylight, sawing off old water pipes and drainpipes, or trimming or notching studs to make way for new electrical cables or heating ducts. A recip saw is also a delight at demolition time, hacking through concrete-soaked wooden foundation forms or nail-embedded packing crates and pallets.

Introduced in the early 1950s by the Milwaukee Tool Company as the Sawzall®, the reciprocating saw is now made by several companies in both corded and cordless models. A plug-in recip has the power for the most demanding jobs, like sawing through cast-iron sewer pipe or several layers of flooring or old roofing. A battery-powered model lets you leave the extension cord behind—handy when you're wriggling through a cramped attic or crawl space or balancing atop a tall ladder.

Corded and cordless saws share many features, including toolless blade change (a *very* handy feature), variable speed, and a multiposition adjustable shoe (as teeth wear out on one part of the blade, repositioning the shoe lets fresh teeth go to work, extending blade life dramatically). More expensive models have a built-in counterbalance mechanism, which reduces

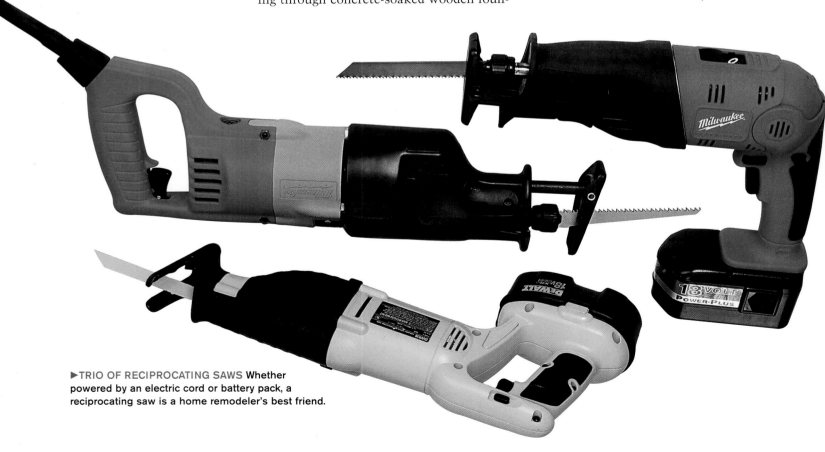

▶TRIO OF RECIPROCATING SAWS **Whether powered by an electric cord or battery pack, a reciprocating saw is a home remodeler's best friend.**

The Correct Extension Cord

Power saws need a strong and steady supply of electricity to keep their motors humming along and to produce the torque and power necessary for the job, especially when cutting tough, dense hardwoods or exotic woods. Using an extension cord that's too thin or too long compromises the electrical power flow to the saw and can lead to poor performance, overheating, and possible motor damage—even fire. This chart shows how to match extension cords of the right size with the amperage of a machine's motor.

EXTENSION CORD GAUGE, LENGTH, AND CAPACITY

Cord Length	Rated Amperage of Tool					
	Up to 2.0	2.1–3.4	3.5–5.0	5.1–7.0	7.1–12.0	12.1–16.0
25 ft.	18 ga.	18 ga.	18 ga.	18 ga.	16 ga.	14 ga.
50 ft.	18 ga.	18 ga.	18 ga.	16 ga.	14 ga.	12 ga.
75 ft.	18 ga.	18 ga.	16 ga.	14 ga.	12 ga.	10 ga.
100 ft.	18 ga.	16 ga.	14 ga.	12 ga.	10 ga.	8 ga.
150 ft.	16 ga.	14 ga.	12 ga.	10 ga.	8 ga.	8 ga.
200 ft.	16 ga.	14 ga.	12 ga.	10 ga.	8 ga.	6 ga.

vibration and user fatigue and makes the saw easier to control. Some cordless saws also offer adjustable blade orbit (see "Jigsaws" on p. 88) and an electronic brake, which stops the blade instantly after shut-off to help prevent accidents and broken blades.

Jigsaw and Reciprocating-Saw Blades

Modern blades for jigsaws and reciprocating saws are often packed with as much clever technology as the tools themselves. You can find special blades for cutting just about any material, including steel, reinforced plastics, cast iron, drywall, and even cement board and tile. General-purpose blades are good for everyday cuts in wood and sheet materials, such as Masonite® and MDF (medium-density fiberboard).

The most popular blades these days are bimetal, made by a process that bonds hardened carbon-steel teeth to a high-speed-steel blade body. The result is a blade with durable teeth that stay sharp while the blade remains flexible and resists breakage. Bimetal blades are ideal for both general work and demanding operations, such as cutting through nail-embedded 2x4s with a recip saw—say, when remodeling a kitchen—or cutting tight curves in dense, exotic woods with a jigsaw.

Fine-tooth metal-cutting blades are designed to cut through pipes and sheet metal effectively. But for tough materials—such as cast iron, cement board, and ceramic tile—fit a blade embedded with tungsten-carbide grit.

While most jigsaw and reciprocating-saw blades have teeth measured in standard teeth per inch (tpi) (see the tip at right), some blades feature progressive tooth pitch, with smaller teeth at the shank and larger teeth at the end. In wood, this pro-

Pro Tip

The overall length and number of teeth per inch (tpi) of any given blade affects both its maximum cutting depth and the fineness or raggedness of the cut it produces. Longer blades with fewer teeth cut deeper, rougher, and more aggressively; shorter blades with more teeth make shallower cuts more slowly but leave a smoother cut surface.

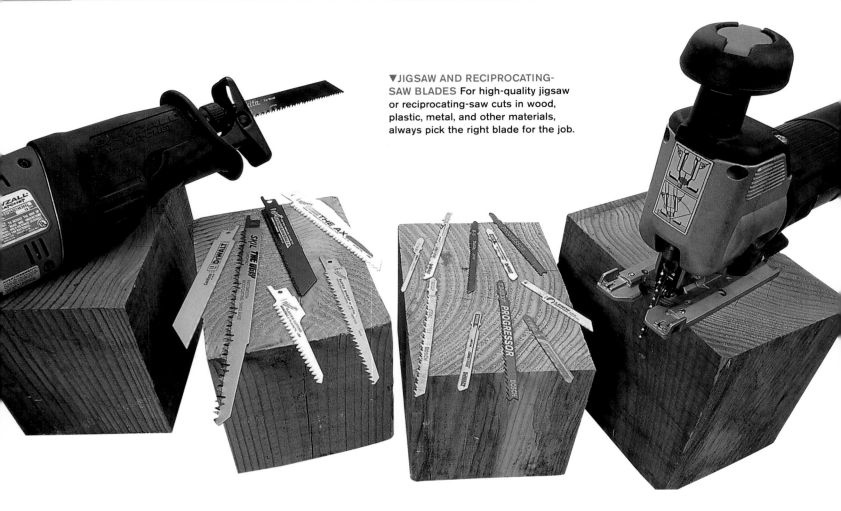

▼JIGSAW AND RECIPROCATING-SAW BLADES For high-quality jigsaw or reciprocating-saw cuts in wood, plastic, metal, and other materials, always pick the right blade for the job.

▲PORTABLE CIRCULAR SAWS Whether plugged into an outlet or powered by a battery pack, portable circular saws are fast wood-cutting machines.

duces a more aggressive cut with less splintering. There are also special blades with variable-size teeth, specifically designed to coax the best cutting performance from cordless saws.

Portable Circular Saws

Although they aren't exactly the most versatile of power tools, portable circular saws (sometimes generically referred to by the brand name of Skilsaw®) do one thing extremely well: make straight cuts in wood. Fitted with a sharp sawblade, a circular saw can rip or crosscut solid lumber, cut up a sheet of plywood, trim moldings, and do lots more. If you can only afford a single power saw, a circular saw will handle most of the cuts you'll need, whether you're remodeling your home or building a doghouse.

Circular saws are sized by the diameter of their blades. The larger the blade, the thicker the wood a saw can cut. The largest (10-in. to 16-in.) beam saws are used to cut big construction timbers, while 3⅜-in. to 4½-in. trim saws are handy for light cuts in paneling, plywood, and trim. The most popular are 7¼-in. saws because they're big enough to cut through 2x construction lumber in a single pass yet small and light enough to carry and use without excessive strain.

Circular saws come in two basic body styles: worm drive and sidewinder (see the Pro/Con box on p. 94). Both styles, as well as cordless saws (see "Cordless Circular Saws" at right), have most of the same features: a depth-of-cut adjustment, a tilting base for bevel cuts, and a self-retracting blade guard to sheath the blade before and after each cut. Newer models often have built-in ports for connection to a shop vacuum. To save weight and user fatigue, some models are built with high-tech fiberglass-reinforced plastics or featherweight magnesium alloys.

Circular-Saw Blades

If the only circular-saw blade you've ever used on your powered portable, table, or compound miter saw is an old, rusty steel blade that came with the bargain saw you bought at the local flea market, you're in for a pleasant surprise. It's true that steel-tooth blades are inexpensive and easy to resharpen, but modern blades with hard, carbide teeth are more durable, stay sharp longer, and can cut difficult materials—wood with knots, dense hardwoods, and man-made sheet goods, like Melamine® and Masonite—with ease.

An all-purpose, carbide-tipped blade is all right for general carpentry chores, but for specific sawing jobs, a specialty blade produces better results. For example, decking and framing blades for portable circular saws are Teflon®-coated, which reduces

STRAIGHT-SAWING ACCESSORIES

Guiding a portable circular saw along a straight line is no easy feat and can take a bit of practice and a steady hand to accomplish. Fortunately the three accessories shown here make the job of taking a straight, square cut across a board or wide sheet of plywood a lot easier. For trimming or ripping a narrow board or panel, a rip fence (shown at front) is a standard accessory that mounts to a circular saw's sole and adjusts in or out to set the width of cut. For cutting a large panel or sheet to size, an edge-clamping guide (center) provides a straight fence that guides the saw through the cut. To make square or angled cuts across the width of a board, a por-

table crosscut guide (left rear) abuts the straight edge of the stock and has a fence bar that guides the saw for a straight, precise cut. Adjusting the guide's protractor-like gauge changes the angle of the fence bar for making 45-degree miters and other angled cuts.

CORDLESS CIRCULAR SAWS

THE FIRST CORDLESS PORTABLE CIRCULAR SAWS looked more like toys than tools, with petite blades and small battery packs (shown at front in the photo) that limited their cutting to thin plywood and trim. However, the latest saws feature large-diameter blades and high-voltage batteries that enable them to do serious work. The largest cordless models, with 6½-in. to 7¼-in. blades and big battery packs, have enough power to rip and crosscut a small project's worth of 2x lumber on a single charge.

Equipped with thin-kerf blades that require less power to drive (see "Circular-Saw Blades" at left), high-voltage (18-volt to 24-volt) models are the most energetic performers—even professional carpenters are using them daily. Lower-voltage (12-volt to 15.6-volt) models with 5⅜-in. to 6-in. blades are lighter and more compact. Although most of these low-voltage saws won't cut through 2x lumber in a single pass, they are handy for many smaller jobs, such as cutting paneling and molding for a family room facelift, trimming sheathing or flooring, or sawing plywood or ¾-in. lumber to size.

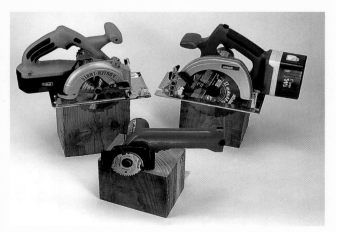

PRO CON

THE WORM DRIVE–STYLE SAW (shown at right in the photo below) has a long, narrow body with its motor at a right angle to the blade. The sidewinder saw (shown at left in the photo) has a more compact body with its motor on axis with its blade. What's the difference and which saw is better for you?

SIDEWINDERS

Pros:
• generally less expensive than worm drive styles
• less maintenance required than worm drive styles
• lighter than worm drive styles
• readily available in cordless models

Cons:
• not as much torque as worm drive styles
• most models' blades mounted to the right of the motor, which can obscure the cut line for a right-hand user
• louder than worm drive saws

WORM DRIVE STYLES

Pros:
• generally more powerful than sidewinders
• enough torque from gearing to prevent the blade from stalling on heavy cuts
• quieter than sidewinders
• blades located to left of motor, making it easier for a right-hand user to see the line of cut (some sidewinder models have left-mounted blades, too)

Cons:
• heavier than sidewinders
• more expensive than sidewinders
• more maintenance required due to oil-filled gear cases that need to be drained and refilled

▲CIRCULAR-SAW BLADES Each of these circular-saw blades is optimized for a different type of job. From large to small: 12-in. 60t combo; 10-in. 60t aluminum; 10-in. 80t Melamine; 10-in. 24t thin-kerf rip; 10-in. 80t ultra cutoff; 10-in. 60t sliding compound miter saw; 7¼-in. 16t framing/decking; 6½-in. 30t thin-kerf combo; and 4½-in. "problem material" blade (fine steel teeth).

friction and prevents pitch buildup when sawing wet or pressure-treated construction lumber, and their extrastout carbide teeth slice through the occasional nail without self-destructing.

On a table saw, a dedicated ripping blade has chisellike teeth that shear through the wood's long fibers quickly, while crosscut blades with a high number of teeth yield ultrasmooth cuts across the grain. Special plywood, panel, and laminate blades let you cut those delicate materials with a minimum of chipping and splintering. You can also cut plastic or aluminum on a table saw by using blades especially designed for those materials. There are even circular-saw blades made for specific machines; a sliding compound miter saw-blade, for instance, crosscuts cleanly without the teeth pulling aggressively into the wood, allowing safer cuts with that saw.

An increasing number of blades made for both portable and stationary circular saws (table saws, compound miter saws, etc.) is the thin-kerf variety, with slender teeth that take a narrower bite during the cut. The thinner the kerf, the less sawdust, and the less motor power needed for the saw to make the cut—a win-win situation. As with all toothed sawblades, the fewer teeth there are, the rougher—but more quickly—a blade will cut.

Rotary Saws

Originally designed to cut out holes in drywall for mounting light-switch and outlet boxes, trimming wallboard around window and skylight cutouts, or running pipes for plumbing or electrical wiring, rotary saws (also called rotary cutters) are interesting hybrid tools. Basically a rotary tool (see "Rotary Tools" on p. 182) with a larger, more powerful motor and a special spiral-cutting bit, a rotary saw plunges into materials with a drill-like action. Then, by moving the tool sideways, the spiral bit cuts with a sawing action.

◄ROTARY SAW A rotary saw uses a spinning spiral bit to quickly and cleanly make cutouts in drywall for electrical boxes and fixtures.

▼GAS-POWERED CHAINSAW For felling small trees or chopping logs to firewood length, nothing beats a gas chainsaw's power and portability.

A rotary saw is handy for cutting out either straight or curved patterns in drywall or plaster, wood, plywood, fiberglass, and—with the right cutter—other materials, including masonry and tile. It's particularly handy to use with a circle-cutting guide, good for cutting large holes to mount can lights and other fixtures. Often promoted as an all-purpose tool, you could even make long, straight cuts or rout grooves with a rotary saw, but those jobs are better left to a circular saw and router, respectively.

Chainsaws

When it's time to saw through thick wood in a hurry, nothing beats the speed and voracious efficiency of a chainsaw. While the majority of owners use their chainsaws for cutting firewood, pruning branches, and removing dead trees, a chainsaw can also be a useful tool for cutting beams and large-dimension construction lumber, rough-trimming fence posts, or even carving large sculptures. (Whatever you use it for, make sure you work safely; see "Chainsaw Safety" on p. 96)

GAS CHAINSAWS While electric-powered chainsaws are also available (see p. 96), chainsaws powered by small, gasoline engines are handier for yard work, because they're quite powerful but don't require an extension cord. Gas chainsaws are distinguished by both their motor size and bar length. It's simple: Bigger engines are more powerful, and longer bars can cut through thicker stock. Chainsaws come in a startling range of engine and bar sizes, from tiny pole pruners, which are mounted on long extension handles, to enormous, twin-engine beasts with bars long enough to cut through huge logs in a single pass. Unless

◀ELECTRIC CHAINSAW Like its gas-powered cousin, an electric chainsaw will cut light timber or construction lumber anywhere you can reach with an extension cord.

you have tree felling or another special use in mind, a midsize chainsaw with a 40cc to 50cc engine and a 16-in. or 18-in. bar is a good bet, as it's compact and relatively light but still has the strength and capacity to handle most jobs around the home and yard.

Modern gas chainsaws have features that make them easier and more pleasant to use than models of a decade ago. These features include electronic ignitions, automatic chain oilers, decompression valves (for easier starting), improved air filters, and quieter mufflers. An optional feature that's worth having is a quick chain adjuster. This device lets you retension the chain (it stretches in normal use) by hand without wrenches or other tools, saving you both time and trouble.

ELECTRIC CHAINSAWS

Although they don't get much respect from professional lumbermen, electric chainsaws are lightweight, powerful, and have most of the same features that gas models, but they don't require nearly as much maintenance. If you can live with the inconvenience of using a long extension cord when cutting away from the house or barn (see "The Correct Extension Cord" on p. 91), small and mid-size electric chainsaws can do virtually anything that comparably sized gas models do. Best of all, electric saws are *much* quieter than gas models; your family and neighbors will thank you! If an electric cord cramps your style—and you can limit your chainsawing to small branches and logs under 6 in. in diameter—you can even find cordless models on the market (shown at upper left in the photo on p. 88).

STATIONARY POWER SAWS

What has a voracious appetite for wood and four feet but can't walk? Stationary power saws, of course. Thanks to the power of electric motors, a variety of wood- and metalworking saws are available to modern woodworkers, making everyday cutting

---

CHAINSAW SAFETY

Along with a chainsaw's aggressive cutting power comes great danger: Losing control of a chainsaw is a terrifying—but statistically real—possibility that carries grim consequences. Therefore, familiarize yourself with the saw you choose and maintain it carefully. When cutting, always wear specially designed chainsaw safety gear (see "Specialized Chainsaw Protection" on p. 274) and use good sense. To avoid kickback, always make sure the chain teeth are sharp, start all cuts with the engine running at top speed, and never cut into wood with the top area of the bar's tip, where the teeth travel away from you.

chores easy, safe, and accurate. Table saws, miter and sliding compound miter saws, bandsaws, and scrollsaws all have toothed blades, but each makes a slightly different type of cut, best suited to a different job in the workshop.

Table Saws

If there's room in your workshop for only one stationary tool, a table saw should be your first choice. This single machine is the master of wood-cutting versatility, tackling a great variety of cuts with aplomb, including rips, crosscuts, bevels, miters, compound-angle cuts, and rabbets. By employing special blades and jigs, you

can put this multitalented saw to work cutting grooves and dadoes (see "Dado Blades" on p. 100), shaping moldings and panel edges, and even forming wood joints, such as box joints and tenons.

Despite its wide range of abilities, the single most important job a table saw does is rip wood (cut parts to width along the grain). To accomplish this, all saws have rip fences—a bar that slides on and locks to a pair of rails mounted to the tabletop, guiding the work past the spinning blade. A pair of slots cast into the saw's table allows you to crosscut parts using a miter gauge to align and support the work as it's cut. While a good gauge lets you make accurate

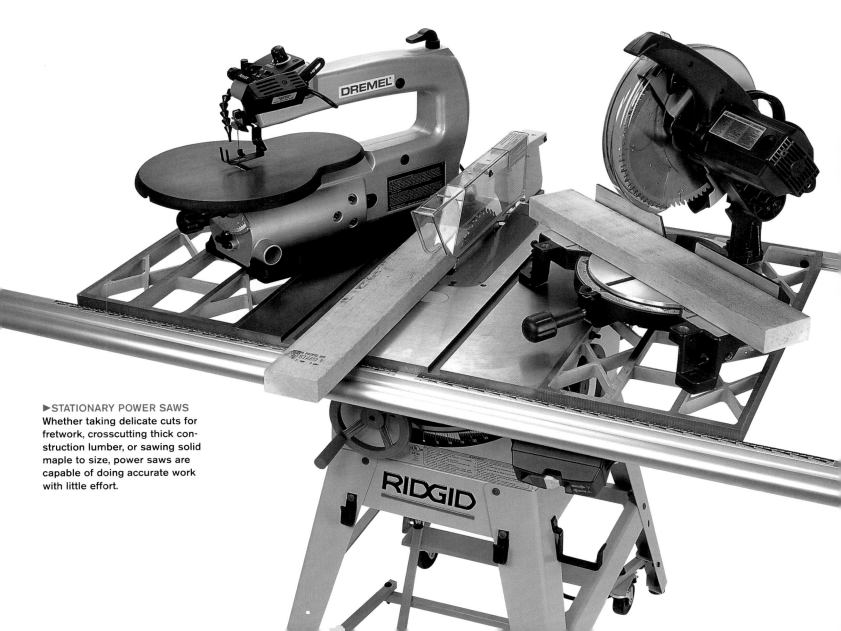

►STATIONARY POWER SAWS
Whether taking delicate cuts for fretwork, crosscutting thick construction lumber, or sawing solid maple to size, power saws are capable of doing accurate work with little effort.

►CONTRACTOR'S TABLE SAW
More powerful than a benchtop saw but more affordable than a cabinet saw, a contractor's table saw is a practical choice for a do-it-yourselfer's home workshop.

cuts (see "Aftermarket Miter Gauges" on the facing page), long and wide work is better crosscut with a miter saw (see "Compound Miter Saws" on p. 102).

Modern table saws all have two handwheels: One raises and lowers the blade; the other tilts the blade (right or left, depending on the model) relative to the tabletop to cut wood at an angle and create beveled edges on frames, panels, and the like. A large compass-scale and cursor indicate the tilt angle, and built-in stops make it easy to set the blade to 90 degrees or 45 degrees, the two most common settings.

A clear guard covers the blade area, preventing accidental contact, and has spring-loaded fingers with serrated points, which scrape against the top of the passing work, acting as one-way devices that block kickback.

Since "one size fits all" is definitely not true of table saws, they come in three basic types. Cabinet saws are the heaviest-duty, most powerful, and most expensive style, designed primarily for serious professionals, and thus they aren't discussed here. The other two types—contractor's saws and benchtop saws—are more practical choices for the majority of home-workshop craftsmen, and each is discussed below.

CONTRACTOR'S TABLE SAW A quality contractor's table saw packs most of the features of an industrial-strength cabinet saw into a machine that's powerful yet more affordable, while being light enough to drag or roll around the shop (important if your shop is in a multiple-use area, such as the garage). Contractor's saws typically take 10-in.-dia. sawblades, capable of cutting wood a little more than 3 in. thick. They have cast-iron tables and rip-fence assemblies large enough to accurately rip sheet goods—plywood, particleboard, etc.—that are 24 in. to 30 in. wide, depending on the model. (Rip fences can have a big impact on how easily and accurately cuts are made; good ones are easy to slide, lock solidly to their rails, and have built-in tape measures and cursor assemblies, ensuring that parts are cut to accurate width quickly and without fuss.)

Better contractor's saws come with strong, 110-volt, 13-amp to 15-amp induction or universal motors. That's enough power to rip wet construction lumber or to saw thick, hardwood parts. The motor and covered drive belt hang off the backside of the saw, which is bolted to a sheet-metal, open-legged stand. The open stand allows sawdust to drop below the saw, although accessory dust-collection shrouds (that connect to a shop vacuum or collection system) are available for some models.

BENCHTOP TABLE SAWS Good things do come in small packages. Modern benchtop table saws are compact and portable enough to cart around easily and tuck away under a benchtop or wide shelf when not in use. Yet they have enough power and versatility to suit the needs of all but the most demanding home-workshop craftsman. Though originally underpowered and with small blades, useful only for their portability, benchtop saws have evolved into full-

Cool Tools   **AFTERMARKET MITER GAUGES**

AFTERMARKET MITER GAUGES take angled cutting to the next level. Practically all table saws come with a small miter gauge that's adequate for crosscutting short wood parts. But if you'd like to cut longer, wider stock safely and accurately, you'd do well to purchase an aftermarket miter gauge. This accessory has a large compass head with accurate, positive locks at commonly used angles: 90 degrees, 60 degrees, 45 degrees, 33 degrees, and 22½ degrees. The head is mounted to a bar with threaded inserts that adjust, allowing for a snug fit in the table saw's slot, while maintaining a smooth sliding action. A large fence bar slides back and forth on the head and adjusts to support workpieces up to a few feet long close to the sawblade as they're cut.

Another handy feature is a scale mounted to the top of the gauge that works with a small flip-down stop. Lock the stop at a setting—say, 12 in.—and you can cut any number of parts to that length without measuring and marking them individually.

featured machines capable of many jobs a contractor's saw can handle. Most models use a standard 10-in. sawblade and have the same depth-of-cut capacity (about 3 in.) as a contractor's saw.

How do benchtops differ from other saws? To keep them light and portable (most weigh between 40 lb. and 65 lb.), cast-iron parts are replaced by light aluminum-alloy castings, and universal motors are used in lieu of induction motors. Different benchtop-saw models also employ various unique and useful fea-

▲BENCHTOP TABLE SAW Lightweight construction and powerful universal motors make modern benchtop table saws easily portable yet capable of some serious work. The optional folding stand keeps the saw at the perfect height for use.

DETENTS: A FUNNY NAME FOR A USEFUL FEATURE

All powered crosscut saws feature small, spring-loaded stops called detents (pronounced DEE-tents) that make setting mitered angles easier. Also called click stops, detents allow you to quickly find and lock the saw at commonly used cutting angles—15 degrees, 22½ degrees, 30 degrees, 45 degrees, and square. Simply rotate the turntable toward the angle you desire (as read on the saw's large compass-scale) until you feel the detent click in place; then turn the locking handle, and you're ready to cut. Many saws also have a vernier scale, which allows you to set odd angles (such as 33.7 degrees, used in cutting crown molding) with great precision.

tures not found on other types of table saws. These include telescoping rip-fence rails (which pull out to allow wide panel cuts, then slide in for transport or storage); a sliding table for easier crosscutting; an extension wing with a built-in router table; a paddle-style on/off motor switch, which is easy to shut off; and onboard storage to keep the rip fence, miter gauge, and other accessories handy.

DADO BLADES A regular table-saw blade takes just a narrow slice (called a kerf), but you can replace the standard blade on most table saws with a special blade designed to cut dadoes (grooves for joinery or decoration). There are four basic kinds of dado blades. An adjustable dado head is a single-piece blade with an eccentric hub that lets you change the width of the groove by rotating the hub. A stacking dado set sandwiches 2-tpi or 4-tpi chipper blades between a pair of outer sawblades. You change the width of a cut by adding or removing the chipper blades. The most expensive choice, a hybrid dado blade, combines an adjustable hub with chipper blades. Finally, short-arbor dado blades are designed specifically for benchtop saws, which have arbors too short for other kinds of dado blades.

Powered Crosscut Saws

Their name says it all. A powered crosscut saw is primarily designed to cut wood parts across the grain, thus trimming parts to length: a chair leg, a fence post, a bookcase shelf, or a 2x4 stud for a new garden shed. Unlike crosscuts on a table saw, where the part must be moved over the spinning blade, a crosscut performed on this specialized saw is achieved by moving the blade in a precise straight path over a stationary part, ensuring effortless accuracy on heavy or long stock.

Crosscut saws come in many different types, including powered miter saws, compound miter saws, and sliding compound miter saws (radial-arm saws, once the crosscutting tool of choice for home craftsmen, are now scarce—probably because they are difficult to set and adjust). Crosscut saws are easily portable and affordable cutting machines capable of both square and angled cuts, although the capacity and particular abilities of each type of saw varies. All crosscut saws have rotary angle–setting turntables and detents (see "Detents" on the facing page), work clamps, self-retracting blade guards, and dust bags or ports. Most also have an electronic blade brake, which stops the blade instantly after the motor is switched off.

POWERED MITER SAWS Often referred to by pro carpenters as chopsaws, miter saws offer a powered crosscutting alternative to using a handsaw and miter box (see "Backsaws" on p. 80). A relatively simple machine, a powered miter saw has a blade that's driven by a universal motor on an arm that pivots down to take the cut. The work butts up against a fence that's mounted to a turntable, which rotates and locks in position for square cuts or angled (miter) cuts to at least 45 degrees left or right. Unlike compound or sliding compound miter saws (discussed on p. 102), miter saws don't tilt, so they can't make beveled or compound-angle cuts.

Pro Tip

Although they may lack the raw power and cutting capacity of corded models, the latest battery-powered cordless compound miter and sliding compound miter saws are lighter and easier to carry and move from room to room—perfect when you have baseboards, trim, or moldings to cut and install.

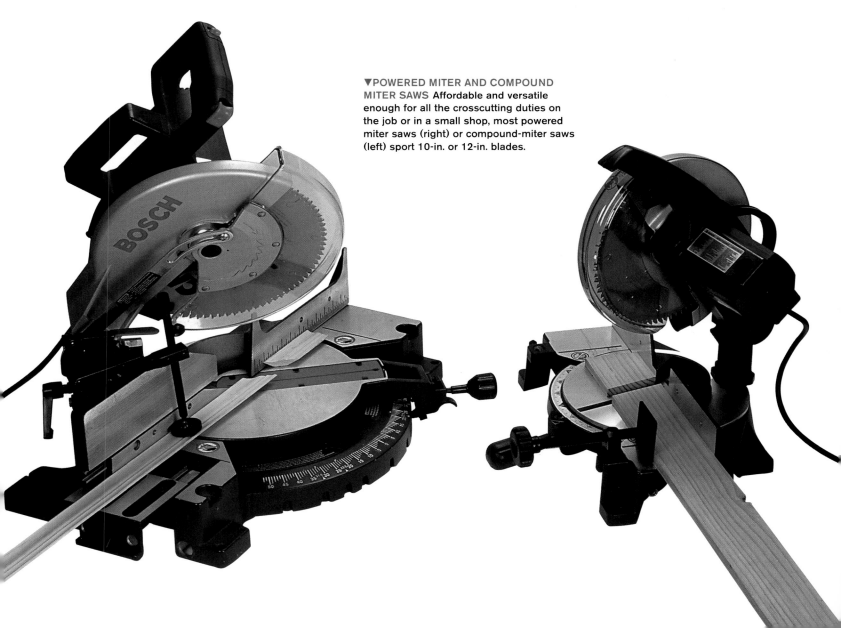

▼**POWERED MITER AND COMPOUND MITER SAWS** Affordable and versatile enough for all the crosscutting duties on the job or in a small shop, most powered miter saws (right) or compound-miter saws (left) sport 10-in. or 12-in. blades.

Tool Helpers

SUPPORTS AND STANDS FOR CROSSCUT SAWS

Because powered cross-cut saws are designed for portability, they don't have bases or fences long enough for safely cutting stock more than a couple of feet long. Optional extensions, available for most saws, slip into holes in either side of the tool's base and support workpieces a few feet long.

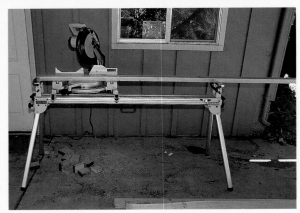

If you need to cut even longer stock, consider buying a miter-saw stand. In addition to supporting long boards and even large, heavy construction lumber, a miter-saw stand has saw-mounting brackets that mount the saw at the proper working height, creating a stable crosscutting workstation. When the job's done, remove the saw and the stand's folding legs and telescoping support arms collapse for easy transport and storage (collapsible stands are also a good idea for portable table saws).

The support arms on most stands also feature length stops. By setting the distance between the stop and the sawblade carefully, you can cut multiple parts to accurate length without measuring and marking each board separately.

Pro Tip

If you're planning to use a powered crosscut saw for cutting wide stock, it's important to note that all saws lose some capacity when their blades are angled or tilted. For example, a saw with a 12-in. crosscut capacity at 90 degrees typically can cut only 8¾-in.-wide stock at a 45-degree miter. Thickness-cutting capacity also diminishes when a compound miter or sliding compound miter saw's head is tilted for bevel or compound-angle cuts.

Although not as versatile as other cross-cut saws, miter saws are less expensive and terrific for making basic square and mitered cuts in construction lumber and trim—the kind of cuts most of us make most of the time. Even the smallest model with a 10-in. blade makes square crosscuts across 4x4 or 2x6 lumber. Move up to a model with a 15-in. blade and you can put a 45-degree miter on a 4x6 or square-cut a 4x8.

COMPOUND MITER SAWS Basic angled miter cuts are all that are needed when making picture frames, trimming moldings for room paneling, or building boxes, book-cases, and the like. But there are times a basic miter isn't enough, such as when cutting framing members for a new dormer or roof or when installing crown moldings around a room. That's where a compound miter saw comes in (see the photo on p. 101). In addition to having a rotating turntable like a miter saw, a compound-miter saw has a tilting arm that angles down for bevel cuts. By both rotating and tilting the blade, you're ready to take com-pound-angle cuts.

Most compound miter saws sport 12-in. blades, large enough to miter or bevel up to 2x8 lumber. They're a good choice if you only occasionally cut compound angles and don't need the wider-stock capacity of a more expensive, sliding compound miter saw. But there is a hitch: Most compound miters tilt only to the left. Hence, life gets a little more complicated when you're cutting both right- and left-hand compound-angle parts. If you plan to take lots of complex compound cuts, look for a dual-compound saw that tilts in both directions.

SLIDING COMPOUND MITER SAWS Talk about a machine that's more than the sum of its parts! A sliding compound miter (SCM) saw has the turntable of a miter saw, the tilting arm of a compound miter saw, and the sliding carriage of a radial-arm saw. The result is a machine that's portable, has improved cutting capacity, and handles practically any kind of cut across wood grain—square, miter, bevel, compound-angle, and even stopped-depth cuts for grooves and dadoes (however, SCM arbors are too short for dado blades; see "Dado Blades" on p. 100).

Operating an SCM saw is simple: For narrow stock, just pivot the saw's head down to take the cut; for wider stock, pivot the head first, then pull the blade carriage (which slides on one or two rails) through the cut. Depending on the brand and model, SCM saws have blades between 8½ in. and 12 in. in diameter. Oddly, although bigger-bladed saws have greater capacity when cutting thick stock, all SCM saws crosscut to about the same maximum width: between 11¾ in. and 12 in. (see the tip at left).

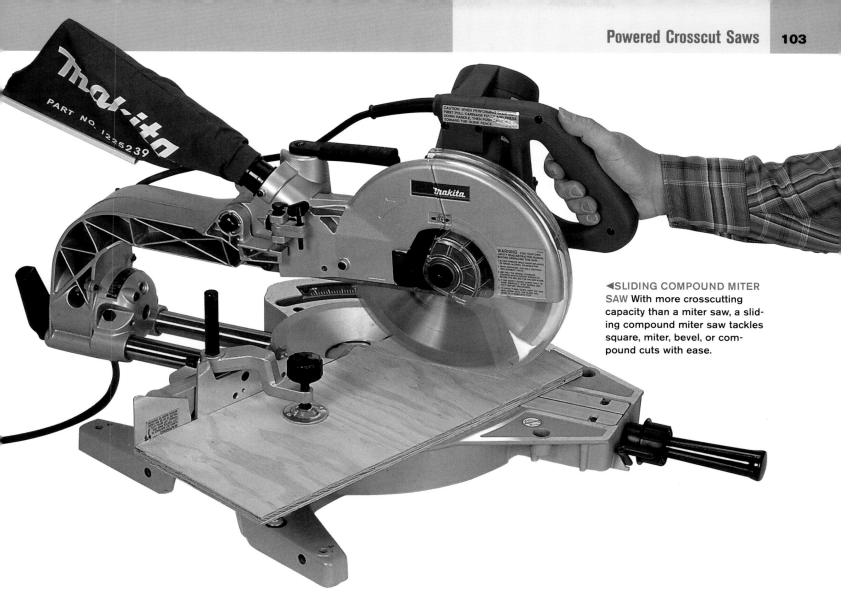

◄SLIDING COMPOUND MITER SAW With more crosscutting capacity than a miter saw, a sliding compound miter saw tackles square, miter, bevel, or compound cuts with ease.

Since SCM saw brands and models vary tremendously in their design and feel, this is one power tool that's good to try out before buying. If you plan to cut lots of crown molding or other complex trim, look for a sliding dual-compound model with a head that tilts both left and right.

METAL-CUTTING CROSSCUT SAWS

Resembling a standard crosscutting miter saw, metal-cutting saws (also known as cutoff saws or machines) are designed to cut metal bars, pipes, channels, angles, and other stock to length. Standard equipment in commercial welding and machine shops, metal cutoff saws are compact, portable, and even affordable enough for a home shop.

Cool Tools | **LASER-EQUIPPED CROSSCUT SAWS**

LASER-EQUIPPED CROSSCUT SAWS are the ultimate accuracy insurance. Lining up the cut line on any crosscut saw can be time-consuming and tedious; get it wrong, and you're liable to cut a part too long or, worse, too short. The latest compound miter saws, like the Sears Craftsman® 12-in. model shown here, include a futuristic feature: a laser beam that shines down on the work marking the exact position of the line of cut. The beam emanates from a doughnut-shape module mounted next to the sawblade. It turns

on automatically when the saw is switched on, producing a bright, dotted red line (it shines through holes in the blade guard) that makes it easy for you to line up with a pencil line marked on the work.

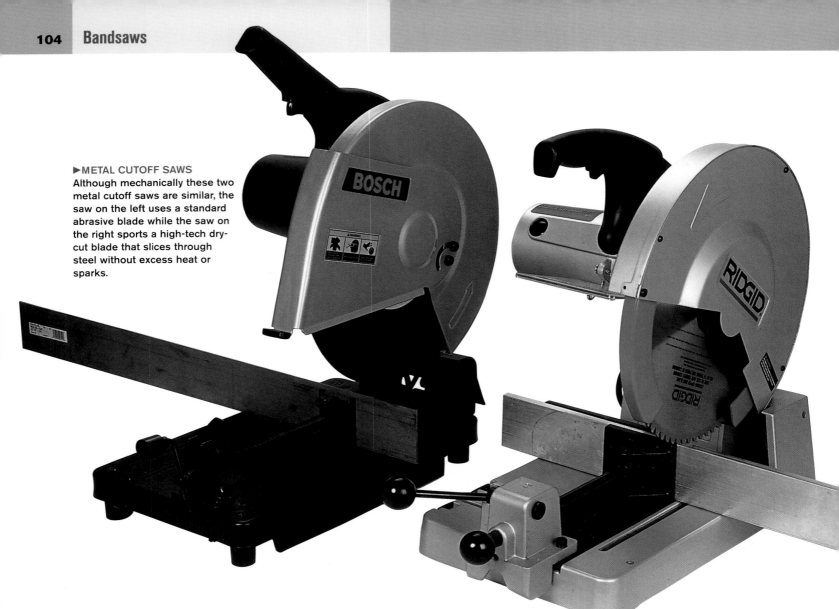

▶METAL CUTOFF SAWS
Although mechanically these two metal cutoff saws are similar, the saw on the left uses a standard abrasive blade while the saw on the right sports a high-tech dry-cut blade that slices through steel without excess heat or sparks.

Pro Tip

Although regular wood-working miter and compound miter saws aren't designed for daily metal-shop duty, you can cut the occasional piece of mild steel pipe or angle iron by fitting your saw with a bonded abrasive blade. Just make sure to cut outdoors or in an area free of debris and sawdust, as the plume of sparks thrown by the saw can easily cause a fire.

The most common type of cutoff machine (shown at left in the photo above) has a 14-in.-dia. abrasive blade that's like a thin grinding wheel, which wears its way through steel and iron (nonferrous metals, such as aluminum and brass, clog up the abrasive). A clamping vise holds the work firmly against a short fence that can be angled for miter cuts.

Similar in features and capacity, more advanced dry-cut metal saws use a 14-in. blade with remarkably durable carbide teeth in lieu of an abrasive blade. Although considerably more expensive than abrasive models, dry-cut saws (shown at right in the photo above) slice through mild steel quickly yet leave a cleaner-cut edge while producing far less heat and noise. Better still, dry-cut blades don't wear down and don't produce a shower of sparks—even during the deepest cuts.

Bandsaws

A bandsaw, which cuts via two wheels that spin a band of metal between them, is a relatively simple but highly versatile shop machine. Although most bandsaw owners use this tool for cutting out curved parts, a bandsaw is also a champ at cutting wood joinery, ripping thick stock to width, and sawing planks thickness-wise (called resawing) into thinner boards or veneers. With its table tilted, a bandsaw can also cut beveled edges—say, for decorative plaques, bases, and signs—and even cone-shaped parts. Overall, a bandsaw is more versatile, quieter, and less space-consuming than a table saw, making it a useful and practical machine for small workshops.

All bandsaws are sized by their wheel diameter, which indicates how wide a part can be cut between the saw's blade and frame. There are two basic types of bandsaws: floor models and benchtop models. Floor models have heavy cast-iron or welded-steel frames, large tables, and powerful induction motors. A saw with 14-in. to 16-in. wheels powered by a ¾-hp or 1-hp motor has enough capacity and power for cutting or resawing thick hardwood planks and parts (using blades up to ¾ in. wide; see the tip at right), making it a great all-around choice for any small woodshop.

Benchtop bandsaws with 8-in. to 12-in. wheels have a smaller cutting capacity and less power than floor models, but they're also portable and a lot less expensive. Made with cast-alloy frames and tables, benchtop models are also compact and light, making them easy to stow under a bench—important for small workshops or shops in shared spaces. All benchtop bandsaws sport universal motors to power blades up to ½ in. wide—adequate for light-duty cutting and hobby use; just don't expect them to resaw thick hardwoods.

Pro Tip

When it comes to cutting on a bandsaw, wider blades (½ in. to ¾ in.) are better for straight cuts and resawing, while thinner blades (⅜ in. and smaller) are better for curved cuts. (Many bandsaw users keep a ¼-in.-wide blade on their saws for general cutting duties.) For most cuts, choose a blade that has at least three teeth constantly in contact with the stock you're cutting (that is, use a 4-tpi blade to cut 1-in.-thick stock).

▲BENCHTOP BANDSAW Small enough to fit under a workbench when not in use, a benchtop bandsaw still has enough power and capacity to make curved or straight cuts in 2-in.-thick hardwood lumber.

◄SCROLLSAW Unlike a band-saw's continuous blade, a scroll-saw's narrow blade is held at each end by a clamp that may be released, allowing you to insert the blade through a hole in the workpiece for an inside cut.

Pro Tip

One of the scrollsaw's neatest tricks is the inside cut—where the center area of a board is cut out. One of the saw's blade clamps (which secure the end of the blades) is loosened, and a blade end is slipped through a hole drilled through the work. Be sure to choose a saw with easy-to-operate, quick-change blade clamps, that don't require wrenches or tools.

Scrollsaws

For curvy cutting, some bandsaws will run a blade as small as ⅟₁₆ in. wide. But when you need to cut out intricate patterns with lots of twisty lines, there's no substitute for a scrollsaw. A scrollsaw's rapid, up-and-down arm motion powers a narrow blade with fine teeth that cut extremely tight curves and leave wood edges amazingly smooth and splinter free. While some models come with floor stands, all scrollsaws are benchtop machines in terms of size and capacity, making them compact and quiet enough for even the smallest home workshop. Although occasionally used by furniture makers and cabinetmakers, scrollsawing is a practice and hobby unto itself, and there are many projects—corner knick-

knack shelves, plate racks, trivets, dollhouse furniture, etc.—that require only a scrollsaw and a few hand tools to build.

Scrollsaws are sized by their throat capacity, which ranges from 14 in. to 30 in. deep. Big throat capacity and an ample-size saw table aren't essential if you primarily plan to cut small parts. Most scrollsaw tables tilt, but if you often tackle beveled cuts, you'll want a large trunnion with stops for commonly used angles (0 degrees, 15 degrees, 30 degrees, and 45 degrees). Variable-speed models are more expensive but add versatility, allowing you to cut delicate materials at slower speeds or do fast or rough work at high speed.

Electric Tile Saws

Cutting tile isn't like sawing through wood or slicing through metal. Tile and other masonry materials are both abrasive and brittle and are best cut with a diamond blade while cooled and lubricated with a steady stream of water. A wet-cutting electric tile saw is designed specifically to do these two things, as well as to eliminate noxious dust created during cutting. Although it's an expensive tool ($300 to $1,000) that you might want to rent rather than buy, you'll want to have one if you plan to tackle a big tile job—cutting granite for kitchen counters, cutting tile for bathroom vanities, or laying an entire marble or slate floor. An electric tile saw will cut and trim all the pieces you need faster, cleaner, and easier than you could by any other means.

Most saws have a motor-driven blade mounted above a tub-style base that serves as a water reservoir. The tile rides on a sliding-track assembly and is pushed through the stationary blade as it's cooled with water squirted by a small submersible pump. A fence guide aligns the tile for perfect square cuts, though it can also be positioned at an angle for mitering tiles or trimming corners. A saw with a 7-in. blade, as shown in the photo below, can cut thick or thin tiles and pavers up to 14 in. wide, as well as cut 10-in. tiles diagonally in half.

▲ELECTRIC TILE SAW Water pumped up from a plastic tub beneath a tile saw provides cooling and lubrication for the blade, to ensure clean cuts and less tile breakage.

CHAPTER 4

Tools That Snip, Slice & Thread

S aws are good for cutting things like wood and thick metals, but on thinner flexible materials—paper, cardboard, wire, etc.—they're overkill. Scissors, shears, snippers, strippers, cutters, and knives are an extensive family of hand-operated tools made to make dozens of cutting tasks swift and painless. From cutting out a cardboard mask and trimming flashing around a chimney to slicing wires to length (or removing their insulation), there is a snipping or slicing tool right for the job. Threading tools also do a kind of slicing, creating spiral threads on bolts, nuts, or pipes that create strong, easy-to-assemble connections between parts.

▲SHEARS, SCISSORS, AND SNIPS Whether you're cutting paper, cardboard, plastic, fabric, leather, or thin sheet metal, there's a pair of shears, scissors, or snips that will do the job cleanly and quickly.

SHEARING TOOLS

There are lots of thin materials around the house that a pair of scissors will cut, everything from paper and cardboard to foam and fabric. But thicker or harder materials—including leather, hardware cloth, and sheet metal, require stouter shears or special snippers: Tin snips, aviation snips, and even power shears can handle all those heavy-duty cuts—straight and curved.

Utility Shears

Shears are basically heavy-duty scissors with blades that are stout and strong enough to slice through tough materials, such as linoleum, leather, and carpeting. Large utility shears often have a compound cutting action like aviation snips (see p. 110). This gives them enough power to easily cut through thin (18 ga. or thinner) aluminum flashing and sheet metal.

Utility shears with serrated cutting edges are the easiest to use for long cuts in heavy stock. The serrations act like little grippers, which prevent the blade from pushing the material away during cutting. Unfortunately, serrated shears are difficult to sharpen and don't produce perfectly clean cut edges; switch to scissors when you need to cut precise parts or create fine paper projects, such as origami.

Tin Snips

Called tinner's snips by some, tin snips are to sheet metal what scissors are to paper: the best hand tool for most cuts. Although you can cut large-radius curves, too, a tin snip's wide, flat blades help guide the tool through long, straight cuts. Large tin snips have enough leverage for cuts in fairly thick semirigid materials, including sheet metal and flexible plastics. They're a great choice for a variety of metal-cutting jobs: trimming aluminum flashing when sealing around a window or chimney, cutting out new mesh or chicken wire for a screen door, lining a flower planter or bak-

◄UTILITY SHEARS The compound cutting action and serrated edges of these utility shears allows them to more easily cut through tough, thick materials, including aluminum flashing.

Cool Tools | **POWER SHEARS**

POWER SHEARS may look like corded jigsaws, but they don't have much of an appetite for wood—they munch metal, and they do it quickly without creating sparks (like an abrasive cutoff saw) or filings (like a hacksaw). One style of power shears, which will cut flat stock up to 14 ga. to 18 ga. (mild steel, depending on the model), plows through a sheet by removing a thin, $7/32$-in.-wide strip that curls up as the cut progresses.

Another style called stroking-blade power shears, cuts with a scissorlike action that slices a flat sheet in two without removing a strip. Lighter-duty stroking-blade shears handle up to 14 ga. or 16 ga. mild steel, while heavy-duty models cut steel up to 8 ga.—that's more than ⅛ in. thick! If you need to cut corrugated steel siding/roofing, look for a power nibbler—a power shear with a small cutting head that can munch across uneven surfaces and cut tight corners.

Pro Tip

Better-quality scissors have a screw pivot pin that you can tighten or loosen to adjust the tension between the halves, allowing you to fine-tune their cutting performance. The screw pivot pin also lets you take the halves of a scissors apart for easier sharpening.

▲TIN SNIPS Although this pair of tin snips has hardened-steel cutting blades, the rest of the tool is cast from aluminum alloy, making it light as well as strong.

ing drawer with sheet copper, or building a metal box for an electronics project. If you need a large pair of tin snips, look for a pair with cast-alloy handles and hardened-steel cutting edges; they're half the weight of forged-steel snips, and thus easier to wield.

Aviation Snips

The blades on a pair of tin snips pivot on a single pin like a pair of scissors. But aviation snips have multiple pivot pins that create a compound cutting action that gives you the leverage to cut thicker mate-

rials with less hand pressure. Unlike tin snips, aviation snips have a spring that pushes the handles apart after each cutting motion (like pruning shears), creating less hand fatigue. Available with either smooth or serrated edges, the strong blades of aviation snips are great for slicing through sheet metal (up to 18 ga. mild steel or 22 ga. stainless steel) as well as steel ductwork, vent pipes, and aluminum or vinyl siding.

There are three basic kinds of aviation snips, each made for a different type of cut. For user convenience, most snips have color-coded handles: yellow for straight cuts, red for left-curving cuts, and green for right-curving cuts. (Snips without colored handles have an "L" or an "R" stamped into the tool itself, specifying which cutting direction is appropriate). Aviation snips' duckbill blades allow you to cut much tighter-radius curves than you can with wide-blade tin snips. Less common bulldog aviation snips have a pair

▼AVIATION SNIP TRIO The color-coded handles on aviation snips indicate their cutting design: yellow for straight cuts, red for left-curving cuts, and green for right-curving cuts.

of serrated blades, made from tough, wear-resistant steel, designed for notching or trimming extra-heavy metal parts and sheet stock.

Offset Snips

Offset snips have the same high-leverage, compound-cutting action and spring-loaded and color-coded handles as left- and right-cutting aviation snips. But offset snips are distinguished by their bent blades, which cut at a sharper angle relative to their handles than curve-cutting aviation snips. This offset puts your hands higher above the work surface, helping prevent nasty cuts from the sharp edges of sheet-metal parts.

CUTTERS AND NIBBLERS

This diverse group of tools includes various handled implements, including diagonal cutters, cable cutters, bolt cutters, and pipe cutters. Each tool is designed to slice though either a specific material or a range of materials such as wire, cable, hose, tubing, bolts, or chain links. Unlike shears, which can take long cuts across wide, thin stock, most cutters use a snipping action to slice through narrower yet thicker work in a single stroke. Other cutters, made specifically for glass and tile, cut by scoring the surface of the material, so it can be snapped cleanly in two. Nibblers, which gnaw through sheet metal, and nippers, which nibble tile, round out this diverse group.

Multipurpose Cutters

When you want to cut the end of a rope, rubber hose, vinyl trim, or piece of flexible plastic tubing, try a pair of multipurpose cutters. Built like pruning shears, these cutters have a single, razor-sharp steel blade that pivots into a flat brass or plastic anvil. This lets you snip through relatively thick materials easily and leave a clean, flat end on the mate-

◄OFFSET AVIATION SNIPS
Unlike straight tin and aviation snips, offset aviation snips (which come in right-cutting and left-cutting models) have bent handles that provide more finger clearance when cutting curved sheet-metal parts.

▼CUTTERS AND NIPPERS
Handled cutting tools belong to a large family, including (left to right): tile nippers, tubing cutters, bolt cutters, cable cutters, and diagonal cutters.

── **Pro Tip** ──

After buying a pair of diagonal cutters (from a store that guarantees your satisfaction), keep the receipt and make a test cut on the largest-diameter wire you will work with (within the tool's capacity range, of course). Then, hold the jaws up to a lamp and look carefully. If you see a point of light where the wire has dented the cutting edges, trade the dikes in for a better pair. This test also works for bolt and cable cutters as well as pliers with built-in wire cutters.

▼MULTIPURPOSE CUTTERS Like a pair of stout pruning shears made for the workshop, multipurpose cutters have a blade-and-anvil design that cuts many materials, including garden hose.

rial. Some pairs feature a replaceable blade, a retractable anvil (so you can use the blade like a utility knife), and even a wire cutter.

Diagonal Cutters

While they're colloquially known as dikes, diagonal cutters are so named because their blades run diagonally to their handles. Depending on their size, a pair of dikes can cut through anything from thin wires to small screws or cables. Many models have a built-in return spring that opens their jaws between cuts, which really cuts down on hand fatigue when you have dozens of cuts to make. Dikes with pivot pins located close to the jaws have greater leverage and create more cutting pressure than tools with the pins close to the handles. The best dikes are forged from chrome-alloy steel with cutting edges hardened by high-frequency or induction-hardening methods. Just remember that all dikes have their limits; switch to cable cutters (see the facing page) for cutting large wires and electrical cables or to bolt cutters (see the facing page) for thick or hard-steel cable and bolts.

Small, 4-in. precision diagonal cutters are just right for cutting thin wires, like in electrical or jewelry work. Larger dikes, with 6-in.- to 8-in.-long handles and stout jaws, are good for heavier-duty work, such as trimming small (#4-40 or #6-32) machine screws, $1/16$-in. music wire, and $1/8$-in. braided cables.

End cutters (also called end nippers) are a variation of regular diagonal cutters. They have cutting edges turned 90 degrees to their handles and are good for trimming wires and small-diameter rods close to a surface or for pulling out bent nails.

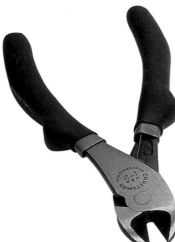

▲DIAGONAL CUTTERS Since wire comes in many sizes, so do diagonal cutters (or dikes): large for thick electrical wires, medium for general use, and small for delicate electronics work.

Cable Cutters

When you need to cut sheathed cables (such as Romex®), multistrand wires, and appliance cords too thick or bulky to cut with regular diagonal cutters or side-cutting pliers, reach for a pair of cable cutters. These sturdy tools have long handles and large, curved jaws that generate lots of power, slicing cleanly through even the thickest cable. With a little finesse, you can also use a cable cutter's concave jaws to cut lightly through and then strip back a cable's outer sheathing in lieu of special cable strippers (see p. 120).

Some cable cutters have handles with protective flairs to keep your hands away from the jaws, as well as serrated cutting edges that help grip the material during cutting. Despite their prodigious capacity and powerful jaws, cable cutters are only designed to cut through electrical cables with soft copper or aluminum wires—cutting through steel wires or cables will damage their cutting edges.

Bolt Cutters

This isn't a tool you're apt to use everyday, but when you need one, it's a lifesaver (remember the time you couldn't find the key to the padlock on the garden shed, and you needed to mow the lawn before the big barbeque?). Also known as rod cutters, most bolt cutters are shaped like giant shears, with short blades and long handles, to create enormous leverage and the power needed to cut through thick, hard, steel rods, bolts, chain links, and hardware. For example, a 36-in. bolt cutter converts 50 lb. of hand pressure into more than 4,000 lb. of cutting pressure at the jaws.

While older style cutters use a blade and anvil–type shear, modern center-cut models have a pair of blades that meet at the edge, with a simple screw mechanism to

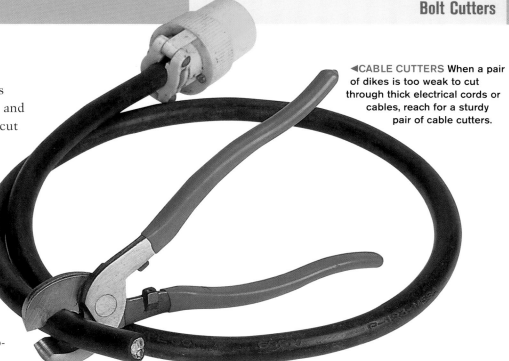

◄CABLE CUTTERS When a pair of dikes is too weak to cut through thick electrical cords or cables, reach for a sturdy pair of cable cutters.

▲BOLT CUTTERS You don't have to be a bicycle thief to benefit from the metal-shearing power of a pair of bolt cutters. This large pair can easily slice through thick steel rods and chain links.

realign them if they need adjusting. Bolt cutters come in several sizes (handle lengths), and each has a maximum cutting capacity. When dealing with mild steel, typical capacities are as follows: 36-in. models cut up to ½ in. to ⅝ in.; 24-in. models cut up to ⅜ in. to ½ in.; 18-in. models cut up to ¼ in. to ⅜ in. Capacities are about ⅛ in. less when cutting hardened-steel parts, which, with less expensive imported tools, may dent the cutter's jaws (precise capacities are usually printed on the tool's handle). The jaws on inexpensive models aren't hardened to the high degree as more expensive ones, the latter of which can cut hardened hasps and chains (up to a hardness of Rockwell®).

Glass Cutters

Most hardware stores cut single-thickness glass to size for a nominal charge. But if you'd rather cut your own custom glass for windows and picture frames or if you're taking up stained-glass work as a hobby, you'll need a glass cutter. An inexpensive cutter (shown at left in the photo below) has a metal handle with a small steel wheel at one end for scoring (scratching) the glass and a ball at the other end for tapping the glass, coaxing it to break cleanly (see the tip at left).

Lubricating the cutting wheel makes scoring easier, thus producing cleaner breaks. Therefore, better glass cutters have a built-in, refillable reservoir that releases a small amount of oil to the cutter wheel when the handle is depressed during cutting. Professional-quality glass cutters have carbide cutting wheels, which outlast by far the steel wheels in inexpensive models. The most advanced models have shapely, easy-to-hold handles that create less hand fatigue (shown at right in the photo below) and feature improved oil-flow control and an ingenious self-vibrating cutter wheel. The vibration creates a deeper scoring crack in the glass, which engenders a square break, leaving smooth and clean-cut edges.

►GLASS CUTTERS Inexpensive glass cutters (left) do an adequate job of scoring glass. More advanced models (right) have a built-in oil reservoir that lubricates during scoring, producing cleaner breaks.

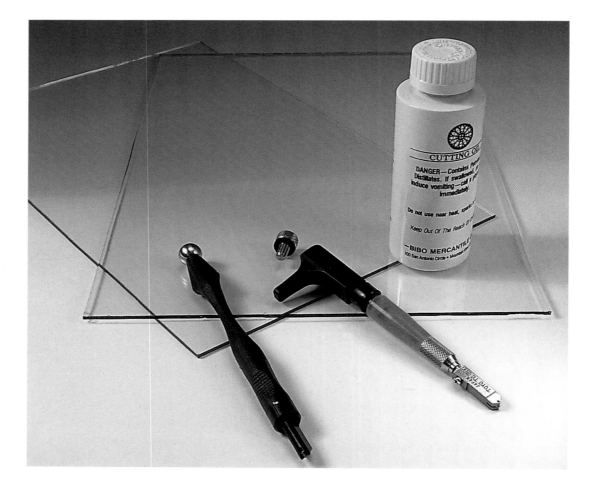

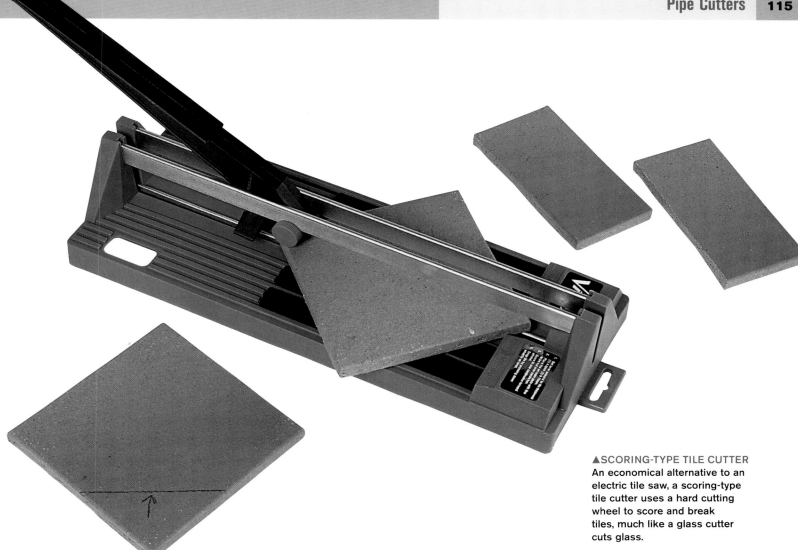

▲SCORING-TYPE TILE CUTTER
An economical alternative to an electric tile saw, a scoring-type tile cutter uses a hard cutting wheel to score and break tiles, much like a glass cutter cuts glass.

Scoring-Type Tile Cutters

Planning to lay a tile floor in your kitchen, bathroom, or family room? A good, economical tool for accurately cutting tiles to size is a scoring-type tile cutter. A fraction of the price of an electric tile saw (see p. 107), a tile cutter is quite useful for trimming tiles to fit around the corners and edges of a room. This simple tool has a scoring wheel (like the one on a glass cutter) attached to a handle that's supported and aligned by a pair of guide bars.

Quarry or mosaic tiles lie on the tool's foam-padded base and bear against a short fence that aligns them. The cutter handle, which adjusts to tiles of different thicknesses, is pulled across the tile to score the surface. Pressing down on the handle snaps the tile in half. A tile cutter is best for simple square cuts, although diagonal cuts are also possible with some care.

Pipe Cutters

You can cut black- or galvanized-steel water or gas pipe with a hacksaw or a metal-cutting chopsaw. But a pipe cutter will produce a cleaner cut than a hacksaw and will be quieter than a power saw (shown at top in the top photo on p. 116). This heavily built tool (not to be confused with a tubing cutter; see p. 116) uses one or more hardened-steel cutting wheels and a pair of guide rollers to pinch the pipe and actually slice through it.

Metal Tubing Cutters

Though not designed to cut thick-wall steel pipe, a tubing cutter is a handy tool for cuts in copper, brass, and aluminum tubing, as well as thin-wall steel conduit (used for electrical wiring). Most tubing cutters (shown at bottom in the photo at left) are affordable tools that are small enough to use at the workbench, and handy for cutting tubes to length in a crawl space or wall cavity. Even the smallest models can cut all the copper tubing used for a household water system (⅛ in. to ⅝ in. dia.). Large tubing cutters have enough capacity to cut tubing with diameters between ⅛ in. and 1⅛ in. Some models have a built-in reamer blade for removing sharp edges left after cutting.

Plastic Pipe Cutters

One of the joys of working with plastic PVC, PE, or ABS pipe is that it's easy to cut with a handsaw or power saw. But if you'd rather slice pipe without creating noise or sawdust, use a plastic pipe cutter. Resembling a strange pair of pruning shears, this special tool has a single cutting blade and a ratcheting handle mechanism that produces enough leverage to easily cut through thick-wall plastic pipe up to 1⅝ in. in diameter. The blade leaves clean, square edges on pipe, ready to glue into fittings. Sometimes called a PVC cutter, this handy tool is convenient to use either for new pipe right off the rack or for trimming pipes already in place in walls or crawl spaces.

Nibbler Metal Cutters

When building a sheet-metal case to house an electronics project or when adapting a metal rack or stand to hold special tools, you occasionally need to cut out square or odd-shaped holes. The cleanest, easiest way to accomplish this is with a nibbler. This tool has a spring-load cutter that bites off a

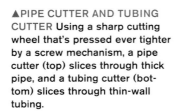

▲**PIPE CUTTER AND TUBING CUTTER** Using a sharp cutting wheel that's pressed ever tighter by a screw mechanism, a pipe cutter (top) slices through thick pipe, and a tubing cutter (bottom) slices through thin-wall tubing.

▼**PLASTIC TUBING CUTTER** With its large, progressive-action shear, a plastic tubing cutter slices through PVC or ABS pipe quickly, leaving a clean, square end.

The tool is rotated around a stationary pipe (clamped in a pipe vise; see p. 55) as the cutter wheel is advanced into the pipe by slow degrees after every turn. The pipe cutter's long handle provides lots of leverage to turn the tool and cut through thick pipe walls, leaving a clean, square end ready for deburring with a pipe reamer (see the bottom right photo on p. 76). To handle nearly all home pipe installations and repairs, look for a pipe cutter sized to handle up to 2-in. pipe.

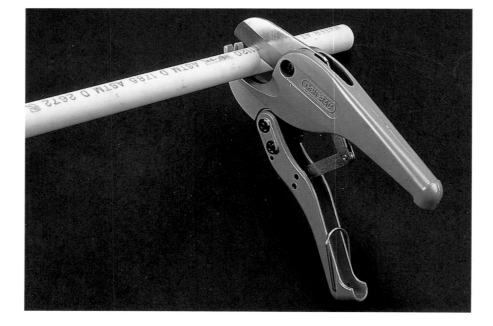

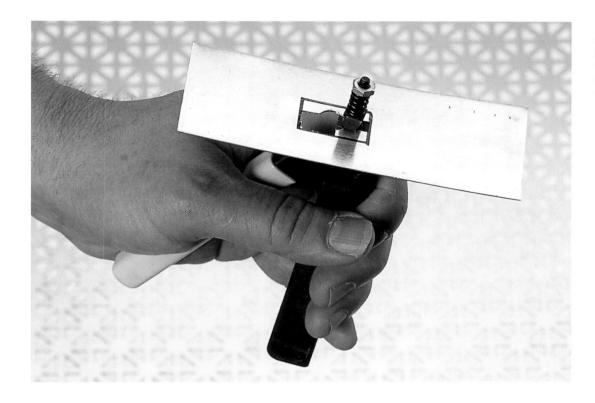

◀NIBBLER TOOL **Making slots or square cutouts in sheet metal is a breeze with a nibbler tool, which has a small spring-loaded cutter to munch through thin metal a small bite at a time.**

▼TILE NIPPERS **A tile nippers' hardened jaws neatly chip away tiles for trimming and for fitting tiles around pipes, wires, and moldings.**

small bit of sheet metal every time you press its plierlike handles together; it can handle up to 18 ga. steel or ¹⁄₁₆-in.-thick aluminum, copper, or plastic. You can start nibbling at the edges of a sheet or insert the cutterhead through a ⁷⁄₁₆-in.-dia. hole drilled somewhere in the middle. You can carve out large openings of any size and shape just by working the cutter in a straight or curved path, one small nibble at a time. You can also use this tool to increase the size of existing holes, slots, and cutouts.

Tile Nippers

A pair of tile nippers provides a quick and easy way to trim off just the corner of a tile or to notch it to fit around a pipe or molding. Resembling a pair of end cutters, a tile nipper has large handles, for leverage, and straight jaws with sharp tips that bite into tile, breaking it off a little bit at a time in a controlled fashion. Better pairs have carbide tips that stand up to even the hardest ceramic tile.

WIRE AND CABLE STRIPPERS

You can strip the plastic or rubber coating from an electrical wire, jacketed cable, or coaxial cable with a pair of dikes, a knife, or even your teeth (I've seen it done, but yeouch!). However, unless you're skillful, you run the risk of nicking a wire and weakening it, which can lead to electrical

▶WIRE STRIPPERS Basic wire strippers (right) will cut, bend, and strip several different sizes of wire. A combination stripping tool (left) not only strips and cuts wire but also crimps connectors, cuts small machine screws, and more.

shorts or connection failures. A good pair of wire or cable strippers removes insulation faster and more easily than less specialized tools, and it does it without harming the wire.

Wire Strippers

Inexpensive adjustable wire strippers have been around for years, but you have to reset them each time you strip a different-size wire—a time-consuming process. More efficient are strippers with separate, semicircular stripping slots for each wire gauge, as shown at right in the photo above. They are much quicker to use than adjustables and tend to do a better job. For added convenience, these strippers also cut wire and have a plierlike nose for pulling and forming wires. As with other plier-handle tools, choose a model with a return spring, which opens the jaws after each cut, reducing hand fatigue.

Slotted wire strippers come in several sizes, each designed for a specific range of wire gauges, specified as AWG (American wire gauge) sizes. The 10–18 AWG strippers are good for wiring most household AC circuits. A 16–26 AWG pair is right for stripping wire commonly used in audio, computer, and electronics projects.

Multipurpose Strippers

If you're looking for a single tool that will strip and cut wire, crimp connectors, and more, choose a pair of multipurpose strippers, as shown at left in the photo above. These plierlike tools have jaws with separate wire-stripping slots, a wire cutter (for cutting copper wire only!), and serrated nose jaws that can bend, shape, or pull wires. In addition, there are crimping dies just above the handles for fastening electrical connectors to wire ends (see "Crimping Pliers" on p. 38). Some multipurpose strippers add even more features, including holes in the sides of the jaws that create looped ends on wires for fastening around screw terminals and threaded cutting holes that trim the length of small machine screws used to attach outlets and switches to electrical boxes.

Automatic Wire Strippers

Although about three times as expensive as basic strippers, automatic wire strippers work with a single-squeeze action that strips up to an inch of insulation without nicking or fraying the wire. To use them, insert the wire into a cutting slot (wire sizes are stamped above or below each slot); the wire butts up against an adjustable wire stop, ensuring a uniform, precise strip length. Press the handles together and the wire is automatically gripped and stripped with the same motion. Release pressure, and the jaws automatically open and release the stripped wire without crushing the stripped end. Just like other wire strippers, each automatic model handles a specific range of wire gauges (10–22 AWG, 16–26 AWG, etc.). They're worth the investment if you've got a big wiring project to do—say, wiring all new outlets in a room addition—and want consistently stripped ends with the least amount of hassle.

Cable Strippers/Cutters

The quickest, cleanest way to strip back the outer jacket from a nonmetallic-sheathed electrical cable (such as the commonly used Romex) is to use a cable stripper/cutter. This tool strips off the plastic jacket with a single cut and pulling action, exposing the wires inside and leaving their insulation intact. If you're wiring new electrical outlets or lighting fixtures, this single tool can save you hours of hassle and frustration.

Pro Tip

Never assume an electrical power cord or wire is safe to strip or cut unless you've verified that it's not connected to live power. Even if you're working with a single live wire, you may accidentally complete a circuit to ground, risking electrocution.

▲AUTOMATIC WIRE STRIPPER All it takes is a single squeeze of the hand to remove a length of insulation from the end of an electrical wire if you're using an automatic wire stripper.

Cool Tools | COAXIAL CABLE STRIPPERS

COAXIAL CABLE STRIPPERS are worth owning if you do a lot of wiring jobs around the house. Of all the different kinds of wire and cable that snake through our homes, coaxial cables (coax), used for cable-television and satellite-dish connections, are probably the hardest to strip correctly. The outer jacket and inner wire must be stripped back to an exact distance in order for the connector that's crimped on the end to work.

Although they can be hard to find, coaxial strippers have multiple cutters that are spaced and aligned to remove just the right amount from both the outer jacket and the inner insulation at one time. You can get a stripper that works on a single size of coax (shown at left in the photo below) or an adjustable model (shown at right in the photo), which works on several common coax sizes (#6, #58, and #59 are the most popular).

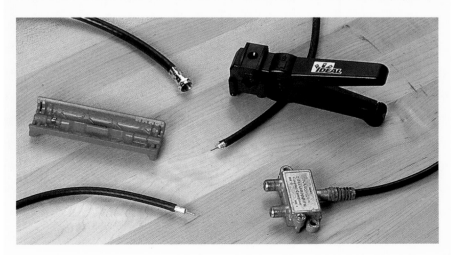

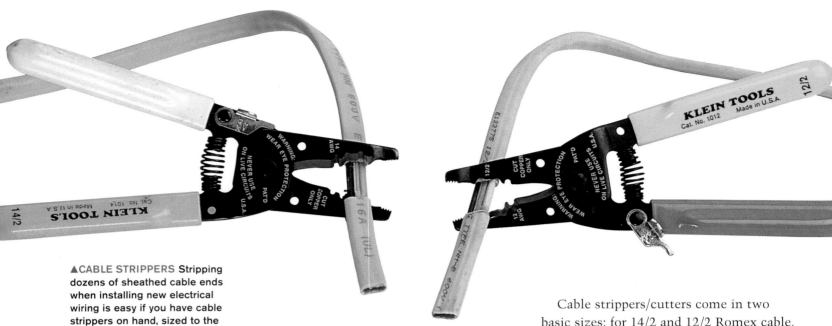

▲CABLE STRIPPERS Stripping dozens of sheathed cable ends when installing new electrical wiring is easy if you have cable strippers on hand, sized to the cable you're using.

Cable strippers/cutters come in two basic sizes: for 14/2 and 12/2 Romex cable, which are the most common in household installations. The tool's curvaceous stripping slot is shaped to accommodate the three wires these cables contain: two insulated wires and one bare wire for ground. Note that they will only strip interior-type cables; exterior cable has a thicker sheath that the tool won't cut through. Some models include a multiple-stage cutter, specifically designed to slice through thick cable progressively, so it's cut cleanly without requiring excessive hand pressure.

MULTIPURPOSE KNIVES

Lots of complex tasks, such as repairing a roof or building a balsa-wood airplane, involve the simple job of slicing thin materials—paper, cardboard, plastic, rubber, fabrics, etc. While old-world craftsmen never left home without the handmade knives they used for everyday cutting and slicing jobs, mass-produced utility and hobby knives are tools of choice for contemporary craftsmen and do-it-yourselfers, and they belong in practically every kind of tool kit. To free their users from constant honing and sharpening, modern knives sport disposable blades, which come in a variety of styles suitable for various appli-

▲UTILITY AND HOBBY KNIVES To take care of everyday cutting and slicing jobs, utility knives, hobby knives, and other multipurpose knives belong in every toolbox, belt, and kit in the home and shop.

cations. In addition to the multipurpose knives discussed here, there are special knives made specifically for carving wood, described on p. 70.

Utility Knives

Among all the multipurpose tools that fit in a toolbox, few are as versatile as the utility knife. In capable hands, a utility knife is handy for everything from slicing open a postal package and cutting roofing felt to size to carving a thick leather sheet into narrow strips. Its standard trapezoid-shaped blades are reversible, disposable, and razor sharp, and they will straight- or curve-cut soft and semisoft materials, deburr and trim plastic tubing or sheet goods, shave or mark wood parts, score drywall for breaking to size, chamfer holes in a variety of materials, and more.

RETRACTABLE BLADES The most popular type of utility knife has a retractable blade, allowing it to be kept in a pocket or apron. A small lever or button slides the blade forward, exposing it a little—say, for slicing into thin packaging without scarring what's inside—or a lot—say, for cutting through thick materials, such as carpet or foam insulation. Some models have rubberized handle inserts that make them comfortable

to grip, especially when the tool is cold. Most models will store several blades inside the handle, where they're readily accessible. Some allow toolless blade changes, so you don't have to find a screwdriver before swapping blades, which is very handy. At least one model features a loop guard built into the handle (shown at bottom right in the photo above) to help prevent scraped knuckles.

FIXED BLADE The simplest kind of utility knife has a fixed blade. Why buy one instead of a retractable-blade model that's easier to carry around (fixed-blade models require a protective sheath or pouch)? There are three reasons. First, fixed-blade knives, such as the one shown at bottom center in the photo above, have a blade that extends about ¼ in. farther than a retractable type, allowing you to cut through thicker materials or cut thin materials while using a board or strip of plywood as a straight edge. Second, the firmly-mounted fixed blade doesn't wiggle around, like a retractable blade can. This makes it easier to use the knife accurately for cutting, scoring, or marking materials. Third, a fixed-blade utility accepts a useful collection of blades, each designed for a different purpose (see the following section).

Pro Tip

Disposable razor knives are so inexpensive that you can afford to keep one in every tool kit or area of the workshop. Made from cheap plastic, this disposable tool's handle holds a strip of snap-off blades. When the blade is spent, simply snap it off sideways (carefully, and wear eye protection) to expose a new, sharp point.

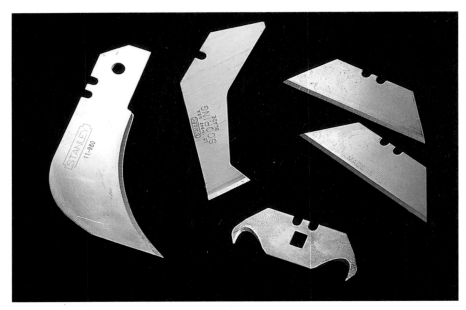

▲**UTILITY-KNIFE BLADE ASSORTMENT** To coax a wider range of jobs from a lowly utility knife, fit it with a different blade. The assortment here includes (clockwise from left): linoleum, plastic scoring, standard (two), and hook blades.

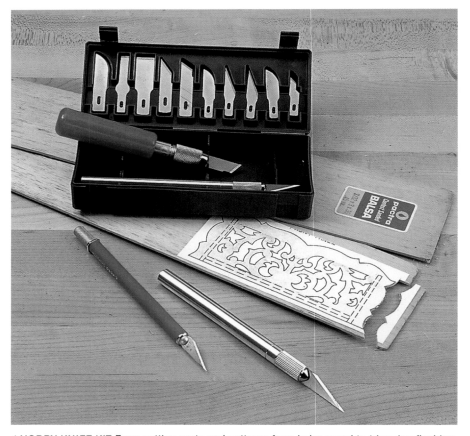

▲**HOBBY KNIFE KIT** From cutting parts and patterns from balsa wood to trimming flashing from plastic model parts, a hobby kit contains an assortment of surgically sharp razor knives and handles to get the job done.

SPECIAL BLADES In addition to a regular all-purpose blade, a fixed-blade utility knife accepts a whole slew of special blades adapting it for specific tasks. Hook blades (shown at bottom in the top photo at left) are good for slicing through cardboard packaging, tape, and twine quickly and cleanly without damaging what's underneath. Hook blades are reversible, rendering multiple sharp edges on every blade.

Plastic scoring blades (shown second from left in the top photo at left) let you score and break Plexiglas®, Lexan®, and other sheet plastics, much as you would cut glass (see "Glass Cutters" on p. 114).

Linoleum blades (shown at left in the top photo at left) have a large, concave cutting edge designed to slice through and trim vinyl and other plastic or rubberlike flooring tiles or sheet stock. This blade's sharp point can start a cut in the middle of a sheet or trim in tight spaces, like a corner or under a cabinet's kick space.

Hobby Knives

Sometimes called X-Acto® knives, referring to a popular brand name, hobby knives use disposable blades made from surgical steel that is honed to a razor-sharp edge, like a surgeon's scalpel. These interchangeable blades come in two basic sizes (large and small) and a staggering array of curved and straight-edge profiles, as shown in the bottom photo at left.

Not as large or stout as a utility knife blade, most hobby blades are sharply pointed, allowing for delicate work: cutting plastic friskets for spray-painted graphic artwork; paper for mobiles or pop-up greeting cards; leather for belts, moccasins, and clothing; and even thin copper sheet for stained-glass work. Other blades are specialized for etching and carving.

Although hobby-knife handles come in several styles and sizes, each accepts only small- or large-size blades. The blades are firmly held in a securely locking two- or four-jaw chuck (lever action–ended knives allow quicker blade changes than screw-chuck types). An economical way to buy hobby knives is in a set, which may contain two or three handles and a dozen or more blades.

AXES, HATCHETS, AND MAULS

Until the industrial revolution changed the way goods are produced, country folk used axes and hatchets to shape a variety of household items, including bowls, spoons, chair parts, and farm implements. They also used these tools to hew logs and create square beams and joinery for their houses and barns. Although few people use them this way now, modern felling axes and hatchets, along with splitting axes and mauls, are still vital tools for many backyard and rural tasks, such as removing and pruning trees, dressing logs, and splitting firewood. Like other contemporary handled tools, axes and their cousins come in both traditional forms—with forged-steel heads and wood handles—and as high-tech tools—with Teflon-coated blades and plastic composite handles.

Felling Axes

With a little skill and stamina (having strong, muscular arms doesn't hurt either), you can use a good, sharp ax to cut down trees, shape logs into furniture or shelter, and split firewood (see "Splitting Axes" on p. 125). All felling-ax blades are hollow-ground to a concave profile that's thinner near the edge and gradually wider toward the body (see the bottom photo on p. 125). This allows the sharpened edge to pene-

▼AXES AND HATCHET From big and brawny to small and handy, axes and hatchets are made for many lumber-cutting jobs. Shown here from top to bottom: double-bit felling ax, splitting ax, single-bit felling ax, Scandinavian forest ax, and camp hatchet.

▼FELLING AXES For heavy-duty log cutting without power tools, use either a single-bit (right) or double-bit (left) felling ax.

Tool Helpers OVERSTRIKE GUARD

When splitting wood, an overstrike—missing the log and hitting the handle near the head—can ruin an ax handle in a hurry, which is time-consuming to replace and refit. You can buy an ax with a composite handle or a built-in protective sleeve near the head, but a rubber overstrike guard is easy to install and will extend the life of any ax, sledgehammer, or any other large striking tool. You heat the guard by immersing it in hot water for a few minutes, and then you slide it onto the handle all the way up against the tool's head.

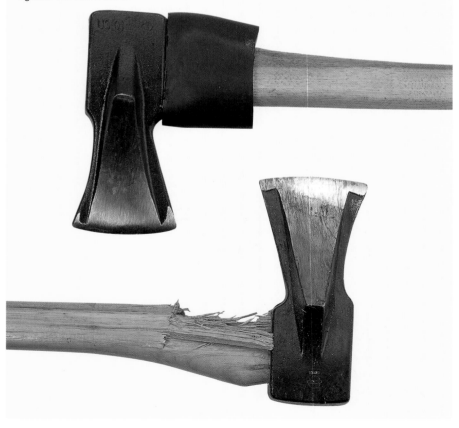

trate wood quickly yet create a cleft as it penetrates deeper, which helps split the wood fibers, making the ax head easier to pull out after each strike.

Felling axes come in both full-size models and in shorter, smaller-head forest-ax models (see the photo on p. 123), which are useful for removing limbs from felled trees and for other light chopping duties. Full-size, long-handle axes come in one of two varieties: single bit (one edge) or double bit (two edges). The beauty of a double-bit ax is that it lets you do twice as much chopping before you need to resharpen its twin blades.

Despite the handicap of having only one edge, single-bit axes are somewhat safer to use, since the cutting edge faces away from you during chopping. Also, single-bit models have a flat rear face, called a poll, which can be used for lightweight striking tasks, such as driving wooden or plastic stakes and tent pegs. *Never* use this poll for striking metal wedges or for other heavy pounding; that's a job for a splitting maul, which is described on p. 127.

CHOOSING A FELLING AX When buying a full-size felling ax, choose one with a handle that's about the same length as the stretch from your armpit to the tip of your fingers. Although it may take a little more effort to swing, it's better to buy an ax with a larger, heavier head than a lighter one that's easier to heft. Ideally, you should build the momentum of each swing, letting the weight of the head (and the sharp edge) do all the work, rather than winding up like a major leaguer pitching a 100-mph fastball and trying to propel the ax through the wood via sheer brute force. If you plan to carry or store the ax in your garage or shop, buy a sheath that fits your ax head to prevent accidental nicks and cuts—on both you and the blade.

Splitting Axes

Unless you prefer the quiet romance of wielding a felling ax to the modern efficiency of tearing through trees with a chainsaw, chances are the only woodchopping you'll ever do is splitting firewood. You can split logs with a regular ax if that's all you have on hand, but the job is easier with a splitting ax. Instead of slicing wood fibers, this specialized ax's head has wide cheeks on both sides of the blade that act like a wedge to split wood fibers apart.

▲SPLITTING AXES Transforming short logs into firewood is a job for a splitting ax. The three styles shown here are (clockwise from bottom): traditional, high-tech, and patent design.

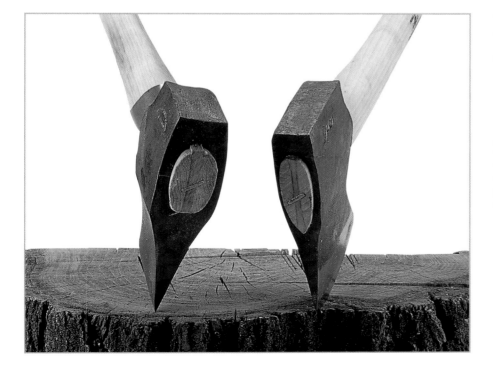

◀SPLITTING-AX AND FELLING-AX HEADS The thin felling-ax head (right) is made for slicing through wood fibers, while the thick splitting-ax head (left) is designed to cleave wood fibers apart.

▶ SPLITTING MAUL AND WEDGES Combine a sledgehammer and a splitting ax, and you have a splitting maul (right), useful for chopping firewood or driving wedges.

▶ HATCHETS Home is where the hearth is, and a small hatchet is good to keep on hand for splitting kindling or chopping small branches to length.

A splitting ax is just right for splitting short (12-in. to 18-in.) green-wood logs to be dried and used as firewood. Splitting axes come in many styles, including traditional wood-handle axes with hand-forged heads, patented models with unusual tapered cheeks, and ultramodern axes with high-tech reinforced-plastic handles and antifriction-coated heads.

Splitting Mauls and Wedges

When log rounds are big, gnarled, and cross-grained or have dried too long (which makes them harder to split), you'll want to tackle them with a splitting maul. Sometimes called a hammer-poll ax, a maul's heavy, 5-lb. to 6-lb. wedge-shaped head has lots of driving power for big jobs. Opposite its single blade is a stout poll for pounding wedges.

Wedges are still the best way to cleave big logs and tough hardwoods. A pair of wedges makes a good splitting team: Drive one in to start a split, then use the other to widen it enough for the first wedge to be removed, and repeat until the log or plank is split. There's another kind of wedge called a Wood Grenade®, which is shaped like a fat cone (shown at left in the top photo on the facing page) and designed specifically for pounding into the end of a short log (with a maul or sledgehammer) to split it apart.

Hatchets

Although some folks incorrectly call it a tomahawk, a scout or camp hatchet looks more like a miniax, with its short (12-in.- to 16-in.-long) handle and light (1-lb. to 1½-lb.) head. Always single-bit, hatchets come fitted with a variety of different handle materials, from traditional wood and steel with a laminated leather handle to fiber-reinforced plastic. Hatchets have a much narrower blade than felling axes, but they're still effective for many smaller chopping jobs around the house, like prun-

▲ THREADING TOOLS Nuts, bolts, studs, and pipes all have one thing in common: They have threaded ends that are cut with taps or dies. These threads allow for quick assembly while creating strong connections.

ing trees, removing overgrown or dead branches in the garden, and splitting small logs for kindling. Outdoorsmen also love hatchets because they are compact and light enough to carry in a sheath or back-pack to campsites or into the wild.

THREADING TOOLS

Threaded screws, nuts, and bolts have amazing holding strength yet make it easy for us to assemble or take apart all kinds of things, from gas barbeques and scooters to children's swing sets. Threading tools allow us to tap holes for screws and bolts, cut threads on rods or pipes, and repair threaded parts. These tools aren't just for professional plumbers and mechanics; having a small set of the right taps and dies can save the day when you're assembling a new project or fixing something around the house.

Taps and Dies

You need at least two separate tools to create a threaded fastening connection: a tap or die to cut threads of a particular size and a handle that holds the tap/die during the threading process. Taps cut internal threads in a hole drilled into metal, plastic, MDF, and even dense hardwoods like maple. You can also use a tap to restore threads in a nut or threaded socket.

Dies cut external threads on metal rods, or extend or repair threads on bolts, studs, and machine screws (also see "Thread Restoring Files" on p. 130). Dies are made from hard tool steel and are quite durable, but taps tend to be brittle, so care is required when handling them—especially the smaller sizes.

Although metric sizes are also available, the more commonly used fractional taps and dies come in sizes that consist of two numbers: The first is either a size number (#8, #10, etc.) or fraction of an inch (¼ in., ⅞₆ in., etc.) that indicates the tap's/die's diameter; the second indicates the number of threads per inch (24, 28, etc.). Common fractional taps and dies range from very small

(#4-40 or #6-32) up to ½-20 in size (see the facing page). Most taps and dies come in both fine- and coarse-threaded versions. For example, ¼-in.-dia. taps/dies come as both ¼-20 (coarse threads) and ¼-28 (fine threads).

Both taps and dies are held in a special handle that provides the leverage necessary for rotating the tap/die during thread cutting. Tap handles have a basic T shape, with a chuck that grasps the square end of the tap. A die handle, called a diestock, surrounds the round- or hexagonal-shaped die and holds it with a setscrew. Better diestocks feature adjustable guide fingers that keep the die properly aligned to the rod or bolt during threading.

Both tap handles and diestocks come in two sizes: small for #4-40 to #12-24 threads and large for ¼-in. to ½-in. threads. There's a ratcheting handle available for small-size taps (shown at center in the photo below) that allows a back-and-forth stroke, like a ratchet wrench, to make tapping small holes easier and quicker (you can also use a cordless drill to drive taps; see the tip at left).

▲ TAP AND DIE HANDLES You can't thread with a tap or die without holding it in a handle. Diestocks (right) come in two sizes, while tap handles come in two styles: standard (left) and ratcheting (center).

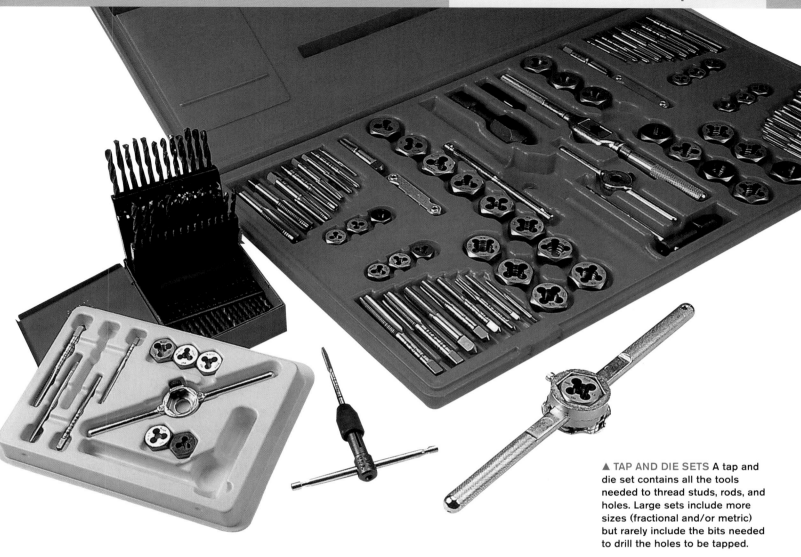

▲ TAP AND DIE SETS A tap and die set contains all the tools needed to thread studs, rods, and holes. Large sets include more sizes (fractional and/or metric) but rarely include the bits needed to drill the holes to be tapped.

BUYING A TAP AND DIE SET A tap and die set contains a collection of taps, dies, and handles, which allow you to create threads of various sizes, in either (or both) fractional and metric sizes. Small sets (shown at left in the photo above) contain just a few taps and dies and handle a narrow range of fasteners—say, machine screws used for building radio-controlled cars or robots. A large set has everything you need to cut both coarse and fine threads, in sizes ranging from very small to very big (some sets also contain metric taps and dies).

A big set is a worthwhile purchase if you're a weekend mechanic restoring a vintage car or building a model steam engine. Most sizes of taps and dies also come individually packaged, so you can buy one to suit just the job at hand or to fit an odd thread size your set doesn't include. For heavy-duty use, look for taps and dies coated with titanium nitride (TiN), which cut easier and last longer than regular taps and dies made from high-speed steel.

THREADING ACCESSORIES Sometimes included in larger tap and die sets, there are a few accessories that make threading jobs easier. A thread-pitch plate or gauge (see front and middle tools at left in the photo on p. 127) allows you to easily check the thread pitch (number of threads per inch) of a screw or bolt, so you can choose a tap or die to match. A tap drill-selector chart

Cool Tools | **THREAD-RESTORING FILES**

THREAD RESTORING FILES allow you to rejuvenate the mashed threads on a bolt, stud, or machine screw as easily as you would file your fingernails—particularly handy if you bung up the threads on a bolt that was special in size or type and crucial to the assembly of a motor, pump, or bicycle. This double-ended tool has eight different files—one on each face of each end—that correspond to common thread pitches (pitch is the spacing of the threads along the length of the screw). Even badly scarred threads can be made serviceable via a few careful strokes with the correct-pitch file.

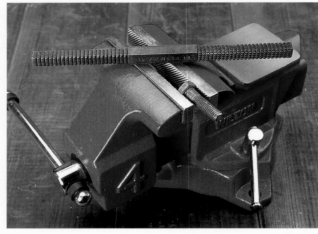

▼ PIPE-THREADING TOOLS Much heavier than standard screw-threading dies, pipe diestocks have adjustable, replaceable teeth and lock into a long ratcheting handle that provides leverage during thread cutting.

helps you quickly determine the right bit size required for drilling a hole for a particular tap size (most taps also have the drill-bit size stamped into their shanks). Special-size drill bits—such as lettered, numbered, or metric bits (often specified for tapping)—come individually and in indexed sets (see "Drill Bit Selection" on pp. 136–137). Cutting fluid (or threading fluid) lubricates and extends the life of taps and dies (see the tip on the facing page).

Pipe-Threading Tools

Also known as plumber's die and diestock, threading equipment allows you to thread the ends of steel (galvanized or black) or brass pipe. This lets you cut and thread straight pipes of any length, as is necessary when installing or repairing water-supply or irrigation piping, a pool's pump and filtration equipment, or a workshop's compressed-air system. Pipe threading requires a diestock for each size of pipe (½ in. and ¾ in. are the most common) and a ratcheting handle, which holds the diestock and provides the leverage you need when cutting threads.

With the pipe held securely in a vise (see "Pipe Vises" on p. 55), the diestock presses over the end of the pipe, which is lubricated (see the tip on facing page). You turn the handle repeatedly through a partial stroke, like a ratchet wrench, to advance the diestock and cut the pipe threads. By reversing the ratchet's direction, the diestock turns in the opposite direction. This is necessary to occasionally clear metal shavings (created as the threads are cut) and to remove the diestock from the pipe. Once the threads are cut, you must clear burrs from the end with a pipe reamer (see the bottom photo on p. 76) before connecting the pipe to the fittings.

◄ TUBE-FLARING TOOL **When special compression fittings are used to join threaded plumbing components, a flaring tool is used to form a flared end on copper tubing.**

Tube-Flaring Tools

Copper tubing, commonly used for residential water-supply piping, isn't threaded like steel pipe. Most tubes and fittings are soldered together (see "Soldering and Brazing" on p. 228) or joined to threaded plumbing components (on filters, faucets fixtures, etc.) with special compression fittings. To seal tightly, these fittings require a flare to be formed on the end of the copper tubing. A flaring tool does this by pressing and stretching the copper into a shape similar to the bell of a trumpet.

The tool has a hinged clamp that accommodates several tube sizes, anything from ⅛ in. to ¾ in. After the end of the tube is cut, deburred, and clamped firmly in the tool, a turnscrew assembly locks in place, and a tapered swage is forced onto the end of the tube, rotated by a handscrew. It just takes a few turns to create a perfect flare (just remember to slip half the compression fitting onto the tubing before you flare the end). Some flaring tools come in a set that includes adapters for forming double flares, necessary for certain special fittings.

CHAPTER 5

Tools That Drill & Drive

I f you look at the incredible number of different drilling and fastener-driving tools found in an average hardware store today—drill presses and corded and cordless portables with variable speeds, torque-adjusting clutches, and hammering functions—it's hard to imagine how you ever got along with an old-fashioned single-speed drill. Portable drills now include com-pact, right-angle, and heavy-duty models, and some perform double duty as both drilling and driving tools. And there's a plethora of powered screwdrivers, screw guns, and impact drivers and wrenches to choose from. Even standard handheld screw-drivers now come with ergonomic handles and tips that fit half a dozen different styles of fasteners.

POWER DRILLS There is no shortage of power tools designed specifically for drilling holes and/or driving screws. Shown here are (clockwise from bottom): cordless, heavy-duty, corded, and right-angle drills.

▲VINTAGE AND MODERN DRILLS Early power drills like this Skil® heavy-duty drill (left) were giant monsters that took two hands to control. While not as powerful, a modern pistol-grip drill (right) is compact and easy to use.

ELECTRIC DRILLS

Tools that are specifically designed to drill holes through materials neatly and controllably have been around since ancient times, but modern electric-powered drills have made the job of drilling faster and easier than ever. Essentially a geared-down electric motor with an adjustable chuck on one end and a handle and trigger on the other, an electric drill not only spins bits that will bore holes in all kinds of materials but also drives a plethora of accessories, including sanding disks and drums, small buffing wheels, wire wheels, grinding points, and even fastener-driver bits.

So versatile and popular is the concept of powering a drill bit with an electric motor that it has spawned a whole class of drilling tools. These range from compact drills for light hobby work to large, heavy-duty drills that bore huge holes through thick material. In addition to general-purpose drills, which are good for everyday shop duties, there are specialized models made for specific duties: right-angle drills, which bore holes in tight places; hammer drills, which power through concrete and masonry; and drills/drivers, which are equally adept at boring holes and driving screws. With the exception of heavy-duty drills, most drill types come as both corded models and battery-powered cordless models.

Pistol-Grip Drills

Although not as handy as their cordless offspring (described on p. 138), corded pistol-grip drills are lighter and more powerful, thanks to the lack of a heavy battery and amperage-rich AC power, respectively.

Originally developed as heavy drilling machines that took two strong hands to wield, modern corded drills are far more compact yet still surprisingly powerful. The modern tool's pistol-grip–shape body lets you hold the tool with your palm at

Pro Tip

It's all too easy to split narrow hardwood moldings unless you drill pilot holes before nailing the moldings in place. But instead of using small (1⁄16-in.) drill bits, which are easy to snap, try this trick. Clip off the head of a nail of the size you're using to attach the moldings. Chuck the nail, clipped side out, in a drill and use it like a bit to make the pilot holes. A few strokes on the clipped end with a mill file should keep it drilling all day long.

PRO CON

WHEN PURCHASING a new drill, one of the features worth considering is whether to buy a tool with a keyed or keyless chuck. Although there's not much choice when buying a heavy-duty drill—virtually all models come with keyed chucks—keyless chucks are found nowadays on both corded and cordless drills.

KEYED CHUCKS
Pros:
• strong and dependable
• easy to tighten and loosen
• if chucks jam, easy to loosen with keys

Cons:
• bit changes can be time-consuming
• keys are easily lost

KEYLESS CHUCKS
Pros:
• bit changes are lightning fast
• force of motors can be used to tighten or loosen chucks
• no keys to lose

Cons:
• if chucks jam or are overly tightened, they can be extremely difficult to get loose
• can get nasty friction burns from chucks' outer sleeves using the drill's power to loosen

the top/rear of the motor housing, in line with the bit, offering better control. To support this grip, the drills have wide triggers that you can activate with one or two fingers—a convenient arrangement when gripping the drill in line. The side handles found on some models provide a two-handed grip, allowing for better control.

Good for all kinds of light and medium drilling jobs, pistol-grip drills are driven by reversible motors packing enough power to bore good-size holes in most materials. They come with either keyed or keyless chucks (see the Pro/Con box at left) large enough to accept bits with up to ⅜-in.- to ½-in.-dia. shanks.

Heavy-Duty Drills

Sometimes hole-drilling needs or fastener-driving tasks are too big for a pistol-grip drill to handle. For boring really large (1-in.- to 3-in.-dia.) holes, as you would through house framing to fit pipes and electrical wiring, you need a D-handle or spade-handle heavy-duty drill. These corded drills have large chucks and special low-speed, high-torque gearing for more power and boring capacity than smaller drills can muster.

However, if you're running pipes or wiring in existing walls, floors, and ceilings, it's unlikely that a D-handle or spade-handle drill will fit between narrowly spaced wall studs or floor joists. The electrician's drill or stud-and-joist drill (see the photo below) is made just for this application. Its powerful motor drives a big chuck at a right angle to the drill's body. The motor's low speed and exceptionally high torque allows you to easily bore large-diameter holes in cramped quarters for running electrical conduits or pipes through walls.

▲HEAVY-DUTY DRILLS Big holes call for powerful drills, like this ½-in. heavy-duty drill (bottom) or right-angle electrician's drill (top).

▲HAMMER DRILL Light masonry drilling jobs, such as installing plastic or metal anchors in brick or stone, is a good job for the pulsating and rotating action of a hammer drill.

Pro Tip

Tired of getting sloppy holes and poor alignment when installing hinges, latches, and other hardware? You'll get great results by chucking a special vix bit in your drill. First, clamp or tape the hardware item in place, then engage the bit's floating alignment sleeve in one of the hardware's chamfered mounting holes, and press down to drill. Drive one screw in place and repeat the drilling process for the other holes.

Hammer Drills

While a heavy-duty drill has the power to bore through many tough materials, boring dense, abrasive masonry materials requires a different kind of drilling strategy. A hammer drill not only rotates its bit but also applies a rapid pounding action that helps the bit break through concrete, brick, and tile much faster than with rotary action alone. Resembling regular drills, hammer drills are compact but powerful enough to bore up to ⅝-in.-dia. holes in concrete.

Rotary Hammers

A hammer drill's big brother, a rotary hammer uses a special gear mechanism that delivers a strong, pulsing impact force to the drill bit. Most models can be switched into a "hammer without rotation" mode that drives a special chisel with a rapid back-and-forth action.

This allows you to use the tool to chip, chisel, and break apart thin concrete, bricks, and other masonry, as long as your job is of a modest size. You'll still need a sledgehammer (see p. 164) or a full-size jackhammer (you can rent them) to break up a thick concrete sidewalk or foundation.

▼ROTARY HAMMER When you need to drill big holes in concrete or do light demolition work on a brick path or patio, a rotary hammer's power and versatility make it the best tool for the job.

Drill Bit Selection

While even a small nail can serve as a drill bit in a pinch, your ability to drill holes cleanly and quickly directly depends on the type of bit you choose. Bits come in a staggering array of sizes, types, and styles, which can easily confuse even a seasoned do-it-yourselfer. A basic set of fractional twist bits (sizes ¹⁄₁₆ in. to ½ in., organized in a drill index storage box) that drill through wood, plastic, and most metals will allow you to get through a wide assortment of household jobs.

But there are occasions when more specialized bits are necessary—when you need to bore through difficult-to-drill materials, such as hard metal or concrete, or when you need really clean holes in splintery or dense hardwoods. You may also occasionally need specially sized bits. To guide you through the choices, the chart shown here lists many of the most popular drill types and styles, describing each one's particular range of sizes and applications.

▲DRILL BIT ASSORTMENT You'll drill the cleanest, truest holes in any material if you choose the right bit: twist bit, bullet-point bit, auger bit, multispur bit, masonry bit, Forstner bit, or hole saw.

DRILL BITS

Bit Type	Range of Available Sizes	Material/Best Application	Notes
Twist bits: fractional and metric	Standard fractional set: 1/16 in. to 1/2 in. (in 1/64-in. increments); metric set: 1mm to 13mm (in 0.5mm increments)	General drilling in most metals, plastics, and wood	Bits coated with titanium nitride (TiN) last longer; cobalt twist bits are stronger and harder. Good for tough jobs (e.g., drilling stainless steel or titanium)
Twist bits: lettered	A to Z (0.234 in. to 0.413 in.)	Precision metalworking; drilling for tapping holes	Most economical to buy as an indexed set
Twist bits: large-numbered wire-gauge	#1 to #60 (0.228 in. to 0.040 in.)	Precision metalworking; drilling for tapping holes	Most economical to buy as an indexed set
Twist bits: small-numbered wire-gauge	#61 to #80 (0.039 in. to 0.0135 in.)	Precision metalworking and model making; drilling for tapping holes	Most economical to buy as an indexed set
Twist bits: bullet-point	Standard index set: 1/16 in. to 1/2 in. (in 1/64-in. increments)	Drilling wood, most metals, and plastics	More aggressive than regular twist bits
Brad-point bits	1/8 in. to 1/2 in.; 3mm to 18 mm	Making clean holes in softwoods and hardwoods	Most precise way to bore hardwoods with minimal tearout
Spade (flat-boring) bits	1/4 in. to 1 1/2 in.	Making quick holes in softwoods	Inexpensive way to drill large holes that need not be precise
Tapered bits	1/8 in. (for #5 screws) to 5/32 in. (for #12 screws)	Drilling tapered pilot holes for standard wood screws	Kits come with countersinks and stop collars
Forstner and multispur bits	3/16 in. to 4 5/8 in.; 10mm to 40mm	Making clean-bottom holes and pockets in hardwoods and softwoods	Available in both high-speed steel and carbide-tipped
Hole saw	Set: 7/8 in. to 2 1/2 in.; individual bits up to 6 in.	Drilling large holes for pipes or electrical wiring	Larger sizes require a different arbor
Power-auger (ship's and electrician's) bits	5/8 in. to 1 1/2 in.	Making fast, rough holes through construction lumber for pipes and electrical wires	Category includes ship's auger, cable, and electrician's bits
Masonry bits	1/8 in. to 2 in.	Drilling concrete, brick, tile, and other dense masonry materials	Most bits for rotary hammers have special SDS shanks
Stepped (multihole) drills	Each drill has a range of hole sizes (e.g., 1/8 in. to 1/2 in., or 1/4 in. to 3/4 in., etc.)	Drilling a number of different-size holes in sheet metals up to 1/8 in. thick	Safe, economical way to handle sheetmetal drilling tasks

ACORDLESS DRILLS The size and voltage of a cordless drill's battery pack offers a good indication of how long and strong it will run.

PRO CON

IF YOU'VE DECIDED to purchase a cordless drill or other power tool, a basic decision you've got to make is what voltage to buy. Big 18-volt, 19.2-volt, and 24-volt models are powerful and impressive, but 9.6-volt, 12-volt, 14.4-volt, and 15.6-volt models have similar features and are more affordable. Whatever size you choose, it's usually most economical to buy the tool as a kit, which generally comes with two batteries and a charger.

HIGH-VOLTAGE (18-VOLT TO 24-VOLT) CORDLESS TOOLS
Pros:
• deliver lots of torque
• longer running time
• best for heavy-duty work

Cons:
• tools and extra batteries are more expensive
• heavier and bulkier than low-voltage models

LOWER-VOLTAGE (9.6-VOLT TO 15.6-VOLT) CORDLESS TOOLS
Pros:
• tools and extra batteries are more affordable
• lighter and less fatiguing to use
• best for light-duty daily jobs

Cons:
• less power and torque than high-voltage models
• shorter running times

Cordless Drills/Drivers

If you're new to the tool game, you probably think a drill is a drill is a drill. But look carefully, and you'll notice that cordless drills are different. Not only are these battery-powered tools extremely handy—no power cords to tangle or extension cords needed—but they've also got useful features that most corded drills can only dream about.

First and foremost among these features is an adjustable clutch—an indexed ring just behind the chuck (on most drills) with which you set how much torque gets to the bit before the motor automatically shuts off. This feature allows a cordless drill to function as a fastener/driver as well as a drilling tool. By dialing the clutch to a low setting, you can drive small screws without snapping them off or stripping them out and tighten them all to the same, exact degree. Pick a high-clutch setting for driving big screws or lock it out for drilling jobs.

ACORDLESS-DRILL ADJUSTABLE CLUTCH One of the best features found on cordless drills is an adjustable clutch, which lets you set how much force the drill will exert on the bit.

Other conveniences that make cordless drills/drivers such remarkably useful tools are: trigger-operated variable-speed control, which let's you start screws or bits slowly; reversibility, for removing screws or backing out drill bits that have gotten stuck; two-speed gearboxes, which allow slower speeds and high torque (for driving big bits) or high speeds (for driving screws quickly); and keyless chucks, for faster bit changes (see the Pro/Con box on p. 134).

Cordless drills come in different battery voltages, from light-duty, 7.2-volt bargain models to heavy-duty, 24-volt professional models. The latest cordless drills sport some innovative elements, such as three-speed gearboxes, quick removable chucks that work with right-angle drilling accessories, and even built-in electronic level indicators that help you drill holes that are precisely square or plumb to walls and floors.

▼RIGHT-ANGLE AND CLOSE-QUARTERS DRILLS To drill in tight quarters, use a right-angle cordless drill (top) or a close-quarters corded drill (bottom).

Tool Helpers DRILL HOLSTERS

Getting the best use from your cordless drill means keeping it handy (and not letting it get buried in benchtop clutter). Just like a gunfighter's six-shooter, putting a cordless drill in a holster puts it at your fingertips, ready to draw at a moment's notice. While some holsters fit around your chest, like an FBI agent's shoulder holster, the majority clip or slip onto a regular belt or tool belt. A snapped strap prevents the drill from falling out, while small pockets found on some holsters provide storage for drill and driver bits.

Angled Drills

There are lots of times you need to drill a hole or drive a screw in a hard-to-reach spot, like deep inside a cabinet. Angled drills, of both the corded and cordless variety, are lifesavers in these situations.

A right-angle cordless drill (shown at top in the photo below) has its chuck mounted perpendicular to its long, slender body. Like a compact version of an electrician's drill, a right-angle cordless will reach into the deepest of recesses, drilling/driving in constricted spaces as narrow as 4 in.

Close-quarters drills (shown at bottom in the photo at left) are lightweight corded tools with angled chucks, paddle on/off switches, and easy-to-grip bodies. While they won't fit into spaces as narrow as those served by a right-angle drill, close-quarters drills are somewhat easier to control since you grip the tool so close to the chuck (they're great for installing drawer glides inside assembled cabinets).

Pro Tip

Because of its trigger-controlled variable speed and reversible motor, a cordless drill makes an excellent driver for tapping threaded holes in lieu of a tap wrench. Simply chuck the round part of the tap's shank in the drill, apply a little tapping lubricant, and carefully drive the tap into the hole you're threading. Go slowly, occasionally reversing the drill to back the tap out and to clear shavings.

Advanced Battery-Charging Technology

A cordless tool is absolutely useless without a charged battery to power it. Regardless of voltage, modern cordless tools have improved features and performance due to advances in both battery and charger technology.

Battery Packs

Many tools now use high-capacity nickel cadmium (NiCd or nicad) battery packs, which carry more power for their size than batteries produced just a few years ago, thus enabling tools to run for a longer time between charges.

The NiMH (nickel metal hydride) battery packs found on some tools have an even greater energy density than nicad cells, so they hold 25 percent to 50 percent more power. NiMH batteries are also more environmentally friendly than nicads, which are considered hazardous waste and must be properly recycled after they expire.

Battery Chargers

The battery chargers used by many cordless tools now have microprocessor-controlled circuitry that not only reduces charging time to as little as 15 minutes but also monitors the condition of the battery, preventing damage and extending battery life. Advanced chargers have tune-up modes or use battery packs equipped with microchips to optimize their charges for peak performance. When buying a cordless drill or other tool, it's wise to choose the tool with the most advanced battery charger, which you can identify by looking at the plug-in part of the battery pack; computerized chargers use batteries with at least three or four electrical contacts.

▲**COMPUTERIZED BATTERY CHARGER** Getting top performance and long life from a cordless-tool battery pack is much easier when you recharge it with a computerized charger. The impact driver (right) uses a sophisticated NiMH battery pack that contains a microchip.

▲ANGLED DRILLING ACCESSORY A compact angled drilling accessory fits into any drill and accepts quick-change bits, allowing you to drill holes or drive bits in cramped spaces.

Either kind of angled drill is a good choice for furniture-making projects and for those who need to refurbish or repair built-in cabinets. If you don't have the extra cash to buy one of these special drills, an angled drilling accessory (see the photo above) chucks into any drill to allow angled drilling or driving in a pinch.

Drill Presses

For demanding tasks—boring large holes in metal or hardwood, drilling angled holes accurately, locating holes in exact positions on a part—is the specialty of a drill press. This stationary power tool drives a large chuck with a powerful motor via an ingenious quill mechanism (a hand lever presses the spinning chuck down into the work, then retracts it) atop a steel column that also supports an adjustable worktable. This arrangement keeps the chuck and bit aligned square to the work's surface or,

with the table tilted, at an exact angle. The workpiece clamps to an adjustable table, which moves up and down on the column to accommodate workpieces of different thicknesses.

An adjustable depth gauge and stop mechanism let you set the downward travel of the quill so you can bore holes to a precise depth. To adjust the rotational speed of the chuck to the operation, drill presses have either adjustable variable speed or stepped-pulley transmissions, the latter of which allow you to change the position of the V-belt(s) to change speeds.

There are two types of drill presses: tall, floor-standing models and shorter benchtop models. Both kinds are sized by their swing (twice the distance between the column and the centerline of a bit), which indicates the widest workpiece you can drill a hole in the center of.

Pro Tip

To get the best performance and longest life from your expensive cordless-tool batteries, buy at least two—or better yet (for heavy-duty users) three—batteries: one to use, one to sit and cool immediately after use (before recharging), and one to recharge while the others are cooling or in use. You can save big bucks by buying aftermarket battery packs from an online retailer. Try this website: www.batterybarn.com.

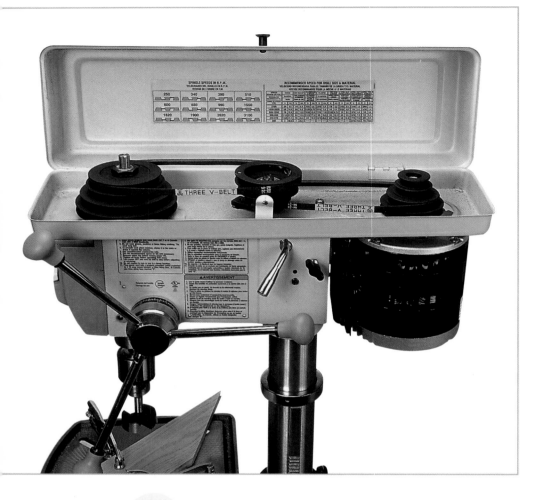

Pro Tip

Boring clean, straight holes requires the right speed and feed rate (how fast the bit is fed into the work). Large-diameter bits need to run and be fed slowly, or they'll overheat and get ruined or burn the material. Conversely, thin bits should be run and fed faster—too slow and they won't cut cleanly and may wander, resulting in a crooked or uneven hole.

FLOOR-STANDING DRILL PRESSES Floor-standing presses range from affordably priced home-workshop models with a 12-in. swing to serious cabinet-shop models with 15-in. to 17-in. swings. Floor-standing drill presses also have a long quill travel, typically between 3¼ in. and 4½ in., so you can use them for boring deep holes.

Incidentally, you can use a drill press for more than just drilling holes. With the right jig, bits, and equipment, you can use them for hollow-chisel mortising (drilling square holes—a neat trick), inverted pin routing, biscuit joinery, shaping (with a rotary rasp), drum or flap sanding, rosette cutting, and light milling and stock surfacing.

◀▶DRILL PRESS For drilling holes with power and precision, nothing beats a floor-standing drill press. Changing the speed on most drill presses involves moving belts on pulleys. A speed chart on the top cover (see photo top left) shows the speeds that various belt-position combinations yield.

▲BENCHTOP DRILL PRESS Offering all the features of a full-size floor model in a more compact tool, a benchtop drill press is perfect for small shops.

BENCHTOP DRILL PRESSES If a drill press has a column that's too short to use without being mounted on a stand or table, it's a benchtop model. However, not all benchtop drilling machines are the same: Some have the same head (motor, quill and chuck, and table) as their floor-standing cousins and are simply mounted to a

shorter column. Other small drill presses have compact heads with shorter quill travel, less powerful motors, and a smaller swing (usually between 8 in. and 12 in.). Although intended mainly for light-duty work, these scaled-down presses are affordable and capable of satisfying the needs of many small shops.

BRACES AND HAND DRILLS

If you're a purist—or you just never got around to running power to your barn workshop—you'll favor a brace or hand drill for boring holes. A tool that's been around since at least Roman times, a bit brace is gracefully simple, with just a big chuck at one end, a flat handle at the other, and a U-shaped crank in between. They're great tools for driving large-diameter auger-type bits or even slotted screw-driving bits. Their alligator-type two-jaw chucks are designed to hold tapered square-end bits. All modern braces have ratcheting drives, allowing you to reverse the drive direction for backing out big bits if they get stuck.

Eggbeater-style hand drills are meant for finer work with smaller bits. Their three-jaw chucks typically hold bits with up to ¼-in.-dia. shanks, and their gear drives generate enough power for holes up to that diameter in wood, plastic, drywall, and even soft metals. Just crank the drive handle in reverse to back a bit out. Buying an

▼BRACE AND BITS A brace provides a traditional but effective way to bore holes in wood.

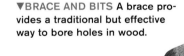

◄**EGGBEATER-STYLE DRILL**
Resembling a hand-turned eggbeater, the vintage-geared drill (right) provides the basic design for the modern version (left), which has enclosed gears that won't foul from debris or accidentally pinch your skin.

►**CORDLESS SCREWDRIVERS**
Cordless screwdrivers aren't all powered the same way. Different models use replaceable cells, rechargeable internal batteries, or rechargeable battery packs.

►**YANKEE-STYLE PUSH DRILL**
A set of spiraling grooves on a push drill's shank rotates the bit every time you push down on the handle.

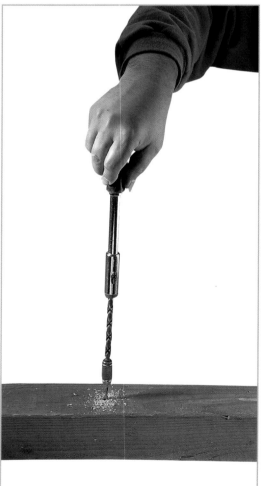

Pro Tip

To get the best long-term performance from a cordless screwdriver with unremovable (nicad) batteries, don't recharge it (or return the tool to its charging base) after every single use. Instead, fully charge the screwdriver (or drill/driver) and use it until the batteries start to run down noticeably—not totally dead—then recharge it fully. This is also a good practice for other small cordless tools.

eggbeater drill with enclosed gears (shown at right in the top left photo above) prevents you from accidentally catching your clothing (or skin—ouch!) in the gear train.

Push Drills

In a toolbox, a push drill (or Yankee drill) looks a lot like a long, fat screwdriver. But this old-timer's favorite is actually a hand-powered drill/driver that's good for boring small holes (up to ¼ in. dia. or so) and driving smallish screws. The tool has an ingenious crosshatched shank with spiraling grooves that rotates the tool's interchangeable bits every time you push down on the handle. Like a ratcheting screwdriver (see p. 150), the push drill has a small lever that reverses rotation for backing out screws or drill bits. The drill's unique collet accepts only special drill and screwdriver bits, which, on some models, store in a compartment in the tool's handle.

POWERED SCREWDRIVERS AND SCREW GUNS

Mass-produced steel and brass screws provide an incredibly strong, economical way of joining all kinds of things together, from construction projects and furniture to cameras and computer cases. While every tool kit should have a good set of screwdrivers (see "Screwdrivers" on p. 148), a powered screwdriver makes everyday tasks that require installing or removing screws quicker and easier. When extra power or efficiency is needed for difficult jobs or projects that use a ton of screws—say, when building a deck—screw guns and impact drivers offer unparalleled speed and consistent driving performance.

Cordless Screwdrivers

Even if you're all thumbs, it's hard to get through daily life without driving a few screws now and then: to assemble a swing set for your child, to attach a mirror to the closet door for your spouse, or to install license plates on your new car. A cordless screwdriver is only slightly fatter and heavier than a manual screwdriver, but it makes these jobs go so much faster and more smoothly. Although less powerful than a drill/driver (see p. 138), a cordless screwdriver is easier to use and to tote around the house or workshop.

Most models have a single toggle switch. Push one side to tighten screws and the other side to loosen them. While not

▲ SCREW GUN A dedicated tool for driving screws when mounting drywall or building decks, a screw gun's adjustable nosepiece assures that all screws are driven to the same depth.

Cool Tools   AUTOMATIC SCREW GUNS

AUTOMATIC SCREW GUNS are the fastest possible way of driving a bushel of screws. This specialized tool has an automatic-feed mechanism that, when pressed against the stock, feeds screws to the bit, so they're always ready for driving. There's no quicker way to build with screws—every time you press down, you drive a screw. Some models offer an optional extension arm, so you can drive screws while standing, saving yourself from knee and back strain.

If a specialized screw gun doesn't fit your budget, you can buy the special attachment shown here, which transforms a regular drill into an automatic-feed screw gun.

Unfortunately, both the accessory and the dedicated guns use special screw strips, which are more expensive than regular screws.

every model has an adjustable clutch or removable battery pack, all cordless screwdrivers hold standard ¼-in. hex bits in a quick-change collet, so you can change from driving Phillips-head screws to slotted-head or square-drive in a flash. Some models also have a body style that hinges in the middle, making the tool easier to control, especially when driving hard-to-turn screws.

Screw Guns

If you need to tackle a job that requires driving hundreds of screws—like fastening redwood boards on the joists of a backyard deck, plywood sheathing to the side of a house or barn, or drywall to the walls and ceiling of a room—you'll appreciate the speed and convenience a screw gun offers. Although it resembles a typical drill/driver, a screw gun is specialized for driving screws only.

◀**IMPACT DRIVER AND IMPACT WRENCH** The heavier the driving job, the more you'll need a powerful driving tool. The light, cordless impact driver (left) is best for driving screw-style fasteners, while an air-powered (bottom) or cordless (top) impact wrench has the brawn to handle big nuts and bolts.

Also known as a drywall screwdriver, a screw gun has a dedicated driving head and bit (instead of an adjustable chuck) that's regulated by a clutch and depth-control mechanism. When a screw is driven, the clutch automatically disengages the bit so it doesn't strip out the screwhead. By adjusting the depth mechanism, you can control the depth to which the head of the screw is driven into the work. This is especially important when installing drywall because screws can't stick out or be driven too deep (they tear the material's paper covering).

Impact Drivers and Wrenches

If a standard drill/driver or screw gun is too slow or weak to handle your tough fastening needs—say, running long, fat screws into dense woods or hard building materials—consider buying a cordless impact driver (shown at left in the photo above). An impact driver not only spins its

bit (Phillips, slotted, etc.) but also produces strong torque pulses when resistance is encountered. Some models have an adjustable torque setting, so you can limit driving force and avoid snapping or stripping small screws.

Need even more power for driving lag bolts and for tightening nuts and bolts for construction or mechanical repairs? An impact wrench (shown at top in the photo above) looks and works like an impact driver, but it's built with a more powerful motor and gearbox. Available in corded and cordless models, these beefy tools deliver up to 250-ft. lb. of torque—enough power to remove lug nuts from rusty car wheels. Like pneumatic impact wrenches, cordless models have a square ½-in. drive shank that accepts standard impact sockets and accessories.

►ASSORTMENT OF SCREW-
DRIVERS Screwdrivers not only
come with tips to fit common
slotted and Phillips fasteners,
but square-drive and Torx screws
as well.

▼SCREWDRIVER SET A com-
plete set of screwdrivers should
include slotted and Phillips drivers of at least two sizes, as well
as in the shorter stubby size.

SCREWDRIVERS

Even if you own a top-quality electric
screwdriver or drill/driver, nothing replaces
a set of screwdrivers. Handheld screwdrivers let you carefully tighten and loosen
torque screws in sensitive materials—
plywood, particleboard, fiberboard, etc.—
so you can drive them without stripping
their heads.

In addition to having different-size and
shape tips, screwdrivers come in a variety
of styles: Basic styles include machinist's,
electrician's, cabinet (or London), and stub-

by. (Other styles—including precision,
offset, and ratcheting—are discussed on
pp. 150–152.) A machinist's screwdriver
has a square shank, or a round shank with
a square or hex-shape section near the handle. This allows you to use a wrench on the
shank for greater driving torque.

An electrician's screwdriver has a long
shank with no flair near the tip, allowing
you to drive deeply recessed screws, which
are often found in electrical switches, outlets, and fixtures. For user protection, some
electrician's screwdrivers have special
plastic-covered shanks which meet VDE
standards for protection up to 1,000 VAC.

A cabinet screwdriver has a flat or round
shank with a flared head at the tip. This
tool is good for general duties, such as driving wood screws when assembling cabinets
or installing hardware.

Stubby screwdrivers are shorter than
regular-size screwdrivers and good for driving screws in confined spaces where a full-
size screwdriver is just too long to fit.

The biggest difference between older
screwdrivers with wood or hard-plastic
handles and contemporary models is
ergonomic handles. Modern handles have

Screw Removers and Extractors

The downside to using powerful tools for driving is that if you don't work carefully, you can easily break a screw or strip its head. If you're lucky enough to have a screw snap off above the work's surface, a pair of locking pliers will usually remove it. Otherwise, you need a screw remover or extractor.

Screw Removers

Designed to work in a variable-speed drill, a screw remover (third from right in the photo) has a tapered head that digs into a stripped screwhead—Phillips, slotted, Torx, square-drive, etc. Simply press the remover against the screwhead as you run the drill counterclockwise to back the screw out. All types of extractors and removers come in sets that include several sizes, suiting a range of fasteners.

Screw Extractors

Screw extractors can remove broken wood or machine screws, small bolts, and studs without damaging the threaded holes. They come in both power and hand-driven models. Power extractors (second from right in the photo) are double-end bits for use in a power drill. One end has a short, bell-shaped bit that drills into the head/shank of the damaged fastener; the other end is a spiral extractor you drive into the hole to back the fastener out.

Hand-driven extractors (far right in the photo) work the same way, but you must first use a separate bit to drill into the fastener (the correct drill size is stamped into the extractor). The spiral- or straight-flute extractor chucks into a tap handle (see "Buying a Tap and Die Set" on p.129) for screw removal.

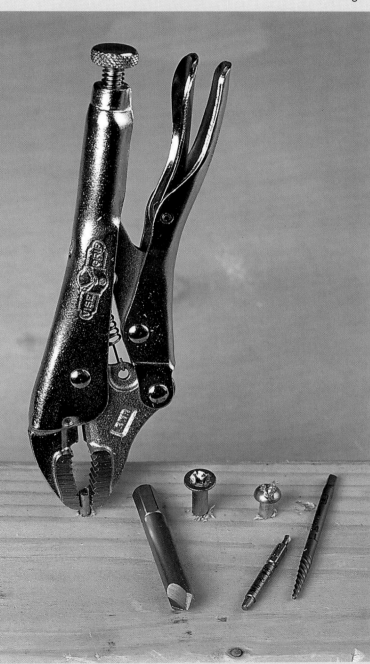

◄EXTRACTING SCREWS **When screws snap or strip and a pair of locking pliers won't get them out, it's time to use a screw remover or extractor.**

▲INTERCHANGEABLE-BIT SCREWDRIVERS An interchangeable-bit screwdriver is like having a whole set of screwdrivers at hand but in a more compact—and cleverly designed—package.

top photo on p. 148. For occasional home or hobby use, or for compact tool kits for your car or boat, choose a multidriver—a single handle (sometimes ratcheting) with interchangeable tips.

Although most screwdriver sets look alike, they aren't. Inexpensive screwdrivers have soft tips that easily distort and ruin the screws you drive with them. For best performance, look for screwdrivers made from chrome vanadium or other strong, alloyed steels. They should have durable tempered shanks and hardened tips ground for a precise fit. Ribbed tips are also desirable, as they grip screwheads better than smooth tips do. Some screwdrivers have built-in screw holders or are magnetized, which allow you to drive screws single-handed in cramped locations.

Ratcheting Screwdrivers

The problem some people have with regular screwdrivers is that you must release and regain your grip on them for every turn you take, thus increasing the chances the tip will slip off the fastener. Ratcheting screwdrivers work differently: You keep

---

Pro Tip

A regular straight-slot screwdriver should match both the width and length of the screw slot, with a tip that's square-edged; file or grind a bent tip to fit as necessary. Check to see that the tip of a Phillips driver goes deep into the recess of the head socket without bottoming out; any given-size driver will partially engage a Phillips screw, and can easily cam out (slip and destroy the screwhead).

contours designed to fit human hands snugly, allowing more driving torque with less hand fatigue. Many newer screwdriver handles feature soft, rubberized coatings or inserts, which reduce slippage and increase user comfort.

Buying a Set

A mechanic's toolbox or a workshop tool kit should have a complete set of full-size and stubby screwdrivers, as shown in the

▲RATCHETING SCREWDRIVERS By allowing you to work without changing your grip, a ratcheting screwdriver lets you tighten or loosen screws quickly and with less chance of stripping out screwheads.

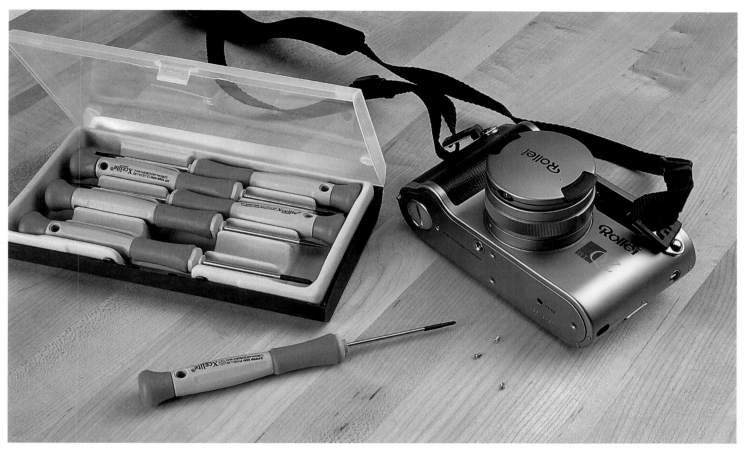

▲PRECISION SCREWDRIVER SET When full-size screwdrivers are just too big, choose a precision screwdriver with a tip that fits the tiny fastener snugly.

your grip comfortably and firmly on the handle and just twist your wrist back and forth to drive the screw. Just like a socket wrench, a mechanism inside engages the driver in one direction but allows it to spin without turning in the other direction. On most tools, a switch controls the ratcheting direction, so you can loosen screws as well as tighten them.

Some models look like regular screwdrivers with the addition of a ratcheting mechanism (shown at left in the photo on the facing page). Others are ratcheting multidrivers that use interchangeable driver bits (shown at right in the photo on the facing page).

Precision Screwdrivers

When you must retighten the miniscule screws on your eyeglasses, install new tuning pegs on your guitar, or take apart your point-and-shoot camera, full-size screwdrivers are simply useless. Precision (or jeweler's) screwdrivers have tiny tips made just for these kind of jobs.

To fit a wide range of small fasteners, precision screwdrivers usually come in a set of four to eight screwdrivers with different-size straight-slot and Phillips tips. These small screwdrivers have rotating end knobs that let you maintain down pressure with your palm or finger while turning the tool for faster driving and less chance of stripping out tiny fasteners.

Although you may be tempted to buy a bargain set, inexpensive precision screw-

Pro Tip

If you're buying a set of precision screwdrivers for work on computers, audio equipment, or electronics projects, make sure they're ESD (electrostatic discharge) safe, so you won't accidentally ruin sensitive components. Wearing a grounded wrist strap will further help prevent electrostatic damage to electronic equipment.

▲RIGHT-ANGLE SCREWDRIVERS When there's just no room to reach a screw with a regular driver, reach for a right-angle screwdriver. The two tools at top have different-size tips at each end, while the bottom tool is a ratcheting-style screwdriver.

> ### Pro Tip
>
> If you find yourself lacking the hand strength to drive big screws, buy screwdrivers with square shanks or with a hex-shape section near the handle. By slipping a wrench onto the shank, you can easily increase driving force while using your other hand to press the screwdriver down, thus preventing the tip from lifting out and possibly damaging the screwhead.

drivers with soft tips are apt to distort or strip out delicate screwheads, which makes any job miserable. It's best to buy a high-quality set made from good steel with hardened tips. A more economical alternative is to buy a single-handle tool with interchangeable drivers, as shown in the tool kit on pp. 4–5.

Offset Screwdrivers

Also known as a right-angle or crank screwdriver, an offset screwdriver has its driving tip bent at 90 degrees to its handle. It's the tool you need for tightening or loosening screws in a confined spot where you can barely fit your hand—underneath a kitchen-sink cabinet, inside a toaster oven, or deep down in an automobile's engine bay. Most offset screwdrivers are made in the shape of a zigzag, with a slotted driver on one end and a Phillips on the other.

Handier still are ratcheting offset screwdrivers (shown at bottom in the photo above), which drive screws with a reversible, back-and-forth motion, like a ratchet wrench. Since you don't need to lift the head from the fastener, you can work without even seeing the screw you're driving.

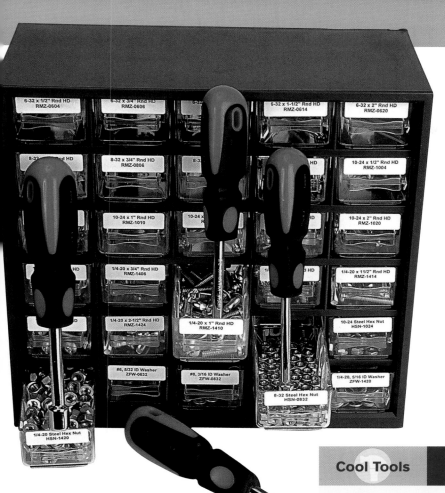

◄NUT DRIVERS Small wrenches aren't nearly as handy as nut drivers when it comes to tightening and loosening small nuts, bolts, and machine screws.

NUT DRIVERS

Like a screwdriver in appearance, a nut driver has a hex-screw socket head at the end of a shaft that's mounted to a round handle. This tool is easier and quicker to use than a wrench whenever you have lots of small nuts to drive. It's a great tool for assembling any project with sheet-metal parts: a gas barbeque grill, table-saw legs or a tool stand, storage shelves and cabinets, etc. As with regular screwdrivers, nut drivers with soft, ergonomically designed grips that fit your hands are the most comfortable to use. Less expensive when purchased as a set, nut drivers come in sizes ranging from ³⁄₁₆ in. to ½ in. (fractional) and from 5mm to 13mm (metric). For model making or watch repair, a technician's precision nut driver set includes sizes as small as ³⁄₃₂ in. or 2.5mm.

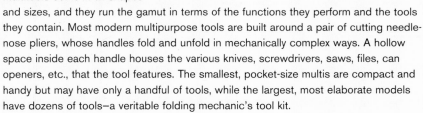

Cool Tools **MULTIPURPOSE TOOLS**

RESONATING WITH our most primal survival instincts, multipurpose tools are terrific to have in an emergency or for makeshift repairs in a pinch. It's prudent to keep one of these tools handy—in your vehicle, tackle box, camera bag, or desk drawer—to save the day when things go kerflooey.

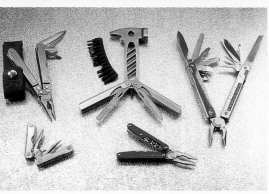

Multitools come in all shapes and sizes, and they run the gamut in terms of the functions they perform and the tools they contain. Most modern multipurpose tools are built around a pair of cutting needle-nose pliers, whose handles fold and unfold in mechanically complex ways. A hollow space inside each handle houses the various knives, screwdrivers, saws, files, can openers, etc., that the tool features. The smallest, pocket-size multis are compact and handy but may have only a handful of tools, while the largest, most elaborate models have dozens of tools—a veritable folding mechanic's tool kit.

Many multitools, like the original Leatherman®, have handles that open with sharp edges facing out. Newer tools, such as the Victorinox® (shown at right in the photo), open in the opposite fashion, which make their handles more comfortable to hold. A significant feature to look for in a multitool is locking blades, which makes it safer and easier to use.

CHAPTER 6

Tools That Pound & Pry

People have called the hammer the "king of tools," since, in the skillful hands of a blacksmith, it can be used to forge all other metal tools—saws, pliers, wrenches, and more. A tool with ancient origins, hammers (along with mallets, sledges, and their other "pounding cousins") are still important tools today for myriad construction and fabrication jobs, which include: pounding nails; shaping metal hollowware and auto bodies; driving chisels, wedges, or punches through metal, wood, and masonry; and setting stakes and posts into the ground. Working in concert with pounding tools are wrecking bars, prying bars, nail pullers and sets, and punches, all of which serve to help build—or tear down—all kinds of construction projects.

▲ CLAW HAMMER No carpenter's tool bag or kit is complete without a good claw hammer, indispensable for driving and pulling out nails, pounding and aligning parts, and even doing light demolition work.

CLAW HAMMERS

Probably the most widely used type of hammers, claw hammers were developed specifically for carpentry jobs—building birdhouses, luxury hotels, and everything in between. Claw hammers combine a striking head for driving nails with a rear-facing claw for pulling nails.

Since nails come in many sizes, from delicate brads for tacking molding to gargantuan spikes for fastening construction timbers, claw hammers also range considerably in size. Claw hammers roughly split into two camps: smaller finish hammers and larger framing hammers.

A finish hammer usually has a head between 7 oz. and 16 oz. with a smooth striking face (see the following section), good for nailing up trim (primarily used to finish construction jobs, hence their name) and for general household duties, driving a range of fasteners from small tacks to nails up to 2 in. long.

Framing hammers have longer handles and heavier heads (usually in the range of 18 oz. to 32 oz.) that deliver the pounding force necessary for driving big nails—8d, 16d, or larger—used in framing and wood-frame construction. The chart at right shows various hammerhead weights and the kinds of tasks they're best suited for.

In addition to its basic style (finish or framing) and head weight, a claw hammer has several other variables that distinguish different types. Striking face, claw type, and handle material and style all vary from hammer to hammer; these factors are discussed in the sections that follow. Even head material is a variable these days, since claw hammers are being manufactured with titanium heads (see the Pro/Con box at right). The particular blend of features you choose will affect the suitability of a hammer to your personal style and the types of jobs you do.

CHOOSING THE RIGHT CLAWHAMMER

Head Weight (Steel-Head Hammers)	Best Use
7 oz. to 10 oz. Framing hammer with rip claw 	Light-duty household driving of pins, tacks, and brads
10 oz. to 13 oz.	Household use for brads and small nails; cabinetmakers use for driving brads and small dowel pins
12 oz. to 16 oz. Finish hammer with curved claw	Best for general use and for small workshop projects with nails up to 16d
18 oz. to 22 oz.	Heavier carpentry and framing jobs
24 oz. to 32 oz.	For professional framers driving big nails in fewer strikes

Note: Long-handle Japanese and titanium-head hammers have lighter head weights relative to the amount of work they're designed to do. For example, a 16-oz. titanium framing hammer generates striking power equivalent to a 20-oz. to 24-oz. steel hammer.

Striking Faces

Claw hammers come with one of two basic striking-face designs: serrated and smooth. Framing hammer faces almost always have a serrated pattern milled on them, also called a waffle face (shown at right in the top photo on p. 156). A few specialized hammers have serrated faces as well (for example, drywall and roofing). Like car tread on a slippery road, the raised waffle pattern gives a hammer better traction on the nail as it's struck. This not only provides more control when toenailing (driv-

FOR DECADES, carpentry hammerheads have been made from steel that's either forged or cast into shape. The bigger and heavier the head, the greater the striking force—but the more muscle it takes to swing it. However, space-age technology now brings us an interesting alternative—a hammerhead made of strong, lightweight titanium (see photo below).

TITANIUM-HEAD HAMMERS

Pros:
- lighter; easier to carry and swing with less fatigue
- faster to swing; will more readily change direction
- transmits less shock than steel, which lessens likelihood of stress injuries

Cons:
- considerably more expensive
- fewer styles available than regular steel-head hammers

STEEL-HEAD HAMMERS

Pros:
- considerably less expensive than titanium-head hammers
- many sizes and handle styles available

Cons:
- much heavier
- more likely to produce fatigue and stress injuries

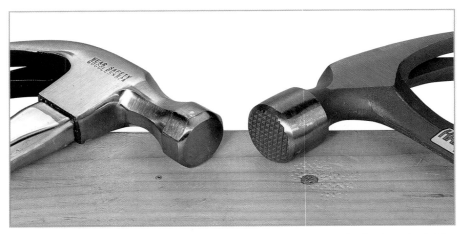

▲ **WAFFLE AND SMOOTH HAMMERHEADS** A smooth-face hammer (left) is best for finish-nailing jobs, while a waffle-face hammer (right) gives you more control when driving big nails into construction lumber.

Cool Tools — CONVERTIBLE HAMMER

A **CONVERTIBLE HAMMER** is the perfect solution if you can't decide if you want your hammer to have a smooth or serrated (waffle) face. These unique hammers allow you to do either finish or framing carpentry jobs simply by screwing on the appropriate striking cap—either smooth or waffle face—to the front of the hammerhead (the overall weight of the head stays the same). Although they can be more expensive than buying a pair of framing and finish hammers, convertible hammers allow you to do most hammering jobs with a single tool.

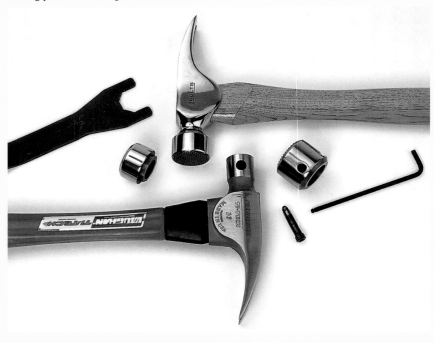

ing nails at a steep angle) but also can even help coax nails to straighten after they've bent or hit a knot. However, serrated faces will shred the wood's surface on contact and are a poor choice for finish-nailing tasks, where the work must remain unscarred.

A finish hammer's face is smooth (shown at left in the photo at left), so errant blows don't leave pockmarks on the work. Smooth-face heads are slightly domed (also know as a bell-shaped), which allow skillful users to drive nail heads flush without leaving so much as a dimple.

Claw Types

Believe it or not, Roman claw hammers made more than 20 centuries ago are just like modern claw hammers: They have striking faces opposite a pair of claws for removing nails when things go wrong (how do you say "!@#*+%!!!" in Latin?). Modern claw hammers come in two styles: curved

▲ **CURVED-CLAW AND RIP-CLAW HAMMERS** If you need a hammer with the leverage to pull out bent nails, choose a curved-claw model (right). Rip-claw hammers (left) can also pull out nails but are better for prying up boards or tearing up walls and floors.

▲ HAMMER SIDE CLAW Long end claws found on most carpentry hammers are fine for pulling up large nails, but a side claw is handier for removing small nails and tacks.

claw and rip claw. Most finish hammers have curved nail claws, which provide good leverage for pulling nails directly from the work without massacring the surface. Rip claws can also pull out nails, but their pointier shape is primarily designed for prying up boards (the straight claws slip between planks easier than curved ones do) as well as for tearing up shingles or chopping holes in drywall and wood paneling. Some claw hammers have heads with a side notch, helpful for extracting small nails and fasteners (see the bottom right photo on the facing page).

Handle Materials and Styles

Claw hammers—as well as hammers of any size and type—need to have comfortable handles before they're ready to take on seri-

KEEPING YOUR HEAD

Believe it or not, one of the biggest shortcomings of hammers before the middle of the 19th century was that the fit between the wood handle and iron head loosened, and they lost their heads all too often. Norwich, New York, toolmaker David Maydole changed all that when he created the adze-eye hammerhead around 1840. It featured a wider socket where the handle joined the head (shown at right in the photo), similar to the one found on an adze—an ancient chopping and shaping tool. Most hammers made today retain the basic adze-eye style, although some modern designs buck this tradition (shown at left in the photo).

ous pounding jobs. Long gone are the days when you'd buy a forged hammerhead from your village blacksmith and whittle a wood handle for it yourself. Nowadays, the extensive array of claw hammers at a typical hardware or home-supply store feature handles in an extensive—and often confusing—array of materials, shapes, and lengths. What's more, the latest, most advanced ergonomic engineering has produced claw and other hammer handles that not only are more comfortable and less stressful to use (see "Ergonomic Handles" on p. 163) but also that actually absorb pounding vibration (see "Stanley® Anti-Vibe® Hammer" on p.159).

Pro Tip

West Coast professional carpenters often prefer framing hammers with wooden ax handles. Besides feeling good and looking really cool, the hammer's flared handle end, according to many, helps prevent you from losing your grip and having the hammer accidentally fly out of your hand.

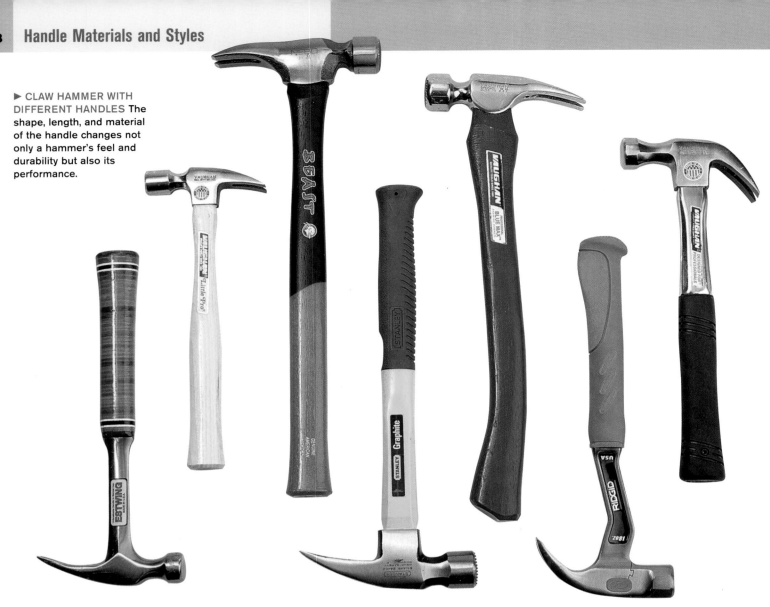

▶ CLAW HAMMER WITH DIFFERENT HANDLES The shape, length, and material of the handle changes not only a hammer's feel and durability but also its performance.

Tool Helpers

ELECTRONIC STUD FINDERS

You can't drive big nails into household walls without finding the studs inside them. If you've had your share of misses when using the old-fashioned wall-tapping method, you'll appreciate the latest electronic stud locators on the market. Using special density-sensing circuitry, these devices can find not only hidden studs and joists but also metal pipes, plates, and conduits. Top models, such as the one shown here, will also detect AC power, so you can trace live wires and avoid accidentally pounding nails into them—a most shocking discovery. (What's next: electronic X-ray vision?)

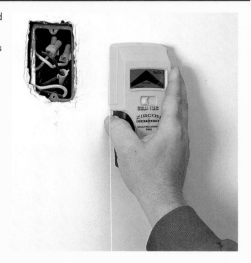

WOOD Wood is still the most common—and affordable—handle material found on hammers of all kinds. Hickory is the species of choice, prized for its strength and durability. Unfortunately, wood handles are particularly prone to overstrike (missing the nail and hitting the handle near the head), which can splinter, split, and ruin a handle in a hurry; at least wood handles are easy to replace. Wood handles come in straight or curved ax-type styles (see the tip at on p. 157).

SYNTHETIC Synthetic handles made from fiberglass- or graphite-reinforced resin are real durability champs and are popular with professional users who pound nails for a living. This kind of handle is actually glued to the head with epoxy resin, making it practically impossible for the head to come loose during regular use. Synthetic handles always have a rubberized grip for comfort and to help dampen striking vibrations. Although the tough resins resist shredding due to overstrikes, some handles come with a molded overstrike guard as well, which further protects the handle.

STEEL Steel-handle hammers are made one of two ways: as a tubular steel shank mated to a standard hammerhead or as an integrated head and handle that are a single casting. Both kinds have leather or rubberized comfort grips. The tubular handles found on bargain-bin hammers are usually of poor quality and poorly made; better-quality tubular handles contain a wood core that adds strength and absorbs vibration. Since integrated steel transmits vibration more than other handle materials, several manufacturers have developed clever technological innovations that reduce the impact on the user's hand and arm (see "Stanley Anti-Vibe Hammer" at right).

SPECIALIZED HAMMERS

If you're used to thinking of a claw hammer as a universal tool to pound parts into submission when all other tools fail, here's a revolutionary thought: Using a hammer specifically designed for the job at hand increases your chances of successfully completing the job (and with less expletives uttered). Specialized hammers have evolved for a variety of tasks, from furniture upholstering to cabinetmaking, drywall installation to brick setting, and metal shaping and mechanical assembly to tool driving and demolition work.

Pro Tip

Some old-timers bore a ¼-in. to ⅜-in. hole in the ends of their wooden hammer handles and fill them with beeswax. Quickly jamming the sharp end of a nail into wax provides a little lubrication, so the nail glides more easily into hard lumber.

▲ **FIBERGLASS-REINFORCED HAMMER HANDLE** Fiberglass-reinforced plastic is a lightweight, durable material for a hammer handle. To protect against damage, the hammer here also features a resilient plastic overstrike guard.

Cool Tools   **VIBRATION-REDUCING HAMMERS**

THE STANLEY ANTI-VIBE HAMMER is the tool of choice for those concerned with the long-term, ill effects of hammer use. To the weekend warrior installing window trim or building a doghouse, swinging a hammer all day long means a sore arm, but to a professional carpenter framing a house or rebuilding a deck, daily nail pounding often leads to hand, wrist, or arm damage due to repetitive stress syndrome (RSS).

While researching the effects of RSS, ergonomic engineers at Stanley Works came up with a novel approach to reducing nerve-damaging hammer vibration. After measuring the frequency of hammer impact, they created a simple vibration-absorbing device: a tuning fork. The steel fork extends through the handle of the tool (see the photo at right), absorbing the shock of every blow and significantly reducing its transmission to the user. Not to be outdone, other manufacturers have developed their own hammerhead designs for reducing pounding vibrations (see the Robo Hammer® antivibration head, shown in the photo at left).

SWING WITH LESS STRESS

To prevent a sore arm and pock-marked surfaces every time you nail something together, make sure you're swinging your hammer properly. First, check your grip: Choking up on the handle (grasping it an inch or two up from the bottom) helps control a heavy hammer better. Next, instead of trying to slam the hammer down with your wrist, try to swing the head through a full arc using your whole arm. Don't jerk the hammer downward; allow the weight of the head to build momentum as it travels toward the nail. Don't fight the impact as the head strikes the nail—this energy helps the hammer rebound, thus returning your arm to its starting position with less effort.

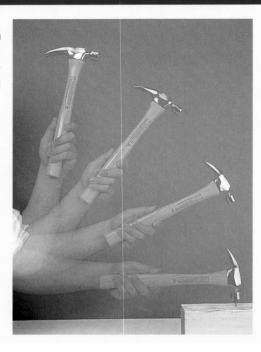

Tack and Upholsterer's Hammers

When even the smallest carpenter's hammer is overkill for driving tiny fasteners, it's time get out the tack hammer. A basic tack hammer has a magnetized, round face on one end for picking up steel brads, finish nails, and tacks, and a squarish face on the other end for driving them. The tool's light, narrow head and "magnetic personality" make it handy for driving nails single-handed and for reaching into places that are hard to get to—for instance, when fastening baseboards in a closet or setting thin moldings around the tops of cabinets, windows, and doors.

If you want to pry up tacks as well as drive them, choose a tack hammer that pairs a magnetized face with a small claw on the other end. And if covering (or recovering) furniture is your pleasure, opt for a specialized upholsterer's hammer: a tack hammer with a larger, slightly curved head that sports magnetized and nonmagnetized faces, made for driving tacks to hold fabric, webbing, and padding in place.

Bricklayer's Hammers

Also known as a brick or mason's hammer, this modern tool couples a chisellike curved pick with a smallish, square striking face (its predecessor, the bricklayer's scutch, had chisel tips at both ends). The chisel end of a bricklayer's hammer is primarily used for trimming bricks to size: You tap the brick on all four sides with the chisel, splitting it apart at that point. It's a quick and useful trick, but it takes some finesse and practice to master.

Contrary to what seems obvious, the striking face of this hammer isn't designed for hitting a brick chisel or pry bar; in fact, you should never do this, as it can shatter the face. Instead, it's used for tapping bricks into place when setting them into fresh mortar and for tweaking their alignment.

▶HAMMERS FOR DRIVING TACKS Here are three different hammers good for driving tacks and small nails (from top to bottom): upholsterer's hammer and regular- and claw-style tack hammers.

Pro Tip

Having trouble driving small nails into thin moldings, strips, or trim without splitting the material? Try flattening the tip of the nail before you drive it by tapping it lightly with a hammer. The blunt end crushes wood fibers instead of cleaving between them, causing splits.

▲BRICKLAYER'S HAMMER A bricklayer's hammer has a wide pick end for trimming bricks and a striking end for tapping bricks into position when they're set in mortar.

Drywall Hammers

Also known as a wallboard hammer, a drywall hammer pairs a hammer with a stubby hatchet. It was originally developed as a tool for chopping thin wood lath to length, and then nailing it in place for a lath-and-plaster wall (old-timers still call them lath hammers). Although do-it-yourselfers primarily use this tool for driving drywall nails, skillful users employ the hatchet for scoring and snapping drywall and for quickly chopping out notches and rough openings for pipes and fixtures. The narrow hatchet can also be handy for wedging a sheet of drywall or lifting it at the bottom to position and holding it while it's tacked in place. A small notch in the underside of the hatchet pulls out bent nails.

Drywall hammers have an angled head, which allows you to nail into corners. Some have a flat side on the upper end of the face (see the photo at right) to further aid nailing

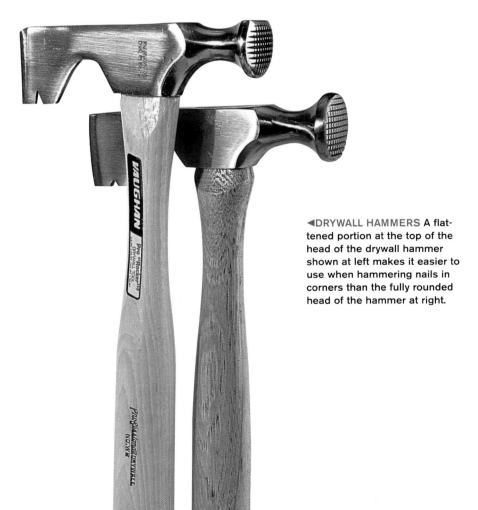

◄DRYWALL HAMMERS A flattened portion at the top of the head of the drywall hammer shown at left makes it easier to use when hammering nails in corners than the fully rounded head of the hammer at right.

▶DRYWALL HAMMER FACE
Specialized for driving cup-headed nails, a drywall hammer's slightly convex head leaves a slight dimple, allowing the nail to be hidden by joint compound when the drywall is finished off.

Roofing Hammers

At first glance, a roofing hammer (or shingling hatchet) has a serrated nail-striking face and short hatchet like a drywall hammer. However, it has three holes and a little stud on the hatchet part. The stud, called a guide pin, provides a simple distance gauge for setting the overlap of consecutive courses (called the exposure) of wood or composition shingles (see the photo below). (When I was just out of school and working on a remodeling crew, I thought the stud was there to limit the hatchet's penetration when chopping wooden shakes to size . . . so much for a college education.) To use the guide, hook the pin on the course of shingles you've just nailed, set the bottom edge of the next row against the hammer, and then use the tool's milled face to nail them in place.

The hatchet is also useful for splitting wood shingles to width and for chopping out old roofing cement or flashing when replacing a roof. Some hatchets have a small razor edge designed to cut roofing felt or to score composition shingles before they're bent and split to size.

Pro Tip

To deal with the ragged edges of cutouts or notches in a sheet of wallboard, a professional drywall installer will use the milled waffle face of a drywall hammer like a small rasp to smooth the rough edges.

close to inside edges and corners. The hammer's serrated face lends more control when driving nails (see "Striking Faces" on p. 155). The prominently domed face creates a dimple in the gypsum wallboard as special cup-headed drywall nails are driven home. This dimple creates a hollow, which is filled with joint compound (a standard part of finishing drywall) to hide the nail heads.

▲ROOFING HAMMER Also known as a shingling hatchet, a roofing hammer's adjustable-gauge peg provides a handy way of spacing subsequent rows of shingles evenly.

Ball Peen Hammers

Although they're used primarily for metal-work and auto-body work, the ball peen—or pein—hammer (also called an engineer's or machinist's hammer) is a versatile tool and a jack of many trades. Ball peens have a smooth striking face (like a finish hammer's) that's specially hardened so that it won't chip or shatter when used to hit a hard tool or surface. These hammers are just the ticket for pounding the end of a cold chisel (see the bottom photo on p. 69), center punch, or nail set when tackling jobs like bolt cutting, rust descaling, or slag chipping (after welding).

The ball peen's other face has a hemispherical head (hence the tool's name) because it was originally intended for peening rivets: flattening the end to set it tight in its hole—a traditional way of joining bridge girders and structural framework. Nowadays, the ball end is more commonly used for forming parts from soft metals or for creating a decorative pattern of concave hammer marks.

Ball peen hammers come in a wide range of weights, with heads weighing from 2 oz. to 3 lb. For chiseling or punch-driving duties, choose a hammer with a face approximately ⅜ in. larger in diameter than the head of the chisel or tool you wish to strike.

Cool Tools **ERGONOMIC HANDLES**

THE MAJORITY OF HAMMERS—ball peen, claw, drywall, etc.–have been fitted with a straight, wood handle since their origin. But the modern science of ergonomics has put an entirely new spin on handle design. The latest ergonomic hammers have bent handles and, in some cases, special grips to allow the user's hand and arm to remain in a more neutral position during pounding. The result is greater striking accuracy with less shock and muscle tension, thus significantly reducing fatigue and pressure on the user's palm. If you hammer a lot, these ergonomic handles also help prevent carpal tunnel syndrome and other repetitive stress injuries.

▲BALL PEEN HAMMER FACE
A ball peen hammer gets its name from its half-round striking face, which can be used to form metal parts or to decorate surfaces with a pattern of overlapping dimples.

◄BALL PEEN HAMMERS
Whether you're driving a chisel or punch, you'll get the best results by selecting a ball peen hammer of the right size and weight.

▶SLEDGEHAMMERS Both large and small sledgehammers are perfect for many heavy pounding and demolition jobs.

SLEDGEHAMMERS

When it comes to the overgrown hammers known as sledges, one size definitely doesn't fit all. These heavy hitters vary in length and weight from short, 10-in.-handle models with 1½-lb. heads, to supersize, 36-in.-long swingers with massive 20-lb. heads. While each size has its own range of usefulness, all sledges have large striking faces with generously beveled heads that are specially heat treated to minimize the chance of chipping or shattering when used to strike other tools. As with all hammers, *never* use a sledge to strike another hammer face or other hardened-steel tool, as it may shatter and shower you with shards (say *that* three times quickly).

Big Sledges

Big sledges are the tools of choice for circus gangs driving the wooden stakes that hold up the big top, as well as for prison chain gangs swinging and singing their way through the rock pile, turning boulders into rubble. And when it's time to break up an old, cracked sidewalk or to demolish a reinforced masonry wall, a big sledge quickly separates the men from the boys—although smashingly effective, a big sledge is tough to wield blow after blow (see the tip on the facing page).

Small Sledges

Smaller sledges, with short handles and 2-lb. to 4-lb. heads, have a variety of colorful names: club hammers, drilling hammers, and single jack hammers. Regardless of the moniker, a small sledge is a versatile tool that's good for lots of jobs: driving smallish wedges and heavy chisels into wood, punching holes in masonry with a star drill, splitting bricks with a brick chisel, cleaving thick metal with a big punch or cold chisel, driving hardened masonry nails or pins into concrete or brick, and performing light demolition work. Small sledges are also just right for pounding in stakes when laying out a building foundation (see the photo at right) and when setting forms for concrete pours.

MALLETS

Unlike ball peen hammers and sledges with steel striking faces, mallets have heads and faces made from softer materials, making them perfectly suited to pounding on a variety of materials without denting or damaging them. Most mallets have largish heads and wide faces, which can be used for striking a tool, such as a chisel or

▲DRILLING HAMMER Resembling a small sledge-hammer, a drilling hammer is handy for medium-size pounding jobs, like driving stakes and small posts.

▲MALLETS Although they're not good for driving nails, mallets come in many styles and materials perfectly suited to pounding other tools or parts without dinging or damaging them.

Pro Tip

If you plan to use a rubber or plastic mallet to pound light-color parts together, as when making a raw blonde wood cabinet, for instance, choose a mallet with a white rubber or light-color plastic head. A black or dark head will leave marks, just like black shoe heels do on a light floor.

punch, or for pounding parts together, as when assembling picture frames or boxes. Mallets are also useful for shaping malleable materials, such as sheet metal and plastic.

Mallet heads come in a variety of materials—wood, rubber, leather, plastic—each suited to a particular range of tasks. There are also specialized mallets designed for specific jobs, such as removing the bat-ear knockoff nuts that secure the wire wheels to vintage sports cars.

Wood-Head Mallets

Also called carpenter's mallets, these are relatively inexpensive and are great for basic bench duties, such as pounding wood chisels when shaping joinery or chopping mortises for hinges and other hardware. They're also perfect for driving mechanical assemblies apart with some force but without damaging or dinging up metal parts.

The bigger the head, the more driving power there is. Most woodworkers find a 1½-lb. to 2½-lb. head (shown at top left in the bottom photo on p. 165) good for general-duty tasks. Just keep an eye on the head; once it splits or mushrooms to the point where it's splintery, it's time to replace it.

Rubber-Head Mallets

An old workbench staple, mallets with solid rubber heads are inexpensive, long lasting, and a good choice for all manner of pounding duties. Smaller mallets are great for pounding sensitive materials, such as veneered furniture parts, because they're

not likely to create dents. Choose a heavy-head (2-lb. to 3-lb.) rubber mallet for banging apart a crate or for driving parts home. For really forceful banging, buy a mallet with a weighted, metal head and replaceable rubber inserts (shown at middle front in the bottom photo on p. 165).

Plastic-Face Mallets

Plastic-face mallets have a metal head with plastic inserts on the striking faces. These may be made from hard plastic or soft plastic. Soft-plastic mallets are useful in jewelry and metal fabrication when you need to pound parts but don't want the impact to unduly mar the material's surface finish. Hard-plastic mallets deliver a more authoritative blow without leaving a mark. They're good for jobs like pounding small chisels and punches or for setting rivets for leather crafts.

Some plastic mallets come with one hard and one soft face, so you can switch between jobs as necessary. For even greater versatility, get a mallet with interchangeable tips. Then, you can choose the exact hardness or softness you need for the task at hand.

Dead-Blow Mallets

These tools usually have a plastic or rubber head that's loaded with a loose weight, such as sand or lead shot, which transfers more of the driving impact to the piece being struck, while preventing the head from bouncing—and rebounding toward the user. A hollow cavity in the mallet's head is only half filled so that the internal load flies forward as the hammer is slammed down. When the head connects, the mass of the load adds oomph to the hit and counteracts the mallet's natural tendency to rebound.

A dead-blow mallet is absolutely the best for driving large cabinet parts and

▼INTERCHANGEABLE-FACE MALLET To increase its versatility, this mallet with interchangeable faces lets the user screw on harder or softer faces to suit the task.

other assemblies that are being glued together because it delivers tons of driving force without marring the parts. They're also tops for driving assemblies apart—in case your glue-up goes awry.

Rawhide Mallets

Featuring a head made of tightly wound leather, rawhide mallets are used in many different kinds of craft work. In fine-metal smithing, they are used extensively in the process of forming metal vessels, such as silver bowls and brass platters. These soft metals are pounded over a form (an anvil or sandbag) with the mallet, which shapes the metal but doesn't leave prominent strike marks. Rawhide mallets are also frequently used in leather work for setting brass rivets, snaps, and other fasteners as well as for driving punches and other leather-cutting and shaping tools. A basic rawhide mallet has a solid, hard leather head on a wooden handle, but heavier, internally weighted heads are available for more demanding jobs, such as pounding dents from metal auto-body parts.

▲DEAD-BLOW MALLET With a weighted head designed to minimize bounce back, a dead-blow mallet packs a potent wallop— great when driving parts together during project assembly.

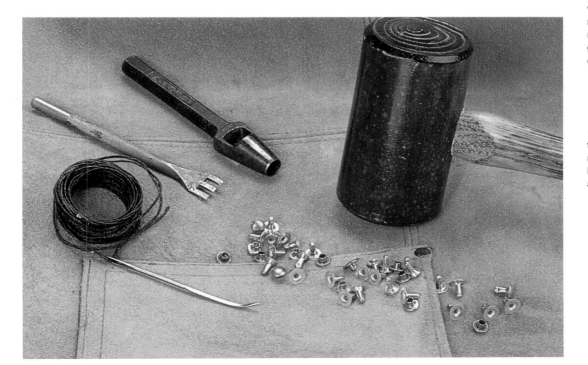

◄RAWHIDE MALLET A traditional tool for leather working, a rawhide mallet's tough head can pound hole punches or set brass rivets and snaps without marring them.

►NAIL SET ASSORTMENT All nail sets are made to drive finish nail heads below the surface, but designs vary (from left to right): right-angle, Japanese, and standard straight (three sizes) styles.

NAIL SETS AND PUNCHES

Of all the tools you can strike with a hammer, few are more important for carpentry and metalworking jobs than nail sets, center punches, and pin punches. All three are used to make indentations, yet each is uniquely suited to a specific kind of work: recessing nail heads in wood, creating dimples in sheet metal, and driving pins in mechanical assemblies.

Nail Sets

Good carpenters can pound finish nails (headless nails for moldings, trim, and other finish woodwork) neatly flush just by dishing out a last well-metered whack with their hammer. We who are mere mortals typically flush-up finish nails using a nail set, a dedicated punch with a small head that mates with the nail's diminutive head. A nail set looks like an awl or pin punch—a shaft with a point. They come in several sizes to fit different-size finish nails and brads. Nicer tools have a plastic coating on the shank, making them more comfortable to hold.

An interesting variation is the right-angle nail set, which has a driving point mounted at a 90-degree angle to the handle. Because the driving point is shorter and closer to the nail head, this design (tradi-tional for Japanese nail sets, shown second from left in the photo above) gives the user good control and reduces the chance that the point will slip off and punch a hole in the wood next to the nail—yeow!

Center Punches

Any time you need to start a drill bit on a hard surface (metal, hardwood, or plastic), creating a little dimple with a center punch prevents the bit from skipping around and marring the material. A simple center punch (shown at bottom in the photo below) is like a cold chisel that tapers to a point; you strike it with a mallet. An automatic center punch (shown at top in the

▲CENTER PUNCHES Creating a dimple on a metal surface or other hard material with a center punch makes it much easier to drill without the bit slipping. Center punches come in standard (bottom) and automatic (top) styles.

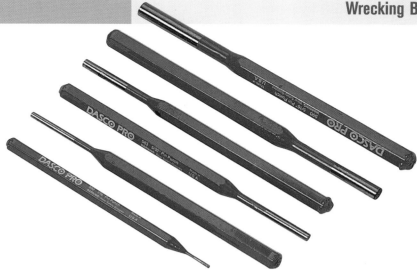

bottom photo on the facing page) has a powerful spring inside that fires when the top of the handle is compressed, eliminating the need to smack it with a mallet. The impact force is adjustable—stronger for punching metals and softer for woods and plastics.

Pin Punches

Many mechanical parts, such as the motor-shaft pulley on your lawnmower or the chain wheel on your child's pedal car, are held in place with a small pin. Split or rolled pins are tightly driven through the wheel, gear, or pulley to hold it firmly on the shaft. To remove them for repairs, you need to drive them out with a pin punch, pounded with a mallet or ball peen hammer. Having a set of punches on hand (see the top photo at right) lets you choose just the right size to fit the diameter of the pin.

WRECKING BARS, PRY BARS, AND NAIL PULLERS

Everyone knows that successfully putting a project together takes careful planning and craftsmanship. But it's easy to forget that tearing it apart can require a surprising amount of effort and strategy—not to mention the right tools. Wrecking bars, pry bars, and nail pullers are all part of a deconstructionist's tool kit, and each tool has its own specialty.

Wrecking Bars

Although these hefty tools often make guest appearances on television shows like *Cops*, they're primarily used for breaking or ripping up concrete and lath-and-plaster and for prying up lumber and other building materials. A basic wrecking bar, or pike (shown at front in the bottom photo at right), is made from a long, heavy bar with a pointed or chisellike tip. You use a pike by simply lifting and hurling it down repeatedly on a horizontal surface, like a sidewalk, to break it up for removal.

Gooseneck wrecking bars, commonly called crowbars, have bent or curved ends with wider, wedge-shaped tips. They're useful for tearing up old flooring, tearing out concrete forms and old walls and ceilings, and tearing apart cabinets, crates, and pallets (small ones are also handy for prying off the tops of big cans). There's usually a claw at one end for prying up nails. Twin-claw wrecking bars (shown at left in the photo below) are specially designed for lifting up flooring or shingles from joists or for prying siding off studs.

▲**PIN PUNCH SET** To remove the pin holding a wheel, gear, or pulley in place on its shaft, choose the correct-diameter pin punch from a set.

▼**WRECKING BARS** Whether you're tearing down a whole house or just pulling up a few boards, a wrecking bar is stout enough to handle any demolition job.

►PRY BARS AND RIPPING CHISELS Pry bars and ripping chisels come in all shapes and sizes, but all have a common purpose: to demolish wood constructions and remove nails.

Pry Bars

You can rip out boards and pull nails with a wrecking bar, but a general-purpose pry bar helps you accomplish these feats without destroying the work in the process, making it a great all-purpose tool for do-it-yourselfers and homeowners doing light demolition and nail removal. A pry bar combines a curved, often flat, bar with two or more nail claws and/or teardrop-shaped nail slots.

The beefy, chisellike ends on some pry bars (sometimes called ripping bars or chisels) are not only useful for prying between boards but also can be pounded directly into them to literally rip wood and other materials apart. The wide, thin tips found on some bars easily slip into narrow crevices, so you can pry off baseboards and moldings (you can even scrape with them in a pinch). Miniripping bars (shown at bottom in the photo above) are the tools of choice for removing thin moldings and opening stubborn paint cans.

Nail Pullers

Pry bars do a good job pulling up nails when their heads stick up a little. But to get at recessed nails, finish nails, or nails with broken-off heads, you need a nail puller. Heavy-duty impact nail pullers and lighter-duty cat's paw nail pullers and

| Cool Tools | **ROOFING MUTT** |

A ROOFING MUTT is a lifesaver when it comes to dirty destruction jobs, like tearing off an old shingle roof or ripping up dilapidated linoleum flooring. Specialized for these kinds of home demolition jobs, the roofing mutt has a wide, curved steel blade designed to dig under shingles and roofing—or old flooring—lifting it up and ripping it off. The mutt's long wood handle gives you lots of leverage, and a row of serrated teeth on the blade slice through roofing felt or underlayment film, catching and pulling up nails as well. There's also a tapered nail slot in the middle of the blade for yanking out longer nails.

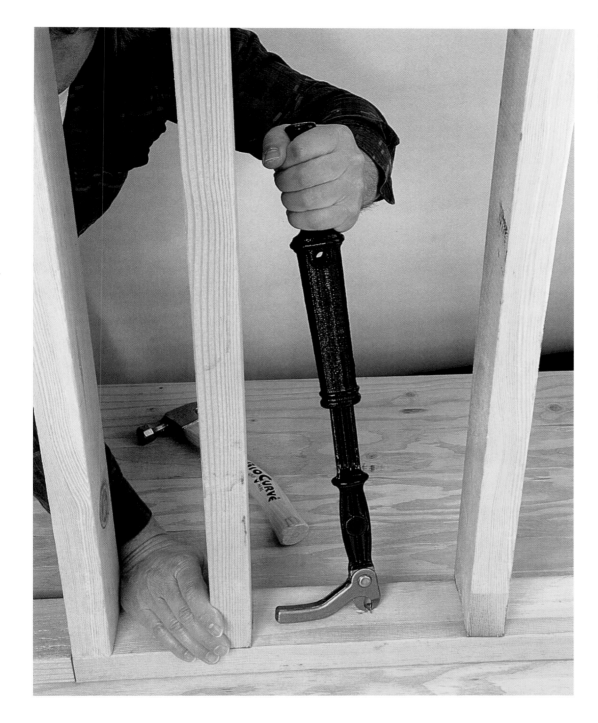

◀IMPACT NAIL PULLER When nails break or are driven below the surface of the wood, it takes the strong gripping jaws and hammer-action handle of an impact nail puller to extract them.

tack pullers all have sharp claws designed to be driven into wood deeply enough to grab whatever is left of the nail and then lever it out.

IMPACT NAIL PULLERS This heavyweight tool lives for only one purpose: to extract deeply embedded spikes and large nails. Made from cast steel, an impact nail puller has special pincerlike jaws and a heavy handle that acts as a sliding weight. After positioning the open jaws over the nail, you slide the weight quickly down the handle to bang the jaws into the wood. Pivoting the handle forward presses the jaws shut, grabbing firmly around whatever's left of the fastener. It leaves a wicked

▲**NAIL PULLERS** Bent nails are no match for nail and tack pullers, which come in many sizes and styles, including (clockwise from left) cat's paw/pry bar combo, cat's paw, Japanese (large), Japanese (small), tack puller, and Japanese with wide prying end.

hole in the work but gets the nail out when all other methods have failed.

CAT'S PAWS This essential carpenter's tool has one or two ends shaped like—you guessed it—a cat's inverted paw, with two, pronglike claws that have a rounded bottom (see the photo above). You work the claws down over the nail by forcing the tool into the wood. If the fastener is headless, hammering the back of the head forces the claws deeper. Japanese-style cat's paws have claws on a rocker head that's bent at 90 degrees to the shank of the tool. This provides greater mechanical advantage when levering the nail out.

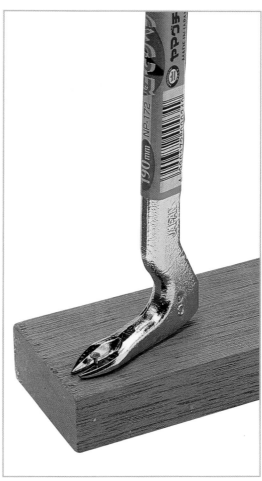

▲JAPANESE-STYLE CAT'S PAW By having its nail puller at the end of a bent arm, a Japanese-style cat's paw has more leverage than the equivalent Western-style tool.

TACK PULLERS This screwdriver-handled tool (shown second from bottom right in the photo above) is small but effective for yanking out little nails, brads, tacks, and escutcheon pins (little brass brads with rounded heads used for mounting plaques and hardware). A tack puller's wide, flat claws firmly grab the heads of small fasteners, but it doesn't work well on embedded fasteners. In such cases, use a small Japanese cat's paw or a fine-tipped pair of dikes (see "Diagonal Cutters" on p. 112). A thin scrap of wood placed under the tool protects the work as you lever the fastener out.

CHAPTER 7

Tools That Sand, Grind & Sharpen

Who would guess that you could do serious work with a bunch of little rocks? "Rocks" in this case refers to abrasive grit bonded to a sheet, belt, drum, disk, or wheel used for sanding or grinding wood, plastic, metal, and other materials. Whether used by hand or in a portable power tool, such as a random-orbit or benchtop disk sander, modern abrasive materials are an important part of many workshop and home-improvement projects. Although most sanding is done to smooth a rough surface in preparation for finishing or polishing—an automobile fender, or a walnut table or dresser—abrasive tools are also useful for flattening and shaping parts, as well as for sharpening and honing bladed tools.

▲ **PORTABLE POWER SANDERS** Belt, random-orbit, and orbital sanders are portable power tools that make short work of any wood-flattening or smoothing job.

PORTABLE POWER SANDERS

Although you can sand by hand, an electric- or air-powered sander really speeds up the process of sanding. Regardless of the type and size of the job, there's a sanding machine that will do the task. The three most useful, versatile machines for a home workshop are the belt sander, random-orbit sander, and orbital sander. Other, more specialized sanding tools—including profile sanders and detail sanders—handle shaped edges and moldings, details, and odd nooks and crannies. With the right accessories, power sanders can even perform nonsanding jobs, like sharpening tools or scraping off old paint.

Belt Sanders

A portable belt sander uses a loop of sandpaper spun between two wheels to make many difficult sanding jobs a lot easier, and it can be used on wood, metal, and some plastics. You can use a coarse-grit belt to remove old finish from an antique dresser or to trim the bottom of a door. A medium-grit belt will scour off heavy rust from a cast-iron stovetop or will sand nail and

screw heads flush. And a fine-grit belt will sand out scratches from a Corian® countertop or smooth a kitchen cabinet's worth of door panels.

Belt sanders come in a range of sizes to suit sanding jobs of any scale. Models that use 3-in. by 24-in. or 4-in. by 24-in. belts have enough motor power to make quick work of flattening a rough burl-wood tabletop or of smoothing house siding that's been puttied and repaired. Smaller 3-in. by 21-in. belt sanders don't have the power of big 4-in. by 24-in. units, but they're much lighter. In-line models have their motors centered over the belt, making them well balanced and easier to control.

Variable-speed models let the user adjust the aggressiveness of the sanding action to suit the job: faster for heavy stock removal, slower for delicate work or for sanding metal,

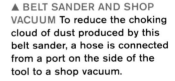

▲ BELT SANDER AND SHOP VACUUM To reduce the choking cloud of dust produced by this belt sander, a hose is connected from a port on the side of the tool to a shop vacuum.

◄ BELT SANDER This belt sander uses a large 4-in. by 24-in. belt ideal for quickly smoothing large surfaces, such as door panels, countertops, and even small floors.

Tool Helpers   BELT-SANDER STAND

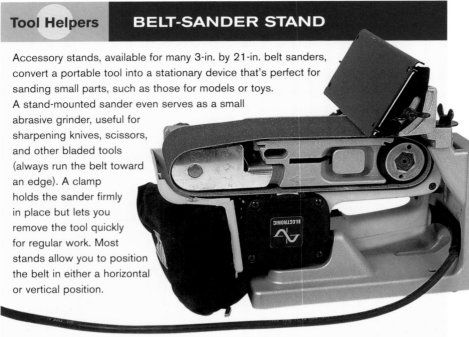

Accessory stands, available for many 3-in. by 21-in. belt sanders, convert a portable tool into a stationary device that's perfect for sanding small parts, such as those for models or toys. A stand-mounted sander even serves as a small abrasive grinder, useful for sharpening knives, scissors, and other bladed tools (always run the belt toward an edge). A clamp holds the sander firmly in place but lets you remove the tool quickly for regular work. Most stands allow you to position the belt in either a horizontal or vertical position.

Pro Tip

It's instinctive to push down on a power sander to get it to work more quickly. The problem is, it only slows the tool's motor down and can lead to deep scratches, gouges, or swirl marks (little semicircular scratches) in the workpiece. It's best to let the weight of the tool do the work and move the sander slowly and evenly to achieve the best results.

plastic, and painted surfaces. Since these machines churn out a steady stream of dust, all models incorporate a dust port, where a shop-vacuum hose or canvas dust-collecting bag can be attached.

Random-Orbit Sanders

Characterized by a spinning sandpaper disk and a wobbly circular motion, a random-orbit (RO) sander creates a hybrid sanding action that removes wood faster than an orbital sander but doesn't leave circular scratches like a disk sander can. ROs are great for sanding rough wood surfaces, quickly removing tool marks, and flattening surfaces. With the right abrasive disk or plastic abrasive pad (such as Scotch-Brite®), you can use

an RO for smoothing and polishing metal and plastic surfaces as well. Random-orbits are least effective when sanding parts with sharp edges, as the spinning disk can easily catch and tear.

Most random-orbits have either a 5-in.- or 6-in.-dia. pad that accepts either sticky-back or hook-and-loop sandpaper (see the Pro/Con box on the facing page). ROs that are 5 in. are lighter, more agile tools, while 6-in. ROs are better for conquering large surfaces more quickly. Models are configured in one of three distinct styles.

Palm ROs are compact sanders, with rounded, cylindrical bodies and a single-hand grip above the pad, providing excellent balance.

In-line random-orbit sanders sport a pair of handles—a rear, pistol-grip handle, with the tool's on/off trigger, and an overhanging front grip that's removable on some models (good for sanding corners).

Right-angle ROs look like small angle grinders and have powerful motors, which give them plenty of muscle for demanding jobs, like stripping thick, peeling paint and varnish.

Variable-speed ROs are more versatile than single-speed models. Lower disk speeds are better for sanding metals and

▶ RANDOM-ORBIT SANDER The top grip of this random-orbit sander makes it easy to hold in your palm. The tool's aggressive sanding action is great for all kinds of wood-smoothing chores.

◄ RANDOM-ORBIT SANDER AND POLISHING BONNET A right-angle random-orbit sander is normally fitted with a backing pad for sandpaper. But dial the variable speed down and fit a polishing bonnet, and the tool's ready for rubbing out a finish.

plastics and polishing clear finishes. With a special applicator pad or polishing bonnet (shown at right in the photo above), an RO will even apply wax, rub out scratches, and buff your car's paint to a sparkling shine (for best results, turn the tool's speed down to about half of maximum).

AIR-POWERED RANDOM-ORBIT SANDERS

If you want a powerful yet compact random-orbit sander and have an air compressor on hand, it's worth trying a pneumatic model. Commonly used in auto-body shops for smoothing repaired fenders and sanding primer and paint, air-powered ROs (known as jitterbugs because of their eccentric sanding action) sand aggressively, but they're lighter than most electric models. Their low profile and compact size let you sand in cramped spaces—inside cabinets and drawers or under cabinet kick spaces, for instance. While even a small portable (2-hp to 3-hp) compressor supplies enough air for short sanding sessions, you need a fairly large compressor (4 hp to 5 hp) to run an air RO continuously (see the air chart on p. 220).

Orbital Sanders

Spinning an eccentric weight mounted directly above its sandpaper-covered pad, an orbital sander creates a small circular scrubbing action that sands the work surface in all directions. Its sanding action is less aggressive than a random-orbit's, but its square or rectangular pad sands into right-angle corners—something a round pad

PRO CON

THE PADS ON all models of random-orbit sanders come ready to accept one of two kinds of sanding disks: stick-on paper disks coated with a pressure-sensitive adhesive (PSA) (at right in the photo below) or press-on disks with hook-and-loop fastening (at left in the photo). Both kinds also come in square sheets that fit the pads on many newer orbital sanders. If you can't decide which pad system to choose, buy a PSA-model sander because you can always retrofit the pad with a stick-on hook-and-loop adapter.

PSA SANDPAPER
Pros:
- less expensive than hook-and-loop
- more convenient for projects that require a lot of sanding and only a single grit

Cons:
- difficult to reuse

HOOK-AND-LOOP SANDPAPER
Pros:
- can be reused
- more convenient for projects that require frequent changes of paper grits

Cons:
- more expensive than PSA

▲ PNEUMATIC RANDOM-ORBIT SANDER Compressed air drives this pneumatic random-orbit sander, which is more compact than a comparable electric model but just as powerful.

▲ ORBITAL SANDERS Great for all kinds of sanding jobs, orbital sanders come in several styles, including the palm grip (left) and in-line models (right) shown here.

can't do. You can use coarse-grit sandpaper with an orbital, but most users find the tool is best suited to finer sanding duties, such as smoothing surfaces previously rough-sanded with a belt or random-orbit sander.

The size of an orbital sander's pad is based on the portion of the standard 9-in. by 11-in. sheet of sandpaper it uses. The most common sizes are ¼-sheet and ½-sheet models. A pair of spring-loaded paper clamps secures the ends of the sheet.

A ¼-sheet model, called a palm sander (shown at left in the photo above) is highly maneuverable and easy for most people to use single-handed. They're great for rounding sharp edges and smoothing smaller parts.

Considerably larger ½-sheet models resemble in-line random-orbit sanders, with a trigger handle and front grip for two-fisted control of the

tool's powerful sanding action. These big orbitals are best reserved for sanding large surfaces: wood room paneling, tabletops, and kitchen cabinets, for instance.

Detail Sanders

If a project requires sanding in snug spaces, such as between the slats of a louvered door or shutter, a detail sander is just the tool. The tips of the sander's small triangular pad easily reach into tight corners and between obstructions, making it indispensable for jobs such as smoothing stair treads around balusters. Extending beyond the front of the tool, the low-profile pad can sand down into slots and grooves and can smooth or remove finish from hard-to-reach areas.

Most detail sanders use a hook-and-loop backing pad to let you remove and rotate

▶ DETAIL SANDER WITH ACCESSORIES Although primarily made for sanding between obstructions and into corners and cramped areas, a detail sander fitted with an accessory can handle cutting or scraping jobs as well.

the triangular paper when the grit at the front tip wears out. Most sanders accept steel wool or plastic abrasive (Scotch-Brite) pads as well, handy for cleaning up rusty steel or iron parts or for polishing most metals.

Accessories for these tools make them even more useful. Outfitted with a scraper blade (shown at left in the bottom photo on the facing page), a detailer transforms into a small power scraper that removes old paint and window-sash putty or cleans the glass on freshly painted doors and window frames. A small semicircular blade accessory even allows you to do light cutting jobs, such as flush-trimming pegs and dowels or trimming the bottom ends of door casings and moldings when laying a new floor (see the flooring Tool Kit on pp. 30–31).

Disk Sanders

When you want to quickly remove rust or finish from metal surfaces or to shape and refine curved wood surfaces, a disk sander fits the bill. Using a coarse sandpaper disk attached to a hard-rubber or flexible-plastic backing disk, the tool scours stock quickly, yet with deft operation, you can sand down into crevices and hollows or can shape complex compound surfaces—say, for creating a sculpture. Coarse-grit disks, however, tend to leave deep, semicircular scratches, especially in wood, which require subsequent stages of sanding to remove.

Heavy-duty disk sanders, which resemble large angle grinders, sport big, 7-in.- to 9-in.-dia. disks that take some muscle to control. Pistol-grip models, shown in the bottom photo at right, have smaller, 5-in. to 6-in. disks and less sanding power, but they're more maneuverable and easier to handle. If you're not ready to buy a dedicated disk sander, try chucking an arbor-mounted sanding disk into an electric drill.

Cool Tools — FESTOOL® IN-LINE PROFILE SANDER

THE FESTOOL LS 130 EQ, an in-line profile sander, uses interchangeable pads that match a variety of profiles, both convex and concave, to sand dowels, rods, moldings, or shaped edges without distorting their shape. Pads snap into the tool's base and are able to be interchanged quickly. With a strong electric motor driving the pad rapidly back and forth, the sander smooths shapely wood, plastic, or metal surfaces more quickly and precisely than you could by hand. A special kit lets you create custom pads to fit odd or complex shapes; after covering the workpiece with stick-on sandpaper, the blank foam pad (shown at right in the photo) is formed by abrading it against the workpiece until the foam has worn down to fit the contour exactly.

◄ DISK SANDER The lightweight and pistol-grip handle of this disk sander makes it easy to maneuver when shaping wood or smoothing metal surfaces.

Benchtop Sanders

When a job is just too much for a portable electric sander, you'll appreciate the extra power of benchtop machines—an oscillating spindle, disk, belt, or combination sander. Although in the strictest sense they're stationary machines, benchtop sanders are

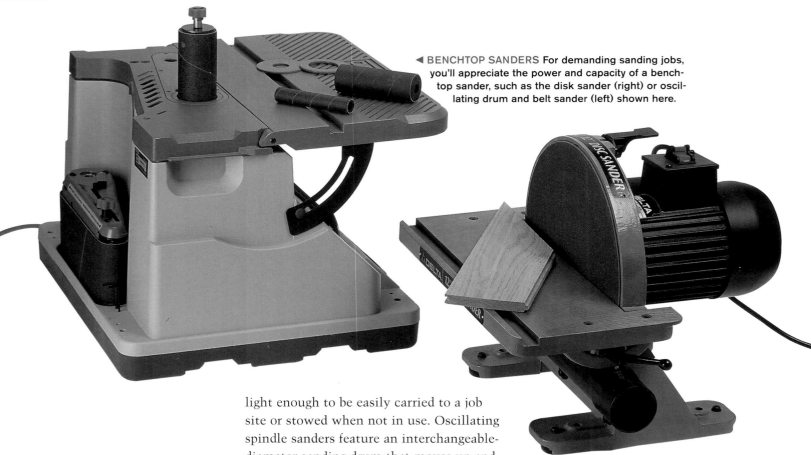

◄ BENCHTOP SANDERS For demanding sanding jobs, you'll appreciate the power and capacity of a benchtop sander, such as the disk sander (right) or oscillating drum and belt sander (left) shown here.

light enough to be easily carried to a job site or stowed when not in use. Oscillating spindle sanders feature an interchangeable-diameter sanding drum that moves up and down while spinning, great for shaping and smoothing curved wood parts and edges. Benchtop disk sanders handle smoothing and trimming jobs on flat or convex parts and joinery, while belt sanders can be used to sharpen edge tools and sand wood. More versatile still, combination models combine two different sanders in one benchtop machine, such as a belt and disk or an oscillating spindle and belt, as shown at left in the photo above.

GRINDERS AND BUFFERS

While the sanding process is good for flattening and smoothing most materials, some jobs need work that's either coarser or finer than what a sander is suited for. Grinding tools— including angle grinders, die grinders, rotary tools, and bench grinders—allow you to rough-shape, rough-cut, and abrade metal tools and components, as well as wood, plastics, and other materials. A power buffer—or a rotary tool

fitted with a buffing wheel or point—will polish all sorts of metal objects, from jewelry and silverware to sundials, and will rub out finishes and painted surfaces to boot.

Angle Grinders

If you've ever strolled into an auto-body repair or welding shop, you've probably seen portable grinders in use, slinging a steady stream of sparks and dust into the air. With their bonded Carborundum® grit abrasive disks, angle grinders make short work of many metal-munching and Bondo®-sanding chores.

Smaller models that use four to five ½-in. disks are light and much easier to handle than the heavy-duty 7-in. to 9-in. disk models used in body shops. Small angle grinders rapidly clean up pitted or heavily rusted iron surfaces and remove metal splatter and slag around welded parts.

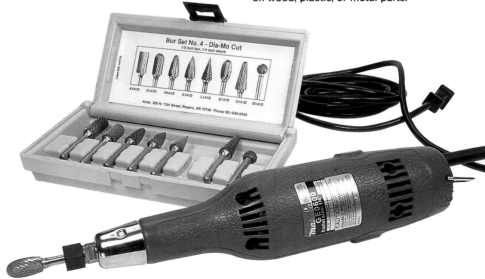

◄ **ANGLE GRINDER** A metal-worker's best friend, a small (4½-in.) angle grinder is compact yet powerful enough to grind away rust and weld splatter, ease sharp cut edges, or smooth rough surfaces.

There are also wheels, brushes, and accessory disks that turn small angle grinders into sanding, carving, cleaning, and cutting tools. Cutoff wheels are thin abrasive disks that allow an angle grinder to cut off rusted bolts or slice through padlock shanks. A wire wheel or cup brush (shown at top in the photo below) scrubs rust from iron or steel parts and creates a brushed finish on brass, copper, or aluminum hardware. Fitted with a coarse-abrasive flap wheel (shown above), an angle grinder is ready for rough wood shaping and sanding jobs, zipping through hardwoods like they're butter.

Die Grinders

Although they get their name from their use in grinding and shaping dies for fabrication of pressed or molded parts, die grinders are one of the most multitalented tools around. Fitted with a hefty ¼-in. collet (the part that holds the bit), a die grinder can be used with large burrs, bits, wheels, and a slew of other grinding, sanding, and polishing accessories. Unlike compact rotary tools, die grinders have motors powerful enough to drive larger (up to ½-in.-dia.) bits for demanding work, such as removing thick flashing from cast-metal parts or shaping or smoothing dense plastics or hardwoods. The slender design of the tool lets you work deep into areas that are hard or impossible to

▲ **ANGLE-GRINDER WHEEL AND BRUSH ASSORTMENT** You can use an angle grinder for more than just metal grinding by fitting it with a different wheel or brush. Here are several options (clockwise from front): flap sanding wheel, abrasive cutoff wheel, wire cup brush, and standard grinding wheel.

▼ **DIE GRINDER** Basically an oversize rotary tool, a die grinder fitted with a cutting burr or grinding point is a versatile tool for fine shaping and smoothing jobs on wood, plastic, or metal parts.

Pro Tip

Instrument and furniture makers know that the best tool around for creating recesses for small decorative inlays is not a router but a rotary tool fitted with an accessory router base. The whole setup is so light and maneuverable that you can rout the most delicate patterns with great precision.

reach using other power grinders or sanders. Fitted with a rotary rasp, diamond burr, or structured-tooth carbide burr, a die grinder handily roughs out carved figures and sculptures from wood and even soft stone. And small sanding drums and grinding points will sharpen or restore the cutting edges of tools with bent or curvaceous edges, such as adzes, inshaves, and other timber-framing and woodworking tools.

Rotary Tools

A rotary tool is just like a die grinder shrunk to about half the size. Although they have less powerful motors and will only accept small shank bits (less than ⅛ in.), rotary tools deserve a place in every home workshop. Their usefulness is due to two things. Rotary tools are so lightweight and compact that you can easily work freehand, reaching into cramped spaces. And by employing the full range of bits and accessories designed specifically for rotary tools (see the following section), you can tackle an endless stream of tasks and hobbies, from woodturning and tile setting to taxidermy.

Consisting of little more than a motor with a collet at the end of its arbor, rotary tools come in both corded and cordless models. Most feature a

variable-speed motor, allowing you to adjust the speed to suit the size of the bit and the nature of the cut (very important!). High speeds work well when carving wood or engraving bone or brass with tiny burrs, while slower speeds are better when running large buffs and wheels for cutting or polishing metals and plastics.

BITS, BURRS, AND WHEELS Part of what makes rotary tools such versatile performers is the plethora of bits, brushes, drums, wheels, buffs, and burrs available for them. A small sampling of these ⅛-in. shank bits (see photo below) reveals a few of the many tasks at which rotary tools excel: grinding bits for smoothing metal, ceramic, or glass parts; wire wheels for removing rust or cleaning metal wares; abrasive drums and disks for sanding and shaping wood and plastic; cutters and minirouter bits for routing recesses for inlays and hardware; felt and muslin wheels for polishing jewelry or hardware; structured-tooth carbide and serrated cutters for carving wood, wax, and plastics; small precision burrs and

▶ **ROTARY TOOL Easy to hold and control, a rotary tool's versatility is due to the wide assortment of grinding, cutting, polishing, and sanding wheels and burrs designed for it.**

diamond points for engraving initials or security identifications; and small abrasive cutoff wheels for severing bent nails and stripped screws.

Bench Grinders

A bench grinder has two, large-diameter grinding wheels driven directly by a powerful motor on a base that mounts either on a compact pedestal stand or on a small area of a workbench. Fitted with coarse and medium (or medium and fine) wheels, a bench grinder is de rigueur for maintaining all manner of shop tools (refurbishing the jaws of pliers, the tips of screwdrivers, crowbars, etc.) and for removing nicks and restoring the beveled edge of many cutting tools (chisels, knives, bolt cutters, etc.) in preparation for finer sharpening.

A grinder is also essential for most metalworking duties, such as removing burrs, rounding or shaping sharp edges and corners, cleaning up the ends of cut bolts or rods, and chamfering pipes and tubing.

Tool Helpers | **ROTARY TOOL BASES AND ACCESSORIES**

To put their various bits to the best use, tool manufacturers offer an interesting complement of bases and accessories that fit their rotary tools. These accessories transform simple rotary tools into specialized machines. Shown in the photo (clockwise from the right) are: a mini drill press, a cutout tool, a router, and flexible-shaft tools (see also "Rotary-Tool Chainsaw Sharpeners" on p. 190).

The drill press accessory works just like a full-size machine but lets you drill really tiny holes for delicate work—such as models and electronics projects—with great accuracy. The cutout tool uses a spiral cutter in a rotary tool for plunge cutting drywall and other soft materials. A router base holds the rotary tool vertically and controls the depth of cut, so you can create precise grooves, slots, and inlays. A flexible shaft transmits the rotary tool's power to a remote hand piece fitted with a standard collet. The slender hand piece is light and easy to maneuver, allowing you to do extrafine carving, engraving, and inlay work with superlative control and dexterity.

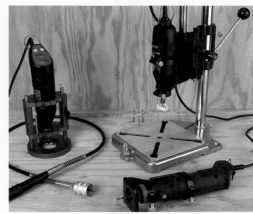

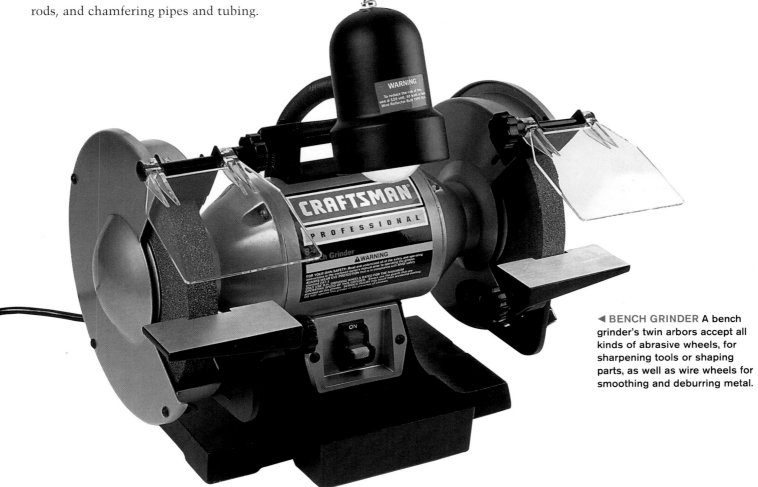

◄ BENCH GRINDER A bench grinder's twin arbors accept all kinds of abrasive wheels, for sharpening tools or shaping parts, as well as wire wheels for smoothing and deburring metal.

▶ GRINDING WHEELS
The color of a grinding wheel indicates the kind of grinding jobs and materials the wheel is best suited for.

Bench grinders are sized by the diameter of the wheels they use; 6-in. and 8-in. models are the most common and useful. Larger-diameter wheels are wider and more expensive but last longer and grind big parts much faster than smaller wheels. In addition to wheels of various grits, colors, and composition (see the chart below), you can also mount wire wheels or buffing wheels on a bench grinder for metal derusting, cleaning, and polishing jobs.

Power Buffers

Polishing is the last step in creating a lustrous and shiny finish on clear-coated or painted surfaces. You can hand-finish with polishing compounds and waxes, but a power buffer does the job more effectively and in a fraction of the time.

Power buffers (or power polishers) fitted with lamb's wool or synthetic polishing bonnets also make quick work of shining up metal and plastic, buffing up waxed furniture and floors, and rubbing out newly finished projects. (Keep in mind that most clear finishes—lacquer, varnish, etc.—take days or weeks to cure before they're ready for rubbing out.) By using rubbing compound or polish on a power buffer's bonnet, you can even restore your car's dull, weathered paint back to its original showroom shine.

Most of the newer power buffers have a variable-speed control, letting you dial in just the right speed to suit your activity (typically between 1,000 rpm and

GRINDING WHEEL CHARACTERISTICS

Color of Wheel	Material/Characteristics	Best Grinding Uses
Bluish gray	Carborundum	General use with all metals
White	Friable* aluminum oxide	Tool steel, particularly high-carbon steel
Pink	Friable* aluminum oxide	Tool steel, particularly high-carbon steel
Green	Silicon carbide	Tungsten carbide-cutting tools

*"Friable" means the wheel's grit particles break readily, revealing new cutting edges.

3,000 rpm): faster when polishing hard surfaces, slower when rubbing out thin or delicate finishes.

HAND-SHARPENING TOOLS

It's a basic fact: Sharp tools cut more safely and predictably—producing better results—than dull tools. There are about as many different methods and tools for sharpening and maintaining an edge as there are edged tools. Power grinding (see "Bench Grinders" on p. 183) provides the first step toward creating a properly shaped beveled or tapered edge and is necessary for restoring tools with nicked, rusted, or broken edges. Although there are powered machines designed for further refinement of coarse-ground edges (see "Sharpening Machine" on p. 188), hand-sharpening—using benchstones, abrasive plates, honing rods and devices, and other special tools—provides the most effective way to maintain cutting tools.

Tool Helpers   **DRESSING A GRINDING WHEEL**

To grind a straight edge, a grinding wheel must be well dressed, meaning the rotating face must be ground flat and true. A dressing tool removes any signs of irregular wear, or glazing (where the abrasive gets clogged), to restore the wheel's face. There are three kinds of tools commonly used to dress bench grinders: a star-wheel dresser, a diamond dresser, or a Carborundum stone.

The star-wheel dresser works the fastest (see photo) but takes some practice to control and is generally best on coarse- or medium-grit grinding wheels. A diamond dresser works slower than a star wheel, but it leaves a clean, flat surface; diamond dressers are relatively expensive and are best for dressing medium- and fine-grit (120-grit and finer) wheels. They're also useful for reshaping a wheel's face—say, for grinding the edge of a carving or turning tool into a special profile. Carborundum dressing sticks do a pretty good job on any grit wheel, and they're affordable and easy to use.

◀ POWER BUFFER For polishing a lacquered dining-room tabletop or rubbing out auto paint, nothing beats the speed and effectiveness of a power buffer fitted with a compound-charged polishing bonnet.

Pro Tip

Diamond, synthetic, and natural stones—all but Japanese waterstones—must be lubricated with honing oil before and during use. The light oil acts to flush out tiny metal and abrasive particles, which keeps a stone's surface from glazing over (the particles pack down into the stone's pores). You can buy special honing oil or economize by using light mineral oil, available from any drugstore.

Sharpening Stones

When you think of a really sharp blade, you probably think of a straight razor that's been honed on a leather strop. But the most practical way to maintain a sharp edge on most home-workshop cutting tools is with a benchstone. Made from both man-made and natural materials, stones come in different sizes, from small, 3-in.-long pocket stones, good for sharpening pocketknives, to large benchstones that are up to 10 in. long—big enough to handle the largest chisels and even jointers and portable planer knives. An 8-in.-long, 2½-in.-wide stone is probably the best choice for general use.

Buying a high-quality benchstone is not only likely to be expensive but confusing as well. Natural stones, synthetic stones, and waterstones are readily available (as are diamond stones, discussed on the facing page), but which is best for you? Each has advantages as well as shortcomings, so the following sections are designed to help you determine what will work best for your specific needs.

NATURAL STONES Natural benchstones are quarried, like granite and marble, from novaculite rock and sold as Washita, soft Arkansas, hard Arkansas, and black hard Arkansas stones, ranging in grade from coarse to fine, respectively. Because of inconsistency in quarried stone, older stones are highly coveted and are worth buying should you run across one in a junk shop or at a flea market. Although professionals and old-timers prefer them, it's more difficult and time-consuming to get a fine, honed edge on a natural stone than on a waterstone or diamond stone.

SYNTHETIC STONES Bonded together from both man-made and natural abrasive particles, such as silicon carbide and aluminum oxide, synthetic stones are generically referred to as oilstones because oil is the preferred lubricant (see the tip at left). Synthetics are the most economical stones, but because finer stones tend to glaze and don't perform as well as other stones, most woodworkers buy them only in coarse grits. The exceptions are man-made ceramic stones and honing rods, which come in very fine grits and are excellent for maintaining edges sharpened on other benchstones.

WATERSTONES While there are some expensive natural Japanese waterstones, most are made from synthetic bonded abrasives. A waterstone should be immersed in water in a plastic container between uses (see the photo in the Tool Kit on p. 25), which keeps it lubricated and produces a slurry (a mixture of water and abrasive paste from the stone) when the stone is used. This lets you really feel the cutting action when sharpening. Japanese stones

CHOOSING A SHARPENING STONE

Like sandpaper, the fineness or coarseness of stones is specified by their grit. The process of sharpening a cutting tool properly requires carefully abrading the tool's edge with finer and finer grits until it's smooth and very sharp. This requires subsequent passes on at least two or three stones. An economical way to get the grits you need is to buy either a two-sided man-made stone or a diamond honing plate that combines two different grits, one on each side. Another option is to buy a three-sided sharpener, a tool that holds three stones—coarse, medium, and fine, as shown here.

▲ FOUR BENCHSTONES Each of these four benchstones uses a different kind of grit to sharpen steel blades. They are (from left to right): diamond stone, Japanese waterstone, two-sided synthetic stone, and natural Arkansas stone.

cut quickly, but unfortunately they're quite soft and wear down faster than other stones. They must be flattened often (using a circular rubbing motion on a coarse diamond stone or abrasive plate) to maintain their performance.

DIAMOND STONES AND HONES Diamond sharpening stones quickly sharpen and hone cutting tools, thanks to the incredible hardness of their diamond grit. The stones have thousands of diamonds, in the form of tiny flakes, bonded to a metal (or metal and plastic) surface. Just like sandpaper, the bigger the diamond grit, the coarser the abrasive action. Diamond grits range from coarse (220 grit), handy for flattening and deglazing other stones, to extrafine (1,200 grit), good for putting a surgical edge on fine knives and chisels. Diamond stones come in dozens of shapes and sizes, from small pocket stones and large, two-sided benchstones to honing rods and tapered gouge hones and files.

Cool Tools | **ANGLE JIGS AND HONING GUIDES**

ANGLE JIGS AND HONING GUIDES are ingenious tools that help you maintain a consistent angle as you hone a blade or chisel on a benchstone or abrasive plate, which is crucial to achieve a keen edge. The five-sided angle jig (see the photo at left) positions the blade in the honing guide according to its degree of edge bevel (bevels typically are between 15° and 35°). With the honing guide (see the photo below) clamped onto the blade, the jig rolls on (or aside) the stone, thus keeping the blade at a fixed angle as it's honed and making the sharpening process nearly mistake proof.

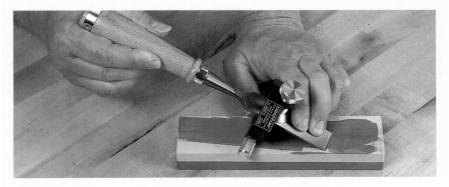

Pro Tip

When you want to buy a high-quality diamond sharpening stone or honing rod, make sure its precious abrasive grit is monocrystalline (check the product literature). Although similar-looking and less expensive, stones and hones with polycrystalline grit wear out more readily, at which point they're spent and must be replaced.

▼DIAMOND STONES AND HONES Diamonds are, indeed, a sharp tool's best friend. Each of the benchstones, pocket stones, rods, and hones shown here has a surface covered with diamond grit, designed to abrade and sharpen steel or carbide blades and cutting edges with speed and efficiency.

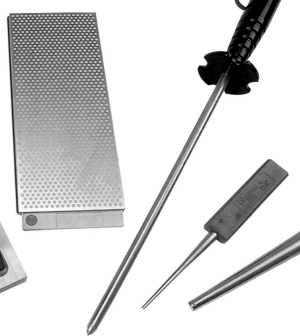

Cool Tools   SHARPENING MACHINE

A SHARPENING MACHINE provides a powerful alternative to sharpening tools by hand. It's designed solely for sharpening steel-edged tools, such as chisels, knives, and plane and spokeshave blades. Fitted with a sliding tool rest, a sharpening machine can even handle planer and jointer knives. This benchtop machine combines a white aluminum-oxide grinding wheel with a horizontally mounted, slow-rotating waterstone.

The machine's 2-in.-wide, 120-grit grinding wheel first removes nicks and restores the bevel on a tool's edge. Then, the 8-in.-dia., 1,000-grit waterstone hones the edge to final sharpness. As the waterstone rotates slowly, the plastic tub mounted above it drips water, keeping the stone properly lubricated. An adjustable tool rest supports the tool or blade at a consistent angle to the waterstone during honing. Although the machine costs as much as a good circular saw, it could save you a lot of time if you have a workshop full of edge tools that need regular sharpening.

Although they're considerably more expensive, diamond stones abrade tool steels more quickly than other benchstones. And their grit is hard enough to sharpen solid carbide cutters and carbide-tip router bits. Because of their aggressive cutting action, diamond stones are especially good for lapping (flattening and polishing the back side of a tool's blade) plane and chisel blades. Also, diamond hones don't clog readily and don't need flattening like natural and synthetic benchstones.

Honing Devices

A sharpening steel or diamond honing rod is good for touching up knife blades between sharpenings. But if you lack the skill to use one properly, you can still get good results with a honing device. These tools use a pair of carbide inserts or ceramic rods or disks fitted into a slotted handle or base. Draw the tapered edge of a knife through the slot a few times and the insert/rod/disk abrades or scrapes the tip, honing it to sharpness in seconds.

Honing devices can damage or ruin top-quality shears as well as the brittle edges of Japanese cutlery or laminated steel blades. Send your good scissors and shears out for professional sharpening, and hone high-carbon blades only with diamond or ceramic hones and benchstones.

▲HONING DEVICES To touch up the edge of a kitchen knife or a pair of scissors, all it takes is a few swipes past the ceramic or carbide inserts of a honing device.

◄SHARPENING AN AX WITH A FILE A flat mill file makes a good tool for touching up the edge of an ax or hatchet, taking out nicks and restoring the blade's sharpness.

Some tools, such as the handheld device shown at left in the top photo above, include a separate sharpening slot for honing scissors and many kinds of shears with nonserrated edges (see pp.109–111). Although results are good with most knives and scissors (see the tip at right), honing devices eventually blunt the edges they're used on, and the tools must be reshaped using benchstones or abrasives.

Files

Although stones are the most commonly used sharpening tools, files also have their role in maintaining sharp edges on axes, handsaws, chainsaws, and other edge tools. A few strokes with an 8-in. flat mill file quickly cleans up and restores an ax, hatchet, or splitting maul blade.

►DRILL BIT SHARP-
ENER Keeping drill bits
sharp is a task made
simpler with the use of a drill-
bit sharpener. This motorized tool
holds the bit in a special chuck
that guides it past a diamond-
abrasive covered drum, thus
restoring a twist drill's tip to pris-
tine condition.

ening drill bits, for example: It takes lots of practice and a steady hand to make a dull bit sharp again using conventional tools. But a special drill-bit sharpener can do it perfectly every time. The same is true for rotary-tool chainsaw sharpeners and jointing and burnishing tools used with scrapers.

Drill-Bit Sharpeners

A sharp drill bit zips through hardwoods, plastics, and even mild steel with ease, while a dull bit takes lots of pressure to burn its way through even soft materials. Since most of us don't have the skills to sharpen drill bits freehand, a drill-sharpening machine offers the only practical way to resharpen twist and masonry bits.

The complicated sharpening process is considerably simplified by the machine's design and jigging: The bit is first aligned and clamped into a special multijawed bit holder (chuck) and then inserted into a series of two tubes in the body of the machine. The tubes align the bit for sharpening and shaping the point, which is achieved on a motorized, diamond-abrasive wheel inside. A clever system of complimentary convex and concave shapes on the end of the chuck and tubes moves the bit in and out to sharpen the drill's cutting point perfectly. The ease of the process lets you touch up your bits often (after every few holes, if you're drilling hard metal) to keep them performing well job after job.

Rotary-Tool Chainsaw Sharpeners

Among its many other talents, a rotary tool becomes a handy chainsaw sharpener when fitted with a special jig and grinding stone. The jig screws on in place of the tool's end cap and guides the position and angle of

Two kinds of files are needed to sharpen a handsaw: a flat, 8-in.-long mill file to joint the sawteeth (file them all to the same level so they'll be in line and cut evenly) and a triangular file to actually sharpen the teeth. Depending on the size of the saw's teeth, this file should be 4 in. to 7 in. long and of a regular, slim, or extraslim profile. (Sharpening a handsaw is a fairly complicated process; for a full account, refer to Leonard Lee's excellent book, *The Complete Guide to Sharpening* [Taunton Press, 1995].)

Files have also traditionally been used for sharpening chainsaw teeth. A round file, sized as specified in your saw's owner manual, reshapes and sharpens each cutting tooth; a small flat file might also be needed to resize and shape depth-gauge teeth. (If you're looking for a faster chainsaw sharpener, check out the rotary-tool jig discussed below).

SPECIALIZED SHARPENERS

Bench grinders, stones, and files are great for many sharpening duties, but sometimes, specialized tools are called for to get the job done more efficiently. Take sharp-

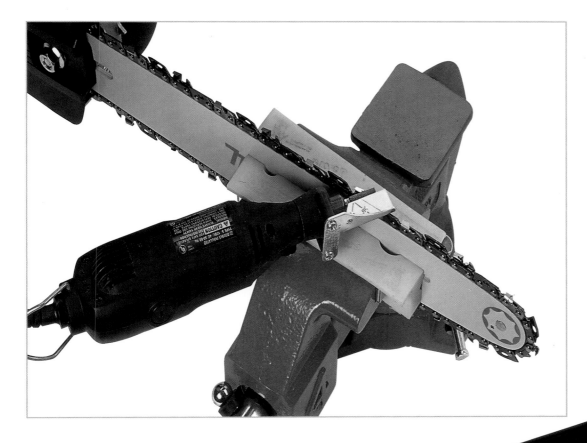

◄ CHAINSAW-BLADE SHARPENER By fitting it with a special jig and cylindrical grinding point, you can use anordinary rotary tool as a motorized chainsaw-blade sharpener.

the tool relative to the chainsaw blade. The small cylindrical stone grinds away at the semicircular face of each cutting tooth, restoring its shape and sharpness.

Scraper Jointing and Burnishing Tools

A scraper blade isn't sharpened like other cutting tools—its edge usually isn't honed like a chisel or knife. Instead, the edge is first jointed (filed straight and flat) and then burnished (rolled by rubbing with a hard rod) to form a hooked edge.

The easiest way to sharpen a cabinet scraper or the blade for a scraper plane (see p. 65) is to joint it with a flat mill file held in a special jig tool (shown in top photo at right) that keeps the file square (or, for scraper plane blades, at 45 degrees) relative to the edge of the blade.

To burnish the blade accurately, use a burnishing tool (shown at bottom in the photo at right), which has a small burnish-ing rod mounted in a jig that allows you to set the burnishing angle to form a perfect, hooked cutting edge: Use a 5-degree hook for general wood scraping and a 10-degree to 15-degree hook for scraping off old paint and varnish.

▲SCRAPER JOINTING AND BUR-NISHING TOOLS Sharpening a cabinet scraper blade is a job made a lot simpler with these two handy tools. The jointing tool (top) uses a file to redress the edge of the blade, while the burnisher (bot-tom) creates a perfectly hooked edge ready for scraping.

CHAPTER 8

Tools That Measure & Mark

Wouldn't it be great if we could simply "will" our saws, drills, and planes to make all the parts for our projects, with no planning required? Nice as that would be, reality dictates that every part must be carefully measured and marked if it's going to fit. Hence, we depend on tools such as tape measures, squares, levels, calipers, and marking gauges. Electrical testers are a different kind of measuring tool, but they're essential for many wiring and electronics jobs.

▲MEASURING TOOLS Accurate measuring tools are part of any quality job, from building furniture or a balsa-wood airplane to putting up a fence or a henhouse.

MEASURING TOOLS

When you consider that the world has seen innumerable measurement standards come and go over the centuries, it's remarkable that only two standards are in primary use today: the English (imperial) system of inches, feet, and yards (defined in 1845) and the metric system of millimeters, centimeters, and meters (developed in France in the 1790s). Hence, all the various tools that help us measure parts for the projects we build—rulers, tape measures, folding rules, measuring calipers, etc.—bear scales and divisions based on one or both of these two systems.

Rules

Whether it's short enough to fit in your pocket or long enough to measure the height of a wall, a rule is a dual-purpose tool. You can use a rule either to measure the length of a part or as a straightedge for drawing pencil lines or guiding razor or knife cuts. Although you may find rules made of wood, plastic, and bamboo, with some specialized models for drafting, model building, or accurate layout work (see the bottom photo on p. 199), the most useful rules for general home and shop work are made of steel, with markings etched on one or both sides in fractional or metric subdivisions.

It's handy to have rules of several lengths on hand: A 6-in. (15cm) pocket rule is short enough to carry around and handy for measuring small parts; a 12-in. (30cm) foot rule or 18-in. (45cm) cabinetmaker's rule fits in a toolbox and will serve many layout and measuring tasks; a 36-in. yard-stick (or meter stick) serves larger, longer work.

FOLDING RULES Some people prefer using a rigid rule rather than a flexible tape measure, but a long rule won't fit into confined spaces (it's also difficult to fit a yard-stick in your back pocket). A folding rule is easy to carry around and yet takes only a second to expand into a tool that will measure parts 12 in., 18 in., or even 24 in. long. Some folding rules have special features, including scales for measuring scale drawings and plans, built-in protractors for determining angles, or slide-out end calipers for checking the thickness of boards and the dimensions of small parts.

For even longer measurements, the multisection folding extension rule (or zigzag rule) has six sections that pivot at the ends to fold up into a pocket-size 8 in. or unfold into a rigid 6-ft. rule (shown in the top photo on p. 194). One advantage to this tool's adjustable length is that you fold out only as much as you need for the measurement at hand: The same rule can check the distance between walls inside a closet or can fit into a narrow hall-way to check a 3-ft.-wide doorjamb. The

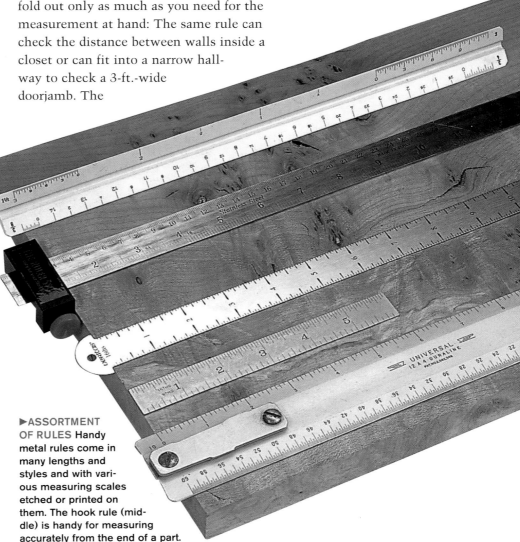

►ASSORTMENT OF RULES Handy metal rules come in many lengths and styles and with various measuring scales etched or printed on them. The hook rule (middle) is handy for measuring accurately from the end of a part.

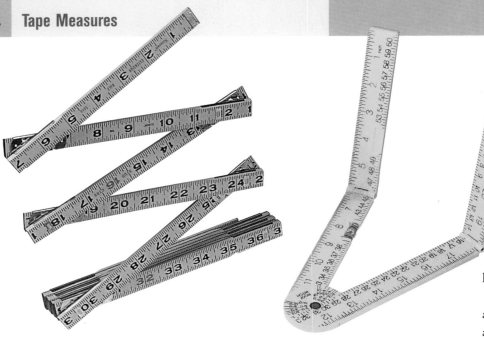

▲FOLDING RULES Essentially rigid rules that collapse to fit into an apron pocket (shown here: the traditional zigzag, left, and modern RascalRule®, right), has a built in protractor.

tool's 6-in.-long caliper, which slides out of the end of the first section, can be used to measure the depth of holes and grooves or the thickness of parts.

Tape Measures

Most construction and household renovation projects require a longer and more convenient form of measurement than a ruler or yardstick can provide. The handy, metal-cased pocket tape was first developed in the 1880s and is still the most practical tool for longer measurements. While early tape measures had narrow, flimsy tapes (blades), and small round cases, modern

tapes have strong, wide, plastic-coated metal blades and D-shaped cases, which prevent the tool from flopping over when it's set down. Other common features on a modern tape measure include a blade-locking button, a belt hook, and a sliding end hook. The latter allows accurate readings both inside (pushing the end of the blade up against a wall, for instance) and outside (slipping the hook over the end of a board).

Tape measures come big and small, long and short, with various types of imperial and/or metric scales printed on them (see "Choosing the Right Tape-Measure Scale" on the facing page). A 25-ft. model is long enough for most carpentry jobs or home-remodeling/improvement projects. Most users prefer models with a wide, 1-in. blade because you can extend it 8 ft. to 10 ft. or more without having to support the blade midspan. Since big tapes have strong, speedy retraction springs, models with built-in shock-absorbing blade bumpers help prevent damage to the end hook, ensuring the tape stays accurate.

Small tapes, with 10-ft.- to 12-ft.-long ½-in.-wide blades are useful for daily measuring tasks around the house or home workshop because they're compact and easily fit into a pocket.

WINDUP TAPES The first tape measures, developed in the mid-1800s, were large, leather-cased tapes for carpenters and other tradesmen. These had fragile fabric blades that the user had to retract with a windup crank on the side of the case. Flash forward 150 years, and this basic design hasn't changed, it's just been re-created with better materials.

Modern wind-up tapes have strong, nonstretching fiberglass or stainless-steel blades and tough metal or impact-resistant plastic cases or reels. Fitted with blades 50 ft. long, 100 ft. long, or longer, windup

Tool Helpers   MAGNETIC TAPE HOLSTERS

If you're tired of yanking your tape measure from your belt or apron pouch, a magnetic tape holster could be your new best friend. Good for self-retracting tape measures from 16 ft. to 35 ft. in length, one half of this magnetic device mounts to the tape case, replacing the belt clip. The other half is a holster that clips to your waistband or a tool belt. The magnet holds the tape measure firmly in the holder but allows it to snap off easily when needed.

◀WINDUP TAPE A windup tape measure has the length necessary for measuring large rooms, building foundations, and other large objects.

tapes are best for large-scale projects—such as laying out the foundation for a new deck, a fenced flowerbed, or a bedroom addition—or for measuring big objects, like boats, trailers, etc. For faster retraction, look for a tape with a geared windup crank mechanism: A 3:1 gear drive turns its reel three times for each time you turn the crank once.

Sonic and Electronic Measuring Tools

Sonic range finders and electronic tape measures are packed with modern technology, and they're worth reaching for when a standard tape measure just won't do.

SONIC RANGE FINDERS Employing a narrowly focused ultrasonic beam, a sonic range finder (shown at left in the photo on p.196) is a small, handheld device that bounces sound to measure the distance between surfaces—ideally large, smooth surfaces, such as walls, ceilings, and floors. A great tool for quickly checking the dimensions of a room (realtors love them), most models can read distances from 2 ft. to 60 ft. They also have built-in functions to add, subtract, and multiply measurements or calculate the area and volume of a room, cabinet, large crate, etc.

Capable of impressive accuracy of up to ¼ in. (±0.5 percent of the distance measured), sonic range finders are also easily foiled; aiming them at surfaces that are angled, soft, or convoluted (such as window

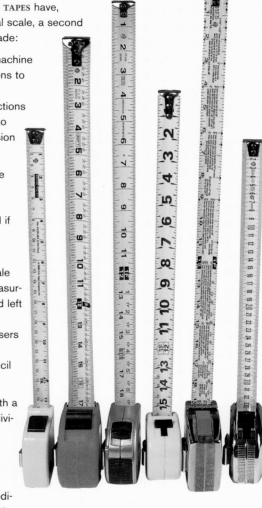

Which One? **CHOOSING THE RIGHT TAPE-MEASURE SCALE**

The majority of tape measures have imperial scales marked with ¹⁄₁₆-in. subdivisions. They also usually have red-boxed numerals at 16-in. intervals to make laying out the spacing of wall studs or ceiling joists easier. However, there are other tape measures that feature different scales. Here are a few that you may find useful, depending on the kind of work you want to do.

DECIMAL-SCALE/FRACTION-SCALE TAPES have, in addition to a standard fractional scale, a second scale on the other edge of the blade:
- the decimal scale is useful for machine work, or when converting fractions to decimal measures
- a fraction scale with marked fractions (⅛ in., ¼ in., ⅝ in., etc.) is easier to read than one with only subdivision markings

METRIC TAPES have a metric scale with only meter, centimeter, and millimeter subdivisions. They are:
- less cluttered and easier to read if you work primarily in the metric system

RIGHT-READING TAPES have a scale that reads right side up when measuring right to left (regular tapes read left to right). They are:
- easier to handle by right-hand users than standard tapes
- more convenient for making pencil markings with the right hand

BLINDMAN'S TAPES are printed with a series of large numbers and subdivisions, which are:
- easy to read in poor light
- good for persons with impaired vision
- marked by diamond-shaped subdivisions that taper for better marking accuracy

CENTER-FINDING TAPES have different scales on each edge. The upper one measures the span and the lower scale shows half the span. They're great for:
- finding the center point of panels, circles, polygons, etc.
- dividing parts in half

HANDICAPPED TAPES have dozens of the most common measurement regulations and codes specified by the Americans with Disabilities Act printed on the blade. They're good for:
- correctly sizing wheelchair ramps and installing grab bars
- construction projects for disabled family members

▶ELECTRONIC MEASURING DEVICES Both the laser-guided sonic measure (left) and electronic tape measure (right) use modern electronics to measure distances quickly and accurately.

Pro Tip

Y ou can measure a dis-
tance up to twice as
long as the length of a rule
or tape measure by making
a small mark at the middle,
measuring in both direc-
tions, and then adding the
measurements together.
To expand the usefulness of
a sonic range finder, use it
from the center of a room,
which effectively doubles
its range.

drapery or a cottage-cheese ceiling) or that are too small usually results in incorrect readings. To prevent these problems and to aid accuracy, look for a model that has a built-in targeting laser, which helps you see exactly where the ultrasonic beam is aimed.

ELECTRONIC TAPE MEASURES An elec-
tronic tape measure (shown at right in the photo above), looks like a regular tape measure, but it has a small, battery-powered electronic brain that reads a special bar code from its metal tape, then displays the measured distance on a liquid crystal display (LCD) screen atop the case. You can set it to show the distance between the end of the tape and the front or back edge of the case for easy inside measurements. There's also a memory button that holds measurements, making it easier to work in dark or tight spaces. Like a sonic range finder, an electronic tape measure easily displays (or converts) readings in fractional, decimal, or metric measures.

Calipers

Regardless of their style, size, and shape, all calipers perform the same kind of job: they measure, check, transfer, or compare the dimensions of raw materials and parts (the thickness of plywood, the length of a bolt), as well as the size of the slots, grooves, and holes that we make in (or for) those parts and materials. This section

includes the three kinds of measuring calipers: inside and outside legged calipers and proportional calipers.

MEASURING CALIPERS

Measuring calipers are extreme-ly handy tools because they're simple to use and produce an accurate measurement that you read directly from a scale or display on the caliper. Need to know the diameter or depth of a hole or the length of the dowel that's supposed to plug it? A caliper is just what you need. Most measuring calipers have three ways of checking a measurement: a pair of outside-measuring jaws for part lengths and thick-nesses, a pair of inside-measuring jaws for slot width or hole diameter, and a depth rod for the depth of holes and grooves.

Modern measuring calipers typically come in 4-in. models and the more popular 6-in. sizes and are made from either stain-less steel or fiber-reinforced plastic. Plastic calipers may look like toys, but they're lighter than steel models and usually just as accurate.

The three most common kinds of mea-suring calipers are vernier, dial, and digital. A vernier caliper (named after the French man who invented it) has dual scales on its beam that show both imperial and metric measurements simultaneously. Inches, tenths of an inch, and hundredths of an inch (along with centimeters and milli-meters) are read directly from the scales. Thousandths of an inch (and micrometers) are read (interpreted is a better word) from a special vernier scale and added to the larger measurement (if any) shown on the beam.

Dial calipers have beams just like verniers, but they usually have a single scale. Thousandths of an inch (or micrometers) are shown on a dial similar to a watch face, which is easier and quicker to read than a vernier scale. Although most imperial dial

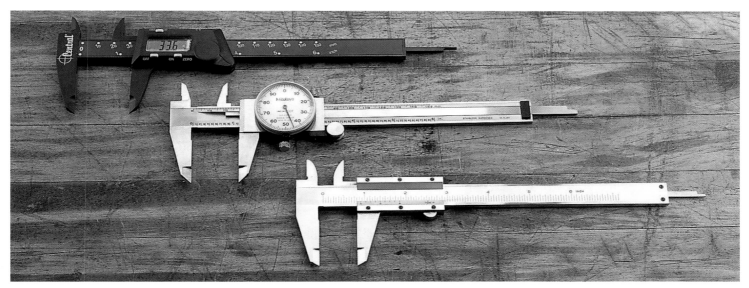

▲DIGITAL, DIAL, AND VERNIER MEASURING CALIPERS Precision measurement of parts calls for a pair of measuring calipers. Shown here are (top to bottom): digital, dial, and vernier models.

calipers read decimal inches (e.g., 2.125 in.), you can buy models that show fractional measurements (e.g., 2⅛ in.), with precision down to ¹⁄₆₄ in.—which is handier for most woodworking and craft projects.

Digital calipers have no scales printed on them. Turn the battery-powered caliper on and take a measurement; it displays the dimensions on a small LCD screen. Push a button and most models instantly show or convert between imperial (decimal) and metric measurements. Another button allows some digitals to be zeroed at any point, which is handy when you want to measure only how much bigger or smaller one part is than another.

LEGGED CALIPERS There are times when you want to check the thickness of a part or compare the size of two parts, and you don't really need to know their dimension. For example, if you want to make a new foot for a blanket chest that's the same as the old one, who cares if they're 3³¹⁄₃₂ in. thick, as long as they both end up the same size. Legged calipers (named for their shape, which resembles a person's legs) are simple tools that check and compare parts

in just that way. (Some 19th-century "dancing master" calipers were actually made to resemble feminine legs; shown in the photo below.)

Legged calipers come in two basic types: Outside calipers read a part's outside dimensions, while inside calipers read the distance between parts or the span of a hole or slot (dividers, close cousins to legged calipers, are discussed on p. 202). A caliper's size corresponds to its maxi-

(dividers, close cousins to legged calipers, are discussed on p. 202).

Pro Tip

Accuracy isn't the same for all measuring calipers, especially digital models. If you're doing precise work, such as machining metal parts, make sure you check the accuracy of a tool before you buy it. Inexpensive digitals may have an accuracy of only ±0.004 in., while high-quality models are precise to ±0.0005 in.

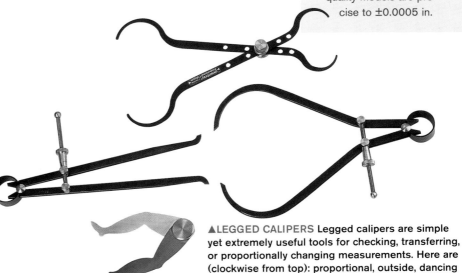

▲LEGGED CALIPERS Legged calipers are simple yet extremely useful tools for checking, transferring, or proportionally changing measurements. Here are (clockwise from top): proportional, outside, dancing (inside & outside) and inside calipers.

mum opening. A 4-in. pair is good for small jobs like model making. The 8-in. size is well suited to general-purpose uses, while a 12-in. pair is for large work. Lathe turners find legged calipers of all sizes useful for both wood and metal turning jobs: from sizing beads on a spindle or checking the wall thickness of a large bowl to sizing an aluminum flange or the opening on a steel socket. Because of their shape and size, legged calipers can take readings in deeper spaces or on larger, bulkier objects than measuring calipers.

Calipers are simple in terms of design, with a strong spring and a threaded rod and nut that adjust the position of the legs. A useful feature to look for in modern calipers is a speed nut, which slides on the threaded shaft when gross adjustments are needed, saving the time it takes to spin the nut several times around.

Proportional Calipers

Originally designed for sculptors and woodturners, proportional calipers (shown in the bottom photo on p.197) are very handy for any crafter or model maker who wants to transform the size of parts from one scale to another. Resembling two pairs of legged calipers joined in the middle, proportional calipers hinge on a pivot screw, which threads into one of five or more pairs of holes. You set the proportion ratio (1:1.5, 1:2, 1:3, 1:4, etc.) by moving the pivot screw in a different pair of holes. Measure something with the tool's smaller jaws (which work for inside or outside measurements) and the larger jaws spread to a proportionally larger size.

Not only can you use proportional calipers to read and compare physical parts, you can also use them to transform scale drawings to full-size parts. For example, to show the actual size of doors and windows on a drawing of a dollhouse drawn in ¼ in. = 1 in., set the calipers at a 1:4 ratio.

MARKING AND LAYOUT TOOLS

Once you know how long a line or how big a circle you want, you need tools to lay it out. Whether you're doing rough carpentry work or fine woodworking (and regardless of whether you're working with wood, metal, or plastic), marking tools—which include straightedges, layout and dividing rules, awls and striking knives, marking and contour gauges, and dividers—are ready to help you get the job done.

Straightedges

Basically a long rule with or without scale divisions, a straightedge is not only useful for marking straight lines but also for drawing long lines on a pattern for a project, as

▲MARKING AND LAYOUT TOOLS Make all your layouts accurate by choosing the right tools for the job. Shown here are: layout rule, chalkline, marking gauge, awl, and straightedge.

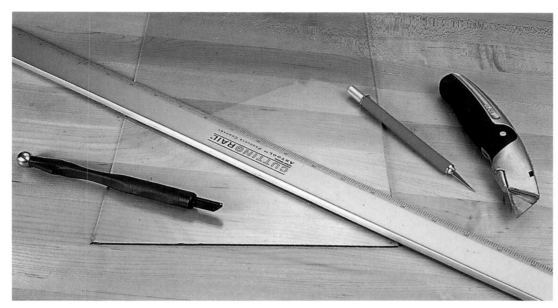

▲STRAIGHTEDGE Whether you want to draw a straight pencil line or make a cut with a utility knife or glass cutter, a straightedge can provide a steady, straight guide.

well as for checking the flatness of edges and surfaces. It's also useful for guiding a utility knife, glass cutter, single-edge razor blade, or other cutting tool when making a straight cut.

While you can use a regular rule or yardstick for these purposes, a well-made aluminum or steel straightedge has a straighter, more precisely formed edge that's often beveled on one side to provide clearance for a short cutter or mechanical pencil to glide along without getting hung up. Some straightedges have a raised lip on the other edge to prevent sharp cutting tools from slipping and causing serious injury. The best straightedges for general use have a thin cork or rubber strip on the underside, which prevents the tool from sliding around during use—especially important when working on slippery surfaces, like plastic laminate or glass.

Layout and Dividing Rules

Marking the length of a part with a standard rule or tape measure is an exercise in eye-hand coordination. You must line up your pencil or marking knife with the right scale line, and the more precision a job requires, the harder it is to line up the marker with those fine scale subdivisions. Layout and dividing rules make this task a lot easier by providing marking holes at exact positions along a scale. For example, some layout rules have holes and narrow slots machined at $\frac{1}{16}$-in., $\frac{1}{32}$-in., and $\frac{1}{64}$-in. intervals. Each slot is precisely sized to fit the lead of a 0.5mm mechanical pencil.

Layout rules with a sliding end stop (shown at left and front center in the photo at right) are excellent for marking parallel or perpendicular to the edge of a part—say, to lay out joinery or an end cut.

A dividing rule (shown at rear center in the photo at right) is used to divide a part into two, three, four, five, . . ., up to 10 equal divisions—handy, for example, if you need to cut cardboard or wood into

▲LAYOUT RULES Rather than just providing a scale to read measurements, layout rules have holes or slots for pencil points to make marking distances and drawing layout lines easier.

strips of equal width. The tool's swiveling pins secure it against the edges of the workpiece, as you mark the divisions through a series of holes clearly labeled along the length of the rule.

Scratch Awls and Marking Knives

The wide line made by the thick lead of a carpenter's pencil is fine for marking cuts that aren't crucial for a perfect fit, but when you want to do your most exacting work—say, to make a picture frame with perfectly mitered corners or cut leather strips to precise width for a woven belt—wide pencil lines won't do. Scratch awls and marking knives create fine lines with great precision.

A scratch awl will score most hard materials and leave a clean line on metals and plastics; lines scored across wood grain are slightly fuzzy but still easy to see, especially on construction lumber and plywood. An awl's sharp point is also good for marking center points for holes, piercing and enlarging holes in flexible materials like leather and rubber, and even for making starter holes in softwoods for tiny screws.

A marking knife is exclusively for marking wood or scoring and slicing thin cardboard and paper. Also known as a striking knife, this tool has a beveled edge with a flat side that rides against a rule or the blade of a square. It makes a fine, clean line that's hard to see, but it may be as precisely located as your steady hand and eye for fine detail allows.

▲AWL AND STRIKING KNIFE When wide pencil lines aren't accurate enough, use an awl (right) or striking knife (left) to mark your work.

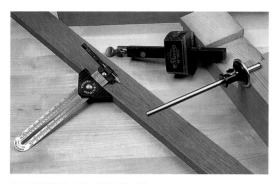

▲MARKING GAUGES Marking gauges come in many styles, including (clockwise from left): pencil, traditional, and modern. The latter marks via a round cutting wheel instead of a scratch pin.

Marking Gauges

If you've ever cut any wood joinery for hand-built cabinets orfurniture, it's likely you're familiar with a marking gauge. The traditional version of this tool (shown at rear center in the photo above) used a small steel pin to scratch a line parallel to, and at a fixed distance from, an edge, marking the amount of material that needed to be trimmed. It was also used to layout wood-to-wood joints, such as mortise-and-tenons joints.

Modern marking gauges (shown at right in the photo above) use a round steel cutter, which cuts rather than scratches, resulting in a cleaner line. Another kind of modern marking gauge (shown at left in the photo above) creates pencil marks rather than scratches and has a built-in scale; other marking gauges must be set with a rule. Although primarily used in carpentry, a pencil marking gauge is also good for many day-to-day layout chores, such as marking a series of holes equidistant from an edge, sizing strips to be cut from leather or rubber, or drawing layout lines on cardboard patterns and parts for small projects.

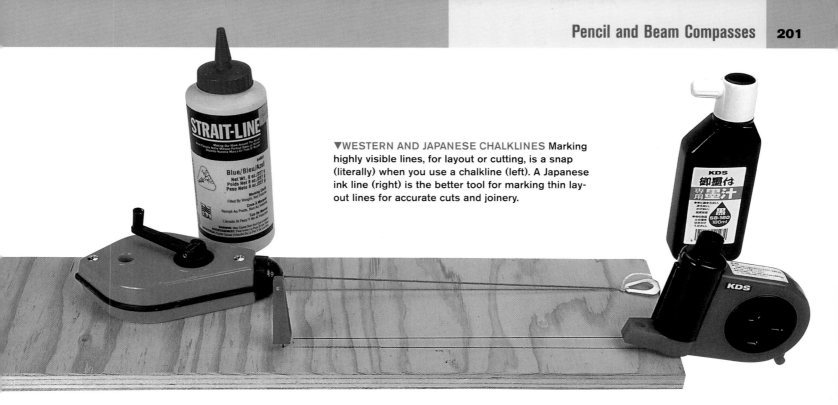

▼WESTERN AND JAPANESE CHALKLINES Marking highly visible lines, for layout or cutting, is a snap (literally) when you use a chalkline (left). A Japanese ink line (right) is the better tool for marking thin layout lines for accurate cuts and joinery.

Chalkline Reels

A long straightedge is great for drawing a 3-ft. to 4-ft. line on your work. But what if you want to draw a straight line 16 ft. long? A chalkline (shown at left in the photo above) is the answer. The tool is basically just a long piece of cotton string that's wound up into a sealed container (chalk reel or box) holding powdered chalk. (The Japanese version, called a *tsumitsubo*, uses a thin, ink-soaked thread to mark fine lines, shown at right in the photo above.)

After hooking the end of a chalkline to the work—a sheet of plywood you're crosscutting, a floor where you're installing tile, a stud wall you're marking for windows or paneling—you pull the line taut and give it a good snap, then reel the line back in with a hand crank. The result is a remarkably straight line that's easy to see and follow when sawing yet may be wiped or washed off. Snap carefully, though; it's difficult to entirely remove chalk from porous surfaces, including softwoods and foam.

The reels come empty and you fill them with blue, red, orange, or yellow chalk,

which is sold separately in a squeeze bottle or jug. A rubber grommet or felt gasket prevents chalk from leaking out of the hole where the line comes out. Most chalkline reels have a lock or clutch that secures the crank handle, allowing you to pull the line taut without having to grab it with your fingers (messy). The lock also lets you use the chalkline as a plumb bob (see p. 213), as most models have a tapered body that ends in a point.

There are two chalkline reel sizes: The smaller one holds 50 ft. of line and is good for most home carpentry jobs; the bigger, 100-ft. model is good for jobs like foundation layouts and roof installations and repairs.

Pencil and Beam Compasses

The compass that came in your high-school drafting set is good enough for drawing small circles on paper or cardboard. But it isn't up to the chore of sketching circles on project materials like plywood, hardwood lumber, or sheet metal. Most pencil

---

Pro Tip

Never use red chalk for marking duties when doing drywall work, as it can bleed through joint compound and latex wall paints. Blue chalk is visible enough to work with yet won't bleed through.

Pro Tip

You can use a pencil compass to transfer a wall's irregular profile to the straight edge of a shelf or countertop so it can be trimmed to fit it perfectly. Butt the work against the wall and set the compass wide enough to span the biggest gap, then follow the wall with the point while drawing on the work with the pencil end.

compasses (shown in the photo below) are easy to adjust and are large enough to draw circles up to 15 in. or more in diameter. They can be fitted with a hard- or soft-lead pencil, or even an ink pen, to suit the material you're drawing on.

If you need to draw even larger circles and arcs, a beam compass is the tool for you. It has a separate pencil holder and center pivot on a long tubular beam. Out of the box, the beam compass (shown in the photo below) comes with a beam long enough to draw a 25-in.-dia. circle. But substitute a longer ½-in. dowel, rod, or tube for the beam, and you can draw much larger circles. Besides creating circles and arcs, a pencil or beam compass can divide a circle into segments—say, to lay out a hexagon or bisect an angle.

▲DIVIDERS **You can use a pair of dividers to scratch a round circle on wood or metal stock or to divide a line or circle into even segments.**

Dividers

Resembling a pair of inside calipers with straight legs and sharp points, dividers are useful for dividing a line, curve, or circle into even segments. For example, to divide the circumference of a circle into six even parts—say, to draw a hexagon—you'd set the dividers to the circle's radius, place one of its points on the circle, then walk the tool all the way around. The sharp points leave small holes in paper and wood and will even mark sheet metal.

Available in the same range of sizes as legged calipers, dividers are also handy for checking and comparing the spacing of holes or pattern elements, as well as for transferring measurements from one part to another (woodturners love them for marking the spacing of elements on spindles). A divider's sharp points also can serve as a compass for scribing circles and arcs on metal and hardwood surfaces.

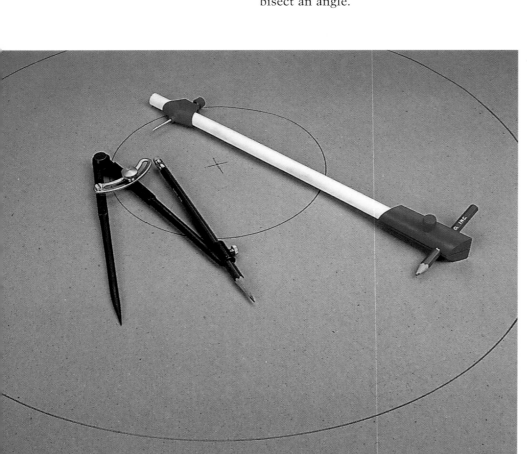

▲PENCIL COMPASSES **Pencil compasses come in legged styles (left), for drawing small circles, and beam styles (right) for drawing large circles.**

◄CONTOUR GAUGE With plastic fingers that conform to convex or concave shapes, a contour gauge is an ideal tool for transferring complex molding or trim profiles.

Contour Gauges

Cutting out one part to fit around the irregular or curvy profiles of another is a job made easy by a contour gauge. This handy tool has a row of fine fingers that are centered by a bar that keeps them tightly aligned but also allows them to slide back and forth. You press the gauge against the part you want to read the profile of—a molding or other shapely object (it works on convex or concave shapes). The gauge's fingers create a template of the profile, which can then be used to transfer the shape onto the part you wish to match.

A contour gauge is invaluable when fitting crown moldings and trim or when laying tile, carpets, and linoleum or wood flooring. You could also use a contour gauge to transfer the shape of an item—say, a precious vase or dueling pistol—to the foam or velvet-lined holder of a presentation box you're making to house it.

Also called profile gauges, contour gauges come in stainless steel and plastic models. Although a steel gauge's fine pins capture intricate details better (there are more pins per inch), plastic gauges are less expensive and come in larger sizes capable of measuring wider profiles.

Cool Tools	DEPTH GAUGES

DEPTH GAUGES are useful tools that will quickly show you the height of a table-saw blade or how far a router bit protrudes beyond the tool's base, so you can accurately set the depth of cut. A depth gauge provides an extremely handy way of setting not only bits in portable routers and router tables but also blades on table saws and portable circular saws, cutters on a shaper, or knives on a jointer. You can also use this gauge to measure the thickness of parts set on top of a flat surface, like a cast-metal saw table.

There are two kinds of depth gauges: fixed and adjustable. Fixed gauges are quick to use, with a series of preset depth notches at ⅛-in. or 1/16-in. intervals (¼ in., ⅜ in., ½ in., etc.). Adjustable depth gauges take more time to use but are more versatile because they can be set for any precise dimension within the range of the gauge.

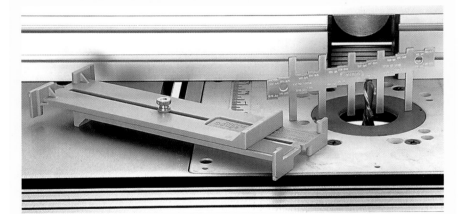

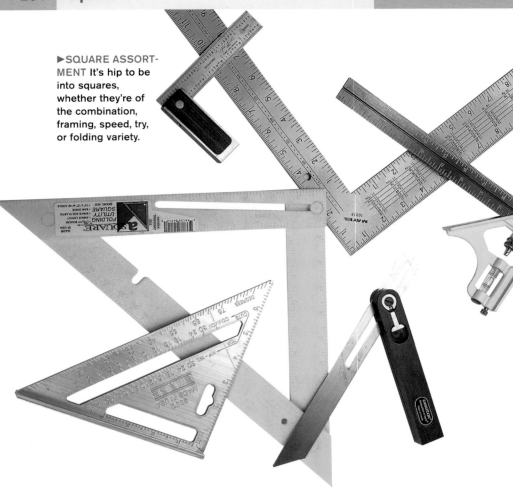

►SQUARE ASSORT-MENT It's hip to be into squares, whether they're of the combination, framing, speed, try, or folding variety.

SQUARES

The built world is full of right angles; just look at a house and the cabinets, built-ins, and trim inside it. Whether you're rough-framing a tree house, carefully trimming out window frames, or cutting out and assembling precise joinery for a fine wood-working project, you'll use a square to mark your cuts and keep your assembled parts true. Although squares have changed little in basic form for millennia, modern squares have construction and features that make them easier to use, more accurate, and often more versatile.

Try Squares

The simplest of all squares, the try square gets its name from the act of trying a frame or corner of a box or cabinet case to see if its members are square. You can also use this L-shaped tool for marking a line perpendi-cular to an edge. Some try squares even have a scale on the blade, allowing you to mark or measure lines of accurate length (shown at lower right in the photo at left). To remain reliably sturdy, a try square's steel or brass blade is firmly mounted to a wood or metal body. Fancy try squares have shiny brass wear plates and ornate rivets connecting the blade and body. All-steel try squares, known as engineer's squares, have accu-rately milled edges on blade and body, making them useful for precision marking and layout work or for setting and aligning workshop power tools. To accom-modate different scales of work, try squares come with blades as short as 2 in., for model work and miniatures, and as long as 8 in. for large-scale projects.

Combination Squares

The Swiss Army Knife® of squares, a com-bination (or combo) square is equally adept working as a try square, a miter square, a short level, and a rule. The tool is primari-ly used for measuring, marking, and laying out either 45-degree or 90-degree lines (some models even include a small pullout scribing awl), but you can also use its slid-ing blade to check the thickness of parts or the depth of slots and larger holes or even remove it entirely and use it as a rule. Although not as accurate as a try square or as large as a framing square, a combo square is just fine for basic carpentry and home projects that require layout. Plus, a combo square is compact enough to hang on a tool belt or fit into a small tool kit.

Basic combo squares (shown at bottom in the top photo on facing page) have a grooved, 12-in. blade that locks into a die-cast metal body. Some models have stamped gradua-tions filled with a contrasting color paint, which makes them easier to read, as well as a powder-coat finish that thwarts rust.

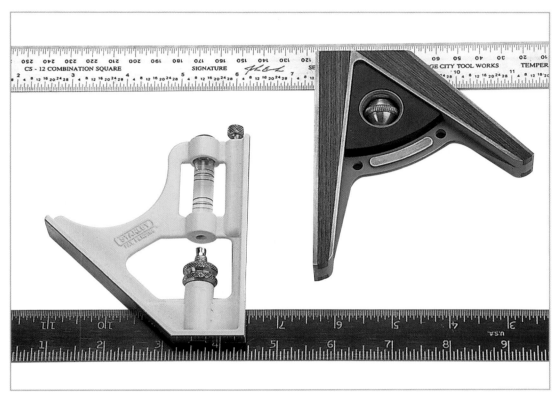

▲COMBINATION SQUARES Whether built plain or fancy, a combination square is really a kind of multitool that features a layout or try square, a miter square (for 45-degree angles), a removable rule, and, on some models, a small level.

Not to be confused with basic carpentry combo squares, fancy combination squares (shown at top in the photo above) have attractive brass and hardwood or crinkle-painted cast-iron bodies and high-quality, machined blades. These are high-priced tools designed for precision wood- or metalwork and machine setup.

Framing Squares

If you're framing a roof or building a large project, you'll appreciate the usefulness of a framing square. Thanks to its big 16-in. by 24-in. size and graduated scales, you can use it to mark a 90-degree line across a wide board, mark the spacing of holes or studs on a beam, and check a large assembly or lay-out—a plywood doghouse, a stud wall, the arrangement of tiles on a bathroom vanity—for square.

Tool Helpers | **STAIR NUTS**

Stair nuts are small accessories that clamp onto the legs of a framing square to make it more useful for angled work. Depending on where they're positioned, the nuts rest against the edge of a board and lock the square at a precise angle. You can use one or both legs of the square to mark the angle of the end of a roof rafter or frame member or use the corner of the square to mark the multiple L-shaped cutouts on a pair of stair stringers for the treads and risers. Either way, stair nuts keep the square's angle consistent, so you can mark numerous parts identically.

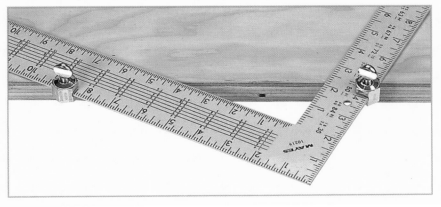

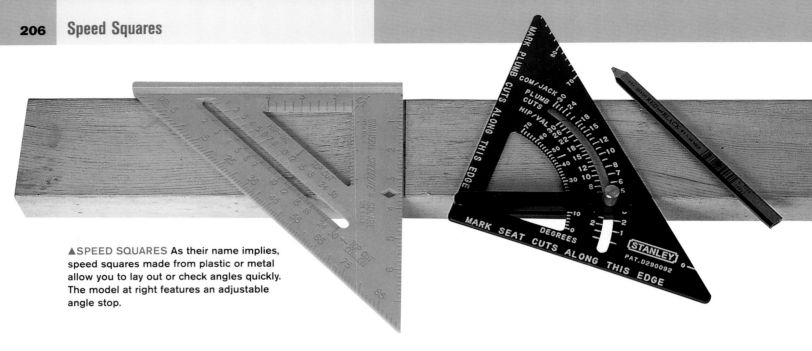

▲SPEED SQUARES As their name implies, speed squares made from plastic or metal allow you to lay out or check angles quickly. The model at right features an adjustable angle stop.

Pro Tip

If the legs of your framing square are no longer at 90 degrees, use a punch and a hammer to readjust it. Set the square on an anvil or the back of a bench vise. If the square is slightly acute, punch a series of dimples near its inside corner (as shown in the photo) to expand its angle. If the square is slightly obtuse, punch the outside corner to reduce the angle.

Beyond these basic tasks, a framing square (also known as a carpenter's square or a rafter square) has informational tables printed directly on its legs, making it easy to perform calculations for many carpentry and woodworking jobs without doing math—figuring the number of board feet of lumber in a long plank, the angles for an octagonal planter box, the roof pitch and length of rafters for a playhouse, or the size of diagonal braces for an elevated outdoor deck.

Framing squares are made from steel or aluminum, with aluminum being the lighter option and steel being the more durable one. A painted steel or anodized aluminum square with graduations and tables printed in a contrasting color is easier to read than the stamped marks on a plain square (painting also prevents a steel square from rusting). However, the marks on a plain, stamped square won't wear off over time as they will on a painted or anodized model.

Speed Squares

At first glance, a speed square (or quick square) looks like a drafting triangle with a lip on one of its short edges. This lip makes it a convenient tool to use for marking 90-degree or 45-degree lines across lumber up to 7 in. wide. You can also stand the square on this lip to use it as you would a try square for checking a frame, box, or other assembly for square or 45 degrees.

But that's only scratching the surface of what a speed square is designed to do. Originally created for use in roof construction, a speed square has scales (and sometimes tables) marked on it for determining the pitch of rafters or stairway stringers and for laying out precisely angled lines. After putting the square corner of the tool (its pivot point) against one side of a board, you can mark or measure angles (either by degree or by rise-and-run slope) by lining up the marks on one of the scales printed on it.

Some models feature an adjustable fence (shown at right in the photo above), which makes it easier to set a particular angle and then mark a series of boards identically. Speed squares are light, inexpensive tools made of either plastic or aluminum. Like framing squares, models that have markings painted in a contrasting color are the easiest to read.

Drywall Squares

Resembling an overgrown draftsman's T-square, a drywall square is designed for making square cuts on sheet goods and for large-scale layout tasks. Its long, 4-ft. beam spans the width of a full sheet of plywood or particleboard, so all it takes is a quick pencil stroke to mark a perpendicular line for snapping the panel to length.

Trimming drywall (also known as Sheetrock or gypsum wallboard) is even easier: You lay the square across the sheet and run a standard utility knife along the beam to score the outer paper covering. Then you simply snap the sheet along the score, using the knife to cut the paper on the other side. It's an incredibly quick and reasonably clean way of cutting sheets to size.

Most drywall squares are made of lightweight aluminum with painted scales on both the beam and head. Better-quality squares have a ¾₆-in.-thick blade rather than the standard ⅛-in. blade, which is flimsy and less durable.

Cool Tools **FOLDING SQUARES**

FOLDING SQUARES lead a double life: They spend most of their time in repose in a flat, narrow package, yet they open quickly into a full-size, highly useful squaring tool. A large (3-ft. by 4-ft.) folding layout square (see the photo at right) helps you set correctly a crucial first row of parquet wood or vinyl tiles across the center of the room, as well as check the squareness of walls at inside corners. Folding squares are also helpful for carpentry layout tasks, for cabinet installation, and when laying out ceramic tiles and pavers on a patio or walkway. The big square conveniently folds down into a long narrow bundle that's easy to carry or hang for storage.

A smaller (12-in. by 12-in.) folding square (see the photo at left) is good for many of the layout or parts-alignment jobs that you'd use a speed square or framer's square for, yet it folds down small enough to fit into a toolbox or tote tray.

▲DRYWALL SQUARE Not only for drawing perpendicular lines, a drywall square is a handy guide for a utility knife, which is used to score drywall sheets prior to snapping them to size.

Bevel Gauges and Miter Squares

Marking and measuring angles is easily accomplished with a bevel gauge. One of the simplest adjustable bevel gauges is the sliding bevel, also called a sliding T-bevel (shown at left in the photo below). This tool's wide body and long, locking blade make easy work of checking angles between parts or marking angles on workpieces. Sliding bevels are also great for reading an angle from a part—say, the beveled edge of a cabinet top—and transferring it to a workpiece or using it to set the angle of a miter-saw or table-saw blade.

A sliding bevel gauge doesn't actually show angles in degrees, so to set the gauge to a known angle, you can either use a protractor or, for really precise work, switch to an electronic bevel gauge (shown at top in the photo below). This modern wonder reads angles with an accuracy down to one-tenth of a degree, displaying them on an LCD screen.

A handy variation of the adjustable bevel gauge is the miter square (shown at center in the photo below), which is like a try square with its blade fixed at 45 degrees to the stock on one side and to the complimentary angle

of 135 degrees on the other. It's a handy, precise tool for checking or laying out miter joints on picture-frame members, cabinet face frames, box corners, etc.

LEVELS AND PLUMB BOBS

Many of the same basic tools that built the great pyramids and temples of antiquity are still around today. Levels and plumb bobs are important for tackling all manner of carpentry and home-improvement projects, from the mundane to the complex. The reason is simple: We like our countertops and tables flat, our pictures and cabinets to hang straight, and our doorways and fence posts plumb to the ground. Today, we have a choice between using traditional gravity-powered tools and choosing modern versions that use lasers and complex electronic circuitry to make our jobs go quickly and easily.

Carpenter's Levels

A carpenter's level is nothing more than a straight stick fitted with a time-honored device: an air bubble trapped in a curved, liquid-filled vial that's mounted in a long, straight body. Gravity makes the bubble rise

►BEVEL GAUGES Measuring and checking angles is what bevel gauges do. Shown here are (from front to back): a sliding bevel, a miter square, and an electronic bevel gauge.

to the highest part of the arc, showing when the level is level. Most levels have a second vial oriented 90 degrees to the first for checking plumb, and some have a third vial for 45-degree angle checks. Others feature an adjustable vial (inclinometer), which reads any angle between level and plumb, handy for setting the correct angle of rafters, for example, or checking the pitch of a roof. The most advanced electronic levels count on battery-powered circuitry rather than a bubble, and they display angles (can check level, plumb, and odd angles) numerically on an LCD screen.

Just as a surfer chooses surfboards of various lengths to handle different-size waves, it's important to choose an appropriately sized level for the task at hand (see "Choosing the Right Level" at right). Most levels are made of light, long-lasting aluminum, although short economy levels are often made of tough plastic. I-beam aluminum levels are good for general carpentry; tubular aluminum levels and wood-and-brass mason levels are best for concrete and brickwork, as their enclosed bodies don't clog up and are easier to clean than I-beam models.

Many modern levels have barrel-shaped vials that read regardless of whether they're right side up or upside down—more convenient than older models with simple curved vials. High-quality levels often have vials made from a rectangular block of acrylic plastic mounted permanently in epoxy and guaranteed not to go out of alignment. Economical models have vials that are replaceable and adjustable, so you don't have to throw the whole tool away if a vial breaks or becomes misaligned (see the tip on p. 210). Shock-absorbing end caps, found on many models, help prevent damage if a level is dropped.

Toolbox- and torpedo-size levels (see the top photo on p. 210) often have a V-groove and one magnetic edge, to hold the tool firmly on a metal pipe, post, or frame. This feature is especially handy when checking plumb or 45-degree angles.

▲LEVELS AND PLUMB BOB
Whether they depend on a laser beam or the forces of gravity to operate, levels and plumb bobs are essential alignment tools for lots of home-improvement jobs.

Which Size? CHOOSING THE RIGHT LEVEL

Go to a large hardware or tool store, and you'll find a rack containing carpenter's levels of all lengths and colors of the rainbow—an impressive but confusing sight. Do you really need a level that's taller than you are? Should you buy two or three? The most popular-size models are listed below, along with some guidelines for picking the best one—or ones—for the kind of jobs you want to do.

FRAMING LEVELS (72 in. long) are not for the average homeowner, but they are good for:
• checking studs, joists, and beams when framing a house or outbuilding

JOURNEYMAN'S LEVELS (24 in. to 48 in. long) are versatile choices:
• longer (36-in. to 48-in.) models are good for projects where accuracy is important
• shorter (32-in. to 24-in.) models are good for general household jobs

TOOLBOX LEVELS (15 in. to 18 in. long) are handy for everyday leveling jobs and:
• can be used in spots too cramped for longer levels
• fit conveniently into drawers or toolboxes and totes

TORPEDO LEVELS (7 in. to 10 in. long) may be the smallest of levels, but they're still very useful. They are:
• easy to carry in a tool belt or apron pouch
• best for quick checks and little jobs around the house, such as leveling curtain rods, where dead-on accuracy isn't crucial

▲TORPEDO LEVEL Although it's short, a torpedo level is long on usefulness; it's a handy tool for many household jobs, such as leveling pictures and curtain rods.

Laser Levels

A laser level isn't meant to replace a carpenter's level, just extend its capabilities. Once expensive, professional tools, laser levels are now affordable and even the cheapest models are accurate to ¼ in. at 50 ft. Most are torpedo-size levels fitted with a small, battery-powered laser (the low-power kind used in laser pointers). The beam is aligned perfectly parallel to its bottom edge, exactly ½ in. above it.

After checking a surface for level with the tool's built-in bubble vial, you use the red point of light emitted by the laser's tightly focused beam to set other parts—joists, cabinets, shelves, etc.—to the same level. The beam extends far enough to a set the height of objects up to 50 ft. or even 100 ft. away. To make the beam easier to see outdoors or in bright light, wear a pair of laser-enhancing glasses (see "Special Eyewear" on p. 262) or use a laser target (see the photo on the facing page).

Pro Tip

Check the bubble vials on all your levels occasionally to make sure they're reading correctly, especially if they've been dropped. With the tool on a relatively level surface, read the vial, then flip the level end for end, and recheck the vial(s) (also check for plumb). If the vial readings differ, adjust, replace, or tape over the bad vial(s) or discard the level.

LASER LEVEL By projecting a concentrated beam of light that's perfectly parallel to its body, a torpedo-size laser level can be used to check the relative level of surfaces that are far apart.

You can use a laser level anywhere you'd use a string level—say, to align framed pictures or kitchen cabinets. Set vertically, you can also use the laser to plumb studs and columns or to transfer points from floor to ceiling or vice versa. Most levels have a ¼–20 threaded hole, allowing you to mount the level on an accessory rotary base or camera tripod to use as a transit (a surveyor's leveling scope)—say, to mark points around a room that are all the same distance from the floor.

Multibeam and Rotary Laser Tools

Multibeam and rotary laser tools don't create a single dot like laser levels, but instead project multiple dots, cross hairs, or continuous lines, making complex leveling jobs for construction, remodeling, installation, and redecoration projects much easier.

MULTIBEAM LASERS A multibeam laser (also called a cross laser, pocket laser, or prism laser) passes its single beam through a prismlike beam splitter, refracting it into up to five individual beams (shown at right in the photo below). Most two-beam models project vertical (plumb) and horizontal (level) lines, handy for the alignment of wall tiles, wallpaper, or stenciling patterns, the plumbing of studs and columns, and the leveling of stairs.

Three-beam and five-beam lasers project orthogonal (90-degree) beams that provide simultaneous plumb, level, and square reference points. These are useful for squaring up concrete foundation forms and deck supports, aligning floor tiles or window and door frames, plumbing walls and posts, and transferring floor and ceiling reference points for the installation of heating/cooling vents, recessed lighting, or skylights.

Surprisingly affordable, multibeam lasers are self-leveling and may be mounted to a tripod or spring-loaded laser pole that wedges between floor and ceiling. An adjustable platform holds the laser at any height.

◄MULTIBEAM AND ROTARY LASERS **Using battery power to generate their ruby-red beams, rotary and multibeam lasers are useful for a wide range of heavy-duty leveling, marking, and layout chores.**

Pro Tip

For eye safety's sake, most laser leveling and measuring tools have beams that radiate less than 5 milliwatts of power. Occasional viewing won't cause eye damage, just irritation, like from a camera's electronic flash.

ROTARY LASERS Also called a rotating laser or laser beacon, a rotary laser (shown at left in the photo on p. 211) has one or two lasers mounted to a spinning armature. Set in the middle of a room or job site, the battery-powered device creates the appearance of a continuous, level line all the way around, perfect for mounting cabinets or drop ceilings indoors or for leveling foundations or pier blocks outdoors.

When working in bright light, a beam detector (shown at center front in the photo on p. 211) must be used to accurately mark the level of the rotating beam. Not self-leveling, a rotary laser's adjustable base allows you to cant the laser line when laying out sloping decks and drain lines. While too expensive for most do-it-yourselfers to buy, a rotary laser is worth renting if you have a large construction or installation project coming up.

Post and Line Levels

If you've got a job to do in the yard or garden that involves setting and/or leveling fence posts, stakes, or poles, post and line levels provide an inexpensive way to get the job done right. A post level (shown at bottom in the photo at right) has three bubble vials: two for plumbing a post when setting it in the ground or concrete and one for leveling rails fastened between posts. The tool's L-shaped body fits snugly against square or round stock, and hinged models open up to fit into corners or against odd-shaped stock. You can hold it in place by hand or attach it temporarily with a rubber band (some models have built-in magnets that stick to steel components).

A line level (shown at top in the photo on the right) lets you easily set a number of objects in a row—posts, piers, stepping stones—to the same height. A line level is basically a single bubble vial in a plastic holder that hangs from a long string pulled taut between two posts or stakes. Once the

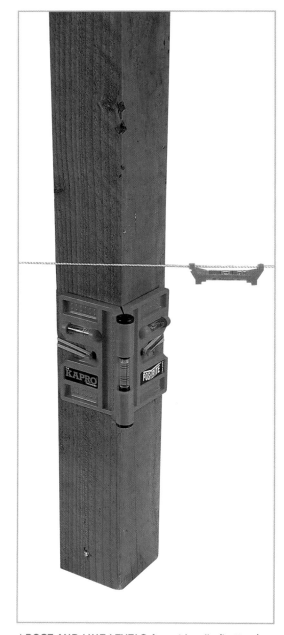

▲**POST AND LINE LEVELS** A post level's (bottom) multiple-bubble vials speed the process of setting a post or column plumb, while a line level (top) helps make setting concrete forms an easier job.

string is level, everything at string height is at the same level. A useful variation, called a pitch level, has grade markings on its vial that show the degree of the string's slope (some standard levels also have this feature). It's a useful tool when laying drainage pipe or a sewer line.

Water Levels

Plain water can provide a remarkably effective means for checking the relative level of parts that are not in line and may be far away from each other. A water level is nothing more than a water-filled hose with transparent vials at both ends. Because of the laws of gravity, the height of the water in one vial will read the same as the height in the other, no matter how the hose twists and turns in between (the hose just can't be higher than the vials).

A modern water level's plastic vials conveniently thread right onto the ends of a standard garden hose of any length—you supply the hose and water. This level can help you finish a multitude of outdoor projects, such as setting deck supports, fence posts, pier blocks, or garden gnomes all to the same level. It's also useful indoors for leveling multiple wall cabinets or shelving. For the most effective use, it's good to work with a helper because the levels in both vials change as they're moved up and down until level is reached. Although considerably more expensive, an electronic version beeps when level is achieved, making it more convenient when working alone.

Plumb Bobs

For millennia, carpenters have used a simple weight on the end of a string, dangling free and aligned by the earth's gravity, to make sure that the walls and pillars of a building were straight up and down. Due to their simplicity and ease of use, plumb bobs are still around today. Modern bobs are sleek, tapered objects cast from metal or machined from handsome bronze; they commonly weigh anywhere from 4 oz. to 24 oz. (8-oz. to 16-oz. models are the most popular for general use). Most bobs have a sharp steel point (to show an exact point of plumb) that's replaceable in case it's badly bent.

▲WATER LEVEL Using the power of gravity to level the water in a long garden hose, a water level is handy for marking distant posts, piers, or stakes all at the same level.

Pro Tip

To keep a plumb bob from twirling endlessly as it dangles, hang it from a thin, braided nylon cord, like the one that comes with a gammon reel, rather than from a twisted string or twine.

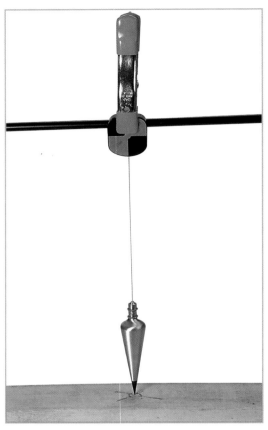

▲**PLUMB BOB AND GAMMON REEL** Controlled by the earth's gravity, a plumb bob hanging on a retractable line from a gammon reel is a basic tool for vertical alignment and measurement transfer chores.

While it's often easier to use a level to check a wall stud or vertical column for plumb, a plumb bob can be used for jobs that a level is too short for—positioning wallpaper or aligning upper and lower kitchen cabinets. It's also a great tool for finding an exact spot below a span—say, to position a new ceiling light directly above your favorite chair.

You can dangle a plumb bob from a simple string wrapped around a stick, but a gammon reel (a small spring-loaded string reel enclosed in a small case) automatically retracts the string after use to keep it clean and prevent it from tangling up in your toolbox.

ELECTRICAL TESTERS AND METERS

Measuring tasks aren't limited to tangible objects; sometimes they also need to be performed on things that defy the visual world—like electricity. It's a simple fact that nobody has ever actually seen electricity—even physicists only know of its presence from the traces that subatomic particles leave behind. But since electricity is such an important part of our daily lives, we have all kinds of testing tools at our disposal to measure electrical voltage or current and detect and monitor its presence. You don't have to be an electrician (or a physicist) to put these meters and testers to good use in home wiring and repair projects.

Multimeters

If your hobby involves electronics—fooling around with ham radios, computers, audio components, or the like—chances are you already know and love multimeters. Versatile and easy to use, a multimeter performs dozens of different electrical- and electronic-testing, diagnostic, and repair duties. Even an inexpensive analog multimeter (the type with a moving needle—once called a VOM, or volt-ohm-millimeter) can be used to measure AC or DC voltage, current (in amps or milliamps), and resistance (in ohms), as well as check for electrical continuity in household circuits, appliances, power tools, motors, or electronic devices.

More expensive but far more accurate and versatile, modern digital multimeters add several other testing functions to their repertoires, including measuring frequency and temperature (usually with a separate probe) and checking the viability of electronic components, such as capacitors, diodes, and transistors. What's more, a digital multimeter (sometimes called a multi-tester) takes readings with much greater precision than older analog meters. Most digitals have large, easy-to-read LCD screens that show readings numerically and

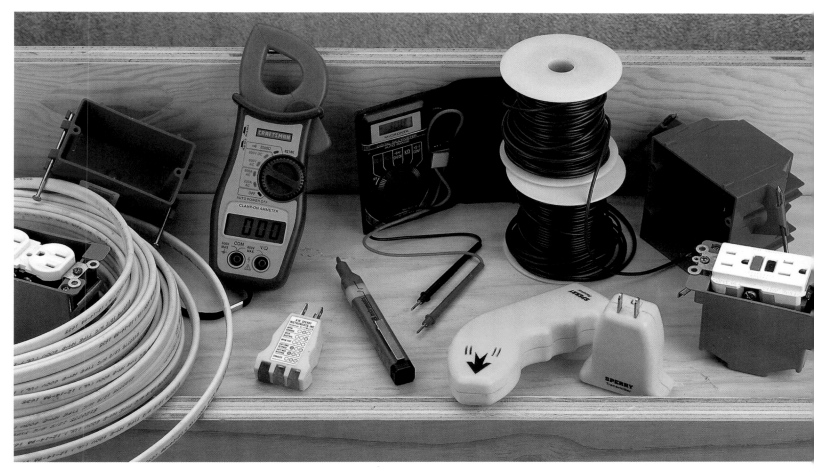

▲ELECTRICAL MEASURING AND TESTING TOOLS Using the right tools with electrical wiring not only helps you get the job done but also prevents accidental shock.

can hold the data, which may only register for a split second.

All multimeters come with test probes that connect via sockets in the meter; better models will show you which sockets to plug into, depending on the testing function you've chosen. Other features and uses are complicated and beyond the scope of this book; it's a good idea to read up on multimeters (Sears' *A Simple and Comprehensive Guide to Multitesters* is a good option) before choosing and using one.

With its pair of plug-in test probes, a clamp-on ammeter measures the current

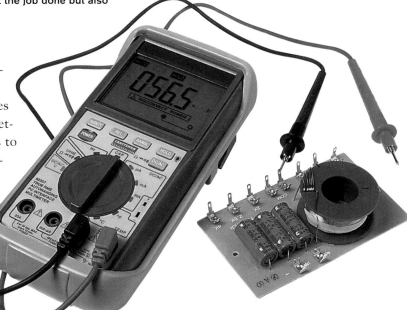

▲DIGITAL MULTIMETER With its large readout that shows measurement clearly, the digital multimeter is a versatile tool for measuring electrical voltage, amperage, resistance, continuity, and more.

▲CLAMP-ON AMMETER To test electrical amperage easily, use a clamp-on ammeter, which can take an accurate reading without the need for clipping wires and connecting test leads.

Cool Tools   ELECTRONIC BATTERY TESTERS

ELECTRONIC BATTERY TESTERS help you get the most out of your batteries. Here's the problem: How do you figure out if any of the semiused batteries floating around your house have any juice left in them? Even a battery that's 90 percent spent will register voltage on a regular multimeter, and inexpensive battery checkers that just have red and green LEDs ("bad" and "good") don't give adequate information about the amount of power left in a battery.

Fortunately, the latest electronic battery testers feature advanced circuitry that's capable of reliably testing more than two dozen different kinds of batteries, including alkaline, rechargeable nicad and NiMH, and lithium. A microprocessor subjects a battery to a load test and then displays the percentage of remaining power (between 10 percent and 100 percent). If you live in the average American household with dozens of battery-operated devices—flashlights, portable video games, CD and tape players, cameras, watches and clocks, etc.—an electronic battery tester is a practical device to have on hand.

flowing though an AC wire (110 volts or 220 volts) without any direct electrical connection to the wire itself. This provides a handy, noninvasive way of measuring the power used by an appliance or power tool—a great diagnostic tool for troubleshooting motors and faulty circuitry.

Electricity Checkers

Before working on any AC wiring or fixtures around the house, it's crucial to verify that there's no power in the circuit. An electricity checker provides an excellent way of verifying that there's no live electricity present. A simple tester (shown at center in the photo at left on the facing page) has two leads connected to a small light bulb. Touch the leads to a pair of 110-volt AC wires (or one hot wire of a 220-volt circuit and ground) or push the leads into an electrical outlet, and if the bulb lights, power is present.

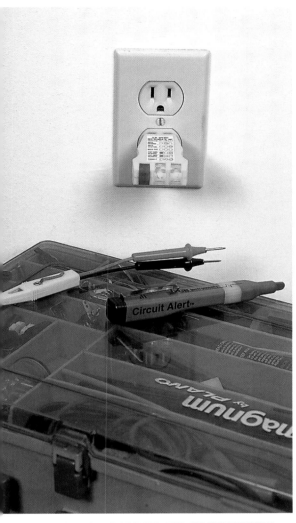

▲ELECTRICAL CHECKER AND CIRCUIT TESTER
To check for live electrical outlets or to make sure outlets are wired correctly, use an electrical checker or circuit tester.

Tool Helpers **FISH TAPE**

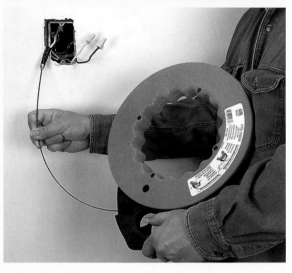

Unless you have a trained pet mouse that can drag wires through walls, a fish tape is an indispensable tool for routing new electrical wiring through finished walls. A fish tape is made from flattened spring steel wire (not fish) that's got enough stiffness to be forced through holes and crevices and snaked through the open pockets between wall studs and floor or ceiling joists.

Once you've coerced and cajoled the tape from point A to point B—say, from the attic down through a wall to a light-switch box—you hook your electrical wires or cable through the tape's slotted head, then pull them into place and wire them up to power. You can use the tape to run 110/220-volt AC wiring, television coaxial cable, or low-power DC wiring (for doorbells and garage-door openers). Fish tapes commonly come in 25-ft. and 50-ft. lengths, with the shorter one adequate for most home-wiring jobs. The tape retracts into a large, covered reel with a locking trigger, which prevents uncoiling.

More sophisticated electricity checkers (shown at bottom in the left photo above) have current-sensing circuitry and are even easier to use; you simply put the tip of the noninvasive probe near wires or outlets, and the tool blinks and chirps rapidly if power is detected—a sure sign that it's unsafe to proceed.

Circuit Testers

After finishing a home-improvement wiring job—say, running new outlets around the family room—ever wonder if you've hooked up all the wires correctly?

While a thrown circuit breaker or blown fuse is a sure sign of a short circuit, you can use a circuit checker to quickly confirm subtler wiring deficiencies.

This three-prong, plug-in diagnostic tool (shown at top in the left photo above) has red and yellow light-emitting diodes (LEDs) that light in combination to quickly show these common problems: if the hot, neutral, or ground wires are disconnected; if the hot and ground wires are reversed; and if the hot and neutral wires are reversed. Two yellow lights indicate that your circuit is wired correctly, offering instant peace of mind.

CHAPTER 9

Tools That Fasten & Glue

Screws or nuts and bolts make strong connections between parts. But there are other methods of fastening that are also strong but speedier to accomplish: Nails or staples driven by an air-powered gun can fasten boards to a frame or shingles to a roof as fast as you can pull a trigger. For heavier-duty jobs, like joining construction lumber to a concrete foundation, there are powder-actuated fastening tools that shoot nails with gunpowder cartridges. Pop-riveting tools, soldering irons, and brazing torches can create exceptionally strong connections between metal parts and wires, while modern adhesives—including liquid wood glues, hot melts, and adhesive transfer tapes—allow a wide variety of materials to be bonded securely together.

▲AIR-POWERED NAIL GUNS Whether for securing structural framing or tacking up light trim, air-powered nailers come in a wide range of sizes and styles made to get the job done quickly and easily.

MECHANICAL FASTENERS

Possibly the strongest, fastest way to join parts is to fasten them together with nails, staples, or rivets. Whether driven by hand (see chapter 6) or with an air-powered gun or other device, mechanical fasteners go into place quickly and provide a lasting connection that's not likely to fail under duress. With the exception of powder-actuated fastening tools, most fastener guns are powered by compressed air fed by a hose connected to a portable compressor.

Air-Powered Nail Guns

Using a powerful cylinder that rams nails home with remarkable speed and accuracy, nail guns allow even rank novices to firmly fasten lumber, plywood, and all kinds of building materials like a professional. Better still, fastening with a nail gun is as accurate as hammering by hand but requires far less muscle power.

Although the special nail clips or coils that guns require are considerably more expensive than loose nails, gun-driven nails take only a trigger pull to apply and don't have the tendency to knock out of alignment the parts being joined, as often happens when hammering regular nails. Air-driven nails also won't disturb existing trim and drywall like hammer-pounded nails do, a real boon when doing delicate remodeling operations.

Nail guns come in a staggering array of types and sizes, from heavy framers that drive big 16d nails used in house framing, to diminutive brad and pin guns for setting moldings and trim, to specialized guns for driving roofing nails or laying tongue-and-groove flooring (see p. 223). Nail guns are terrific for building all kinds of projects, from chicken coops to kitchen stoops. And if you're building or remodeling a house, a nail gun really speeds up the installation of sheathing, siding, subflooring, roofing, drywall, and trim.

Even big nail guns have a relatively small appetite for air and will run off small, portable compressors (see "Portable Air Compressors" on p. 220). Most guns require daily oiling with pneumatic oil (*never* engine oil) to keep them well lubricated and firing smoothly, although some newer guns are oil free.

Although big guns are expensive, you can buy combo kits that pair a gun with a portable compressor often at prices even the occasional user can afford. The next sections examine several popular types of nail guns and describe the range of duties they're designed to handle.

FRAMING NAILERS The heavy artillery of the pneumatic fastening world, framing nailers are built to take on the heaviest construction and remodeling projects. Using nails up to 3½ in. in length, these guns will speedily join studs to plates, assemble trusses and fences, and secure rafters, decking, siding, subflooring and more. Framing guns are especially adept at

---

Pro Tip

Because even small electric-powered air compressors draw up to 15 amps, it's best to plug them directly into outlets rather than feed them with long extension cords, which are both more expensive and less effective than using an air hose to reach your work site. Use ⅜-in. hoses for runs longer than 25 ft. and ¼-in. hoses for runs of 15 ft. or less.

Which One? — **CHOOSING A NAIL GUN**

With all the different nail guns on the market, choosing one can be confusing. Do you need to buy a different one for each construction task? The answer is yes and no. Some guns, such as roofing and brad nailers, are designed for specific tasks. However, many framing, coil, and finish nail guns handle several fastener types and sizes, making them quite versatile.

FRAMING NAILERS typically use 2-in.- to 3½-in.-long nails, so depending on the nail, one gun can:
• fasten 2x lumber
• attach sheathing and subflooring

COIL NAIL GUNS handle nails from ⅞ in. to 2½ in. long and are designed for specific duties, including:
• light framing and utility nailing
• nailing up siding, sheathing, and subflooring
• attaching roofing

FINISH GUNS use 1-in.- to 2½-in.-long nails, so depending on the nail, one gun can:
• tack up trim
• assemble full-size cabinets
• tackle standard around-the-house building projects

Portable Air Compressors

The most powerful nail gun won't penetrate Styrofoam without air pressure—just the thing a portable compressor is designed to supply. Compressors use a pump powered by an electric motor (or, on professional models, a gas engine) to squeeze air into a storage tank. A hose supplies the compressed air to power a nail gun, spray gun, or other air-powered tool (see "Random-Orbit Sanders" on p.176). Traditional compressors have oil-lubricated pumps, which are sturdy but require regular oil changes. However, many newer compressors have oilless pumps, which require less maintenance but are considerably noisier than oil-lubed pumps and tend not to last as long.

Small compressors come in many styles, each with a different storage-tank arrangement. Two styles are particularly popular for their compact size and portability. Pancake compressors (see the photo at right) have their motors and pumps mounted atop a round, low tank. Twin-tank (or twin-stack) compressors have a pair of long, narrow tanks, one located above the other, with the motor and pump off to one side (see the photo above). Both have carrying handles and run on 110-volt household power; it's not a good idea to buy a compressor that draws more than 15 amps because you won't be able to run it on average household circuits.

Compressor Size and Air Requirements

To get the most from your nail guns and air tools, your compressor must have enough power to run them. Air volume—not motor horsepower or pressure—is the most important indicator of any compressor's ability to power tools. Generally, the bigger a compressor's motor and tank, the greater the air volume (stated as scfm, or standard cubic feet per minute) it produces, and the more nails you can fire, or the longer you can use an air tool before the motor and pump must run to fill the tank up with air again.

It's important to choose a compressor that can supply enough air to run the tools you want to use with it. As you can see from the chart, it takes only a small compressor to run most nail guns. Unfortunately, some air tools—especially air random-orbit sanders—use lots of air and require a big compressor to run for extended periods of time. However, even a small compressor lets you run air tools for short stints.

AVERAGE AIR CONSUMPTION OF COMMON PNEUMATIC TOOLS		
Tool	**Air Pressure (psi)**	**Air Volume (scfm)**
Nail gun (forty 2-in. nails/min.)	100	2.2
Staple gun (forty ¼-in. by 1½-ifl. staples/min.)	100	1.8
Blow gun	100	2.5
Finish sander, random orbit	90	4–16*
Jigsaw	90	7–27*
Angle grinder (7-in. disk)	90	7.5–30*
Spray gun (with medium-size nozzle)	30–50	7.8–11½**

* First number indicates scfm with intermittent use; second number is scfm needed for constant use.

** Actual air usage depends on air pressure and type of gun nozzle and air cap used.

Pro Tip

To make toenailing with a framing nail gun more positive and accurate, professionals carefully sharpen the tips of the gun's safety foot (the part that must be pressed against the work before the gun will fire). The sharpened points dig into the wood slightly, allowing you to position and fire the gun without slipping.

▲FRAMING NAIL GUN Deceptively light for its size, a modern framing gun is made from light metal alloys and plastics, so it's easy to handle when doing jobs like toenailing posts to foundation piers.

toenailing—driving nails at a steep angle, a task that often results in bent nails (not to mention expletives) when hammering by hand.

Despite their imposing size, space-age alloys and plastics make framing nailers reasonably manageable (between 7½ lb. and 9 lb.) if your forearms aren't as big as Arnold Schwarzenegger's. Since every ounce counts when schlepping a gun around, choose the lightest gun that has the features you like. You must also choose between models specifically designed for full round–head or clipped-head nails (see the Pro/Con box on p. 222).

COIL NAILERS Much smaller than framing guns, coil nailers come in a variety of models, each designed for a different range of nailing jobs: siding and light framing with 1½-in. to 2½-in. nails, utility nailing with 1¼-in. to 2-in. nails, and roofing with large-head ⅞-in. to 1¾-in. roofing nails.

As their name implies, these guns accept nails packed into spiral-wound coils; most other guns take clips—a strip of nails or staples lightly glued together. Because coils hold about four times more nails than clips, coil nailers are marvelous for installing subflooring, siding, or sheathing because they allow you to work longer before reloading. Coil guns are also compact, making them handy for nailing in cramped locations.

FINISH, BRAD, AND PIN NAILERS If you want to use a nail gun to fasten interior moldings or exterior trim but don't want nails to show, you need a finish, brad, or pin nailer. More compact than framing guns, finish nailers are light (2½ lb. to 3¾ lb.) yet shoot beefy, 15-ga. or 16-ga.

▼COIL NAIL GUN Nailing house siding or subflooring is easy with a coil nail gun, which drives dozens of nails without the need for reloading.

PRO CON

WHEN BUYING a framing nailer, you're faced with the choice of selecting a model that shoots full round–head or clipped-head nails. Clipped-head nails (see the photo below) have a little crescent removed from their heads.

CLIPPED-HEAD NAILS

Pros:
- more nails can be packed into a single clip
- less expensive than full round–head

Cons:
- don't meet building-code requirements in all jurisdictions
- not as strong as full round–head

FULL ROUND–HEAD NAILS

Pros:
- always meet code requirements
- more holding power than clipped-head

Cons:
- a single clip holds fewer nails
- more expensive than clipped-head

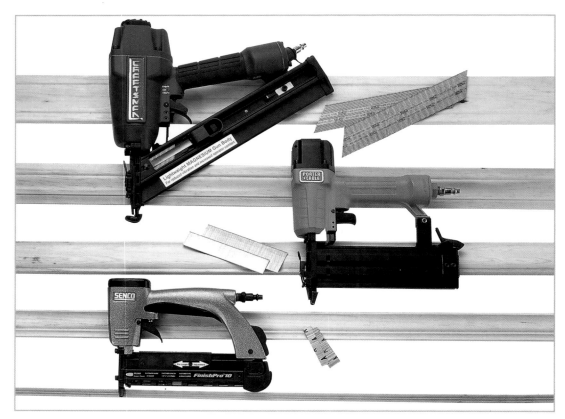

▲FINISH NAIL GUNS For tacking trim and moldings in place, pick a gun that fits the size of the job. The guns shown here are (from top to bottom): finish nail gun, brad gun, and pin gun.

▲FINISH NAIL GUN To clear a jammed or bent nail from the magazine, guns such as the finish nail gun shown here have quick-release access doors.

small-head nails from around 1¼ in. to 2½ in. long. Longer nails are good for structural work, like installing door and window casings. Most models have a steeply angled magazine (the part that holds the nails) to make it easier to drive nails into corners and narrow spaces.

Air-powered brad nailers (shown at middle in the top photo above) shoot thinner, 18-ga. slight-head nails, which are good for lighter jobs, such as attaching thin moldings and trim or building small projects, like a dollhouse. Some models handle brads up to 2⅛ in. long, appropriate for assembling picture frames and small drawers and boxes. For tacking up delicate trim, glazing strips, and window beading, choose a pin nailer (shown at bottom in the top photo above). These dainty-size nail guns use

◄FLOORING CLEATS Specifically designed to nail down flooring planks and prevent squeaks or future loosening of boards, flooring cleats are driven into the tongue portion of tongue-and-groove flooring strips.

▼AIR-POWERED FLOORING NAIL GUN Laying an entire wood-strip floor is a less tedious job if you use a pneumatic flooring nail gun. Striking the knob atop the tool triggers an air-driven plunger that drives and sets a cleatlike barbed nail.

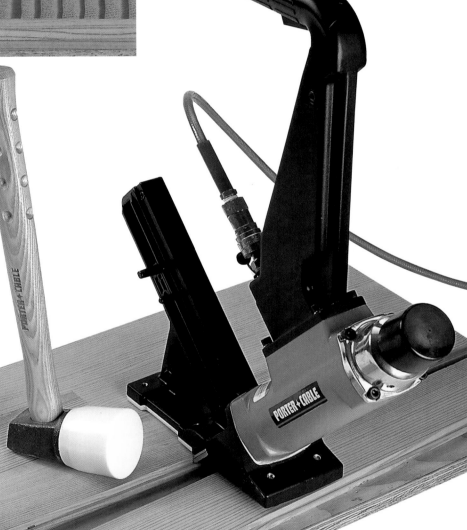

headless fasteners up to ¾ in. long that are so thin (23 ga.), that they leave practically no mark on the surface.

TONGUE-AND-GROOVE FLOORING NAILERS

A specialized tool, the tongue-and-groove flooring nailer is the ideal tool for installing solid hardwood floors milled with tongue and grooves, which lock together when the floor is laid. The nails that hold down each new plank must be driven accurately through the top portion of the tongue, a job that this tool is specifically designed to do. Available in both manual and air-powered versions (the latter shown in the photo at right), a flooring nailer drives special barbed flooring nails (fed automatically from a clip) that resist being pulled out, preventing loose or squeaky boards. It nails flooring strips to subflooring more quickly and accurately than hand-nailing. Both the manual and air-powered models are expensive, so it's probably something you'll want to rent instead of buy.

▶NARROW-CROWN STAPLER AND ROOFING STAPLER These are two air-powered staple guns with very different applications: The narrow-crown stapler (left) is for all kinds of woodworking assembly chores; the roofing stapler (right) is for installing wood or composition shingles on a roof.

Air Staplers

Although they look just like nail guns, air-powered staple guns shoot twin-shank fasteners with a simple advantage over nails: They have twice the holding power. Like nail guns, air staple guns use a specific range of fastener types and sizes. Narrow-crown staple guns fire strong, ¼-in.-wide staples perfect for building kitchen cabinets, assembling drawers, or fabricating all manner of jigs and fixtures.

Wide-crown staple guns (sometimes called roofing staplers) use 1-in.-wide staples great for fastening wood or composition shingles when installing or repairing a roof. Wide-crown staples are also good for tacking up rigid insulation and fastening insulative sheathing on your home.

Hand-Operated Staple Guns

Not to be confused with the stapler you keep in your desk, a hand staple gun is a powerful fastening tool, capable of driving staples into plywood, fiberboard, and other dense materials. It's the perfect tool for about a million different jobs around the house or shop: to tack up birthday-party decorations, reupholster a chair, install insulation, or hold up plastic sheeting when painting your house. Special nose-piece accessories, available with some models, make it easier to do special jobs, such as stapling wire screen to a door frame or fabric to a rollup window shade.

While the majority of staplers use standard T-50 staples, there are models that use special fasteners, such as wire and cable tackers, which shoot U-shaped staples for tacking down telephone, cable-television, or computer-network wiring.

Heavy-duty staple guns not only handle the greatest range of jobs but also require

▲STAPLE GUN Using a staple gun is a quick yet dependable way of tacking up sheet plastic and other light materials.

▲WIRE AND CABLE STAPLE GUN Using special-size T-75 staples, this staple gun is handy for fastening low-voltage electrical wires and cables in place.

more muscle power than light-duty guns (you're compressing a strong spring that, when released, slams the staple down). Many models have handles that are reversed from traditional guns, with your trigger hand pressing closer to the end of the gun where staples fire. Even though they may look backward, many users find the new guns easier to use and control—important when you're atop a ladder and reaching up to staple that last insulation bat in place.

Hammer Tackers

This unique tool combines the fastening power of a stapler with the speed of a hammer. Using regular T-50 staples, a hammer tacker uses a shoe on the bottom of its head to drive staples when the shoe is pounded against a surface.

▼STAPLE GUNS Unlike a traditional staple gun (left), many modern guns have their firing levers reversed so more force is applied over the spot where the staple is driven.

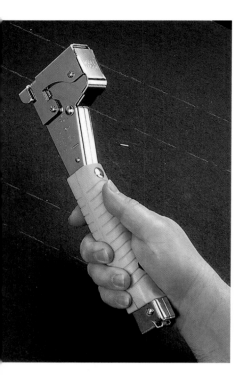

◄HAMMER TACKER A specialized kind of staple gun, a hammer tacker quickly sets staples to hold in place roofing paper, plastic tarps, and other sheeting.

►ELECTRIC STAPLE GUN Using an electrically driven piston to fire fasteners, an electric staple gun will prevent you from getting hand cramps when you have lots of staples to drive.

A hammer tacker will drive a few dozen staples in about half as many seconds to firmly batten down roofing felt, secure building paper and plastic sheeting, or tack insulation bats between rafters or ceiling joists. A hammer tacker has about twice the staple-holding capacity of a regular stapler, allowing you to work for a long time before reloading.

Electric Staplers and Brad Guns

On occasions when you have a big job, an electric stapler or brad gun will save you from a sore arm. Unlike air-powered staple guns, electric staplers don't require a compressor. The tool's electromechanically driven coil spring drives staples with just the pull of a trigger, even into dense materials like hardwoods and Masonite. Depending on the model, some guns drive both staples and small brad nails. Although more versatile, dual-fastener models have one small drawback: The single ram they use to drive both staples and brads tends to leave a wide indentation adjacent to brads.

►POP-RIVETING KIT Pop-riveting is a strong yet easy-to-use method for joining sheet metal and other thin materials. This kit includes a pop-riveting tool and an assortment of rivets to suit various applications.

Pop Riveters

Unless you have a magic wand that can weld without heat, the easiest way to join two thin metal parts together—say, to repair a rain gutter—is with pop rivets. This clever fastening system relies on special metal rivets that insert into holes drilled through thin workpieces. Each rivet's long tail fits into the nozzle of a pop-riveting gun. Squeezing the tool's handle repeatedly pulls the rivet's tail out, flaring the end and cinching it in the hole.

Amazingly, you drill and pop rivets entirely from one side of the workpiece, so you can join parts even when you don't have access to the back side—say, when adding a shelf bracket to the side of a filing cabinet. Some pop riveters come with a swiveling head that allows you to set rivets inside partially assembled boxes and other enclosed forms. Pop rivets come in several sizes to suit various thicknesses.

Although they're often used for fabricating sheet-metal projects, pop rivets also work with other thin materials—plastic, hardboard, leather, etc. There's even a new kind of pop rivet that can fasten thin parts to wood, such as plastic house numbers to a sign. Concentric grooves on the rivet's shank lock into the wood's fibers when the rivet is set.

Powder-Actuated Fasteners

Fastening lumber or steel to masonry materials is a quick and easy job, if you make friends with PAT, a popular nickname for powder-actuated tools. PATs are handheld tools that fire naillike fasteners into concrete and masonry using the force of a gunpowder-filled cartridge. Cartridges come in several sizes, for lighter- or heavier-duty jobs.

Expensive semiautomatic, trigger-operated versions of these tools are used daily by construction professionals to securely fasten wall plates and furring strips to concrete slabs and walls. They're also a quick means of clipping electrical conduits and fastening junction boxes to masonry or even wood shutters to brick walls. But there are also affordable, hammer-fired or twist-action PAT models useful for do-it-yourselfers. Although they need reloading after every shot, these PATs are still much faster to use than regular drill-and-drive concrete anchors. Also, you don't need a license to buy or use one, as required for professional models.

▲POP RIVETER A swivel-head feature allows you to use a pop riveter in a cramped space, such as inside a sheet-metal toolbox or filing cabinet.

▼SPECIAL POP RIVETS Most often used on sheet metal, you can get special pop rivets that allow you to join thin parts and hardware to wood surfaces.

▲POWDER-ACTUATED TOOL One of the strongest, fastest ways of attaching wood or metal components to concrete foundations, a powder-actuated tool uses a gunpowder cartridge to drive a stout fastener.

SOLDERING AND BRAZING

Few things put us more in touch with our primitive ancestry than using fire for useful purposes, such as heating our homes (or caves) and cooking our food. But by far the do-it-yourselfer's most useful application of fire is for joining metal parts—using soldering, brazing, and welding techniques and devices. Both electric soldering irons and propane gas torches create adequate amounts of heat to melt soft metals into liquid form, allowing you to join metal parts much like you'd glued them together—only with much stronger results.

Soldering Irons

As simple as the process of soldering is—melt soft metal solder and use it to bond together hard-metal (steel, brass, silver, etc.) parts—it's terrifically effective for diverse chores, from repairing electrical devices and electronics projects to fastening mechanical parts and jewelry, to assembling pipes and plumbing. In the old days, a soldering iron was literally a piece of iron or copper with a handle that you heated in a small furnace or fire.

Today's electric soldering irons make the process safer and more convenient. Both pencil-style and gun-style irons use 110-volt electric heating elements to heat their metal tips hot enough to melt solder. Pressing the tip against metal objects transfers enough heat to allow molten solder to flow onto the surfaces and bond parts together: a wire to a terminal, an elbow to a straight pipe, etc. The size of a soldering iron is rated in watts; the higher the wattage, the higher the heat capacity of the iron, and the faster it will heat up thicker, larger workpieces.

PENCIL-STYLE IRONS Inexpensive and compact, pencil-style soldering irons are indispensable for home and workshop electrical repairs. Many users prefer their compact, easy-to-hold design to the bigger, bulkier form of a soldering gun.

Typically, electric pencil irons come in different ratings—25 watts, 40 watts, 60 watts, and 75 watts. The higher the wattage, the larger the size of the tip, and the greater the heat output of the iron. For greater soldering versatility, you can buy a pencil-iron handle that accepts different screw-in heating elements, so one iron works for both large jobs and delicate work.

Which One? PICKING THE RIGHT SOLDER

Regardless of the kind of iron you use—an electric gun or pencil iron, or a gas torch—the kind of solder you choose is crucial for achieving good results. There are at least four kinds of soft and semisoft solders available at a well-stocked hardware store. Since all kinds of solder can produce harmful fumes when heated, always work in a well-ventilated area.

ROSIN FLUX-CORE SOLDER is a tin-lead alloy with a flux paste in the core that cleans away oxides and encourages a good bond with metal. It's used for electrical work.
• 18 swg (gauge) is good for general electrical repairs
• 22 swg is best for soldering delicate electronics components on printed circuit boards

ACID FLUX-CORE SOLDER is also a tin-lead alloy with a flux paste in the core, but it is specifically used for metal work—never use it for electrical repairs or plumbing work.
• useful for repairing radiators
• good for soldering radiators or sheet-metal parts

PLUMBER'S SOLDER has no lead in it, so it's safe for sweating pipes.
• safe for copper pipes
• used for fittings in a household water supply

SILVER SOLDER is also lead free. It's harder than other types of solders.
• intended for repairing jewelry
• good for soldering parts made from silver, copper, or nickel alloy

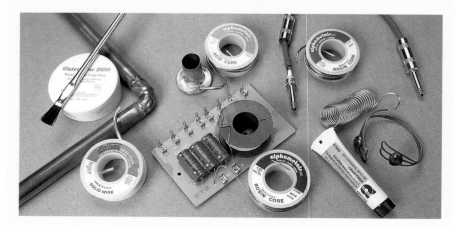

▶SOLDERING IRONS It's easy to take for granted the ease with which a modern soldering iron, such as a pencil-style iron (bottom), heats up, until you consider that early irons (top) had to be heated with a separate torch or furnace.

SOLDERING GUNS Resembling a small electric drill, a gun-style soldering iron contains a high-wattage transformer that heats the gun's tip quickly: Just pull the trigger, wait a few seconds, and you're ready to solder.

Most guns are rated at between 150 watts and 260 watts, so they produce higher temperatures and a greater volume of heat than pencil-style irons do. Having lots of heat on tap makes soldering guns a best bet for heavy-duty jobs, such as soldering sheet metal or hardware and automotive or electrical-wiring repairs (guns produce too much heat for delicate electronics repairs). Better soldering guns have built-in lights for improved visibility and dual heat settings so you can adjust the heat output to match the task.

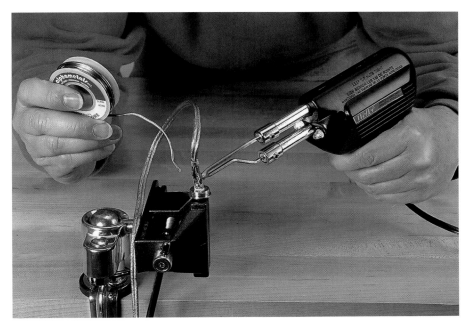

▲SOLDERING GUN A soldering gun heats quickly and has enough power for demanding soldering jobs. Built-in lights help you see what you're doing, even in a dim environment.

Propane Torches

As destructive as fire can be, a controlled, high-temperature flame is an incredibly useful thing (in the hands of a careful user, of course). Propane torches put out a lot of heat given their modest size. The torch itself runs on inexpensive, disposable propane canisters, mixing the gas with air to generate a flame hot enough to sweat copper pipe, braze aluminum, and solder mechanical or electrical joints.

Most torches have interchangeable tips: A smaller tip produces a pencil-point blue flame (it looks like a miniature jet exhaust) that's good for concentrating heat on a joint or

| Cool Tools | **BUTANE-POWERED PORTABLE SOLDERING IRONS** |

BUTANE-POWERED PORTABLE SOLDERING IRONS are the perfect answer if you're away from power and can't plug in your soldering iron. Compact and easy to handle, these clever devices run on the same kind of butane used in refillable lighters. Once ignited by the built-in striker in the cap, the iron fires up quickly and produces a surprising amount of heat, considering its small size. You can use them for all kinds of field repairs, from portable power-tool cords on the job site to audio plugs and cables at music concerts.

►BUTANE TORCH A push-button, instant-ignition feature makes it quick and safe to light the flame on a butane torch.

precise area. Larger tips produce a swirling, dispersed flame that's good for heating larger surfaces to do decorative wood burning or give wood a weathered, antique look (scorch with a torch, then scrub with a stiff, metal bristle brush). Furthermore, a torch will handily start a charcoal fire in your barbeque or even caramelize sugar atop a dessert like crème brûlée.

Most propane torches also work with Mapp® gas cylinders, which generate an even hotter flame than propane, allowing you to tackle small brazing jobs (fastening metal parts with melted bronze) and light welding. Older torches require a spark lighter to ignite the flame (*never* use a cigarette lighter—it could explode), but the latest models feature built-in piezoelectric ignitions. Open the gas valve, push the trigger, and voilà, an instant blue flame.

MINITORCHES Good things often come in small packages, and minitorches are a good example. Small enough to fit into your pocket, they're perfect for small soldering jobs away from home and power outlets. While they don't produce the heat of a full-size propane torch, minitorches mix butane fuel with air to generate enough heat for both soft or silver soldering of small objects.

The precision of a minitorch's microflame is particularly suitable for jewelry work and repairs. It will even melt glass rod and tubing for small craft projects (pipe and cigar smokers say it's also great for lighting up). Most minis refill from a butane canister, just like cigarette lighters, while some (shown at bottom in the photo below) use a standard disposable lighter as a fuel source.

▲BUTANE TORCH WITH MAPP GAS To get a higher temperature flame for brazing and light welding with a butane torch, fit it with a Mapp gas cylinder.

►BUTANE MINITORCHES Handy for all kinds of small soldering and heating jobs, butane minitorches come in two kinds: The blue torch refills from a can of butane, while the red torch runs on a standard disposable lighter.

GLUE APPLICATORS AND GUNS

Glue is magic stuff, isn't it? A little drop between two parts can hold them together with astonishing strength (especially with wood, where glue bonds are usually stronger than the wood itself). But gluing can also be a messy process, which is why there are lots of different kinds of liquid-glue applicators to help spread just the right amount.

To make glue joints even stronger, football-shaped biscuits may be added after the wood is prepared with a plate-joinery machine. Other versatile gluing devices for joining diverse materials include electric hot-melt glue guns and adhesive transfer tape applicators.

Glue Applicators

White and yellow PVA (polyvinyl acetate) adhesives are great for gluing together wood projects, as well as a host of other materials, including leather, foam, cardboard, and porcelain. But to form an effective bond, glue must be spread evenly on both surfaces being joined.

A simple brush works well for applying glue on edges and small parts. A flux brush (sold as a soldering accessory) or inexpensive foam brush is a good choice, since it's disposable if the glue dries on it. Another approach is to buy a glue bottle with a built-in brush, as shown in the top photo at right. The plastic bottle's tight-fitting cap keeps the glue and brush from drying out.

To get strong bonds between edges and surfaces—say, when gluing together boards or panels, glue should be spread in a thin, even layer. A glue roller bottle accomplishes this more neatly and quickly than spreading the glue by brush. A spigot in the top of the bottle lets glue run onto the roller, which then transfers glue to the work (it looks like a tiny steamroller).

Since PVA glues are viscous, it isn't always easy to apply them into holes and narrow slots. An inexpensive plastic glue

◄GLUE BOTTLE AND BRUSHES
Brushing liquid glue onto parts assures a strong, even glueline. Soldering flux brushes (front) make good glue brushes, or you can buy a glue bottle with an applicator brush in the lid.

▼GLUE ROLLER BOTTLE This special bottle, designed for applying an even layer of woodworking glue, has a spreading roller built into its cap.

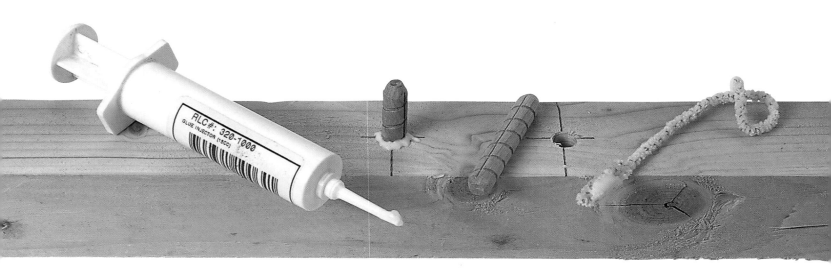

▲GLUE INJECTOR SYRINGE
**To get liquid glues into holes
and deep slots, nothing beats
a plastic glue syringe.**

syringe does the trick nicely. Just push its plunger to squirt out just the amount of glue that's needed. Not only does it inject glue into deep cavities or cracks, a syringe will also sensitively apply a teeny drop of glue on a tiny part—say, when building a ship model or repairing a delicate knickknack.

Hot-Melt Glue Guns

The clever crafter's not-so-secret weapon, a glue gun heats and applies hot-melt adhesives capable of bonding parts for assembling craft projects or accomplishing home repairs. Since they'll stick to just about anything, hot-melt glues are useful in all crafts and are particularly effective when bonding dissimilar materials, such as wood, cardboard, metal, or plastic to one another. Plus, hot melts are water resistant, making them useful for outdoor projects that aren't subject to direct sunlight and high temperatures, which could melt the glue.

The adhesive comes in a ½-in.-dia. stick, which feeds into a chamber inside the electric gun where it melts. Thumb pressure or a trigger-operated feed mechanism dispenses the hot glue through the

gun's nozzle. Better guns come with two or more interchangeable nozzles, allowing you to change the shape/volume of glue output to suit the task: a thin bead for narrow or small parts, a thick stream to coat large surfaces.

Basic glue guns have only one, high-heat setting, which is good for a wide variety of projects from making jewelry and building dollhouses to repairing holes in drywall. High-heat guns work with most types of glue sticks (see the facing page).

Better gun models offer both a high-heat setting and low-heat setting

▲HOT-MELT GLUE GUN TIPS
**Interchangeable tips let you
adapt the flow of adhesive from
a hot-melt glue gun to suit
different bonding tasks.**

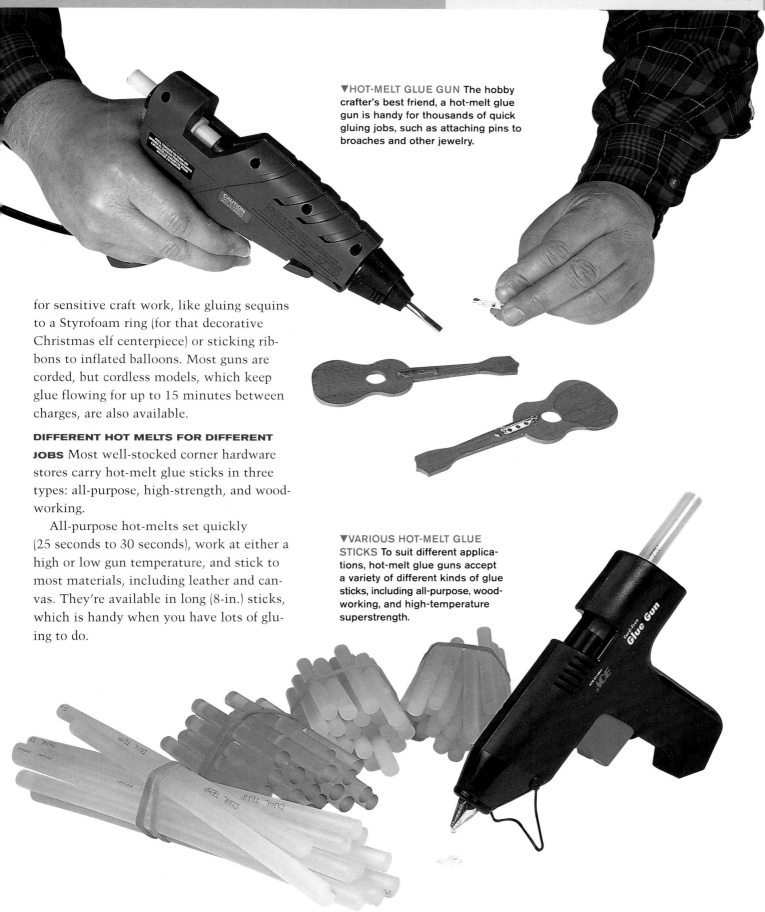

▼HOT-MELT GLUE GUN The hobby crafter's best friend, a hot-melt glue gun is handy for thousands of quick gluing jobs, such as attaching pins to broaches and other jewelry.

for sensitive craft work, like gluing sequins to a Styrofoam ring (for that decorative Christmas elf centerpiece) or sticking ribbons to inflated balloons. Most guns are corded, but cordless models, which keep glue flowing for up to 15 minutes between charges, are also available.

DIFFERENT HOT MELTS FOR DIFFERENT JOBS Most well-stocked corner hardware stores carry hot-melt glue sticks in three types: all-purpose, high-strength, and woodworking.

All-purpose hot-melts set quickly (25 seconds to 30 seconds), work at either a high or low gun temperature, and stick to most materials, including leather and canvas. They're available in long (8-in.) sticks, which is handy when you have lots of gluing to do.

▼VARIOUS HOT-MELT GLUE STICKS To suit different applications, hot-melt glue guns accept a variety of different kinds of glue sticks, including all-purpose, woodworking, and high-temperature superstrength.

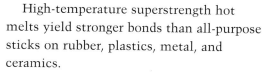
High-temperature superstrength hot melts yield stronger bonds than all-purpose sticks on rubber, plastics, metal, and ceramics.

Woodworking glue sticks have a slightly longer set time than other hot melts, 50 seconds to 60 seconds, which provides enough time to position and reposition wood parts carefully. They're good for many wood projects that don't require enormous holding power—for example, gluing up small picture frames and wooden toys. And they excel at mounting thin moldings, which are easily split with small nails.

Adhesive Transfer Tape

Take double-stick tape, eliminate the thin plastic tape backing, and you have adhesive transfer tape. This useful material comes in rolls like regular tapes, but it must be applied with a special dispenser gun. A rubber roller at the tip of the gun dispenses a layer of adhesive (which looks a bit like the translucent trail left by a snail or slug) from a strip of backing paper as you drag the roller over a surface. A takeup reel inside the gun spools up the used backing paper, which is thrown away when the tape's used up. Adhesive transfer tape is sensational for attaching paper, cardboard, and other thin materials.

Biscuit Joinery

The glue that joins two pieces of wood makes a strong joint. But you can make any joint stronger and easier to align during assembly by adding a biscuit—a special football-shaped wafer made from compressed wood. The biscuit fits into a pair of slots cut into the edges or surfaces of parts, such as the sides of a box, picture frame, or stereo cabinet.

You can cut the slots with a router or by hand with a chisel, but using a plate-joinery

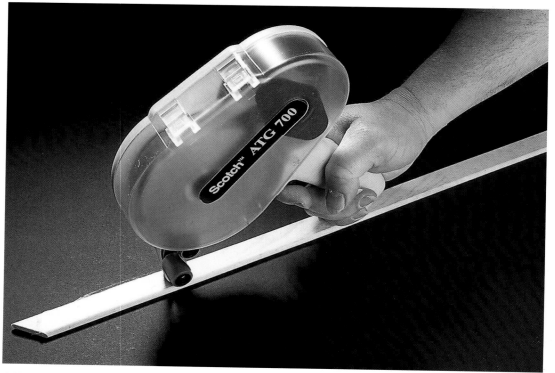

▲ADHESIVE TRANSFER TAPE DISPENSER GUN Resembling a slime trail left by a snail, adhesive transfer tape, applied from a special dispenser gun, is handy for bonding all kinds of light parts, from paper decorations to decorative wood moldings.

▼BISCUIT JOINER AND GLUE
APPLICATOR Football-shaped
biscuits set into slots cut by a
biscuit joiner reinforce all kinds
of wood joints, including miters.
A piston-action applicator bottle
spreads glue evenly into the slots.

machine makes the job practically effortless. Pressing the machine's handle forward plunges the blade into the wood and creates a semicircular slot just the right size for a biscuit. To handle different stock thicknesses, biscuits come in three common sizes: #0, #10, and #20. The #20s are the largest and best for stock that's ¾ in. thick or thicker. A depth stop on the biscuit joiner adjusts the blade-plunge depth to work with each size biscuit. A fence on the front of the machine tilts down, allowing you to cut slots into beveled edges.

When your slotted work is ready for assembly, putting glue (white or yellow carpenter's glue) in each slot makes the biscuit swell until it's wedged tightly in the slot, thus strengthening the joint. Biscuits also help keep parts aligned during assembly. A special applicator bottle with a slot-shaped nozzle lets you squirt just the right amount of glue into each slot, making the job less messy.

CHAPTER 10

Tools That Brush & Spread

You may not think of a paintbrush or roller as a tool, in the same way you think of a chisel or screwdriver, but when it comes to painting your house or putting a coat of varnish on an heirloom rocking chair, shouldn't you select and use finishing tools with the same care and consideration you'd apply to a new table saw or cordless drill? Traditional hand applicators—such as brushes, rollers, and pads—may seem like simple tools, but choosing the right one makes all the difference between success and failure. Power applicators—airless sprayers, spray guns, power rollers, etc.—are even more confusing to choose and use. If surfaces require stripping and preparation, there are other tools to consider as well, including sanders, wire brushes, and heat guns.

▲PAINT BRUSH ASSORTMENT Depending on the size and shape of the job, choose a wide, narrow, or skewed paint brush.

BRUSHES, PAINT PADS, AND ROLLERS

To achieve an impressive final appearance, the tools you use to apply finish to a new shed, mailbox, or doghouse are just as important as the tools you used to build it. A hand applicator, like a brush or paint pad, is inexpensive and relatively easy to use, but you must select the right one to suit the size and nature of the job, as well as the type of paint or finish you're using.

The following section will guide you through the myriad choices you face when selecting a brush (bristle or foam), paint pad, or roller. Regardless of which finishing tools you use, it's always a good idea to wear gloves to protect your hands and shorten cleanup time (see p. 269).

Bristle Brushes

Paintbrushes with bunches of fine bristles fashioned from natural hair or synthetic fibers have been around a long time, and with good reason: A good brush is a simple and effective application tool for a wide range of materials, from house paints and enamels to woodworking varnishes, lacquers, and other clear finishes—not to mention deck stains, concrete and stone sealers, and waterproofers. A strong advantage of using a brush rather than a roller or piece of spray equipment is that its bristles force the finish into all the nooks, crannies, and imperfections found on a surface.

To suit a wide range of finishing jobs and materials, brushes are made with different kinds of bristles (see "The Right Brush for the Finish" at right) and come in several sizes and styles. Wide brushes (4 in. to 6 in.) have the capacity to hold lots of finish and spread it more evenly and quickly over a large surface, like a wall or the side of a barn.

Which One? **THE RIGHT BRUSH FOR THE FINISH**

If you want to get nice results when brushing a paint or finish on your home or other project, you must choose the right kind of brush to suit the type of finishing material you're using. There are many to choose from, including both traditional (hair, nylon, etc.) and modern synthetic bristle blends, designed to handle a full range of finishes. The bristle type is usually printed on the protective holder the brush comes in (sometimes you have to look carefully at the back of the packaging to find it) or on the brush itself, along with application recommendations.

NYLON, POLYESTER, AND NYLON/POLYESTER BLEND BRUSHES have synthetic bristles. They're best for:
• latex and water-based paints
• water-based stains and clear coatings

NATURAL BRISTLE BRUSHES made with hog hair are sometimes called China bristle brushes. They're best for:
• oil-based paints and stains
• oil- and solvent-based clear coatings (e.g., spar varnish)
• mixed hog-hair and ox-hair brushes are best for clear oil-based varnishes, shellac, and lacquers

NYLON/CHINEX® BRISTLE BLEND BRUSHES are the latest all-purpose finishing applicators. They're best for:
• oil-based enamels
• water-based latex paints
• all stains, varnishes, and polyurethane finishes (both oil and water-based)

Narrower brushes (1 in. to 3 in.) are more effective for painting and finishing small projects and trim (moldings, window and door frames, etc.). Really skinny brushes (½ in. to 1 in.) are best for painting models and doing touchup work. Inexpensive flux brushes (also called acid brushes; shown at left in the photo in Pro/Con box on p. 239) are short and narrow and work well for applying glue to edges and into slots, holes, and crevices.

Most projects require two brushes: a large one for covering surfaces quickly and a smaller one for painting trim and details (see p. 238). Choosing the largest brush that fits the size of the area you're working on saves time: It takes fewer strokes to cover the surface, and you don't have to dip it in the finish as frequently.

Pro Tip

You'll get the best brush control, fewer hand cramps, and a smoother, more even finish if you grasp a brush with your fingers spread out across the ferrule (the metal band above the bristles) and the handle resting between your thumb and forefinger.

Tool Helpers — MASKING TOOLS AND PAINTING SHIELDS

It's often impossible to paint one surface (a wall) without getting paint on an adjacent surface (a molding), especially if you're using spray equipment. That's why masking and covering surfaces is an important part of the finishing process. Masking tape applicators make it quick and easy to cover up window frames, doorways, baseboards, chair rails, and the like.

An applicator dispenses tape from a reel and has a serrated blade that cuts the tape cleanly. Most applicators will also dispense masking paper or plastic film along with the tape (shown at top in the photo), which is convenient when you need to cover up wider surfaces, like kitchen cabinets or built-in shelves.

But masking tape isn't a surface-covering cure-all. Finishes can creep under masking tape (especially oil-based paints), leaving behind a messy, difficult-to-clean edge that usually requires further touching up. That's why many experienced painters prefer to cut in with a brush—carefully brush along an edge or corner that's between painted and unpainted surfaces. Although it requires some skill to master, the method is faster than masking, and by using a handheld painting shield (shown at bottom in the photo), you can guard an adjacent surface just in case your brush slips.

STRAIGHT AND SKEWED BRUSH STYLES

Most brushes made for painting and finish application have a straight edge that's square relative to the handle and ferrule (the metal band that surrounds the bristles). The exception are skewed brushes (or sash brushes), which have an angled edge that makes it easier to apply finish in the corners of a window frame, on furniture details, on the raised panels of a door, or in the cramped spaces around the corners of a room. Some people also prefer to use a wide skewed brush in lieu of a straight brush to paint shiplap or clapboard house siding. Brush handles are traditionally made out of varnished or unfinished wood, although modern brushes often feature molded plastic handles with rubberized grips, which are comfortable to hold for long periods of time.

CLEANING AND STORING BRUSHES If
you've gone to the trouble and expense of buying high-quality paintbrushes, you need to clean them thoroughly after every use and store them carefully. Proper storage

Pro Tip

For best masking performance: (1) Choose the right tape to suit the finish: blue tape for long-term masking and a clean, residue-free release; green tape for a crisp finish line. (2) Never tape over a freshly painted surface. (3) Peel tape off shortly after painting, pulling it back at a 30-degree angle away from the painted edge.

▲SKEWED BRUSH With its angled end, a skewed brush makes it easier to apply paint or finish to corners, finish moldings, and raised panels.

◄BRUSH CLEANING AND WRAPPING
Cleaning a brush thoroughly after use and then wrapping it in clean paper keeps the bristles straight and makes the brush last longer.

means putting the brush back into the cardboard holder it came in or wrapping it in brown paper (a cutup grocery bag is just fine) right after washing. This keeps the bristles straight as they dry, so the brush keeps its shape and continues to perform well.

If you don't like to clean brushes after every use (or just want to keep a brush from drying out for a few hours), suspend it in a can of solvent that suits the finish you're using. A covered soaking container, as shown at left in the photo above, is handy, as it holds two brushes and prevents solvent fumes from wafting around the room.

Foam Brushes

If frugality is next to godliness in your book, then foam brushes will certainly appeal to you. Probably the least expensive finish applicator you can buy, a foam brush is really nothing more than a piece of thin foam on a stick, which you use once and throw away. Despite their simple construction, foam brushes are appropriate for a great many jobs around the house. For example, they're good at applying oil finishes, stains, or bleach, as well as a first coat of paint or finish that will be sanded smooth before subsequent coats are applied. Available in several widths, foam brushes are handy for all kinds of small touchups. Because they're disposable, peo-

▲FOAM BRUSHES Inexpensive enough to be disposable after a single use, foam brushes are handy for small finishing and touchup jobs.

THERE'S NO QUESTION that a high-quality brush will outperform an inexpensive one, which is an important consideration when choosing a brush to apply a smooth lacquer finish on a tabletop or a flawless coat of glossy varnish on your prized woody station wagon.

But for every high-quality finishing job you do around the house or workshop, there are probably two jobs that an inexpensive brush will do just as well (see the photo below), and there's definitely an advantage to using a brush once and simply throwing it away—no cleanup time or nasty solvents to deal with.

QUALITY BRUSHES
Pros:
• great for fine finishing jobs
• leave a smooth finish without brush marks
• no loose bristles
• last a long time

Cons:
• expensive
• must be properly cleaned to maintain performance

BARGAIN BRUSHES
Pros:
• inexpensive to buy
• good for applying glue, strippers, and chemicals
• no cleanup (disposable)

Cons:
• leave brush marks; poor choice for finishing
• may leave loose bristles in finish
• don't last

Pro Tip

To save paints and finishes from drying out when you take a break, spread a layer of plastic food wrap directly on top of the finish in the can or tray. Doing this before resealing the can will help prevent finishes from skinning over during storage.

ple also like using them to apply and spread glue and other nasty substances.

What *don't* foam brushes do well? Even professionals find it difficult to accomplish fine work with a foam brush—say, applying a smooth, even coat of varnish on a bar counter or wood boat transom. Because they don't have bristles, a foam brush can't paint down into surface details, such as carvings, flutes, or routed decorations. Finally, you simply *cannot* use a foam brush for applying alcohol-based materials, such as shellac sealer or nitrocellulose lacquer, because their solvents melt foam.

▶PAINT PADS An easy-to-use alternative to brushes, paint pads come in many sizes and shapes, good for applying latex paints, as well as many clear finishes.

Paint Pads

Although it doesn't look much like one, a paint pad is actually like a paintbrush: On close examination, you can see that the pad's furry covering has thousands of tiny bristles which are like short versions of paintbrush bristles. If you're an inexperienced painter, paint pads are an excellent choice. Lighter in weight than most rollers and brushes, paint pads come in all shapes and sizes and are easy to use with latex paints and water-based finishes. They also work well with most oil-based coatings, and better still, they're inexpensive enough that you could throw them away after a single use—convenient if you hate doing cleanup.

Because of their flat shape and short bristles, most paint pads work best on flat surfaces. A big, rectangular pad works well on a large wall, a panel, or exterior siding, though it won't hold as much paint as a well-loaded roller or paintbrush. Smaller paint pads excel at cutting-in or edging work—around window frames, moldings, and trim, as well as touchups. You can paint a reasonably straight line with little paint splatter, even if you don't have a particularly steady hand. There are also special pad models for painting inside corners of a room, ceilings, and high trim (they attach to a long handle). You can even buy a paint pad device (shown at left in the photo at left) that feeds latex paint to its small pad from a spring-loaded reservoir, which is filled by sucking paint right out of the can. Designed for painting trim, the device saves time because you don't have to reload it after every few strokes.

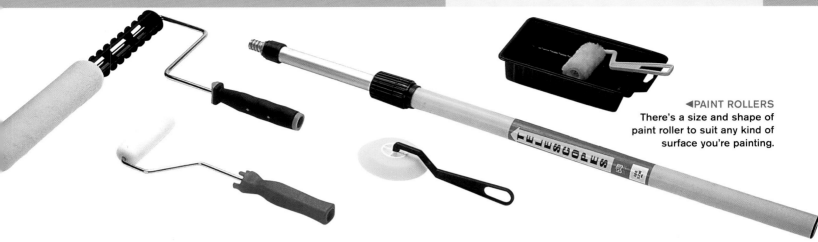

◄PAINT ROLLERS
There's a size and shape of paint roller to suit any kind of surface you're painting.

Paint Rollers

When finishing a large area, such as a wall or ceiling, a paint roller can apply paint almost as quickly as a power sprayer can, but it costs far less and doesn't generate messy overspray. Using a paint roller requires the purchase of several separate components: a roller frame (handle), roller cover, and a paint tray.

FRAMES A good roller frame has a comfortable hand grip (sometimes rubberized) and a metal wire or fiberglass-reinforced nylon cage that holds the cover snugly, preventing it from slipping or walking off during rolling, while still allowing it to be removed quickly and easily (avoid inexpensive roller handles that attach the roller with a wing nut).

Most roller handles have a threaded end that fits an extension pole—handy for lengthening your reach when painting floors without stooping or ceilings without a ladder. Standard roller frames, best for painting large areas, are 9 in. long and 1½ in. in diameter. Smaller 3-in. and 4-in. frames are great for rolling smaller areas and trim, as well as for touchups. You can also find rollers specialized for different jobs—painting inside corners, radiators, or rounded columns, for example.

ROLLER COVERS The cover you put on a roller frame has everything to do with how well (or badly) your finishing job will go. There are dozens of different kinds of standard roller covers to choose from, as well as special textured rollers for decorative

Tool Helpers	**ROLLER TRAY LINERS AND PAINT-CAN LIDS**

These two painting accessories are inexpensive and really make cleanup a lot easier. Plastic tray liners are a must if you use a paint roller to apply latex paints—there's just no sense spending time washing out a tray after every use. The thin liner presses down into the plastic or metal tray to hold the paint—you simply throw it away after the job. Just be aware that each style and size of roller tray uses a different liner—the wrong one won't fit.

A neat new alternative to tray liners is a disposable roller tray (shown at right in the photo below). The tray's clamshell-style lid is designed to close with the roller inside, thus you can stop work for the day without having to empty the tray and wash the roller cover.

Plastic paint-can lids (shown at rear in the photo) solve a couple of common problems inherent with standard 1-gal. paint cans. Most styles replace a can's regular lid and have a built-in vented spout for pouring paint into trays, and they also have a wider opening conducive to brushing right out of the can. The plastic lid seals tightly when not in use—much easier than prying off (and banging on) a regular lid. Best of all, the lid snaps over the can's rim and prevents paint from flooding into it, so the lid won't stick when you replace it after the job's done. You can also buy a simple plastic ring that seals the can's rim.

effects (see "Finish Application Devices" on p. 242). Like paintbrushes, standard covers made from synthetic materials (polyester fabric, foam, etc.) are recommended for applying latex paints and water-based finishes, while natural fiber covers, made with mohair or a blend of polyester and lamb's wool, are recommended for oil-based paints, varnish, and stains.

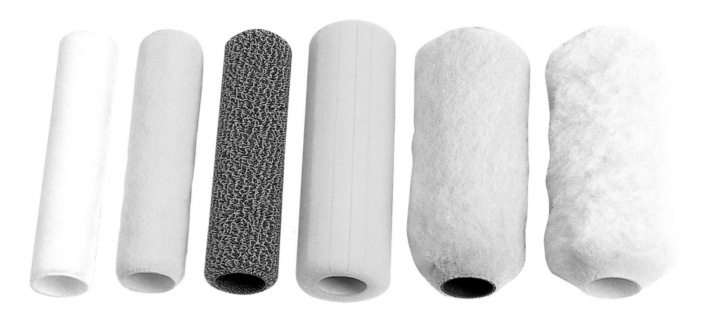

▲PAINT ROLLER COVERS Fitting a paint roller frame with a different cover can completely change the way it applies paint.

Cool Tools FINISH APPLICATION DEVICES

SEA SPONGES AND FAUX AND DECORATIVE FINISHING APPLICATORS are probably the most written about kinds of do-it-yourself finishing tools. Indeed, stroll through the paint department in a big, well-stocked home center and you'll see all manner of finish application devices, each for creating a different kind of decorative finish. Some traditional applicators take considerable skill to use effectively—a feather, for example, which is used in creating a faux veined-marble effect.

Fortunately, there's no shortage of decorative devices that are easy to use and that produce good results—even on the first try. These include: sea sponges, for blotting on an irregular pattern of accents in a contrasting-color glaze; texture rollers, for creating a swirl pattern or deep stipple marks; rag rollers, for applying glaze in a zebra-stripe pattern; accent rollers, for creating a repeating-pattern border around a room; and dragging brushes, for producing a glazed surface with a brushed look.

Both natural and synthetic covers are distinguished by their nap, the amount that their fur sticks up from the tube core (like the pile of a carpet). Nap length ranges from ³⁄₁₆ in. to 1½ in. and should suit the surface and finish. As a general rule, the smoother the surface, the shorter the cover's nap should be, and shorter naps are also better for glossier paints and finishes. For example, you'd typically use a short (¼-in. or less) nap when rolling a gloss enamel on smooth kitchen walls and a longer (¾-in. or more) nap for applying flat latex paint on the textured ceiling in the den. The chart on the facing page shows the proper nap lengths for a variety of household surfaces.

Higher-quality lint-free (or shed-resistant or epoxy-set) rollers shed less fur than bargain covers. It's worth spending more on a cover when you're finishing a high-profile area where small defects are likely to show, like a well-lit entrance hall. Another strategy for hiding surface imperfections is to choose a cover with a longer nap than is usually recommended, which will create a textured effect in the final painted surface.

TRAYS Roller trays are made of metal or plastic and come in many different sizes. Larger, deeper trays hold more paint, but they're heavier and more difficult to move when full. All trays have a textured pattern or grid on them, which helps distribute paint evenly across the roller and wrings out extra paint so the roller won't drip.

Lamb's Wool Mitts and Pads

Chain-link or picket fences, steam radiators, louvered doors, and the spindles on rocking chairs are all difficult to paint or finish; it's hard to work a brush all the way around them, and spraying them wastes too much finish. The applicator that professional painters often use for these tricky objects is a lamb's wool mitt. Resembling an overgrown mitten, a lamb's wool mitt—or its synthetic equivalent, called a painter's mitt—turns your hand into a fuzzy applicator that you can easily wrap around thin rods, spokes, and spindles to finish these objects on all sides. You can also poke the mitt down between slats, around wire mesh, or deep into slots and cubbies.

Lamb's wool and fuzzy synthetics are also commonly used for applicator pads designed for mopping floor finishes, such as clear polyurethanes (on hardwood floors) or sealers (on stone floors). They are the professional floor specialist's choice for a smooth, even finish. For really large floors, you can buy an applicator that's 10 in. to 16 in. by 3 in. wide and fits on a long pole, like a floor sweep. Synthetic applicator pads (as well as synthetic mitts) are less durable than lamb's wool but also less expensive.

Pro Tip

Condition a new roller cover to remove loose fur before using it by loading it with paint, then vigorously rolling it back and forth on a scrap of cardboard. To extend its life, reverse the cover on the roller frame now and then.

ROLLER COVERS

Nap Length	Application Surfaces
$\frac{3}{16}$ in. to $\frac{1}{4}$ in.	Smooth surfaces: smooth wood, metal, untextured plaster, or drywall
$\frac{3}{8}$ in. to $\frac{1}{2}$ in.	Medium-smooth surfaces: lightly textured plaster or wood, sand-textured walls, or paneling
$\frac{3}{4}$ in. to 1 in.	Rough surfaces: unfinished concrete, cement block, masonry floors, rough wood, or lightly textured plaster
$\frac{3}{4}$ in. to 1$\frac{1}{2}$ in.	Extra-rough surfaces: corrugated metal, stucco, textured (cottage-cheese) ceilings, or brick walls

◄**LAMB'S WOOL MITT** To apply a thin finish to an irregular or shapely object, like a stair-baluster spindle, wipe it with a lamb's wool mitt that's been dipped in the finish.

Pro Tip

Some painter's mitts have an inner protective glove to keep finish off your hands when you use them, while others (especially those made of lamb's wool) don't. Wearing a latex, vinyl, or nitrile glove with the latter will keep your hands clean.

POWERED PAINTING DEVICES

Whether it uses a motor-powered piston pump or a compressed-air spray, a powered painting device can cover a large surface with a smooth, even coat of paint or finish in a fraction of the time it takes using conventional brushes, pads, or rollers. There are several kinds of powered devices, each with different features and attributes that suit some finishing jobs better than others. This section, which covers both air-powered and airless spraying devices, as well as electric power rollers and sprayers, provides an overview of which device is best suited to a particular project.

Air-Powered Spray Guns

If you already own a compressor, you can use its powerful air output to spray on finishes by hooking up a hose and a spray gun. The trigger-operated gun takes finish from a container and mixes it with high-pressure air, atomizing it and showering the work surface in a neat, controllable pattern (usually a wide fan). With practice, you can use a gun to apply finishes smoothly and evenly, even to vertical or overhead surfaces, without creating drips and sags.

Spray guns are especially good for applications where a fine finish is crucial—lacquering fine furniture, painting automobiles, etc. By changing the size of a gun's nozzle (tip and air cap), you can use a gun to shoot many types of finishes, including lacquers and varnishes, stains, and thin paints. Unfortunately, most guns can't handle thick latex paints (see "Airless Sprayers" on p. 246).

The most popular style of spray guns siphons finish directly from a one-quart cup attached below the nozzle. These full-size guns (shown at right in the top photo on the facing page) have

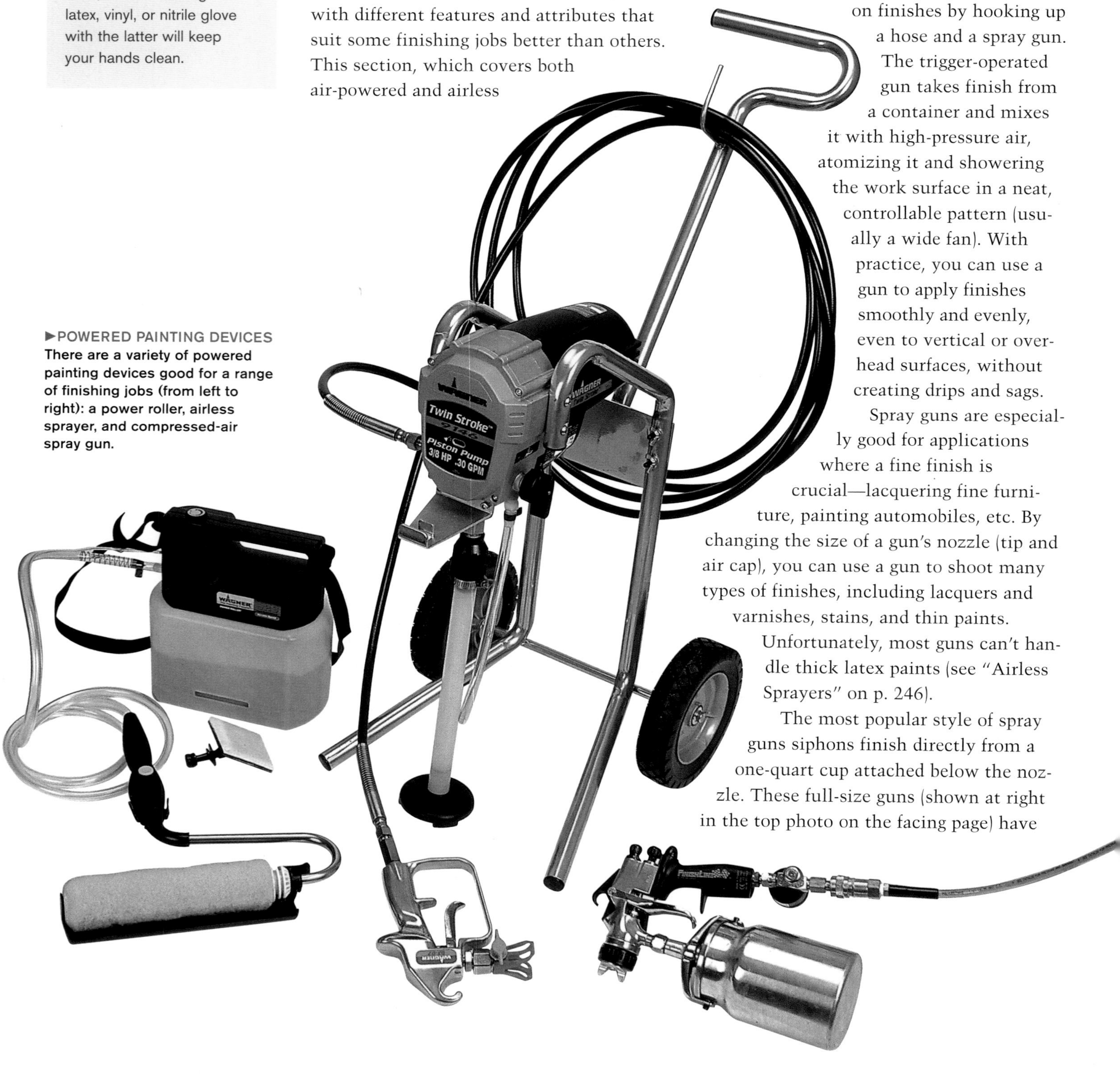

►POWERED PAINTING DEVICES There are a variety of powered painting devices good for a range of finishing jobs (from left to right): a power roller, airless sprayer, and compressed-air spray gun.

▶AIR-POWERED SPRAY GUNS
For spraying clear finishes and enamel paints, it's hard to beat the excellent job an air-powered spray gun will do—at left, a gravity-fed touchup gun; at right, a full-size siphon gun.

enough capacity for fairly large projects (lacquering a few kitchen cabinets, for instance) before the cup needs refilling.

But if your goal is spraying smaller items (woodturnings, model planes and cars, rocking horses) or doing artistic airbrush painting, you may prefer a touchup gun (shown at left in the photo at right), which is physically smaller, lighter, and easier to maneuver than a full-size spray gun. Some touchup guns have a top-mounted cup that gravity-feeds finish to the nozzle. Depending on the model, a touchup gun's cup may hold a pint or less—usually enough for a small project.

STANDARD AND HVLP-STYLE GUNS Both full-size and touchup guns come in both standard and HVLP (high-volume, low-pressure) styles, which are functionally similar. The biggest difference is that the newer-style HVLP guns (sometimes referred to as conversion guns) are more efficient, and they create less overspray. If you do a lot of spray finishing, an HVLP gun can actually save you money in the long run, because you'll use less finish.

Both styles typically require a fairly large volume of air for continuous operation, so be sure to compare a particular model's air requirements to your compressor's scfm output (see "Portable Air Compressors" on p. 220) before buying it. If you don't have an air compressor but want

Cool Tools | SPRAY-CAN HANDLE

A SPRAY-CAN HANDLE provides a cheap way to get a better spray finish, especially if you don't do enough finishing to justify buying a compressor and spray gun. You can get a decent finish with a spray can by shaking it vigorously before and during application and by using good technique (long, even strokes, keeping the can parallel to the surface). To make the job more comfortable, get an inexpensive spray-can handle. It snaps to the top ring of a standard spray can and not only makes it easier to depress the nozzle but also prevents your index finger from getting covered with paint or finish.

to use an HVLP gun, consider an HVLP turbine system, which supplies air to the gun from a special turbine-powered air pump instead of an air compressor.

ROTARY PAINT MIXERS are great devices for thoroughly mixing paints, stains, and clear finishes before application. Doing a poor job of mixing can result in parts that have the wrong tint or sheen, or adjacent walls that don't match in color. Paint sticks are fine for small cans of new finish, but you need more "horsepower" for stirring up old paints and thick materials, such as drywall joint compound, especially when they're in big 5-gal. buckets.

A rotary paint mixer has paddles on the end of its shaft that swirl and stir up thin or thick liquids (even drywall joint compound and topping) with gusto. A regular electric drill provides the power to spin the tool. It usually takes just a minute or two for the paddles to agitate paint and stain pigments (or stearates, which make flat, clear finishes flat) that settle to the bottom, mixing them evenly throughout the can or bucket.

Pro Tip

To avoid clogging delicate nozzle orifices, always stir paints and finishes thoroughly, then pour them through an inexpensive, disposable paint strainer before using them with any kind of spray equipment.

THE DOWNSIDE OF SPRAYING FINISHES
Spraying can make a quick job of finishing a project, but it can also be problematic. Unlike brushing or rolling, where, with luck, all but a few drips of paint or finish end up where they belong—on the work's surface—a significant portion of a spray gun's output ends up as overspray on adjacent surfaces, or it wafts around in the air until it settles.

Unless you do your spraying in a shop with a fan-powered spray booth that exhausts the overspray (as well as fumes from solvent-based finishes), spray guns, as well as airless sprayers, are primarily for outdoor use. Even outdoors, you'll need to cover or mask all nearby surfaces where

you don't want to get paint—windows, doors, light fixtures, small children, and pets—before you spray.

Airless Sprayers

If you'd like to spray-paint to complete larger household-improvement projects but don't own a compressor, an airless sprayer is worth considering. Airless sprayers use an electric motor and powerful pump, which pressurize the paint or finish and then force it through a hose and handheld sprayer nozzle, atomizing it into a fine spray. They're designed to apply paints, stains, and other finishes to large surfaces quickly, making them the tool of choice for professional house painters. Although not as good as air-powered spray guns for fine finish work, airless units spray more efficiently and create less overspray. Some airless sprayers can even be fitted with roller attachments, so they can be used for interior work.

Airless sprayers can be divided into two types—diaphragm and piston models—depending on the kind of pumping device they use. Diaphragm models are less expensive but also tend to be less powerful, and they're typically not as durable as piston sprayers, which are the choice of professionals. All airless sprayers use siphon tubes to suck paint directly out of the can. Some models have their motor/pump units mounted on a wheeled stand that's tall enough to fit over a 5-gal. bucket of paint—convenient for big jobs like house painting.

Power Sprayers and Rollers

Compact and reasonably priced, power sprayers and rollers are self-contained units (no compressors necessary) designed for home-improvement enthusiasts. They dispense paint or other finishing material much like airless sprayers—by pressurizing it with a small pump and spreading it via a nozzled sprayer or roller head. Power

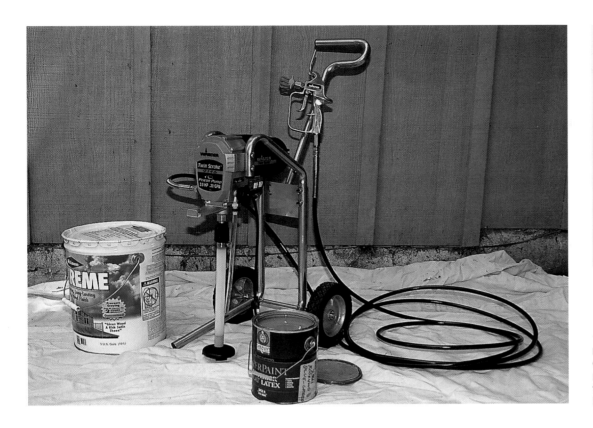

Pro Tip

Since a powerful airless sprayer will probably cost more than you'd want to spend to get a single big job done—like painting a house—consider renting one instead. Airless sprayers are available for rent throughout the country, and when you consider how much time you'll save using one, the rental fee is a bargain.

◀AIRLESS SPRAYER Able to pump paint and thick finishes directly from the can at high pressure, an airless sprayer is the tool of choice for big jobs, like painting houses.

sprayers and rollers are great for small- to medium-size painting or staining projects around the house, such as fences, lattices and shutters, patio furniture, decks and picnic tables, cottages, sheds, and cabins. You could even paint a whole house with one—although an airless sprayer is a better tool for such a large job.

POWER SPRAYERS Depending on the model you choose, power sprayers (also referred to as airless cup guns or Power Painters®—a Wagner® brand name) come in several configurations: a spray gun with a built-in, quart-finish container (shown in the photo on p. 248), a gun with a siphon hose that feeds directly from a paint can, or a gun with a hose fed from a backpack-style container.

Power sprayers don't produce the volume of finish as airless sprayers, so it can take a while to finish a large surface. But you can use one for indoor painting and finishing jobs without creating clouds of

Which One?   CHOOSING AN AIRLESS SPRAYER

When you're comparing airless sprayer models, the type of pump, the power of the motor, the maximum gpm (gallons per minute) of finish delivery, and the size of the tips the gun will accept all determine the sprayer's performance and the type of finishes it's capable of handling. The higher a unit's power and flow rate, the quicker the material is delivered, allowing a larger area to be sprayed in a shorter time. Also, the larger the gun's tip orifice, the thicker the finish the unit can spray. As a general rule, piston pumps are more durable than diaphragm-style units.

SMALL-DIAPHRAGM PUMP SPRAYERS with ⅜-hp or smaller motors, a 0.3 gpm (or less), and a maximum 0.011-in. tip size are good for small projects. They can handle:
• stains and enamel paints
• low-viscosity clear finishes (lacquer, thinned varnish)

MEDIUM-DIAPHRAGM PUMP SPRAYERS with motors between ½ hp and ⅝ hp, a 0.4 gpm, and a maximum 0.015-in. tip are fine for larger home-improvement jobs. They can handle:
• stains and most enamels
• thinned latex paints (they'll spray unthinned latex more slowly)
• clear finishes

LARGE PISTON PUMP SPRAYERS with ¾-hp to 1-hp motors, a 0.5 gpm or greater, and maximum tip size of 0.017 in. or 0.019 in. are professional units that are up to the most rigorous finishing challenges. They can handle:
• unthinned latex paints
• all stains and clear finishes
• some roof coatings

Pro Tip

When spray-painting wood house siding, fences, or decks, spray a small area at a time and then work the paint into the surface with a brush. This back brushing works the finish into the tiny crevices, nooks, and crannies and assures more thorough penetration and bonding.

overspray. Another consideration for indoor work is that power sprayers are as noisy as some portable power tools, so wear earplugs and don't plan to spray at night after your family's gone to bed. Power sprayers also tend to drip and dribble, so be sure you cover and mask anything that you don't want doused in paint.

Different power-sprayer models produce different amounts of pressure, typically 1,300 psi, 1,600 psi, 2,000 psi, and 2,400 psi. The higher the pressure, the faster paint is applied and the thicker the paint the unit can handle. Low-power models (1,600 psi and less) can only spray oil-based paints, semitransparent stains, clear finishes, wood preservatives/water sealers, and other thin materials. More powerful units can handle most water-based paints and finishes and even unthinned latex house paint. If you plan to paint a whole house, get at least a 2,000-psi model, as modern latex interior

and exterior paints are best when applied unthinned. Some models offer two speeds to control the rate at which finish is sprayed: slower for small projects, faster for large surfaces.

POWER ROLLERS Designed specifically to apply latex house paints and water-based stains, power rollers are great for painting interior walls and ceilings or for painting or staining decks and wood fences. The unit's pump forces materials through a hose to a paint roller frame fitted with a special cover that has internal holes to allow the finish to feed through. Some models also accept special paint-pad attachments for finishing trim.

Stationary-base power-roller models run on AC power and pump finishes through a long hose fed directly from a 1-gal. can. Battery-powered models feed finish from a plastic container that hangs from a shoulder strap. Although less powerful than AC

▼POWER SPRAYER A power sprayer can apply even heavy finishes, such as latex house paint, either from a cup attached to the gun or directly from the paint can via a plastic siphon hose (left).

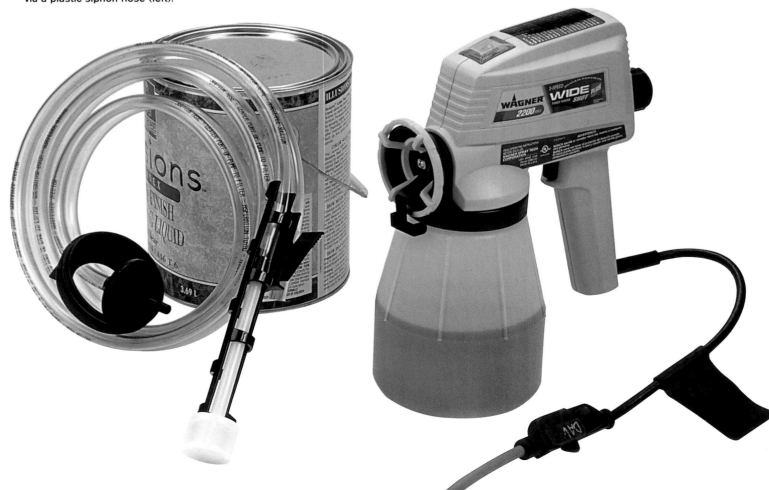

◄POWERED PAINT ROLLER
Running on batteries, this portable, powered paint roller feeds paint from a large reservoir pack that hangs on a shoulder strap.

Pro Tip

Whether you're painting a whole room or just doing a touchup, never dip the application tool in the can; it can contaminate or shorten the life of the finish. Instead, pour it into a separate cup, can, or even better, a disposable plastic tray (rectangular ones are best, as you can touch the brush's bristles off on the side of the tray).

models, cordless units are easily portable and can apply up to 20 gal. of paint using a single set of batteries.

CLEANUP SHORTCOMINGS The most significant shortcoming of power sprayers, and especially power rollers, is that cleanup can be tedious, especially if long paint hoses are used. Typically, a power-sprayer unit must be disassembled and washed in water or solvent, and the pump parts must be oiled before storage. Cleanup is even more arduous for a power roller and involves flushing a significant amount of paint from the hoses and roller handle. Since this cleaning regime is required every time you switch paint types or colors,

Unless you're an NBA all-star, chances are you'll need a ladder when you paint the ceiling or the trim around a skylight. Height is the first thing to consider when picking a ladder: Short stepladders are good for gaining a step or two to reach the ceiling; 5-ft. and 6-ft. ladders are good for general improvement and maintenance work, both inside and outside the house; and adjustable extension ladders help you reach high gutters, eaves, and rooftops safely.

If you only want to buy a single ladder, consider a multiuse model (see the photo below). These versatile ladders have telescoping sections and a hinged middle, allowing easy conversion from a stepladder (with climbable steps on both sides) to a ladder used on stairs (each extension sets to a different height) to an extension ladder. You can even use the extendable sections as a separate support and set up a scaffold with construction lumber for a platform.

Ladders are commonly made from wood, fiberglass, and aluminum; wood is the heaviest (the other two kinds weigh about half as much as wood, although they flex more, which makes them feel less safe to some people). Wood and fiberglass ladders are the safest when you're working around electricity (aluminum is a conductor).

Ladders designed for different levels of use have different ratings, from Type III household-grade models, which are rated to support 200 lb., to Type II commercial models (225 lb.) to industrial-grade Type I models (250 lb.). The rating is on a sticker on the side of the ladder. You need to buy a ladder that's rated to support at least your own weight, not to mention the weight of tools and finishes you might carry with you.

Pro Tip

You can get away with applying most low-viscosity coatings and finishes to decks, fences, and exterior siding with a garden sprayer (normally used for applying pesticides and fertilizers). Thoroughly clean the sprayer before using it, and for best results, use a brush to work the finish in after applying.

---

sprayers and rollers are best when you're using the same finish for the whole job.

SPREADING TOOLS

A brush or roller is great for spreading paint or varnish but isn't usually much help when applying thicker pastes and liquids, like spackle, caulk, or mastic. To do a good job spreading, leveling, and/or smoothing these common house-building and finishing materials, you need special tools, including trowels and floats, joint and putty knives, and caulking guns.

Masonry Trowels and Floats

Trowels and floats come in a staggering array of styles. By selecting the right one of these masonry tools, you're equipped to mix a tub of thinset or grout for a tile job, to level and smooth a concrete sidewalk or patio, or to spread the proper amount of mastic or adhesive on a plywood substrate before laying vinyl floor covering.

While some trowels and floats are good for general uses—such as mixing, spreading, and leveling or shaping pastelike liquids (thinset, mortar, mastic, etc.)—others are highly specialized for jobs such as packing grout into the joints between tiles or grooving concrete to form expansion joints, which help prevent cracking in sidewalks and slabs. The list below is a guide to some of the more popular—and useful—trowels and floats for home-improvement jobs.

EDGING TROWEL This small trowel is used for putting a smooth, slightly rounded edge on a cement pad, sidewalk, or curb.

WOOD FLOAT This tool looks like a flat trowel made from redwood or mahogany. Wood floats are typically 12 in. to 18 in. long and are used to finish the surface of a mortar bed or concrete slab. They produce a coarser final surface than steel flat trowels, which makes them better for leveling mortar beds in preparation for setting tile.

GROUT TROWELS A rectangular steel or plastic trowel with a rubber covering (also called a rubber float), a grout trowel is used to pack thin grout into crevices between tiles without scratching the shiny glaze on the tiles' surface. Stiff-rubber trowels are best for pavers and heavier floor tiles. Soft-rubber trowels often have a foam backing and work well with more delicate tiles that have shiny glaze finishes.

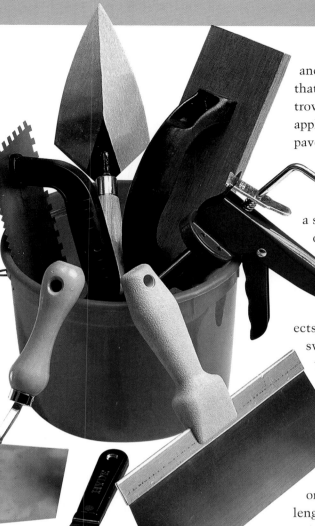

and applying and leveling mortar in areas that are too small to work with a big flat trowel. It's also good for little jobs, like applying thinset to the back of tiles or pavers or packing joints with mortar.

FLAT TROWELS With its rectangular, thin metal blade mounted to a handle, a flat trowel is used to create a smooth final surface on a concrete slab or sidewalk or to float a mortar bed in preparation for setting tile. A 12-in.- or 14-in.-long by 4-in.-wide flat trowel is a useful size for tile and small concrete projects and patch work. A similar tool, a swimming-pool trowel, is rectangular with rounded corners, making it good for work on compound-curve surfaces.

BULL FLOATS (NOT SHOWN) Also called a concrete float, this tool is designed for smoothing and finishing the surface of a large concrete slab, such as for a floor or patio. Between 42 in. and 48 in. in length and 8 in. wide, a bull float has a swivel bracket that attaches to a long handle so you can reach the middle of a big slab. The most popular models are extruded from lightweight magnesium, which sticks less to wet concrete than wood.

BRICK TROWELS Also called a bricklayer's trowel, this tool has a diamond-shape blade between 8 in. and 12 in. long that is attached to an offset handle. Brick trowels are used to "butter" bricks (spread mortar on them) when building a wall. They also can be useful for spreading and leveling mortar in corners. Smaller versions, called pointers, are good for detail work.

MARGIN TROWELS This trowel has a rectangular-shape blade 4 in. to 6 in. long and ½ in. to 3 in. wide that's mounted on an offset handle (it looks a bit like a spatula). It's used for mixing small batches of mortar

◀**SPREADING TOOLS** Whether it's mortar, mastic, joint compound, caulk, or spackle, there's a spreading tool that's right for the job.

▼**TROWELS AND FLOATS** Masonry jobs—like finishing poured concrete, building a brick wall, or doing tile work—require a complement of specialized trowels and floats.

Pro Tip

Uncertain what size and shape of notched trowel to use for the mastic you're applying? Just read the instructions on the can, which always specifies the appropriate notch size and shape.

▲NOTCHED TROWELS To spread mastic and other glues, use a notched trowel (right) or adhesive spreader. Different-size notches provide the right spreading action for different glues.

Notched Trowels

Modern adhesives and mastics are miraculous substances. They stick tenaciously and are made for gluing all kinds of materials—vinyl and composite flooring, tile, wood veneers, and plastic laminates. To apply these adhesives properly, you must use a notched trowel. A notched trowel is not only useful for spreading adhesives on a substrate (subfloor, wallboard, particleboard counter, etc.), but the notches along its edge also comb through the adhesive, leaving behind a series of ridges that ensure the material is evenly distributed and ready for bonding.

Different jobs and types of adhesive need different kinds of notches, so for versatility's sake, most notched trowels have square or V-shaped notches in a range of different sizes (1/16 in., 1/8 in., 1/4 in.) on each edge. Notched trowels designed for tile work are made of metal and have a raised handle. Disposable glue trowels are simple squares of plastic and are inexpensive enough for a single use.

Putty Knives

Trying to patch a gouge in drywall without using a putty knife is like trying to butter bread with a fork—you can do it, but why would you want to? A putty knife's flat, smooth blade is perfect for evenly spreading all kinds of semiliquid materials, from spackle to joint compound, wood filler, glazing material, and auto-body putty. Flexible blades are good for light spreading work on flat or slightly curved surfaces. A knife with a stiff blade and a hefty, solid handle is also great for flat surface work, as well as for lifting off peeling wallpaper and paint or lightly scraping other deteriorating finishes.

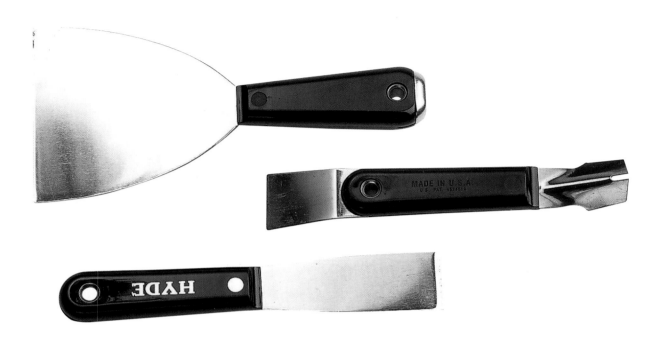

▲PUTTY KNIVES Wide or narrow, a putty knife is good for spreading materials or scraping them off. A glazier's putty knife (center) is specialized for applying putty around glass in window frames.

Basic models come with blades ranging in width from 1¼ in. to 6 in. A narrow-blade knife is good for small repairs—patching holes with wood putty, for example. You can also scoop putty or filler right out of a small can with a narrow knife. A wide-blade model is better for applying materials to large surfaces—say, when spreading joint compound to finish off taped drywall. Stainless steel knives are expensive but won't rust, so they're good when you're working with water-based materials. Plastic putty knives are good for single-use, throwaway jobs, such as applying two-part epoxies.

You can also buy special job-specific putty knives, such as a painter's model, with a built-in can opener and roller cleaning blade, or a glazier's model (shown at center in the photo above), with dual blades for removing and applying glazing putty when replacing glass in wood sash windows.

Joint Knives and Corner Knives

Resembling a big putty knife, a joint knife (shown at front right in the top photo on p. 251) is used for applying joint compound over taped seams between sheets of drywall. The tool's superwide, flexible spring-steel blade (often treated with a tough clear coat to prevent rust) allows you to evenly spread joint compound and feather the edges, making seams easier to sand flat.

Also called mud knives, joint knives come with blades 6 in. to 24 in. wide. A 12-in. to 16-in. knife is good for small household drywall installations and repairs. Some people also prefer to use a narrow (6-in.) joint knife for filling screw or nail holes in lieu of a putty knife.

A companion to the joint knife, a corner knife (shown at front left in the top photo on p. 251) has a short, bent blade designed specifically for spreading joint compound evenly into drywall seams at the inside corners of a room.

Pro Tip

You can't spread compounds, fillers, and putties smoothly with a dirty putty knife, so thoroughly clean the blade after every use. To remove dried-on substances, you may need to soak the knife in a strong solvent, such as lacquer thinner, or scrape it with a razor blade.

Old-fashioned, wood sash windows are lovely and traditional, but they can be a real problem if they break because it's a challenge to remove old, hardened putty without damaging the frame. The Prazi® Putty Chaser™ works with any 2,000-rpm to 3,000-rpm electric drill (with a ¼-in. chuck or larger) to rout away old putty quickly but in a controlled manner. Its carbide cutter works somewhat like a router bit but is designed to chew through rock-hard putty easily. A stepped sleeve just above the cutter (adjustable to suit different windows) guides the tool around the frame and keeps the cutter from straying into the wood.

Caulking Guns

Caulking around the various parts of a house—windows, doors, siding, light fixtures, pool decks, etc.—can not only save on heating and air-conditioning bills but also prevent moisture and even insects from entering your home. Caulking that comes in standard, 11-oz. disposable tubes is the most economical, but you need a caulking gun to apply it. Caulking guns use a racheting plunger to press out the caulk as you pull the trigger.

Basic half-barrel guns (shown at lower right in the photo below) are inexpensive but flimsily made from pressed sheet metal. More expensive guns feature rigid cast parts and a twin-arm frame (shown at upper left in the photo below) that deflects less as pressure is applied to the caulking tube. In addition, the more refined ratchet and trigger mechanisms used on these guns make it easier to apply steady pressure, which means an even flow of caulk.

The bottom line is that better-quality guns are easier to use and more predictable to control, hence you stand a better chance of ending up with neat, clean beads of caulk spread where they belong, rather than wads of goo all over the place. Buying a good caulking gun is worth it when you

►CAULKING GUNS An inexpensive caulking gun (bottom) is made from cheap pressed steel; better guns (top) have cast parts and stronger tube holders.

consider that the same gun will also dispense construction and panel adhesives, lubricating grease, and more.

FINISH REMOVAL TOOLS

New or smooth, undamaged surfaces are always the easiest to paint or finish. But weathered, worn, or just plain aged surfaces usually need a little sprucing up before they're ready for finishing. At best, a little cleaning is all you need to do. More typically, a surface must be lightly abraded with a few strokes from a sheet of sandpaper or wire brush or scuff-sanded with a power sander. At worst, a badly deteriorated surface may need to be stripped completely, using a heat gun and scraper, paint-abrading sander, or chemical stripper.

Heat Guns

Heat softens paint and many kinds of finishes, making them easier to remove with a scraper (see "Box Scrapers" on p. 66). But it's not safe to use a live flame—say, from a propane torch—for this kind of job for obvious reasons. An electric heat gun may look like a regular blow dryer, but it produces much higher temperatures—up to 1,100°F. Not only is it much safer to use than an open flame but also its heat output is easier to control. Most guns offer either a dual-temperature setting or, even better, a variable temperature control to let you regulate the amount of heat for the job—less for light work indoors, more for heavy removal work on exterior surfaces.

The most advanced heat guns have separate controls for temperature and airflow, so you can balance the amount of heat with air volume, which helps ensure that paint softens without burning. These new guns also use electronic circuitry to monitor and display the actual temperature—not crucial for finish removal but handy for many of the other jobs a heat gun's adept at, such as shrinking heat-shrink tubing (for electrical work), thawing frozen pipes,

Cool Tools | **POWERED CAULK GUNS**

POWERED CAULK GUNS produce a steady bead with the pull of a trigger, making quick work of applying caulk, while preventing you from getting a sore arm in the process. To make caulk dispensing highly controllable, both air and electric guns offer rate-of-flow adjustments: Electrics have a flow-adjuster knob or, handier still, a variable-flow trigger; air-powered units have a pressure-regulator knob that adjusts air pressure, and most models have a rod-release button above their triggers, to stem the flow of caulk.

Air-powered guns (see the photo at right) are lightweight and will run on small portable compressors. Battery-powered electric models are heavier (due to their battery packs) and more expensive, but they offer completely untethered performance—good when you're working atop a ladder or in a cramped space. Regardless of battery voltage, which ranges from 7.2 volts to 14.4 volts, depending on the model, electric guns can dispense nearly a whole case of caulk on a single charge.

Tool Helpers | **CAULK FINISHING TOOL**

You don't need to smooth the surface of a bead of caulk as long as you've applied it evenly. Unfortunately, this isn't as easy as it sounds, so people use many techniques to smooth caulking: a finger dipped in water or detergent, the back of a spoon, or even an ice cube. For clean results with less mess, try a caulk finishing tool—an inexpensive device that's pushed over the applied caulk, thus skimming off excess material for a smooth bead. One style (shown at front in the photo below) doubles as a caulk tube cap, providing a convenient way of resealing a partially used tube.

▲FINISH REMOVAL TOOLS Removing paints, varnishes, and other finishes can take as much finesse as applying them. Tools made for this duty include (from left to right): power paint remover, wire brush, random-orbit sander, heat gun, and putty knife.

▲HEAT GUN With sophisticated electronic controls and LED temperature readouts, this heat gun accepts various accessory nozzles to direct its flow of hot air.

dissolving adhesives, and softening old glazing putty when replacing broken windows.

You can get accessory nozzles for most brands of guns, which alter and direct the airflow: Wide, flat nozzles are best for distributing heat over a large surface; small round tips concentrate heat in a specific area.

Paint-Removing Sanders

Abrading a thick coat of paint or varnish with a power sander produces clouds of lung-choking dust that gets over everything. It's a dirty business, but sometimes it's the only practical way of returning a surface to smooth, bare wood. For most projects, a belt, disk, or random-orbit sander (see "Portable Power Sanders" on p. 175) fitted with a coarse (36-grit to 60-grit) belt or disk provides a reasonably quick way of removing the finish, even from a fairly large surface.

The coarser the grit (and the more often you clean the belt or disk), the less likely the sandpaper is to clog up (when finish sticks to the abrasive particles, making them less effective). This problem is at its worst when removing finishes that tend to gum up, like spar varnish and latex paint.

Disk sanders tend to remove finishes more aggressively than either belt or random-orbit sanders, but they're also harder to control and tend to leave deep semicircular swirl marks behind.

A different kind of disk sanding machine, designed specifically for paint removal, is called a power paint remover. Primarily designed for removing damaged, peeling, or blistered paint from exterior surfaces, this machine uses tungsten carbide–impregnated metal disks, which remove the thickest, hardest finishes. Unlike paper sanding disks, the metal disks can be cleaned off when they clog up.

The base of this powerful tool has guides and rollers that help the user control its motion and depth of cut. This allows fast, uniform

---

Tool Helpers | **WHEN NOT TO STRIP**

When most people think about renewing the finish on a piece of cabinetry or furniture— a built-in hutch or yard-sale dresser—they immediately think of stripping it down to bare wood. But stripping isn't always necessary, and as anyone who has seen *Antiques Roadshow* knows, stripping can ruin fine vintage woodwork and reduce its value significantly.

Many finish problems can be repaired, or surfaces renewed, without the time and trouble (and mess) it takes to strip off the entire finish. If the finish on a piece looks and feels solid with no obvious cracking or peeling, you can often apply a new finish directly over the old one. After scrubbing the piece thoroughly (to remove grease, dust, and oil) with a plastic-bristle brush and TSP (trisodium phosphate), rinse it thoroughly with water. Sand lightly to scuff the surface, and dust before applying the new finish.

Stripping with coarse sandpaper or wire brushes and wheels should only be done in cases where finishes are severely damaged; the chipped, cracked, and peeling paint on a building's exterior is a good example. Remember that coarse sanding will destroy the patina of the wood and the aged beauty of an original finish.

▲POWER PAINT REMOVER Basically a strong disk sander with special guides, a power paint remover quickly grinds old paint from a flat or clapboard-covered surface.

removal of old paint from large wood surfaces—even from houses with shiplap siding—without leaving massive swirl marks behind.

Wire Brushes and Wheels

An alternative to using sandpaper or heat, wire brushes and wheels can scour rust, paint, and old finishes from durable surfaces (especially metal), without removing the patina. Their bristles easily get around narrow parts, such as rods on a steel rail-

ing, and down into crevices and shaped surfaces, such as cast back splats on wrought-iron chairs.

Handheld brushes are best for large surfaces or for work in narrow crevices. A 3-in.- or 4-in.-dia. wire wheel chucked in

▲WIRE WHEEL AND BRUSHES **A wire wheel chucked into an electric drill is great for scrubbing corrosion from heavily rusted metal parts. Steel- and brass-wire brushes are handy for cleaning smaller parts.**

an electric drill is fine for powering through rust and old paint on smaller parts and surfaces. Coarse-bristle brushes and wheels are best for steel and iron, while softer bristles will clean aluminum or brass surfaces without leaving coarse scratches behind. Brass bristles are good for cleaning soft metals and delicate objects, as well as for scrubbing softened paint or finish out of corners, carvings, and crevices on hardwood cabinets and furniture being stripped with liquid stripping chemicals.

Cool Tools   PRESSURE WASHER

A PRESSURE WASHER will help you quickly clean outdoor surfaces (house siding, deck, fencing, patio furniture, etc.) that need to be painted or finished—a job that's often more time-consuming than finishing itself. This modern marvel (sometimes called a power washer) uses a small, electric- or gasoline-powered pump to boost the pressure of water from a garden hose, driving it with great velocity through a handheld spray wand. With water propelled through the nozzle at between 1,200 psi and 3,200 psi, a pressure washer easily removes dirt, surface deposits, and even loose paint, thus reducing the amount of scraping and sanding you need to do.

Wand nozzles are interchangeable, so you can pick a wide spray pattern for flat surfaces or a more concentrated spray for narrow objects, like patio chair legs or fence posts. Most models have a siphon hose or compartment where you can add a concentrated cleaner, degreaser, or mildewcide for extratough cleaning jobs, such as under the eaves of a house. With detergent added, a pressure washer is also great for washing your car, boat, or recreational vehicle.

When choosing a pressure washer, it's important to choose a model with enough pressure (stated in psi—pounds per square inch) to get the job done. When comparing two units, the one with a higher water flow (larger number of gpm—gallons per minute) will generally clean a surface more quickly. Here's a quick guide to the pressure required for different jobs.

700-PSI TO 1,000-PSI WASHERS can handle cars, boats, and recreational vehicles

1,000-PSI TO 1,500-PSI WASHERS will tackle house, siding, and decks

2,000-PSI TO 3,000-PSI WASHERS will clean engines and concrete surfaces (3,000 psi)

CHAPTER 11

Tools That Protect

Many handy people would rather spend their money on tools than on gear that protects against the noise, sparks, dust, and flying debris that tools produce. But when you consider that your ears, eyes, and lungs are irreplaceable, the cost of buying personal protective gear is small indeed. No tool kit or workshop—especially one with power tools and machines—is completely equipped unless it includes safety eyewear, protective earmuffs or earplugs, and dust masks or respirators. Beyond this basic safety equipment, other protective gear—such as gloves, knee pads, and back braces—can make difficult or tedious jobs easier and more comfortable to perform safely.

▲SAFETY GLASSES AND GOGGLES Modern safety glasses come in both clear and tinted models, many of which are quite stylish. Safety goggles (center) fit all the way around your eyes, for maximum protection.

SAFETY EYEWEAR

Few of our natural possessions are as precious and remarkable as our eyes, and no other is as delicate and vulnerable. There's really no excuse for not protecting them with safety glasses, goggles, or face shields whenever working with power tools or striking tools, such as hammers, axes, and sledges. Safety eyewear also offers protection from the dust and debris that's a natural result of working with tools and materials.

Safety Glasses

You need not look like a goggle-clad laboratory geek to keep your eyes safe. Modern safety glasses and eyewear now come in a wide range of styles, some of them even fashionable. Many have improved comfort features like soft-rubber nosepieces and adjustable earpieces. Regardless of their look and feel, all safety glasses have shatter-resistant lenses to protect you from direct impact, as well as small side shields, which offer protection from flying debris that may sneak in around the lenses. Although the lenses in most models have anti-scratch and antistatic coatings to keep them clear and dust free, not all glasses have antifog coatings, which can be an annoyance (see the tip on p. 263).

Some safety glasses have replaceable lenses, so you can trade clear lenses with tinted ones when working outdoors in bright sunlight or when using a propane torch. If you wear prescription eyeglasses, you can get special safety eyewear that accepts prescription lens inserts or order a special pair of safety glasses ground to your regular prescription.

Tool Helpers	FLASHLIGHTS AND WORK LIGHTS

You can't drill, drive, cut, or pound what you can't see. Therefore, a good flashlight or work light is just as important a part of a home tool kit as a wrench or a screwdriver. Standard battery-powered flashlights are hand carried, but many people find wearable headlamp-style flashlights more useful because they keep your hands free (see the automobile tool kit on pp. 10–11).

Rechargeable flashlights are more expensive, but they save money in the long run. On the downside, rechargeables wear out and take time to replenish. Accessories for small AA-size battery flashlights have proliferated and include straps, which allow them to be worn on your head, and optical-fiber caps (shown at middle in the photo below), which are useful as a slender inspection light you can insert into a dark hole or crevice.

While flashlights create a relatively narrow light beam, work lights are more like floodlights, illuminating a larger area. Because they don't require a power cord, work lights that run on rechargeable battery packs (shown at left in the photo) are particularly handy. They feature cool-temperature fluorescent bulbs, so you won't get burned, and share battery packs and chargers with portable power tools of the same brand (they'll also run on an AC transformer).

Safety Goggles

A good pair of safety goggles fits tightly against your face all the way around your eyes, and it generally does a better job of keeping debris from getting under or around the lenses than safety glasses. Goggles also provide superior protection from splashing liquids, including solvents or solvent-based paints and finishes.

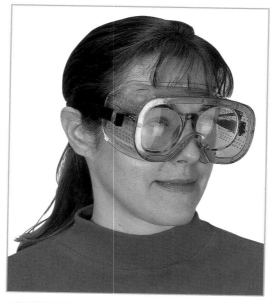

▲SAFETY GOGGLES Goggles afford excellent eye protection from splattering liquids and flying debris and can be worn over regular prescription eyeglasses.

below) provide protection from the blindingly bright light produced during gas or arc welding. These goggles accept interchangeable greenish-tint filter lenses that come in a range of shades to handle light of various intensities; a #4 or #5 shade is a popular choice for light gas-welding and brazing operations.

In addition to providing protection, eyewear can also be used to enhance your vision. For example, special laser-enhancing glasses (at right in the photo below) are tinted a deep red, to help you see the light produced by a laser level or rotary laser when working in sunlight or under bright interior lighting. (They don't provide protection against the laser beam itself, which isn't strong enough to be harmful but should never be stared at for a prolonged period.)

Face Shields

Goggles or safety glasses will keep sharp flying debris out of your eyes, but they don't protect your nose and mouth. A plastic face shield protects your entire face, and it's a good idea to use one when working with power tools or machines that can hurl objects with strong velocity. For example, face shields are de rigueur when turning on a lathe, where a spindle, bowl, or other vessel could split and become a hazardous projectile.

▲WELDING GOGGLES AND LASER GLASSES Welding goggles (left) have interchangeable dark-tinted filters to protect your eyes from the blindingly bright flame or arc of a welding torch. Conversely, laser glasses are tinted red to enhance the visibility of the beam emitted by a laser level or other laser tool.

Prescription eyeglass wearers can usually wear goggles over their regular glasses. While many goggles have a molded soft-plastic facepiece, more comfortable models have a foam gasket, much like a pair of ski goggles, which fits tightly around your face, even keeping dust out.

Special Eyewear

Working safely and effectively sometimes means protecting your eyes from not only flying objects but harmful light sources as well. Welding goggles (at left in the photo

For comfort, choose a face shield with a ratchet-style adjustable headpiece, which is quick and easy to set for a good fit. While most shields are made from thin clear plastic bent into a cylindrical shield, the latest deluxe shields are molded into a compound-curve shape that minimizes distortion while creating more room for glasses or goggles to be worn underneath (face shields aren't designed to fully protect your eyes in case of strong impact; so safety glasses or goggles should also be worn).

If you're looking for face protection but don't want to deal with the condensation and fogging that can be problematic with a plastic shield, an alternative is a shield with a metal or plastic face screen. This protective headgear, which mounts both a face screen and earmuffs to a hard hat, is popular for chainsaw work (see "Specialized Chainsaw Protection" on p. 274). The screen blocks flying wood chips, but it's much cooler than a plastic face shield, particularly in warm or humid weather.

Tool Helpers — **MAGNIFYING GLASSES**

Father Time is merciless when it comes to our eyesight; everyone eventually has a more difficult time reading small text and markings on tape measures, rulers, and project plans and blueprints. Magnifying glasses are a great aid for reading and layout jobs, as well as for seeing details when working on models or other diminutive projects. A magnifying headpiece has lenses mounted to an adjustable band that's comfortable to wear. They come in many different magnifications and focal lengths ranging from 1.5 power at 20-in. viewing distance, to 3.5 power at only 4 in. If you have reasonably good eyesight, a magnifier with 1.75 power at 14-in. viewing distance is a good choice for all-around detail work on home projects.

Pro Tip

Before buying a pair of safety glasses or goggles, do a simple test: Breath on the inside of the lenses to see if they fog up. A lot of the newer lenses are made from an optically clear, ballistic polycarbonate material with an effective antifog coating, such as Uvextreme®. While they still offer adequate eye protection, older glasses with silicon-based coatings are more prone to fogging.

▲**PLASTIC FACE SHIELD** A plastic face shield covers and protects your entire face, a good thing when working with a lathe or other power tool capable of unexpectedly hurling objects with great force.

►**EARMUFFS AND EARPLUGS**
Ear protection devices come as over-ear muffs (rear) or as plugs that are inserted into the ear. Plugs come in both disposable (left and center) and reusable styles.

EAR PROTECTION

Loud music isn't the only thing that can destroy your hearing in a hurry. Power tools, air compressors, and shop machines create enough noise to ruin your hearing, even with only occasional exposure. Hearing protection comes in two basic forms: earplugs and earmuffs.

Earplugs

Earplugs, which fit directly into your ear canal, come in several styles and materials, ranging from disposable foam and wax to molded foam and soft plastic to custom-made plastic plugs molded to the exact shape of your ear.

Plugs are lighter, less expensive, and less conspicuous than earmuffs, and they don't interfere with headgear or the earpieces on eyeglasses. However, plugs typically don't provide the same degree of sound reduction as earmuffs (see "Noise Reduction Rating" at left). They also take time to remove and replace, which can be a hassle if you must answer the telephone or talk to a visitor (speaking of which, it's nice to keep a few packs of disposable foam plugs on hand for the occasional assistant or visitor).

Earmuffs

Although some people feel they are more cumbersome and less comfortable than plugs, earmuffs cover your entire ear, thus protecting them not only from loud sounds but also from flying debris—as well as accidental head butts with shop machines and cabinetry. All muffs come with an adjustable headband that either fits over or behind your head. The behind-the-head design is a good option if you wear eyeglasses or safety glasses, as the band interferes less with the earpieces. The most comfortable muffs to wear for long periods have gel-filled ear cups that mold easily around your ears. Because of their superior fit, gel-filled muffs also shut out more noise—reducing it up to 29 dB (decibels).

NOISE REDUCTION RATING

You can quickly determine how much a pair of earmuffs or plugs is reducing noise by simply looking for the NRR (noise reduction rating) number on the package. Stated in decibels (dB), the higher the number, the better. While even a relatively low NRR, such as 18 dB, is good for occasional use, hard-core handy persons who use really noisy tools—routers, table saws, angle grinders, etc.—for hours at a time should look for a higher NRR, such as 26 dB to 29 dB.

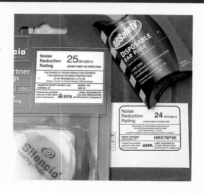

Combination Goggles/Earmuffs

One thing that keeps some people from donning safety gear is the time and hassle of putting it on every time they should (which is *every* time a power tool is switched on or a dangerous substance is handled). One way to save time while defending your eyes and ears is by using combination ear protectors and safety glasses. Combos are quicker to put on and take off, and many people find them more comfortable than wearing separate goggles and muffs.

Two styles are available. One looks like a pair of regular headband earmuffs but with safety glasses attached to them (see the photo below). It features ingenious articulating supports for the safety lens, which can be positioned to suit the user, yet allow the muffs to fold up compactly for storage. The other style adds comfortable foam earplugs to the ends of the eyewear frames on a pair of lightweight wraparound safety glasses. Both feature replaceable lenses that are clear, tinted, or amber in color.

Cool Tools | **WORKTUNES® MUFFS**

WORKTUNES MUFFS, created by Peltor®, combine ear protection with entertainment. These gel-filled earmuffs provide excellent noise reduction as well as a built-in AM/FM radio, allowing you to tune in a ballgame or your favorite music station while you're working. Small knobs on the side of one muff adjust the volume and radio frequency.

RESPIRATORY PROTECTION

When you're using tools that raise clouds of dust or you're working with solvents and finishes, you should always protect your lungs by wearing some kind of respiratory-protection device. Depending on its filter characteristics, a disposable dust mask, reusable respirator, or air helmet can filter out a range of irritants, including particles, mists, fumes, and even unpleasant odors, making your working conditions safer and more pleasant.

Disposable Dust Masks

The easiest way to protect your lungs against fine particles in a dusty environment is to wear a disposable dust mask. Disposables are reasonably inexpensive, light, and relatively unobtrusive to wear. And, of course, they require no maintenance: When a mask gets used, you simple toss it out and don a new one. They provide adequate protection for many common home-improvement tasks, such as installing

Pro Tip

If you have problems with your glasses fogging up whenever you wear a mask in hot weather, try using a disposable mask with a built-in exhalation valve. The mask's one-way valve closes during inhalation to prevent dust from being drawn in, while opening when you exhale your moist breath. This helps prevent fogging due to the moisture in your breath, while also preventing moisture buildup inside the mask, which can make your face feel clammy.

◄COMBINATION EYE/EAR PROTECTORS Combination eye/ear protectors, easy and comfortable to don, team a pair of earmuffs with a pair of safety glasses mounted on articulating arms.

▲DISPOSABLE DUST MASKS Disposable dust masks come in several styles, including (clockwise from bottom): pleated folding, molded shell, standard twin-strap, and single-strap nuisance masks.

MASK RATINGS

With the exception of single-strap nuisance dust masks, the most commonly available disposable dust masks found in hardware stores and home-supply centers are designated as N95 by NIOSH (National Institute for Occupational Safety and Health). This means they'll stop 95 percent of particles down to 0.3 microns in diameter. That's good enough to eliminate serious risks for most people from exposure to the relatively modest dust concentrations found in a typical home workshop. N95 masks are not designed to filter out aerosols, such as spray paints or fumes and mists from oils, solvent-based finishes, or pesticides. When working with those substances, you'll need to wear a reusable respirator fitted with the right filter cartridges (see facing page).

fiberglass insulation, woodworking with power tools, sanding drywall, and breaking up concrete. They can even prevent allergic reactions from pollen, spores, and molds.

Several styles are readily available at hardware and paint stores and at home centers, but there are two major varieties. Single-strap comfort masks (at far right in the photo above) are inexpensive but are only designed for light use against nuisance levels of dust, as is generated by hand-sanding.

For protection against the greater amounts of dust produced when working with machines and power tools—especially wood-sanding tools—look for a two-strap disposable mask (see "Mask Ratings" at left). These masks have a thicker filter and usually feature an adjustable nosepiece that helps seal the mask to your face. Most two-strap masks have a molded shell, which crush fairly easily, but there are also pleated fold-flat fabric styles now available (shown at front center in the photo on the facing page), which you can pocket between uses without ruining their effectiveness.

Reusable Respirators

Most disposables guard you from dust, but what about protection from fumes generated when spray painting enamel paint, toxic preservative finishes, or pesticides? In such cases, you need a reusable respirator fitted with filters rated for the kinds of fumes you'll be exposed to. Reusables are composed of a molded neoprene-rubber or silicone facepiece that holds one or two disposable filters (silicone masks are softer and more comfortable to wear). Air is inhaled through the filters and exhaled through a one-way valve on the facepiece.

Some reusable respirators are designed primarily for woodworking and use a single, disposable, pleated filter (at left in the photo below) to trap dust particles, much like disposable masks do.

More versatile are respirators that accept a pair of screw-in filter cartridges (at right

in the photo below).There are dozens of different kinds of cartridges for these respirators, and each is designed to effectively filter out a particular type of material, such as dust, mists, vapors, gases, chemicals, and various combinations of the above. The availability of different kinds of filters makes reusable respirators versatile since you can use one respirator for protection against a range of irritants and toxins.

Air Helmets

For protection when working in a dusty environment, an interesting alternative to masks and respirators is the air hel-

Cool Tools | **8274 MASK**

THE 8274 MASK by 3M® is the perfect solution if you're tired of sniffing the obnoxious odors given off by latex paints. This disposable mask offers N95-rated protection and contains a thin charcoal filter to soak up nuisance levels of organic vapors. Although it isn't meant to handle strong fumes generated by solvent-based finishes, such as lacquer and varnish (for that, you'll need a respirator with the proper filter cartridge), the 8274 mask will shield you from the stink of latex paints and water-based finishes you're brushing or rolling on.

Pro Tip

It's a good idea to keep a reusable respirator in a sealable plastic bag (a food storage bag works just fine) to keep it clean. That practice is even more important if the mask is fitted with organic-vapor cartridges: The activated charcoal in them continues to work—and will wear out— even if the mask isn't in use.

▲REUSABLE RESPIRATORS The reusable respirator at left has only a single filter designed to handle wood dust, but models such as the twin-cartridge respirator (right) accept cartridges for protection against chemical and finish solvent fumes, oil mists, and more.

Which One? CHOOSING A FILTER CARTRIDGE

Most manufacturers color-code the filter cartridges that fit in their reusable respirators to indicate what substances they will filter out. Filters can also be used in combination. For example, a particulate pre-filter (e.g., N95 dust filter) should always be used in conjunction with an organic-vapor cartridge (see the photo at right); the prefilter captures mist droplets while the cartridge filters out solvent fumes.

BLACK-CODED FILTERS protect against organic vapors, found in solvent-based lacquers, varnishes, etc. This is the cartridge most frequently used by do-it-yourselfers when spray-finishing wood projects or working with epoxy boat paints and resins.

GREEN-CODED FILTERS protect against ammonia gases, produced by industrial cleaners and agricultural compounds.

YELLOW-CODED FILTERS protect against acid gases, which are commonly found in acid-based solvents or cleaners.

met. Officially known as a PAPR (powered air-purifying respirator), an air helmet envelops and protects your entire face—not just your nose and mouth—and provides a steady stream of cool, clean, filtered air to breathe. Although expensive ($250 to $450 plus), air helmets provide a higher level of comfort and breathing protection than standard masks and respirators (see "Air Helmets" on the facing page).

An air helmet uses a small, battery-powered fan to draw air through a dust filter into a plastic shield that loosely seals around your face with a rub-

◄COMPACT AIR HELMET With its plastic visor, built-in fan, filter, and batteries, an air helmet not only guards the user's face but also provides respiratory protection from light levels of dust.

ber or fabric collar. More expensive, professional-model air helmets have their fan and filters in a backpack, using a flexible tube to blow air into a fabric cap or an actual helmet with a flipup face shield mounted to it. More affordable models designed for light home and workshop use mount the fan, batteries, and filter in the oversize crown of a face shield (see the bottom photo on the facing page).

HAND PROTECTION

Regardless of the type of handiwork you do, there's probably a pair of gloves that will make the job safer and more comfortable to perform. When working around the house or workshop, a good pair of basic work gloves protects your hands from abrasions, cuts, and splinters, as well as keeping them clean and free of glue, paint, etc. Gloves also provide padding and can enhance your grip on tools, providing more control for safer power-tool operation.

Basic Work Gloves

Even basic work gloves come in a confusing array of types and materials. The photo at right shows a range of gloves, arranged (from left to right) in order of least to most expensive. Cotton gloves only provide light abrasion protection, but they're lightweight and comfortable in hot weather, and they're cheap enough to dispose of after a really dirty chore. Some cotton gloves are covered with soft-plastic raised dots that improve your grip and control of tools. Knit polyester gloves are also inexpensive, light, and comfortable, and they have a grip-enhancing soft-plastic coating applied in a crisscross pattern over their entire surface.

Canvas gloves with leather palms and fingertips are more durable than cotton and

Cool Tools   AIR HELMETS

WHY CHOOSE AN AIR HELMET when a regular mask or respirator is less expensive? Many bearded woodworkers choose them because they can't get a good face-to-mask seal with regular dust masks. Others prefer them because there's plenty of room under the face shield for prescription eyeglasses, and they provide a constant flow of fresh air, so your eyewear won't fog up. The cool air also feels great when working in hot weather. Some professional models accept organic-vapor cartridges, so you can use your air helmet to filter fumes when applying solvent-based finishes (an air helmet only filters the air—it doesn't supply oxygen, so you can't use it in an enclosed garage with an unvented heater or a running car engine).

▲WORK GLOVE ASSORTMENT **The five styles of work gloves shown here are (from left to right): inexpensive cotton gloves with raised dots to improve grip, knit polyester gloves with grip-enhancing coating, canvas gloves with leather palms and fingertips, full-leather driver gloves, and anatomically designed gloves made from durable synthetic materials.**

Pro Tip

Most work gloves come in several sizes, ranging from small to extralarge; some are even offered in women's sizes small to large. But because of variations in manufacture, I suggest you ignore the size designation and simply try the pair on to check the fit.

The gloves' fingers should be just long enough to fit your fingers without leaving slack at the tips to hamper dexterity. Check fit in the hand by making a fist: The glove should feel snug but not too tight. With your hand relaxed, the glove should be tight enough that it won't fly off if you shake your arm vigorously.

polyester gloves, providing enough protection to make them good for general rough work around the house. Full-leather driver gloves are more pliable than canvas-leather gloves and come in many types of leather. Deerskin and goatskin are the softest and most supple, allowing the sense of touch necessary when doing fine detail work. Pigskin and cowhide gloves come in thicker top-grain and thinner (and more affordable) split-grain styles. Both styles are durable, comfortable, and good for a wide range of do-it-yourself activities.

Anatomically Designed Gloves

The newest and most advanced gloves are built to suit the anatomy of the human hand, for a snug, comfortable fit. They're made from synthetic materials that are light and flexible, allowing better dexterity, while still being tough and abrasion resistant. They're also washable. Stretchable glove backs help them form-fit to your hands, and hook-and-loop cuff fasteners keep them snug yet make them easy to remove quickly. Anatomically designed gloves are offered in both general-use models, as shown at far right in the bottom photo on p. 269 and task-

specific types that have modified features for a particular job. For example, framer's gloves designed for carpentry have open tips on three fingers for better dexterity and control.

Specialty Gloves

There are jobs in the workshop and around the house that demand special protection for your hands. For starters, contact with harmful caustic chemicals can burn or irritate your skin, and exposure to toxic solvents or pesticides can adversely affect your health—perhaps even with grave consequences. Gloves made from (or coated with) neoprene, nitrile, butyl, or PVC (at far left in the photo below) provide protection from a wide range of solvents and chemicals. Thinner gloves with textured fingers and palms offer better dexterity, while thicker, lined gloves are more comfortable to wear.

The latest mechanic's gloves (second from right in the photo below) are made from synthetic materials and have durable palms to protect your hands from sharp edges and burns—from a hot exhaust manifold, for instance. Their padding also makes handling wrenches and other tools more comfortable and less fatiguing.

Thick-leather welding gloves have long gauntlets (shown at left in the photo below) to prevent nasty burns when working around high-temperature torch flames and red-hot metal parts. When woodworking with chisels, gouges, and other sharp cutting and slicing tools, leather gloves with a special Kevlar lining (second from right in the photo below) can prevent serious cuts in case you slip.

Antivibration Gloves

Most handheld portable power tools produce vibration that can lead to hand discomfort, an annoying tingling in your hands and wrists, or worse. Prolonged vibration can cause or exacerbate repetitive stress disorders, including carpal tunnel syndrome. You can reduce vibration and hand fatigue by simply wearing special antivibration gloves, which have a shock-absorbing gel in the palm padding. These gloves often come with cutoff fingers, much like bicycle gloves, for better dexterity (in fact, gel-filled bike gloves usually cost much less than specialized woodworking antivibration gloves and do nearly as good a job).

Tool Helpers **FINGER-PROTECTION TAPE**

Finger-protection tape is a thin tape, with a light tackiness that acts like a glove, which you wrap around the end of your fingertips (or any part of your hand, for that matter). The gauzelike tape provides a light layer of protection for your skin without impeding the nimbleness of your digits. The tape is great for precise work when shaping or smoothing small parts on a stationary belt or edge sander, when sanding and polishing turnings as they spin on the lathe, or when hand-sanding metal parts or wood carvings. While finger tape won't protect you from a major injury, it will prevent you from accidentally sanding away the skin on your fingers.

◀SPECIALIZED GLOVES
Specialized gloves are made to protect the user during specific tasks, including (from left to right): chemical and solvent handling, mechanical repairs, welding, and carving or knife work.

YOU HAVE A CHOICE for hand protection in the home or workshop: reusable latex gloves (at left in the photo below) or disposable gloves (nitrile disposables are shown at right in the photo). The following are some advantages and disadvantages of both.

DISPOSABLE GLOVES

Pros:

• less expensive than reusables

• no maintenance or cleanup

• available in a variety of materials

• nitrile disposables are puncture resistant

Cons:

• not as thick or strong as reusables

• vinyl disposables tear easily

• some people are allergic to latex disposables

• not as protective against solvents and pesticides (although nitrile gloves provide some protection)

REUSABLE GLOVES

Pros:

• thicker than disposables

• generally more protective against solvents and pesticides

• longer lasting than disposables

Cons:

• more expensive than disposables

• require cleaning

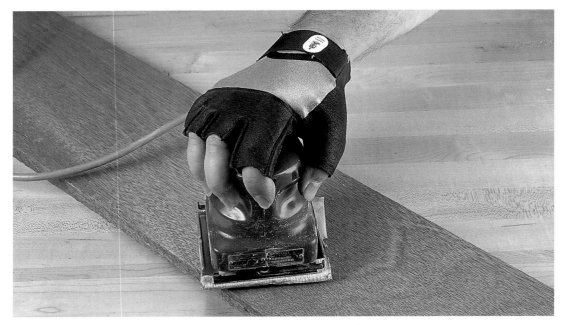

▲ANTIVIBRATION GLOVES To reduce hand fatigue when using orbital sanders and other vibration-generating tools, wear a pair of antivibration gloves, which are padded with a shock-absorbing gel.

BODY PROTECTION

Eyes, ears, and hands aren't the only body parts that need protection during work operations. Knees take a real beating when you're laying a floor or repairing a roof; the legs and groin are subject to severe injury when using a chainsaw; and the spine and back are vulnerable during heavy lifting. Wearing the right protective body gear will prevent not only little aches and pains but also serious accidents that can ruin your day— or the rest of your life.

Knee Pads

For creatures capable of walking upright, it seems that humans spend a lot of time down on their knees. Knee pads provide our boniest joints with the cushioning that nature didn't, and they can be indispensable for jobs that require a lot of kneeling or scooting around on the floor. Inexpensive pads, made from closed-cell

foam (at left in the photo below) make ground-level chores a bit more comfortable, although they won't hold up to a lot of scurrying around on rough surfaces, such as a concrete driveway or composition roof.

For more demanding duties and long-term use, choose knee pads with durable rubberized caps and softer padding. The gel-filled lining in the pads, like the ones shown at right in the photo below, helps distribute body weight and minimize pressure on the kneecaps. Their treaded-rubber outer caps provide traction, which is important when working on a slippery surface or on a roof or elevated scaffolding.

Knee pads with hard-rubber or hard-plastic caps are a good choice for work on rocky, uneven ground or in areas where you need protection from

▲HARD-CAP KNEE PADS **Knee pads with hard-plastic caps provide good protection from pebbles and sharp objects when kneeling on uneven or rocky ground.**

sharp, hard objects, such as a subfloor with protruding nails or screws. These knee pads are also great for floor-laying jobs, where you *want* to slide along on your knees quickly.

Back-Support Belt

Thankfully, few of us will ever be struck by lightning—but back spasms due to stress and strain can leave you feeling like you've been zapped by a thunderous bolt. To prevent overexertion and injury, it's smart to wear a back brace when performing tasks that require lots of bending and/or heavy lifting. Old-fashioned weight lifter–style leather belts are still preferred by many profes-

◀KNEE PADS **Knee pads come in many styles, including inexpensive foam pads (left), which are good for one-time jobs, and high-quality gel-filled pads with threaded caps (right), which are made to last for many years.**

Pro Tip

To assure the best out-
come in times of emer-
gency, post numbers for
the following near your telephone: personal physician,
local emergency room,
poison-control center, and
local hand surgeon (in
case of accidental amputa-
tion of digits). Also, informational charts, such as a
poison/antidote chart or
what to do in a medical
emergency, can be
lifesavers.

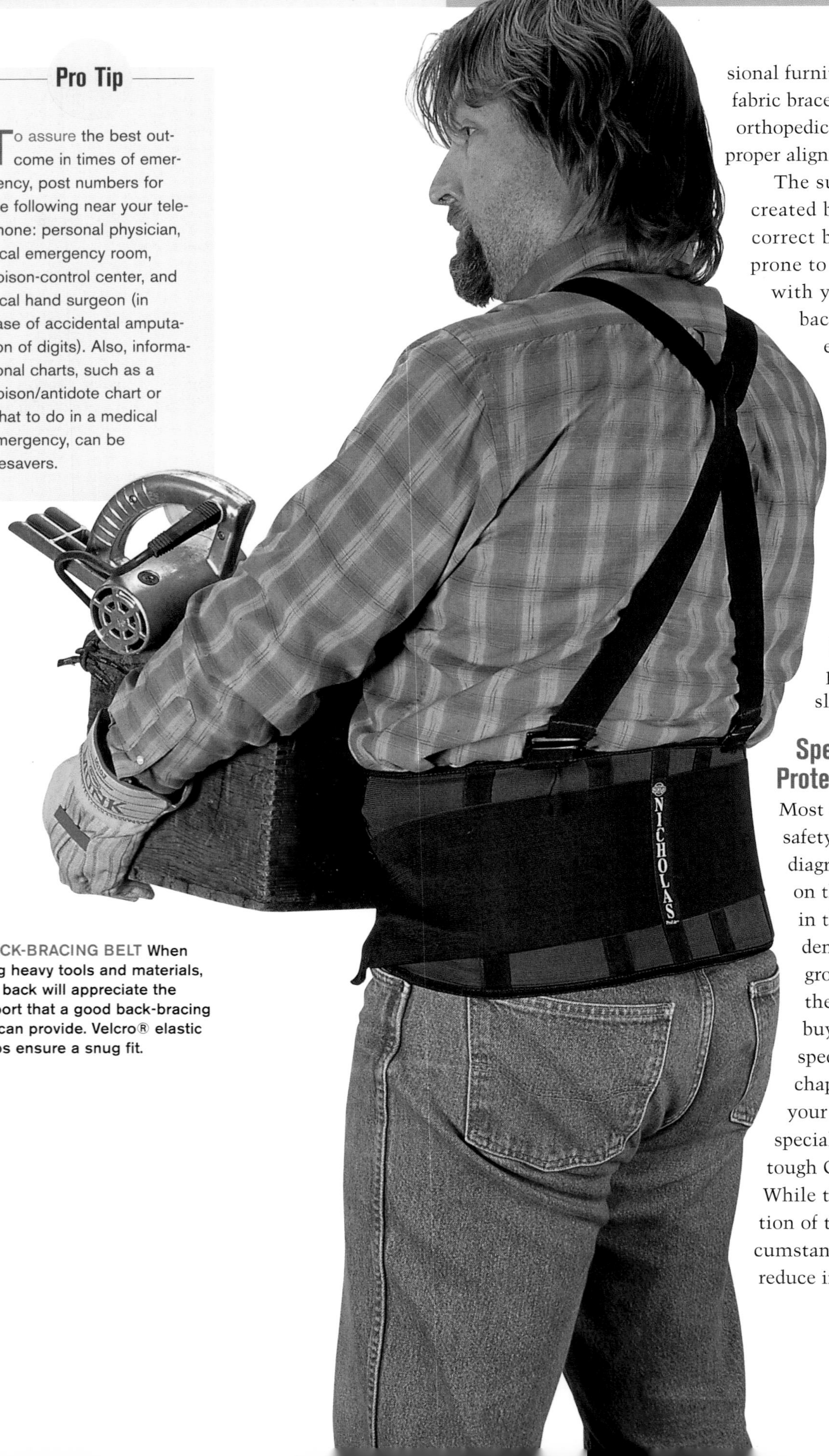

sional furniture movers, but newer fabric braces are designed to be a true orthopedic ally, keeping your back in proper alignment.

The support and alignment created by these ergonomically correct braces makes you more prone to lift things correctly—with your legs instead of your back. Made of stretchy elastic material, they have hook-and-loop fasteners that let you adjust the snugness of the brace around your midriff, for a firm yet comfort-able fit. Light metal stays sewn into the brace support your back and abdomen like a Victorian corset. The brace's integrated sus-penders keep it from slipping down.

Specialized Chainsaw Protection

Most chainsaws come with a safety brochure that includes a diagram illustrating the spots on the body that are involved in the most chainsaw acci-dents; injuries to the legs and groin are rated highest. Could there be a greater impetus for buying and using a pair of special protective chainsaw chaps? Attaching directly over your pants, the chaps contain special cut-resistant pads under a tough Cordura® nylon exterior. While they don't prevent penetra-tion of the chain bar under all cir-cumstances, they're designed to reduce injuries significantly.

▶BACK-BRACING BELT When lifting heavy tools and materials, your back will appreciate the support that a good back-bracing belt can provide. Velcro® elastic straps ensure a snug fit.

Interestingly, they're only meant for use with gas chainsaws; they won't provide full protection from contact with an electric chainsaw because of the continuous high torque of a motorized blade.

To protect your head from falling limbs and flying chips, as well as to shield your ears from noise, there's a special helmet built just for chainsaw users. It features a steel-mesh screen visor and earmuffs mounted to an impact-resistant hard hat. Since it allows air circulation, the mesh visor is cooler than a plastic face shield, but for full eye protection, you must wear safety glasses or goggles under it.

Tool Helpers | **FIRE EXTINGUISHERS**

To prevent a small fire from becoming a full-blown inferno, every home and workshop should keep a portable fire extinguisher on hand. A basic extinguisher that will put out most types of fires will only set you back $25 to $50. Make sure that the extinguisher is ABC-rated (the rating is clearly printed on its label) to handle all common types of home and workshop fires: Class A (combustibles like wood, cloth, paper, rubber, and plastic), Class B (flammable liquids like gasoline, paints, and solvents), and Class C (electrical sources like wires, cords, and outlets). To have adequate capacity for a small fire, the extinguisher you choose should be rated at least Size II for Class A fires and Size I for Class B and C fires (again, check the label). Mount the extinguisher on its quick-release bracket within easy reach—near a doorway, for instance, where you can access it without compromising your egress. Check the unit's gauge every few months and replace the extinguisher if necessary.

▲**CHAINSAW HELMET AND MUFFS** A chainsaw helmet guards the face with a mesh screen. The optional earmuffs, shown here, make it easy to protect your ears from loud gas chainsaws.

◄**CHAINSAW CHAPS** A pair of chainsaw chaps strap over regular pants to protect your legs and groin from one of the most dangerous power tools you can use.

▶FIRST-AID KIT A properly stocked first-aid kit can literally be a lifesaver if you have an accident while working in your home or workshop.

Sterile Gauze Dressing Pads

12 ply - 3 in x 3 in (7.5 cm x 7.5 cm)
Contents: 2 all-purpose gauze pads

Sterility guaranteed unless package is damaged or opened.

FIRST AID

Item# M-215

American Medical Association

First-Aid Guide
Immediate care for injured or ill patients

Knuckle & Fingertip Bandages

Adhesive Plastic Bandages

Burn Relief

Antiseptic Cleansing Wipes

Latex Gloves

Instant Cold Compress

Triangular Sling/Bandage
Non-Sterile
36" x 36" x 51"

FIRST AID

EYE WASH

Sterile Eye Pad

1.5/8 in x 2.5/8 in (4.1 cm x 6.7 cm)
Contents: 1 sterile oval eye pad

Sterility guaranteed unless package is damaged or opened.

FIRST AID

FIRST-AID KIT

A good first aid kit is a convenience if you cut your finger or get a splinter. But if you have a catastrophic accident, such as severing an artery or striking your head, a well-stocked first-aid kit can be a lifesaver. You can buy a ready-made first-aid kit, such as the one shown in the photo above, which comes packed in a wall-mountable metal box. Or, you can assemble one yourself by collecting the items shown in the chart on the facing page into a clean box with a tight-fitting lid that will keep out dust and moisture.

In addition to the basic supplies, other items worth stocking in your first-aid kit include a rescue blanket, inspection mirror, and eyedrops with eye cup to flush out irritants. You may also wish to keep in the kit an asthma inhaler and small quantities of any prescription medications you regularly use or need.

A HOME WORKSHOP FIRST-AID KIT

Essential Items	What They're Used For
Band-aid assortment (including finger tip and knuckle bandages)	To cover small cuts, blisters, and assorted small injuries
Latex gloves	To prevent spreading infection when dressing wounds
Antiseptic or alcohol wipes	To clean dirt from abrasions and lacerations
Sterile gauze roll	To cover burns and wounds and to apply pressure to deep wounds to control bleeding
Triangular bandage and/or large gauze pads	To bandage large wounds
Butterfly closures	To close up large lacerations
Adhesive tape	To hold gauze and large bandages in place
Small, sharp scissors	To cut bandages, gauze, and tape
Disinfectant ointment or solution, such as Mycitracin® or Betadine®	To disinfect small cuts and wounds
Clean, sealable plastic bag	To keep amputated parts clean en route to the emergency room

Recommended Items	What They're Used For
Fine-point tweezers	To remove splinters, thorns, etc.
Eye cup, boric-acid solution	To flush sawdust particles from eyes
Small mirror	To inspect your own eyes for foreign objects
Antiseptic/anesthetic cream or lotion	To soothe burns
Rescue blanket	To cover up and to help retain body heat in case of shock
Instant cold compress	To reduce pain and swelling from injuries and to keep amputated parts cool en route to the emergency room
First-aid guide	To provide instructions on how to handle medical emergencies

Items to Include as Necessary	What They're Used For
Asthma inhaler	To counteract allergic reactions to toxic wood dust, smoke, or solvent fumes
Prescription medications	To remedy an unexpected, sudden onset of symptoms that the medication is prescribed for

Index